# CUSTOMARY LAW IN HUNGARY

# Customary Law in Hungary

## *Courts, Texts, and the* Tripartitum

MARTYN RADY

OXFORD
UNIVERSITY PRESS

**OXFORD**
**UNIVERSITY PRESS**

Great Clarendon Street, Oxford, OX2 6DP,
United Kingdom

Oxford University Press is a department of the University of Oxford.
It furthers the University's objective of excellence in research, scholarship,
and education by publishing worldwide. Oxford is a registered trade mark of
Oxford University Press in the UK and in certain other countries



First Edition published in 2015



Published in the United States of America by Oxford University Press
198 Madison Avenue, New York, NY 10016, United States of America

British Library Cataloguing in Publication Data
Data available

Library of Congress Control Number: 2014959014

ISBN 978–0–19–874391–0

For Ann

Acknowledgements

My first thanks are due to the Leverhulme Trust, which awarded me a two-year Research Fellowship in 2010–12 to support the research and writing of this book. The British Academy and the Hungarian National Research Foundation (OTKA) also funded two collaborative research projects on Werbőczy's *Tripartitum* and the laws of Jagiello Hungary (in 2003–5 and 2008–10 respectively), on which the present work draws. The UCL School of Slavonic and East European Studies (SSEES) funded my visit to the archives in Cluj in 2013.

I owe debts to many people. Of these, the largest are due to János M. Bak and to the late László Péter. Both encouraged me with my research, provided the intellectual context and companionship for its undertaking, and in their very different ways inspired me over decades to seek out new avenues and ideas. David Ibbetson twice read this book in draft, correcting howlers and pointing me in fresh directions. I am also grateful to the anonymous readers of OUP for their careful criticism, which obliged me to recast an earlier draft almost entirely.

I have benefited from discussion and conversation in many quarters, not least with my alleged former and present students, Thomas Lorman, Christopher Nicholson, Robert Gray, Eleanor Janega and Philip Barker. Colleagues at SSEES have listened both attentively and distractedly, but have been always encouraging. I am particularly grateful to Simon Dixon, Rebecca Haynes and Richard Butterwick-Pawlikowski. Trevor Vaughan Thomas has heard more than most. I have learned much from him and from his Socratic probing of my ideas. I have also benefited from conversations and correspondence with Magnus Ryan, Robert Evans, Graeme Murdock, Björn Weiler, William O'Reilly, Peter Sherwood, the late Brian Hodson, Katalin Gönczi, Irina Marin, Andrew Lewis and, again, David Ibbetson. I am particularly grateful to Adrian and Livia Magina in Resiţa and to Alexandru Simon in Cluj for their friendship, deep knowledge of the historical sources and help in locating manuscripts and in introducing me to several archives. György Kurucz and I have spent several decades discussing Hungarian history and its problems and I owe much to his insights. I am also indebted for their advice and knowledge to Damir and Marija Karbić and Suzana Miljan in Zagreb, to Ioan Aurel-Pop, Gelu Fodor, Tudor Sălăgean, András W. Kovács and Florin Ardelean in Cluj, to Balázs Nagy, Katalin Szende, István Kenyeres, Kriszta Arany, Kees Teszelszky, Márton Zászkaliczy and Péter Banyó in Budapest, and to Zsolt Hunyadi in Szeged. Parts of this book were first delivered as lectures in Budapest, at ELTE University, Pázmány University and Károli Gaspar University, in Szeged at JATE University, in Bergen at the Centre for Medieval Studies, in Cluj at UBB University, in Passau at Thomas Wunsch's seminar in the University, in Dublin at TCD, in Leeds at several meetings of the International Medieval Congress, and in London at SSEES, City University, the Institute of Historical Research and the Warburg Institute. I am grateful both for the invitations to talk and for the advice received on each occasion.

I am most grateful to Christopher Wheeler and Robert Faber at OUP for seeing this work through to publication, and to Christopher Summerville for his attentive editing of the manuscript.

Ann has put up with this book for longer than she deserves, but has been unfailingly supportive and understanding. It is dedicated to her.

MR

*UCL SSEES*
*November 2014*

# *Contents*

# *Abbreviations*

| | |
|---|---|
| AO | *Anjoukori okmánytár*, eds. Imre Nagy and Gyula Nagy, 7 vols. (Budapest, 1878–1920). |
| AUO | *Árpádkori új okmánytár*, ed. Gusztáv Wenzel, 12 vols. (Pest, 1860–74). |
| BAR-CJ | Biblioteca Academiei Române Cluj-Napoca (Library of the Romanian Academy, Cluj). |
| Bónis, KJE | Bónis, György, *Középkori jogunk elemei. Római jog, kánonjog, szokásjog* (Budapest, 1972). |
| CLCE | *Custom and Law in Central Europe*, ed. Martyn Rady (Cambridge, 2003). |
| *Corp. Stat.* | *Corpus Statutorum Hungariae Municipalium, A magyar törvényhatóságok jogszabályainak gyűjteménye*, eds. Sándor Kolosvári and Kelemen Óvári, 5 vols. (Budapest, 1885–1904). |
| DRH 1301–1457 | *Decreta Regni Hungariae, Gesetze und Verordnungen Ungarns 1301–1457*, eds. Ferenc Döry, György Bónis and Vera Bácskai (Budapest, 1976). |
| DRMH | *Decreta Regni Mediaevalis Hungariae—The Laws of the Medieval Kingdom of Hungary*, eds. János M. Bak et al., 5 vols. (Budapest, Los Angeles, Salt Lake City, Idyllwild, CA, 1989–2012). The first volume appeared in a second edition in 1999 and is referred to in the footnotes as $1^2$. |
| ELTE | Eötvös Loránd Tudományegyetem (Eötvös Loránd University, Budapest). |
| HO | *Hazai okmánytár*, eds. Imre Nagy, Dezső Véghely et al., 8 vols. (Győr and Budapest, 1865–91). |
| MJL | *Magyar Jogi Lexikon*, ed. Dezső Márkus, 6 vols. (Budapest, 1898–1907). |
| MNL OL | Magyar Nemzeti Levéltár, Országos Levéltár (Hungarian National Archive). |
| MNL OL DL | Magyar Nemzeti Levéltár, Országos Levéltár (Hungarian National Archive), Section Q, Mohács-előtti gyűjtemény (Pre-Mohács Collection). |
| *Monumenta Comitialia* | *Monumenta Comitialia regni Hungariae*, eds. Vilmos Fraknói and Árpád Károlyi, 12 vols. (Budapest, 1874–1912). |
| MZsO | *Magyar-Zsidó oklevéltár*, eds. Armin Friss, Sándor Scheiber et al., 18 vols. (Budapest, 1903–80). |
| OSzK | Országos Széchényi Könyvtár (National Széchényi Library). |
| Pesty-Magina | *Diplome privind istoria comitatului Timiş şi a oraşului Timişoara—Oklevelek Temesvármegye és Temesvár város történetéhez 1430–1470*, eds. Frigyes Pesty, Adrian Magina and Livia Magina (Cluj, 2014). |
| PML | Pest Megyei Levéltár (Pest County Archive, Budapest). |

| | |
|---|---|
| RA | *Az Árpád-házi királyok okleveleinek kritikai jegyzéke*, eds. Imre Szentpétery and Iván Borsa, 2 vols. (Budapest, 1923–87). |
| RL | A Dunamelléki Református Egyházkerület Ráday Levéltára (Ráday Archive of the Danubian District of the Reformed Church, Budapest). |
| SEER | *Slavonic and East European Review*. |
| SJAN-CJ | Serviciul Judeţean al Arhivelor Naţionale, Cluj-Napoca (County Branch of the National Archive, Cluj). |
| SJAN Sibiu | Serviciul Judeţean al Arhivelor Naţionale, Sibiu (County Branch of the National Archive, Sibiu). |
| Trip. | *Tripartitum opus iuris consuetudinarii inclyti regni Hungariae per Stephanum de Werbewcz editum* (Vienna, 1517), publ. as DRMH 5, with English translation. |
| ZsO | *Zsigmondkori oklevéltár*, eds. Elemér Mályusz, Iván Borsa, Norbert C. Tóth et al., 12 vols. (Budapest, 1951–2013). |

# 1

# The Legal Landscape

## HISTORICAL INTRODUCTION

In the last decade of the ninth century the Hungarians crossed the Carpathians, at first mainly settling in the former Roman province of Pannonia and on parts of the Great Plain. Whether the Hungarians, who were a nomadic Turkic people descended from the Onogurs (whence their name), were accompanied by Finno-Ugric tribes of Magyar speakers, or whether they found the Magyars already established in the area of modern-day Hungary, is uncertain.[1] Whatever the circumstances of the conquest, Hungarians and Magyars had within a few decades become a single people. The Hungarians adopted the language of the Magyars; the Magyars embraced the ruling Hungarian house of Árpád and, along with it, the Hungarians' martial and historical lore. The conversion of Hungarians and Magyars to Christianity during the eleventh century contributed to their common identity. The advent to power of saintly kings and scions of the dynasty of Árpád, beginning with the coronation of St Stephen in the year 1000, sanctified the secular power wielded by Hungary's early rulers, aiding the kingdom's political integration. A silver coinage, stamped with the portrait and title of the monarch, provided a visible symbol of the unifying power accumulated by the new royal line.[2]

The Hungarian kingdom was founded on the ruins of earlier Slavonic principalities, from whose previous organization it borrowed. The Slavonic contribution to the kingdom's nascent government and administration is recalled in early Hungarian vocabulary—*megye* (a border or county); *nádor* (palatine); *ispán* (lord); *udvar* (court); *vajda* (voivode); *tárnok* (purveyor, provisioner); *szolga* (servant); *pristav* (bailiff); and even *király* (king). *Törvény* (a law) and *billog* (a judge's seal) are, however, of an older, Turkic provenance.[3] Even so, the traditions of law and justice practised by the nomadic Hungarians did not long survive the conquest. Recollection perhaps survived of ancient forms of contract and treaty,

[1] See Nándor Dreisziger, 'The Lessons of Genomic Research', *The Hungarian Quarterly*, no. 196 (2009), 50–5 (52–5), for a summary of controversial new research. The literary evidence is reviewed in C.A. Macartney, *The Magyars in the Ninth Century* (Cambridge, 1930). See also Gyula Kristó, *Hungarian History in the Ninth Century* (Szeged, 1996).

[2] György Györffy, *Wirtschaft und Gesellschaft der Ungarn um die Jahrtausendwende* (Budapest, 1983), 18; Bálint Hóman, *Magyar pénztörténet 1000–1325* (Budapest, 1916), 171–4.

[3] See thus the relevant entries in Loránd Benkő, ed., *A magyar nyelv történeti-etimológiai szótára*, 4 vols. (Budapest, 1967–84); István Kniezsa, *A magyar nyelv szláv jövevényszavai*, 1, Part 1 (Budapest, 1955). For *billog/bilochus*, see *Lexikon Latinitatis Medii Aevi Hungariae*, i etc. (Budapest, 1987 etc.), i, fasc. 3, 242.

involving the solemn mingling of blood, but the offices of the Hungarians' tribal judges, *gyula* and *karchas*, soon vanished.[4] The words of the Russian chronicler, describing the fate of a previous tribe of nomads that had settled in Pannonia, 'They have perished like the Avars,' might equally well apply to the ancient institutions of the early Hungarians.[5]

The newly founded Hungarian kingdom was plainly possessed of strong central power. During the first years of the eleventh century, St Stephen began the conquest of Transylvania, a territory that had been previously ruled by a rival Hungarian chieftain. His successors would go on to capture Slavonia, which lay between the Rivers Drava and Sava, and then, around 1100, bring the kingdom of Croatia (modern-day Dalmatia) under their sway. In the task of territorial expansion, military roadways were driven southwards through Hungary that supplemented the surviving Roman roads. Farther to the north, in the area of Rábaköz, a complex canal and irrigation work extending over 22 square kilometres had been completed by no later than around 1200.[6] Possibly, this was just part of a much larger scheme of water regulation that involved many thousands of kilometres of channels.[7] The territorial consolidation of the new kingdom was marked by the construction of long earthen ramparts, intersected by gates, which reached across the Great Plain into Transylvania.[8] Throughout the kingdom, earthwork castles were also thrown up, often several hundred metres in length, many of which served as centres of local administration under royally appointed lords.[9] Their function in revenue-collection is suggested by a surviving list of the royal income, dating from the last decades of the twelfth century, that identified the quantity of silver that the castles were expected to contribute to the king's treasury.[10] Plainly, there were pockets of great wealth in the kingdom. The royal court was famously lavish, but the late twelfth-century ground plans of, for instance, the cathedrals of Pécs and Alba Iulia

[4] See the *Gesta Hungarorum* of the Hungarian Anonymus (ch. 5), in János M. Bak, Martyn Rady and László Veszprémy, eds., *Anonymus and Master Roger* (New York and Budapest, 2010), 17, with bibliographical references. A translation of the Anonymus Chronicle, composed *c.* 1200, is also available in SEER, 87, no. 4 (2009), 681–727. For additional information on early oath-taking and its survival in popular culture, see Lajos Rácz, 'Hatalmi szimbolánk nomád gyökereiről', *Jogtörténeti Szemle* (1986, no. 1), 24–32 (24–5); Karl Tagányi, *Lebende Rechtsgewohnheiten und ihre Sammlung in Ungarn* (Berlin and Leipzig, 1922), 99; Daniel Cornides, *Vindiciae Belae regis notariae* (Buda, 1802), 300–1. For the titles of judges, see Gyula Moravcsik, *Byzantinoturcica*, 2nd edition, 2 vols. (Berlin, 1958), ii, 115, 155.

[5] Samuel H. Cross, ed., *The Russian Primary Chronicle* (Cambridge, MA, 1930), 141; discussed in Herwig Wolfram, *The Roman Empire and its Germanic Peoples* (Berkeley and Los Angeles, 1997), 305.

[6] Károly Takács, 'Medieval Hydraulic Systems in Hungary: Written Sources, Archaeology and Interpretation', in József Laszlovszky and Péter Szabó, eds., *People and Nature in Historical Perspective* (Budapest, 2010), 126–33.

[7] Discussed in Péter Szabó, *Woodland and Forests in Medieval Hungary* (Oxford, 2005), 52.

[8] Hansgerd Göckenjan, *Hilfsvölker und Grenzwächter im mittelalterlichen Ungarn* (Wiesbaden, 1972), 9–11, 234 (map).

[9] Erik Fügedi, *Castle and Society in Medieval Hungary (1000–1437)* (Budapest, 1986), 15–39; József Dénes, 'Várak és erődítmények a középkori Magyarországon', *Rubicon,* (2011, no. 1), 36–41, with aerial photographs.

[10] Henrik Marczali, *A magyar történet kútfőinek kézikönyve* (Budapest, 1901), 129–30; discussed by Gábor Barta and János Barta, 'Royal Finance in Medieval Hungary: the revenues of King Béla III', in W.M. Ormrod, Margaret Bonney and Richard Bonney, eds., *Crises, Revolutions and Self-Sustained Growth: Essays in European Fiscal History, 1130–1830* (Stamford, 1999), 22–37.

indicate that the resources available to the church were also considerable.[11] The Romanesque stone churches in southern Transylvania, constructed by local Orthodox communities of Romanians, suggest that this wealth was not confined to the upper reaches of Hungarian society.[12] 'Great in strength and mighty in riches, superior in warlike arms and able to take on any king of the world,' was one early-twelfth-century verdict on the resources and military capacity available to Hungary's early Árpád kings.[13]

These examples of coercive power and of financial means may be matched by equally telling evidence of the kingdom's institutional and material poverty. Otto of Freising, who traversed Hungary in the 1140s, recorded the miserable huts of the people, their primitive weaponry, and the arbitrary justice dispensed by their king. The Hungarian ruler depended for his power, so Otto explained, on a retinue of foreign knights and mercenaries.[14] The impression is thus of a *Gefolgschaft* or druzhina-type organization, whereby the ruler exercised authority through a body of trusted warriors. Some of these were vested with local offices, and put in charge of the kingdom's castles. The king and druzhina, however, maintained through their periodic traversing of the realm a check on these local lords, rotating them from one part of the kingdom to the other, lest through territorialization they accumulate too independent a power.[15] On their journeying, the king and his retinue often stayed as the guests of bishops and chapters, which almost alone at that time had stone buildings that might be used for military protection.[16] As the Mongols demonstrated, at the time of their invasion in 1241, earthen 'mud pies' were easily broken.[17]

* * *

Medieval Hungary illustrates the problem of revelation versus revolution. Before the thirteenth century, the surviving sources are few—a handful of laws, several hundred genuine charters, fragmentary travellers' tales, saints' lives and a lone chronicle of dubious content. After 1200, the volume of available material increases rapidly. Almost all the royal archive perished in the immediate aftermath of the Turkish victory at Mohács in 1526. Nevertheless, more than 300,000 charters survive from the Hungarian Middle Ages, either as originals or as transcripts,

[11] For an example of royal gift-giving in Hungary, see Joachim Bumke, *Courtly Culture: Literature and Society in the High Middle Ages* (New York and London, 2000), 127.

[12] Thus the churches in Haţeg at Densuş, Strei, Streisângeorgiu and Ostrov. See Adrian Andrei Rusu and Ileana Burnichioiu, *Monumente medievale din Ţara Haţegului–Medieval monuments from Haţeg District* (Cluj, 2008).

[13] Cosmas of Prague, *Chronicle of the Czechs*, 3. 42, in MGH SS rer. Germ. N.S., 2, 215.

[14] Otto of Freising, *Gesta Friderici I imperatoris*, 1, ch. 32 (31). Translated in C.C. Mierow, ed., *The Deeds of Frederick Barbarossa* (New York, 1966), 66–7. See also, János M. Bak and Erik Fügedi, 'Fremde Ritter im mittelalterlichen Ungarn', *Quaestiones Mediae Aevi Novae*, 3 (1998), 3–17 (4–12).

[15] Lists of all office-holders in the Árpád period are given in Attila Zsoldos, *Magyarország világi archontológiája 1000–1301* (Budapest, 2011). On the tension between the druzhina and the territorialization of power, see more generally Perry Anderson, *Passages from Antiquity to Feudalism* (London, 1974), 231–3.

[16] RA, 1, nos. 59 (Vác), 63 (Székesfehérvár), 102 (Esztergom), 112 (Eger), 114, 118 (Veszprém), 147 (Esztergom), covering the period 1135–88.

[17] The description is taken from Gyula Pauler, *A magyar nemzet története az Árpádházi királyok alatt*, 2nd edition, 2 vols. (Budapest, 1899), 2, 196.

which is more than for medieval Poland or Bohemia.[18] Of these charters, about 10,000 derive from the thirteenth century. Taken together, this thirteenth-century material suggests a society in crisis—where the royal power was under threat both from lordly ambition and from an emerging class of nobility that was intent upon capturing the royal institutions of government. The grant of royal privileges ceding rights to nobles, townsfolk and other status groups, together with the cession by charter of chunks of the royal domain, adds to the impression of a diminution of royal rights and of a corresponding accumulation of power by the kingdom's nascent estates. Yet an impression is all it can be. In the absence of comparable material from the preceding centuries, we cannot say for sure whether the thirteenth century witnessed a sudden social and political transformation or whether it saw instead the continuation of trends that had been going on for several hundred years.

The Árpád dynasty expired in 1301. For more than 200 years, Hungary was ruled by the so-called 'mixed dynasties', variously Italian Angevins, Polish-Lithuanian Jagiellos, a Luxemburger, several Habsburgs, and, in the second half of the fifteenth century, Matthias Corvinus, who was an elected king of partly Romanian origin with no royal blood in him. Amidst conditions of civil war, confessional strife, a Turkish onslaught and territorial disintegration, Archduke Ferdinand of Habsburg took possession of a part of the Hungarian kingdom in 1526, following the death of Hungary's last Jagiello king in battle with the Turks at Mohács. Ferdinand's successors would rule Hungary for almost 400 years, until the collapse of the Habsburg Monarchy in the late autumn of 1918. The extent to which the government and administration of the kingdom were transformed by the Habsburg succession must, nevertheless, remain as uncertain as the pace of change in the thirteenth century, and for much the same reasons. The archive of the royal treasury or Kammer, instituted by Ferdinand shortly after his accession, occupies today more than a kilometre of shelving in the Hungarian National Archive; the Chancellery archive a kilometre and a half; and the Judicial archive a further kilometre. By contrast, nothing survives of the workings of Hungary's medieval administration, save a summary of royal income and expenditure from the 1490s, drawn up to show that the king's treasurer had been embezzling money.[19] What remains from the Middle Ages are charters, usually recording donations of property or drawn up in the course of litigation over land. They thus convey the impression of a dominant class of landowners, overwhelmingly concerned with rights of property, for whom the ruler served both as the source of landed wealth and as the arbiter of their disputes. By the same token, the relative lack of material for the kingdom's cities (although significant quantities remain from medieval Sopron and Bratislava) may be thought to reflect the weakness of the urban estate, and the dearth of sources on the peasantry as confirming their political marginality.

* * *

[18] Zsolt Hunyadi, '"Scripta manent." Archival and Manuscript Resources in Hungary', *Annual of Medieval Studies at CEU 1997–1998* (Budapest, 1999), 231–40 (232–4).

[19] The summary is published in Johann Christian von Engel, *Geschichte des Ungrischen Reichs und seiner Nebenländer*, 4 vols. (Halle, 1797–1804), i, 17–181.

Whatever the impact of Habsburg rule upon the kingdom's administration, it is plain that medieval Hungary was as under-governed as most European polities of the time. The chancellery and treasury operated for most of the later Middle Ages with only a few dozen officials apiece. Ostensibly 'public' duties were either passed down to local agencies or made into private functions, which officers of the king were expected to discharge using their own servants or *familiares*. *Familiares* were usually noblemen who had entered the service of greater lords in the expectation of patronage and reward. Some offices in the fourteenth century had lands or revenues (*honores*) attached to them. It was from the fifteenth century more usual for those performing tasks on behalf of the king to receive gifts of land or a slice of tax income levied locally. Tax collection was frequently farmed out or made the job of county officials and large landowners to collect in return for a part of the yield. The suspicion that greater men were subverting the revenues of the kingdom was a frequent cause of complaint in the decades before Mohács. In fact, the system of revenue collection in Hungary worked reasonably well and was sufficient in the early sixteenth century to finance one of the largest and best-equipped armies in Catholic Europe.[20] In this respect, under-government was not synonymous with political weakness.

Although Hungary may have been under-governed, it was over-judicialized. The lack of distinction between justice and administration meant that more or less every royal and local agency was also possessed of its own legal jurisdiction. As we would expect, the king's supreme power encompassed both governmental and judicial functions, although the king's justice was usually administered by judges under the fiction of the 'royal presence'. It was to the court of the king's presence or, as it was later known, the Royal Table that nobles usually went to prosecute their suits. The royal council, which advised the ruler, had a similarly double competence, and its principal member, the palatine, was not only the monarch's deputy and chief commander of the army, but also the foremost judge in the realm, next to the king himself. Counties, cities, market towns and villages had their own administrations that similarly functioned as courts. Local officers in charge of markets, grazing and woodland might also act as judges and impose penalties for minor infractions. Military garrisons, communities of miners, clusters of semi-noblemen (*conditionales*, *praediales*), and guilds of merchants likewise constituted jurisdictional units and had their own forums for adjudicating disputes and imposing discipline on their members. Honour courts maintained order among the knightly elite, dispensing a collective judgment over their peers.[21] Jews, foreign merchants, market traders, young men in villages and, later, Roma had their own courts for resolving suits among themselves and for maintaining communal discipline.[22] By the late fourteenth century, landowners were automatically considered to have the right to

[20] Martyn Rady, 'Jagiello Hungary', in DRMH 4, pp. ix–xlvii (pp. xvii–xxix). See also Rady, 'Fiscal and Military Developments in Hungary during the Jagiello Period', *Chronica*, 11 (2011), 85–98; János B. Szabó, 'Mohács-legendáink nyomában', *Korunk* (2012, no. 3), 27–33 (28).

[21] János Karácsonyi, 'Katonai becsületbiróság 1515–1516', *Hadtörténeti Közlemények*, 2 (1891), 482–8.

[22] For Jewish jurisdiction, see Martyn Rady, *Medieval Buda: Municipal Government and Jurisdiction in the Kingdom of Hungary* (Boulder, CO and New York, 1985), 81–5; for Roma courts, see Kamill Erdős, 'Cigány-törvényszék', *Néprajzi Közlemények*, 4, nos. 1–2 (1959), 203–14. I am indebted to Katalin Prajda for her information on the courts operating in late medieval Buda for visiting Italian

adjudicate in matters affecting their peasants, and many possessed the *ius gladii* (*pallosjog*) that allowed them to impose the death sentence for offences. Within the individual counties of the realm, elected noble administrators heard complaints and dispensed justice, eventually establishing subordinate magistrates' courts in the ridings. A few parts of the countryside operated outside the authority of the kingdom's counties, most notably the areas settled by Cuman and Jazyg nomads from the steppe. These had migrated to the Hungarian Plain during, or even before, the first decades of the thirteenth century and were subordinate to the authority of their own princes and captains.[23] Although many Cumans and Jazygs retained their nomadic habits and pagan practices until well into the fourteenth century, their leading families were soon converted and magyarized, adopting many of the legal practices observed within Hungarian noble society as a whole.[24]

The Hungarian kingdom was not territorially unified but constituted, like most medieval polities, a 'composite state'. Transylvania, Slavonia and Croatia were separate realms (called *regna*), under their own officers appointed by the Hungarian king—the voivode of Transylvania, and the bans of Croatia and Slavonia (their offices were from the mid-fourteenth century usually combined).[25] The nobility of the three territories took their plaints in the first instance to the voivode or ban, in much the same way as noblemen of the 'mother kingdom' sued before the king's court. Croatia itself consisted of a myriad of communes and rural districts, of which more than forty followed their own written law, although most of its coastal parts were taken by Venice at the beginning of the fifteenth century.[26] Transylvania contained the privileged territories of the Saxons and Szekels, who first settled in eastern Transylvania during the late twelfth and thirteenth centuries. The Saxons were immigrants, mainly from the Rhineland and the Low Countries; the Szekels were Hungarian-speakers, who were employed as border guards, but whose origins remain speculative. Along the southern frontier were military lordships consisting mainly of Romanians that constituted separate jurisdictional enclaves, having their own local administrations and courts.[27]

merchants. Some of the furnishings of young men's courts are on semi-permanent exhibition in the Ethnographic Museum in Cluj [visited July 2013].

[23] Nora Berend, *At the Gate of Christendom: Jews, Muslims and Pagans in Medieval Hungary* (Cambridge, 2001), 87–92; András Palóczi Horváth, *Pechenegs, Cumans, Iasians: Steppe peoples in medieval Hungary* (Budapest, 1989), 107.

[24] István Gyárfás, *A Jász-Kúnok története*, 4 vols. (Szolnok, Kecskemét and Budapest, 1870–85), iii, 484 (showing the Christianization of names by the mid-fourteenth century), 501, 532 (retained nomadic and pagan practices), 504, 553–4, 622 (grants of nobility), 469, 513, 528, 758 (adoption of legal practices). See also Nora Berend, 'Cuman integration in Hungary', in André Wink and Anatoly Khazanov, eds., *Nomads in the sedentary world* (London, 2001), 103–27.

[25] For the term *regnum* (which does not require a *rex*), see Martyn Rady, 'Voivode and *Regnum*: Transylvania's Place in the Medieval Kingdom of Hungary', in László Péter, ed., *Historians and the History of Transylvania* (Boulder, CO and New York, 1992), 87–101 (87–8, 97–101); and, more recently, Tudor Sălăgean, '*Regnum Transilvanum*: the Transylvanian *congregatio nobilium* and its role as a legal community at the end of the thirteenth century', in Martyn Rady and Alexandru Simon, eds., *Government and Law in Medieval Moldavia, Transylvania and Wallachia* (London, 2013), 21–8.

[26] See now, Damir Karbić and Marija Karbić, *The Laws and Customs of Medieval Croatia and Slavonia: A Guide to the Extant Sources*, ed. Martyn Rady (London, 2013) (electronic resource).

[27] For local jurisdictions in south-eastern Hungary, see Adrian Magina, 'From Custom to Written Law: *Ius Valachicum* in the Banat', in Rady and Simon, *Government and Law*, 71–7.

Within this jurisdictional mosaic, some elements of structure may be detected. Cases might be moved from the counties to the king's court, referred from market and mining courts to the local urban or town council for final adjudication, or moved from village courts to the landowner's manor court. The kingdom's courts existed for the most part, however, not in any hierarchical arrangement, but as a congeries of overlapping competences, permitting opportunities for litigants to prevaricate, sue through several courts simultaneously in the same action, or challenge the execution of court judgments by referring the case elsewhere. It might, therefore happen that the same case was brought before four separate courts in succession.[28] The kingdom's courts would, indeed, continue to remain numerous but jurisdictionally unhewn until the eighteenth century when some order was imposed upon their operation and mutual relations. Even so, the basic form of their organization, which may be first detected in the explosion of sources during the thirteenth century, continued largely unaltered until 1848.

* * *

Medieval Hungary was not only under-governed but also under-legislated. Its kings seldom troubled to institute written instruments of law. After an initial flurry of legislative activity in the eleventh century, principally aimed at establishing a Christian order and at announcing the royal rule, law stopped being made in this way. During the thirteenth century, several charters of liberties were extracted from Hungary's rulers but, thereafter, the legislative momentum again ceased. It picked up again in the late fourteenth and fifteenth centuries, first in consequence of the military and fiscal reforms that were undertaken to meet the Turkish threat, and then as a result of the rise to political power of the kingdom's diet, which by the mid-fifteenth century conceived of itself as possessing a legislative capacity. Laws agreed at the diet were supposedly the joint endeavour of ruler and estates, although in the language of the time they were referred to as royal decrees (*decreta*).[29] In most cases, however, they were negotiated, with the king presenting propositions that were debated, modified, and added to, being eventually concluded in the manner of a treaty. Throughout the kingdom's history, right up until 1918, legislative sovereignty was deemed to lie with the king *and* parliament, not with the king *in* parliament.[30]

Both during and after the medieval period, the legislation agreed by ruler and estates was primarily concerned with the resolution of pressing financial and military concerns, with measures aimed at preserving or restoring order, and with what we might consider 'private' business that affected individuals and corporations. Such legislation as there was dealt overwhelmingly with the needs of the moment, mainly as they impinged upon the nobility, and was accordingly of only temporary significance. The substantive content of the laws was accordingly slender. The law that was followed in the many courts of the kingdom was thus for the most part not legislative in origin, for its provisions were not defined or written down in normative instruments. Instead, the courts observed what they understood to be the

[28] Rady, *Medieval Buda*, 153–4.

[29] The terminological confusion was noted at the time. See Trip., II, 3 [5] (DRMH 5, 229).

[30] See here, László Péter, 'The Hungarian *Diætalis Tractatus* and the Imperial Constitutional Systems: A Comparison', *Central Europe*, 6, no. 1 (2008), 47–64 (58–60).

law and as now best fitted the circumstances before them. To begin with, the law that they practised was conceived as an amalgam of competing rights, *potestates* or *iura*, which attached subjectively to individuals and between which the courts negotiated.[31] From the thirteenth century, however, the law acquired an increasingly objective character in the sense of being understood to comprise general statements of universal application. Borrowing from church practice, this law, which was increasingly invoked in judgments, was called *consuetudo* or customary law, and its history is the subject of this book.[32]

## THE NATURE OF CUSTOMARY LAW

In purporting to originate in popular practice, customary law turns most modern legal positivism on its head. Customary law ostensibly derives neither from the precept of the sovereign nor from the sanction of the legislature, but from the acts of the people by which it acquires the character of law. This was, however, one of the principal ways in which law was understood in Europe for a large part of the Middle Ages. Even so, it was only in the twelfth century that customary law became the subject of systematic analysis, largely as a consequence of the discovery of Roman Law texts that discussed the relation of imperial law to local practices. Although contradictory opinions remained in respect of its nature and scope, many commentators promoted customary law as the highest form of secular law.[33] For Aquinas, therefore, custom was not just akin to enacted law, but superior to it, since customary law, being historically derived, was more stable and had been confirmed over time as being in accordance with the 'interior movement of the will and the concept of reason'. Thus, 'the consent of the whole community in the observance of a single custom has more value than the authority of the ruler'.[34] By locating the customary law in historical action, Aquinas was following an explanatory model favoured by canonists and civilians.[35] When asked to describe the customary law, laymen were apt to give a simpler account—that it was the law which conformed to truth and justice, which gave each man his due and which was harmful to none.[36]

[31] There is little consistency in usage before 1200, but *consuetudo* is rarely employed, except in the extra-legal sense of *mos*. See Synod of Szabolcs: 31 (DRMH 1, 57); *De institutione morum*: 6, given in Levente Závodszky, *A Szent István, Szent László és Kálmán korábeli törvények és zsinati határozatok forrásai* (Budapest, 1904), 137. For *ius*, *iura*, often also in its 'concretized' ablative form, see György Györffy, ed., *Diplomata Hungariae Antiquissimae, 1000–1131* (Budapest, 1992), 79, 101, 119, 155, 172, 214, 217, 236, 267 etc.; for *potestates*, see Györffy, *Diplomata*, 39, 52, 91, 118, 169. The terminology matches German legal materials of the same period, for which see Gerhard Köbler, *Das Recht im frühen Mittelalter. Untersuchungen zu Herkunft und Inhalt frühmittelalterlicher Rechtsbegriffe im deutschen Sprachgebiet* (Cologne and Vienna, 1971), 43–53.

[32] For the ecclesiastical origins of *consuetudo*, see Karl Kroeschell, *Deutsche Rechtsgeschichte 2, 1250–1450* (Reinbek bei Hamburg, 1973), 85; Köbler, *Das Recht im frühen Mittelalter*, 227–9.

[33] See thus G. R. Evans, *Law and Theology in the Middle Ages* (London and New York, 2002), 38.

[34] Aquinas, *Selected Political Writings*, ed. A.P. D'Entreves (Oxford, 1959), 73 (S. Th. 1a 2ae 97. 3).

[35] Köbler, *Das Recht im frühen Mittelalter*, 22–9.

[36] *Les Sources du droit du Canton de Vaud. Époque Savoyard (XII^e^–XVI^e^ siècle)* A. Coutume, 1. Enquêtes, eds. Jean-François Poudret and Jeanne Gallone-Brack (Sammlung Schweizerischer Rechtsquellen/Les Sources du droit suisse, 19: Vaud/Waadt) (Lausanne, 1972), 56, 62, 473, 503.

Much of customary law was unwritten and its substance was communicated orally, sometimes even in poetry, song and mnemonic verse.[37] From the twelfth century onwards, however, local customary laws were often written down and collected. The best known of these, Beaumanoir, Glanvill and the *Sachsenspiegel*, were only the tip of a much larger activity of codification that can be observed across much of Latin Christendom.[38] Where the law was still uncertain, lawyers and officials might in the later Middle Ages be called upon to establish and report upon its content, relaying their findings back to the courts in order to facilitate their deliberations. Advice might also be sought from jurists, learned men and so-called *coutumiers* (*consuetudinarii*) on the customary law's content and application.[39] The process of gathering and sifting customary arrangements of law, and then putting them into writing, altered their content. Lawyerly interpretation made the customary law lawyerly, imposing an order upon it and stiffening it with a vocabulary that often derived from civilian texts and from Romano-canonical procedural practices. Customary law was further shaped by legislative acts in the form of privileges of the ruler or of the statutes issued by representative assemblies, which often sought to abolish 'bad customs' and to promote new legal arrangements. The effectiveness of these instruments rested on the degree to which their provisions passed into practice and were themselves customized. They, nonetheless, communicated the law in the high language of chancellery practice, thereby contributing to its definition and sophistication. In its origin, customary law may have rested on common conviction, but it was also formed by interaction with the learned law and the written word.

Custom was locked into place by writing and by 'notoriety', in the sense of repetitive practice and observation.[40] It was only known to be law, however, as a consequence of its recognition in court judgments. As with statutory legislation or contracts, the courts had to be satisfied that custom was 'clothed with legal sanction' before they could admit its legal character.[41] The declaratory function of the courts often, therefore, melded into a constitutive one, and the interpretative role of jurisprudential action amounted thereby to a determining one. The uncertainty

[37] Bernard Mees, 'Weaving Words: Law and Performance in Early Nordic Tradition', *Amsterdamer Beiträge zur älteren Germanistik*, 70 (2013), 131–50; Katharine Simms, 'The Poetic Brehon Lawyers of Early Sixteenth-Century Ireland', *Ériu*, 57 (2007), 121–32; Sara Elin Roberts, *The Legal Triads of Medieval Wales* (Cardiff, 2007).

[38] Armin Wolf, *Gesetzgebung in Europa 1100–1500. Zur Entstehung der Territorialstaaten*, 2nd edition (Munich, 1996), 46–51.

[39] John Gilissen, *La Coutume* (Turnhout, 1982), 62–80. On the *coutumiers* and *consuetudinarii* and their role as witnesses to the law, see Jean-François Poudret, 'La Composition des courts de justice dans les pays romands et son influence sur la formation de la coutume (1250–1500), in Lloyd Bonfield, ed., *Seigneurial Justice* (Berlin, 2000), 40–75; Simon Teuscher, *Lords' Rights and Peasant Stories: Writing and the Formation of Tradition in the Later Middle Ages* (Philadelphia, 2012), 39–42.

[40] David Ibbetson, 'Custom in Medieval Law', in Amanda Perreau-Saussine and James Bernard Murphy, eds., *The Nature of Customary Law* (Cambridge, 2007), 151–75 (158).

[41] Hans Kelsen, *General Theory of Law and State* (New Brunswick and London, 2006), 127 (XI. B. a. 3) (first published in 1945). The relationship between customary law and contract was noted by medieval jurists. See Siegfried Brie, *Die Lehre vom Gewohnheitsrecht. Eine historisch-dogmatische Untersuchung*, i (Wrocław, 1899), 101.

over whether courts played a declaratory or creative role in the making of customary law not only confused the author of Hungary's sixteenth-century *Tripartitum* but was also the object of scholarly contention elsewhere.[42]

Notwithstanding the ambiguity attaching to the role of the courts, customary law became increasingly judicialized and shaped by the judgments and practices of the courts. We may thus note how in the legal literature of the later Middle Ages the decisions of courts were increasingly perceived as markers that disclosed the content of customary law.[43] It was in England, however, that the process of judicialization was perhaps most complete. By the sixteenth century, therefore the 'divers general Customs of old time used through all the realm' might be contrasted with the 'divers principles that be called by those learned in the law maxims, the which have been always taken for law in this realm'.[44] The conversion of customary law into the Common Law required, however, two preconditions. The first was an institutional memory that recollected and built upon past judicial practice in such a way as to extract the law's substance. The second was the establishment of a professional elite of law men, who accepted certain premises, acted upon them and communicated their decisions to each other, thus disseminating their 'tradition, use and experience'.[45] The fulfilment of these preconditions did not automatically lend stability to the law, but it did give fixity to the way that the law might be known, or at least how it might be said to be known.

These preconditions were largely missing in customary law courts. Their membership was not confined to a caste of professional law men, but included the unlearned, who often went under the name of assessors or sworn men. Lower courts were in places analogous to assemblies, charged both with law-making and with law-giving, and they were crowded. Higher courts were also notably diverse in their composition, drawing on noblemen and others whose expertise in the law derived from personal experience and not from legal study—many were in any case illiterate. The interest of courts of this type lay not so much in developing a body of substantive propositions as in finding remedies to the specific cases that came before them. They thus tended to seek positions that were midway between contending claims, bending principle to expediency. Certainly, there were some fundamental propositions or 'proto-norms' to which the courts usually deferred—the right of sons to inherit, a presumption in favour of widows and orphans, providential modes of proof, and so on.[46] Courts preferred to stick by these since to deviate too freely from them might vitiate the integrity of their past judgments. In this respect, their appeals to past conduct were not rhetorical. Nevertheless, the

[42] Roy Garré, *Consuetudo. Das Gewohnheitsrecht in der Rechtsquellen- und Methodenlehre des späten ius commune in Italien (16.–18. Jahrhundert)* (Frankfurt a/M, 2005), 73–6.

[43] Brie, *Die Lehre vom Gewohnheitsrecht*, 108–12, 144–5.

[44] T.F.T. Plucknett and J.L. Barton, eds., *St German's Doctor and Student* (London, 1974), pp. li–lii, 45, 57 (adjusted). See also A.W.B. Simpson, 'The Common Law and Legal Theory', in Simpson, *Legal Theory and Legal History: Essays on the Common Law* (London and Ronceverte, 1987), 359–82 (374–5).

[45] William Blackstone, *Commentaries on the Laws of England* (Oxford, 1765–9), i. 17, cited in Michael Lobban, *The Common Law and English Jurisprudence 1760–1850* (Oxford, 1991), 16.

[46] For proto-norms, see Garré, *Consuetudo. Das Gewohnheitsrecht*, 17–18.

decisions of courts were also guided by what was thought to be reasonable and just, which sometimes required that the proto-norms be set aside. The repudiation of a custom in concrete cases did not mean its obliteration. After the judgment, the law might revert back instead to its condition of generality, reassuming its previous normative value.[47] Nevertheless, a decision that disregarded an established norm might also yield an alternative way of handling similar disputes that arose in future, to which subsequent judgments might, or might not, defer. It was quite possible, therefore, to have a number of perfectly valid solutions to any one circumstance, between which the courts chose.[48]

Although their determinations were often couched in a learned language, courts in customary law jurisdictions remained tied to communal apprehensions of what the law's content should be, and they were flexible in their application of the law. Courts seldom, therefore, explained their decisions, lest by delivering the grounds of their judgments they constrain their freedom to make equitable determinations in the future.[49] The reluctance of Hungarian courts to elucidate their judgments would, indeed, remain a feature of their operation until well into the twentieth century. At the same time, however, lawyerly approaches to the law filtered through the hierarchy of the courts, adding to the law's complexity. Recollection of previous judgments was often persuasive and resulted in the establishment of a jurisprudence and court practice that became increasingly remote from popular observance. The *Verwissenschaftlichung* of the law, its transition from a supposed *Volksrecht* to the learned law of the courts or *Juristenrecht*, was mostly viewed with suspicion by litigants, who saw in it the law's distortion by partisan judges and crafty lawyers.[50] Much of the theoretical literature composed in the later Middle Ages, and indeed afterwards, continued thus to affirm that customary law was rooted in the repetitive acts of a legally sovereign people, in which the decisions of courts played only a minor role.[51]

* * *

The activity and constitution of Hungary's courts only become visible in the thirteenth century. They were by this time communal in their composition and judgments were given out after collective discussion. The language in which suits were brought and the vocabulary of court judgments were, nevertheless, informed by the larger European *ius commune*, and procedures broadly followed the Romano-canonical practices of church courts. The courts generally acknowledged a set of proto-norms that had their origin not in some 'mysterious birth' or 'unconscious choice' of first principles but from early arrangements of land holding that vested

47 George C. Homans, *English Villagers of the thirteenth century* (Cambridge, MA), 1941, 404; see also, Ian Hamnett, *Chieftainship and Legitimacy: An anthropological study of executive law in Lesotho* (London and Boston, 1975), 14.

48 J.-A. Brutails, *La Coutume d'Andorre*, 2nd edition (Andorra la Vella, 1965), 56–7.

49 Kroeschell, *Deutsche Rechtsgeschichte 2 (1250–1650)*, 124.

50 For the development of *Volksrecht* to *Juristenrecht*, see James Bernard Murphy, *The Philosophy of Customary Law* (Oxford and New York, 2014), 112.

51 Garré, *Consuetudo. Das Gewohnheitsrecht*, 117–18.

property in the male descendants of the *avus* or ancestor who had first acquired it.[52] Much the same disposition of property rights as we will find in Hungary can also be discerned in other medieval societies where land was the primary mark of wealth and prestige—not only in neighbouring Moldavia and Wallachia, but also further afield, in Russia and Ireland, for instance.[53] Although a part of Hungarian legal vocabulary was Slavonic in origin, it is thus mistaken to consider it rooted in older, Slavonic practices.[54] The set of fundamental propositions to which the law usually deferred, included partible inheritance among male heirs, the concurrent rights of the kindred or descendants of the *avus* over the landed goods that had once been a part of the *avus*'s patrimony, and the right of free bestowal in respect of land that someone had acquired by his own efforts. To these we must add the conviction in Hungary that all landed property had its origin in the royal gift and thus should return to the ruler in the event of a nobleman dying without heir or being found guilty of perfidy (*nota infidelitatis*). These customary norms, which were conceived in Hungary under the broad heading of 'ancestral rights' or *aviticitas*, were compelling but not absolute, for to have stuck by them in all circumstances could have led to injustices. The interests of daughters might in particular be offended by prescriptive approaches.

From these substantive propositions, Hungarian courts were able to make logical inferences and to build a body of jurisprudence that became increasingly sophisticated, if only to match the ingenuity of litigants and lawyers. Nevertheless, because court judgments were also reflective of common conviction, the substance of customary law remained uncertain. Conventions built upon the foundations of *aviticitas* might therefore lapse and either fall into desuetude or move into a legal half-life, sometimes being recalled and on other occasions overlooked. By the same token, new practices might acquire legal recognition, or contradictory customs be posited, between which the courts chose. Prudential practice might likewise over time acquire the character of a legal obligation, with the consequence that precautionary clauses inserted voluntarily in charters gradually took on a normative quality, adding to the law's complexity.[55] Although it was generally acknowledged

[52] For these descriptions of the origins of custom, see Jean-Marie Carbasse, 'Contribution à l'étude du processus coutumier: la coutume de droit privé jusqu'à la Révolution', *Droits. Revue française de théorie juridique*, 3 (1986), 24–37 (25). See also, Michel Troper, 'Du Fondement de la Coutume à la Coutume comme fondement', *Droits. Revue française de théorie juridique*, 3 (1986), 11–24 (15).

[53] See Martyn Rady, 'Historical Introduction', in Rady and Simon, *Government and Law*, 1–13 (11); Fergus Kelly, *A Guide to Early Irish Law* (Dublin, 2009), 100–5; Lee A. Farrow, *Between Clan and Crown: The Struggle to Define Noble Property Rights in Imperial Russia* (Cranbury, NJ, 2004), 41–5; R.C. van Caenegem, *An Historical Introduction to Private Law* (Cambridge, 1992), 186.

[54] Cf. Karel Kadlec, *Verbőczyovo Tripartitum a soukromé právo uherské i chorvatské šlechty v něm obsažené* (Prague, 1902), 6–16. Discussed in László Blazovich, 'A Tripartitum és forrásai', *Századok*, 141 (2007), 1011–23 (1014–15).

[55] Hence the *(tanto) melius* formula included in deeds of conveyance and exchange. See 'Decisiones Tabulae' in *Codex Ilosvay*, OSzK, MSS, Fol. Lat. 4023, fol. 123*v*, also in J.N. Kovachich, *Notitiae Praeliminares ad Syllogen Decretorum Comitialium* (Pest, 1820), 404–5; György Galanthai Fekete, *Problemata Juridica seu Quaestiones in causis*, ed. János Csaplovics (Bratislava, 1814), 28. On the movement from 'une prudence habituelle' to 'une obligation impérieuse', see Paul Ourliac and J. de Malafosse, *Histoire du droit privé*, 3 vols. (Paris, 1968–71), ii, 424. See also, David J. Bederman, *Custom as a Source of Law* (Cambridge, 2010), 38.

by commentators that the larger custom of the realm should take precedence over local arrangements of law, courts might take an opposing view, asserting a particular *usus* or understanding to be stronger.[56] This approach, which favoured local arrangements at the expense of uniformity, may be observed in other customary jurisdictions.[57] Written law in the form of statute might also intrude, for a time being considered persuasive, but after a space being forgotten or deemed no longer relevant. The opinion that statutes that had not been absorbed into custom, lapsed with the death of the ruler created additional uncertainty in respect of the written law's application.[58] In this respect, it did not help that the texts of the kingdom's laws were inadequately circulated or miscopied in their transmission, thus rendering their content unsure.

Had Hungarian customary law become more fully judicialized, then a body of enduring rules might have emerged that gave continuity and predictability to the law's application. The reluctance of the courts to give legal grounds for their determinations and their preference for equitable solutions stood in the way, however, of jurisprudential growth. Under these circumstances, it is not surprising that there should have been much opportunistic litigation. Spurious plaints were frequently raised in the hope that the court would find them of legal merit, yielding a windfall to the plaintiff. Or dubious rights were advanced in the expectation that the court would press for an accommodation between the parties. In many cases, the only obstacle to vexatious suits was the cost. By the same token, surety of possession was compromised, for the grounds of legal right were apt to change in accordance with the court's determination of the customary law's content and of its applicability in specific cases.

From the thirteenth century onwards, many civilian commentators posited the customary law as the equivalent to the written statutory law. For these, customary law was not subordinate to, and only explanatory of, statute law, in the manner imagined by many canonists.[59] Both operated instead as equal and interacting sources of legal authority. The dualistic relationship between customary and statute law was often expressed scholastically in the binary oppositions of unwritten and written law, of the law that derived from, on the one hand, the tacit and, on the other, the express consent of the people, and of the gradual authority that the one gathered through use over time, and the immediate authority that the other possessed upon promulgation.[60] Just as the statutory law might be brought together

[56] The relationship between law, custom and *usus* in the practice of Hungarian noble society is cleverly satirized by József Eötvös, *The Village Notary: A Romance of Hungarian Life*, trans. Otto Wenckstern, 3 vols. (London, 1850), ii, 245–6.

[57] Brutails, *La Coutume d'Andorre*, 63; Hamnett, *Chieftainship and Legitimacy*, 13. See also Kroeschell, *Deutsche Rechtsgeschichte 2*, 85–6.

[58] György Bónis, 'Einleitung', in DRH 1301–1457, 9–37 (28).

[59] Willibald M. Plöchl, *Geschichte des Kirchenrechts*, 2nd edition, 5 vols. (Vienna and Munich, 1953–69), ii, 52; James A. Brundage, 'E pluribus unum: Custom, the Professionalization of Medieval Law, and Regional Variations in Marriage Formation', in Mia Korpiola, ed., *Regional Variations in Matrimonial Law and Custom in Europe, 1150–1600* (Leiden and Boston, 2011), 21–41 (23–33); Harold J. Berman, *Law and Revolution: The Formation of the Western Legal Tradition* (Cambridge, MA and London, 1983), 145.

[60] These oppositions can be partly tracked back to the post-classical period. See A. A. Schiller, 'Custom in Classical Roman Law', *Virginia Law Review*, 24 (1937–8), 268–82 (270).

in a single codex, so, it was imagined that, in view of their dualistic relationship, the customary law might also be converted through lawyerly interrogation from an 'unwritten book of the law' to a series of coherent, written propositions.[61] Behind this approach, we may discern the same sort of interest in establishing legal uniformity as generally characterize polities moving in the direction of greater territorial stability and organizational cohesion.[62] In Hungary, the stabilization of the customary law through its concentration in a text did not, however, render the law less customary. Instead, the codified customary law was itself also customized through practice and use, contributing to its malleability and indeterminacy. As a consequence, the law as observed continued to lack fixity and thus the kingdom to retain its character as a customary jurisdiction, right through to the nineteenth century. In what follows, we will examine the interaction of practice and text by analysing the background and responses to the early-sixteenth-century legal code that is known as the *Tripartitum*.

[61] Teuscher, *Lords' Rights and Peasant Stories*, 38.

[62] The process is examined in Franco Ciardo and Jean-Daniel Morerod, 'Les Chartes de franchises du XIIIe siècle et l'histoire des libertés vaudoises', *Revue Historique Vaudoise*, 99, (1991), 9–41 (20–35).

# 2

# Customary Law and the *Tripartitum*

## STEPHEN WERBŐCZY AND HIS *TRIPARTITUM*

Kings and diets in fourteenth- and fifteenth-century Hungary generally shied away from imposing substantive rules of law, for such imposed rules fixed obligations and robbed adjudication of its suppleness. Most of the statutes published during this time were thus almost exclusively concerned with establishing rules of procedure and, particularly in the interregna of the 1440s and 1450s, with devising mechanisms against arbitrary despoliation. With the restoration of order in the second half of the fifteenth century, however, attention turned to the content and application of the law. The demand was thus laid, principally by the diet, that the kingdom's laws be fixed in writing and be no longer indeterminate and contingent.[1] A notary of the chancellery—a certain Magister Adam Liszkai—was in the 1490s duly appointed for this purpose, in vain as it turned out.[2] Soon, however, the diet switched its attention to such statutes as had been already proclaimed and urged that the kingdom's written law be brought together and published in a single volume.[3] It belonged, however, to Wladislas II, or at least to one of his counsellors, to combine these two programmes. At some point towards the end of the first decade of the new century, Wladislas commissioned a quite different work that would unite both the statutes enacted by king and diet and the unwritten customary law of the realm, and thus 'collect into one all the rights, laws, customs and constitutions received and approved of this realm; that is to say, those within this our realm, and especially those that they are accustomed to follow and observe in our royal court in judging and deciding cases, and in making determinations'.[4] The motive that Wladislas II gave for his decision was the confusion and unpredictability attending unwritten law and the opportunities that this gave to unscrupulous litigants: 'for as the laws themselves lacked the support of the power of writing, whatsoever of the law or custom was brought to the fore, they most shamefully confused in respect of the reasonableness of its judgments, either by dragging in a contrary opinion or by asserting that it was otherwise opined and understood by other judges in other cases. Thus, it frequently happened that in one case someone previously had won and in the same or similar circumstance

1 1498: 7 (DRMH 4, 90). 2 1498: 7; 1500: 10 (DRMH 4, 90, 142).

3 1504: 31 (DRMH 4, 172). See also 1507: 20. References given in this way refer to the statute as published in any of the many editions of the *Corpus Juris Hungarici*.

4 DRMH 5, 8–9.

another lost and was defeated.'[5] Wladislas's explanation is testimony to the legal uncertainties inherent within a customary jurisdiction and to the impact that the law's indeterminacy had upon the lives of ordinary noblemen.

Wladislas's commission to unite the kingdom's statute law and its unwritten customary law was entrusted to the chancellery lawyer, politician and spokesman of the common nobility, Stephen Werbőczy (*c.* 1470–1541). The work that Werbőczy presented in 1514 and published three years later was entitled, *The Customary Law of the Renowned Kingdom of Hungary: A Work in Three Parts* (*Tripartitum opus iuris consuetudinarii inclyti regni Hungariae*). It was from the very first known either as the *Tripartitum* or, as a consequence of the reputation it enjoyed, the *Decretum*.

* * *

Much of Werbőczy's biography is uncertain and we do not know precisely when he received his commission to bring together the kingdom's laws.[6] It must, however, have been after 1507, when the diet again requested that work begin on collecting the kingdom's legislation, and there is now good evidence to suggest a later rather than an earlier date.[7] Following Werbőczy, historians have averred that his commission required 'so much study and so many late nights' that the *Tripartitum* was for a long period in gestation.[8] Its preparation was certainly attended by the scrutiny of formulary books, from which Werbőczy subsequently drew.[9] Nevertheless, the *Tripartitum* betrays in its eventual form all the hallmarks of haste. In places, the Latin text is jumbled to the point of opacity; elsewhere, there are contradictions, non sequiturs and omissions. The Prologue, in particular, which many historians have taken as evidence of Werbőczy's extraordinary erudition, is in fact an amalgam of probably no more than half a dozen texts, mostly distillations and *summae*, jumbled carelessly together.[10] Whole chunks of the Prologue were lifted verbatim from a thirteenth-century Neapolitan account, the *Summa Legum* of Raymundus Parthenopeus, which Werbőczy knew from its 1506 Cracow edition.[11] The principal body of the book was similarly ill arranged. Originally, Werbőczy had intended to

[5] DRMH 5, 6–9.

[6] Werbőczy's career is summarized in Martyn Rady, 'Stephen Werbőczy and his *Tripartitum*', in DRMH 5, pp. xxvii–xliv. The standard biography remains Vilmos Fraknói, *Werbőczi István életrajza* (Budapest, 1899).

[7] 1507: 20. See now Gábor Mikó, 'Ismeretlen országgyűlési emlék a Jagelló-korból', *Történelmi Szemle*, 56, no. 3 (2013), 455–80 (471–3), who proposes the end of 1512 as the date of commencement.

[8] DRMH 5, 4–5.

[9] Rady, 'Stephen Werbőczy and his *Tripartitum*', p. xxxiv. See in particular MNL OL DL, 281415, discussed in Ferenc Eckhart, 'Formuláskönyv Werbőczy István hivatali működése köréből', in Ferenc Eckhart and Alajos Degré, eds., *Emlékkonyv Dr. Viski Illés József* (Budapest, 1942), 151–60. The relationship between the so-called 'Werbőczy-féle' formulary, the *Fragmenta iuris* included within it, and the final text of the *Tripartitum* awaits thorough explication. Plainly some parts of the formulary were disregarded. See Bónis, KJE, 217. For textual links between the Werbőczy-féle formulary, the *Fragmenta*, the Somogy formulary book and the *Tripartitum*, see Bónis, KJE, 249–58.

[10] Martyn Rady, 'The Prologue to Werbőczy's *Tripartitum* and its Sources', *English Historical Review*, 121, no. 490 (2006), 104–45 (113).

[11] Rady, 'The Prologue to Werbőczy's *Tripartitum*', 109. The *Summa Legum* itself relied on the thirteenth-century *Summa* of Azo's pupil, Goffredo da Trani. See Péter Bónis, 'Bartolus in Medieval Hungary', *Fundamina*, 18, no. 2 (2012), 11–22 (13).

divide his material into three parts, corresponding to the classical division between persons, things and actions. He was unable, however, to keep to his scheme. The first part thus conjoined persons and property; the second dealt largely with procedure; while the third has all the appearance of a hotchpotch, including materials on Croatia, Slavonia and Transylvania, the condition of the peasantry, and the concept of blameless defence (culled verbatim from Aquinas), before concluding abruptly with the oath to be given in court by Jews.[12] In addition to the Prologue, the main parts of the *Tripartitum* were supported by an Address to the Reader that included the text of Wladislas's commission, Werbőczy's Dedication to the king, a Conclusion and several poems by contemporaries that extolled Werbőczy's achievement. Of these, the thirty-eight-line verse by the humanist poet and churchman, Hieronymus Balbi, is little more than a florid rendering in metre of Wladislas's original commission. Balbi had obviously not read the work that he was recommending.[13]

Werbőczy himself was not an academic lawyer and, although he had briefly attended the University of Cracow, he had received no education in the law.[14] His experience derived from service in the courts and in the chancellery. The content and arrangement of the *Tripartitum* reflected his practical understanding of the law's content and proper application. Thus, although the *Tripartitum* was a work on the law, it was not primarily intended for lawyerly consumption. Certainly, in one place, Werbőczy introduces and solves a legal conundrum which seems more intended for academic debate than for a real situation.[15] Nevertheless, his intended audience was the nobility and it is the law of the nobility with which Werbőczy is mainly concerned. In the first part, he thus addresses his readership directly in respect of the rights of the *paterfamilias* and on another occasion speaks to himself as a nobleman.[16] In the second, he dwells at length upon out-of-court procedures, such as inquests and oath-taking, wherein nobles were more likely to be involved, while ignoring arrangements observed within the courtroom. The details of court practice cannot therefore be discerned in Werbőczy's account. The passage from the written submission of the plaint, to the summons, to the raising and calling of the case, its formal joining and interlocutory decisions, and onwards to the final judgment and execution, are only hinted at. All this was the business of lawyers, not of the noblemen who entrusted suits to their care. In this respect, it is telling that Werbőczy's most detailed account of procedure is given in respect of how a nobleman

12 For Aquinas in the *Tripartitum*, see Rady, 'The Prologue to Werbőczy's *Tripartitum*', 111–12, and DRMH 5, 403, note 292. For blameless defence, see also Péter Bónis, 'A Tripartitum forrásai és az európai ius commune', in Gábor Máthé, ed., *A magyar jog fejlődésének fél évezrede. Werbőczy és a Hármaskönyv 500 esztendő múltán* (Budapest, 2014), 213–42 (229–38).

13 The poems are given in DRMH 5, 434–7, with translations into English. For Balbi's career and relations with Werbőczy, see György Bónis, *A jogtudó értelmiség a Mohács előtti Magyarországon* (Budapest, 1971), 320–1.

14 András Kubinyi, 'István Werbőczy als Politiker vor Mohács (1526)', in Balázs Nagy and Marcell Sebők, eds., *Festschrift for János M. Bak* (Budapest and New York, 1999), 558–82 (559).

15 Trip., I. 50 (DRMH 5, 118–19, with note), although it may derive from a real case. See Erik Fügedi, *The Elefánthy: The Hungarian Nobleman and his Kindred* (Budapest, 1998), 27; Martyn Rady, 'Erik Fügedi and the Elefánthy Kindred', SEER, 77, no. 2 (1999), 295–308 (304).

16 Trip., I. 51 [2] (DRMH 5, 121). See also Trip., I. 97 (DRMH 5, 179).

might sack his attorney and force a retrial on account of lawyerly ineptitude.[17] Neither, it should be remarked, does Werbőczy describe the various competences of the several royal courts before which noblemen might plead, nor explain their collegiate composition, preserving instead the civilian fiction that the courts lay under the mastery of single judges. As Werbőczy saw it, the details of court composition were as irrelevant to his audience as the arcana of their practices and seating plans. For this information, we must instead rely upon later accounts. The contention that the *Tripartitum* was intended either for students or for specialists already familiar with civilian law and the *ius commune* cannot therefore be shown.[18]

In 1514, Werbőczy presented the *Tripartitum* to the diet. In a manner reflecting the divided sovereignty of the late medieval polity, the compilation was sent for inspection to committees appointed respectively by the king and the estates. Reserving the final right of approval to the king, the law that was published at the diet's close authorized Wladislas to seal and distribute the *Tripartitum*.[19] We know that Wladislas gave his consent to the text even before the diet's formal dissolution, but, contrary to expectation, the *Tripartitum* neither received the royal seal nor was it distributed by the chancellery. Werbőczy later explained these omissions by reference to the cares that had beset the king and the subsequent difficulties involved in any royal succession (after a long illness, Wladislas died in March 1516).[20] There may be some truth in this. The task of transcribing the text many times by hand and having each copy sealed prior to distribution, which was the usual way at this time of disseminating the kingdom's statutory laws, required commitment on the part of the chancellery and thus (as Werbőczy recognized) political will.[21] Both the Dedication and one of the appended poems ('Epigram on a Busybody and Zoilus') also suggest contemporary criticism of Werbőczy's work, which may be connected to a brief political setback to his ambitions.[22] Nevertheless, the explanation sometimes offered for Wladislas's delay is implausible—that the barons moved the king to reject the *Tripartitum* on account of the clause that declared them to have rights no greater than those of ordinary noblemen.[23]

Werbőczy's career suffered no lasting check on account of Wladislas's death, and he moved into the service of Wladislas's successor, Louis II, holding the high judicial

[17] Trip., II. 79–81 (DRMH 5, 357–81).

[18] Cf. Alajos Degré, *A Négyeskönyv perjogi anyaga* (Budapest, 1935), 16; János Zlinszky, 'Werbőczy jogforrástana', *Jogtudományi Közlöny*, 48, no. 10 (1993), 374–6; Péter Bónis, 'The commentators and the Hungarian law in the Middle Ages, with special regard to the Tripartitum', in Péter Antalóczy, ed., *Hagyomány és érték. Állam- és jogtudományi tanulmányok a Károli Gáspár Református Egyetem fennállásának 20. évfordulójára* (Budapest, 2013), 116–26 (121).

[19] 1514: 63 (DRMH 4, 206).

[20] Address to the Reader (DRMH 5, 5).

[21] Address to the Reader (DRMH 5, 3).

[22] Bónis, *A jogtudó értelmiség*, 339.

[23] Thus József Illés, *Bevezetés a magyar jog történetébe. A források története* (Budapest, 1910), 133; Bálint Hóman and Gyula Szekfű, *Magyar történet*, 3rd edition, 5 vols. (Budapest, 1935–6), ii, 588; more recently, Béla P. Szabó, 'Stephanus Werbőczy', in Michael Stolleis, ed., *Juristen. Ein biographisches Lexikon. Von der Antike bis zum 20. Jahrhundert*, (Munich, 2001), 668–9 (669). But the *Quadripartitum* drawn up in the 1550s with the aim of superseding the *Tripartitum* retained the same clause (*una eademque*), which it would surely not have done had the clause been controversial. For the criticisms implied in the text and poem, see DRMH 5, 17, 437.

office of *personalis* (the title meant that he substituted in judging for the king's own person). The momentum for publication of his work had, however, been lost in the interregnum. After making a few revisions to his manuscript to take into account the decisions of the 1514 diet, Werbőczy accordingly had the *Tripartitum* published at his own expense by the printing house of Singrenius in Vienna. The printed sheets were then sent by him to the county seats of the kingdom for public proclamation. By the standards of today's computer-aided publication, the typesetting and printing of the *Tripartitum* was achieved in record time, a mere forty days, but is unlikely to have cost the author more than a few hundred florins.[24]

A later account contended that the *Tripartitum* was feted as '*the* Decretum' almost immediately upon its publication.[25] Indeed, little more than a year after its distribution, the diet confirmed its contents and instructed the courts of the realm to adjudicate in accordance with its text.[26] Nevertheless, the authority of the *Tripartitum* rested not on legislation but on use. In the same month as the *Tripartitum* was printed, in May 1517, a Curia court summarized a portion of its text in support of a judgment.[27] We have other evidence of the *Tripartitum*'s text being relied upon in the courts, as is indicated in a compilation of court judgments drawn up in the 1520s.[28] A formulary composed at about the same time for notaries in training likewise contained large chunks deriving from the *Tripartitum*'s text.[29] The earliest surviving Hungarian case file, although it dates only from much later, also records a decision based explicitly on the *Tripartitum*'s text (hence: *Decreti Tripartiti partem secundum titulum quinquagesimum*).[30] The *Tripartitum* additionally gained currency in Transylvania, where it subsequently operated side by side with compendia of local law.[31] In Slavonia, it also became the principal text upon which lawyers relied, although its influence on the Croatian littoral was diminished by the retained efficacy of local codes.[32]

24 The rapidity of its production is noted on the final page of the original 1517 edition, in the *Corrigenda*. The cost of publication is based on Rudolf Hirsch, *Printing, Selling and Reading, 1450–1550*, 2nd edition (Wiesbaden, 1974), 36–40. Presumably, the leaves were sent out uncut and unbound.

25 Nicolaus Istvánffy, *De rebus Ungaricis* (Cologne, 1622), 61.

26 1518 (Bács): 41 [5] (DRMH 4, 234).

27 MNL OL DL, 84630. The judgment (*quod divisiones intra fratribus indivisis non Longe Lite*) borrows from Trip., I. 45 (DRMH 5, 111–13).

28 'Notabilia circa processum Juris in Curiae Regiae Majestatis', *Codex Ilosvay*, OSzK, MSS, Fol. Lat. 4023, fols. 38–9 (see also J. N. Kovachich, *Notitiae Praeliminares ad Syllogen Decretorum Comitialium* (Pest, 1820), 406–15).

29 György Bónis, 'Ungarische Juristen am Ausgang des Mittelalters', in Roman Schur, ed., *Die Rolle der Juristen bei der Entstehung des modernen Staates* (Berlin, 1986), 65–75 (74–5).

30 MNL OL, O 1, *Processus octavales*, Bundle 4, no. 183, fol. 6*v* (1588).

31 Where they are given, the grounds for judgments delivered in Transylvanian county courts rely as much upon the *Tripartitum* as upon the seventeenth-century Transylvanian collections known as the *Approbatae* and *Compilatae*.

32 *Arhivski vjesnik*, Series 1, no. 8 (1939), 51; *Arhivski vjesnik*, Series 2, nos. 7–8 (1964–5), 238; *Arhivski vjesnik*, Series 2, nos. 17–18, (1974–5), 119, 121, 126; Vjekoslav Klaić, *Povijest hrvata od najstarijih vremena do svršetka XIX stoljeća*, 5 vols. (Zagreb, 1980), v, 629–37; Géza Palffy, 'Horvátorszag és Szlavónia a xvi–xvii. századi magyar királyságban', *Fons*, 9, nos. 1–3, (2002), 107–21 (113). Cf. Szabolcs Varga, 'Horvátország és Szlavónia Werbőczy Tripartitumában', in Gábor Máthé, ed., *A magyar jog fejlődésének fél évezrede. Werbőczy és a Hármaskönyv 500 esztendő múltán* (Budapest, 2014), 163–85 (180–1).

The success of the *Tripartitum* is amply demonstrated by the history of its publication. Following the original 1517 printing, there was a hiatus of several decades. At this time, it was still uncertain whether the *Tripartitum* might be reworked or even superseded by a new text, and so there was thought to be little commercial merit in reissuing the original version. By the middle years of the century, these concerns had been at least partly allayed. Accordingly, two further editions were issued by Singrenius in Vienna in 1545 and 1561, with several more printed by other Viennese firms (1572, 1581). A Hungarian-language version under the title of the *Magyar Decretum* was next published in Debrecen in 1565, and a new Hungarian translation in Cluj in 1571 and 1572 for circulation in Transylvania. A Croatian-language edition (in at least three separate print-runs) followed in 1574, and a German edition in 1599.[33] Thus, in the sixteenth century, the *Tripartitum* was published altogether in ten separate editions. We should add that in the 500 years since 1517, the *Tripartitum* has been published more than any other secular work in Hungarian history—fifty-seven times in total, not including mnemonic, rhyming and abbreviated versions.[34]

* * *

Customary law is frequently understood as unwritten law, although (and as Werbőczy himself noted) there were plenty of occasions in the Middle Ages when it was written down.[35] The act of writing does not in itself, however, lend custom permanence. The text so composed may be forgotten or never pass into circulation, or it may be glossed, with the gloss taking on the authority that the original text had enjoyed.[36] The text may be emended, with different versions acquiring a local or temporary currency.[37] It may fall into desuetude or be superseded, which has been the fate over time of most customary compilations.[38] Once a body of customary law has been committed to writing, however, and has passed into use, it will often acquire a strongly normative character, taking on the appearance of legislation.[39] Some customary collections, for instance the codes of Transylvanian

[33] For the Croatian edition, see Nataša Štefanec, 'Pergošić's Translation of the *Tripartitum* into Slavonian', in CLCE, 71–85; also, Nataša Štefanec, *Heretik Njegova Veličanstva. Povijest o Jurju IV. Zrinskom i njegovu rodu* (Zagreb, 2001), 231–2.

[34] Rady, 'Stephen Werbőczy and his *Tripartitum*', p. xxvii. Previous editions are listed in István Csekey, *Werbőczy István–A Tripartitum bibliográfiája* (Acta Juridico-Politica, 2) (Cluj, 1942), 157–94. The latest edition of which I am aware is a translation into Slovak by Erik Štenpien, *Tripartitum* (Bratislava, 2008).

[35] Trip., Prologue [11] (DRMH 5, 35).

[36] The obvious examples here are the Buda *Stadtrecht* of *c.* 1400, which was largely neglected until its discovery four centuries later, and the *Sachsenspiegel* with its Romanized glosses.

[37] As was the case with the fourteenth-century *Zipser Willkür*, in use among the Germans of Spiš. See Béla P. Szabó, *A Zipser Willkür (Szepesi jog) 13 kéziratának összehasonlító elemzése és fordítása*, on-line Project Report, OTKA, 2007; see also László Blazovich, 'A Szász tükör és a Zipser Willkür', *Jogtörténeti Szemle* (2004, no. 1), 1–4; Béla P. Szabó, 'A szepesi jog forrásai', *Jogtörténeti Tanulmányok*, 8 (2005), 443–63.

[38] For Italian examples, see Manlio Bellomo, *The Common Legal Past of Europe 1000–1800* (Washington, D.C., 1995), 84–5.

[39] Alan Watson, *The Evolution of Western Private Law* (Baltimore and London, 2000), 100.

law published in the later seventeenth century, may receive the imprimatur of the legislator, but this is not a necessary condition for custom to acquire the attributes of statute.

Paradoxically, however, by purporting to have its roots in popular practice, written custom can acquire a normative power that is stronger and more compelling than ordinary legislation. Alleging an origin in historic observance and in the popular will, it may become emblematic of the community and the legal expression of its common identity over time. Very often, it will be imbued with a mythic quality, as the 'law of our fathers', or deemed a product of the 'national genius', even though the written customary law may in fact be a text borrowed from elsewhere.[40] By the same token, the original compiler may be vested with grand historical significance, as the true interpreter of the laws, and eventually feted, like Werbőczy, as 'our Hermogenes, Bracton and Tribonian'.[41] Written custom may thus obtain a power that is akin to legislation and yet, as Aquinas saw, be more than legislation, being possessed of a reputation that lends it special moral suasion. Its ultimate authority, however, rests on its use over time, by which its precepts become embedded in social habit, thus confirming its continued validity through repetitive practice. In short, written custom is persuasive and normative to the extent that it is itself considered customary.

## THE *TRIPARTITUM* AND THE SOURCES OF CUSTOMARY LAW

Most descriptions of customary law are brief in respect of their authors' epistemology. A few authors explained the customary law as being known to them through their perusal of the legal record; others by their interrogation of those who might be expected to know. Beaumanoir, Glanvill and, pre-eminently, the Bohemian Land Ordinance of 1500 fall into the first group—in the case of the last of these even to the extent of footnoting individual provisions to the texts of court judgments.[42] To the second belong Bogišić's and Brutails's more recent account of the customs of Montenegro and Andorra, which allegedly built upon popular practices as actually observed—in Bogišić's case through a check list of over a thousand questions.[43] Most authors are, however, content simply to aver that what they write is true. Werbőczy belongs to this category, for most of his text is unsourced and we are invited to take his word on trust. Werbőczy does, however, indicate the

[40] Watson, *The Evolution of Western Private Law*, 99, 103.

[41] Paul Wallaszky (Valaszky), *De Stephano Verbőczio icto celeberrimo dissertatio* (Leipzig, 1768), 15.

[42] Petr Kreuz and Ivan Martinovský, eds., *Vladislavské zřízení zemské* (Prague, 2007), 107–291. Discussed in Christopher Nicholson, *Law and the Estates: the Bohemian Land Ordinance of 1500 in Context*, unpublished PhD thesis (University College London, 2013), 107–14, 219–23. Similar referencing to court judgments may be found in Raymond Monier, ed., *Les Lois, enquêtes et jugements des pairs du castel de Lille* (Lille, 1937), which was composed on the basis of court judgments in the late-fourteenth and fifteenth centuries.

[43] Werner G. Zimmermann, *Valtazar Bogišić 1834–1908. Ein Beitrag zur südslavistischen Geistes- und Rechtsgeschichte im 19. Jahrhundert* (Wiesbaden, 1962), 162–3.

sources from which the content of Hungarian customary law might be known, on account of which it is possible to extrapolate his working methods. As we will see, he not untypically invests these instruments of recognition with a creative function, thus confusing their declaratory and constitutive roles.

A principal difficulty attending Werbőczy's account is his theoretical inconsistency. First, he uses terms indiscriminately, often alternating in his discussion between *ius*, *lex* and *consuetudo*, as if these were synonymous.[44] This inconsistency is less apparent in the Prologue, largely because this part of the work is given rigour by the civilian sources upon which Werbőczy relied, principally the *Summa Legum*. Thus, *lex* or statute is here counterpoised to custom or *consuetudo* and both are presented as equal manifestations of a transcendent and overarching *ius*.[45] In the main part of the *Tripartitum*, however, this neat arrangement is forgotten. *Lex* and *consuetudo* are used indiscriminately, sometimes within the course of a single sentence, and sometimes also in clusters as if the author had suddenly reminded himself of one or the other term. *Ius*, moreover, which had previously united *lex* and *consuetudo*, loses its earlier function, being largely absorbed into *consuetudo*. The shift is apparent at the very beginning of the first part of the main text, where *ius* is conflated with *consuetudo*, initially in the form of *iura et consuetudines*, and subsequently in the conjoined forms of *consuetudo iuris* and *ius consuetudinarium*.[46] Werbőczy does not develop, still less explain, this unexpected shift, largely because he is following at this point the language used by Raymundus at the start of the main text of the *Summa Legum*.[47] The persistence with which he conflates *ius* and *consuetudo* may owe something, however, to chancellery practice which routinely equated the *iura regni* with the kingdom's *consuetudines*, reserving the title of *lex* for statute law enacted by ruler and diet.[48]

Secondly, the account of customary law that Werbőczy gives in the Prologue does not chime with the discussion contained in the main part of the text. We are presented instead with two conflicting accounts of the origins of customary law. The first of these, as given in the Prologue, is a theoretical exposition which largely derives from Bartolus and which posits the customary law as deriving out of the

[44] For much of what follows, see David Ibbetson, 'Custom in the Tripartitum', in CLCE, 13–23 (20–2).

[45] On the historical separation of *ius* from *lex* and *consuetudo*, see Gerhard Köbler, *Das Recht im frühen Mittelalter. Untersuchungen zur Herkunft und Inhalt frühmittelalterlicher Rechtsbegriffen im deutschen Sprachgebiet* (Cologne and Vienna, 1971), 28.

[46] Trip., I. 1; Trip., III. 30 [6] (DRMH 5, 47, 419). *Ius consuetudinarium* is thoroughly glossator. See Siegfried Brie, *Die Lehre vom Gewohnheitsrecht. Eine historisch-dogmatische Untersuchung*, i (no more published), (Wrocław, 1899), 104.

[47] Alexander Gál, ed., *Die Summa Legum brevis levis et utilis*, 2 vols. (Weimar, 1926), i, 151; *Summa utriusque Juris doctoris Raymundi*, published in *Commune incliti Polonie Regni Privilegium constitutionum* (Cracow, 1506), fol. 4. The opening lines of the first part of the Trip. are culled verbatim from Raymundus. Cf. Trip., I. 1 [1] and *Summa Legum*, I, ch 20. Of the preceding chapters of the *Summa Legum*, the first fifteen of Part One constitute a theoretical introduction, and the next four a discussion of privileges, notarial instruments and seals. Chapter 20 marks the point where the first book, *ad personas*, actually starts.

[48] 1500: 10 (DRMH 4, 142); 1514: 63 (DRMH 4, 206); 1518 (Bács): 41 [5] (DRMH 4, 234); 1525 (Hatvan): 23. The relevant article issued by the Hatvan diet is given in M. G. Kovachich, *Vestigia Comitiorum* (Buda, 1790), 609.

people's acts. The second, in the main text, is a more practical account that looks towards statute and court practice as the sources of customary law. In what follows, we will examine the contradictory positions that Werbőczy takes and attempt their reconciliation.

* * *

The Prologue is built up in mosaic fashion from a number of separate authorities, culled for the most part from compendia of passages and quotations as well as from the 1506 edition of the *Summa Legum*. Recent research also indicates a debt to Johannes Andreae's fourteenth-century *Tractatus de consuetudine*, although probably in a mediated form.[49] A further passage, which seemingly gave the courts discretion to judge by either customary law or statute, is similarly derived from a post-glossator discussion.[50] In respect of his treatment of custom, Werbőczy depended largely upon Bartolus, as communicated through one of the other texts that he used. Bartolus had promoted custom as of equivalent force to statute, both being emanations of the popular will and expressions of the larger law or *ius*, which was synonymous with justice. Like Bartolus, Werbőczy makes Gratian his starting point—'It is called custom, for it is, as it were, common practice and human use, because it is in common use.'[51] He goes on, still following Bartolus, to affirm the equality of custom and statute, providing that custom be, like all human law, reasonable and in conformity with divine law, that it advance the common good, and that it not contradict the threefold division of the law given in Justinian's *Institutes*: natural law, the *ius gentium* and positive law.[52] Unlike written statute, however, which obtained immediate force upon promulgation, custom required a period of time or prescription for the people's consent to be determined. Here, Werbőczy proposes a decade: 'The passage of ten years begins from the time the first act is performed by the people', during which the newly introduced custom manifested itself gradually in as many acts as were needed to disclose the people's unspoken consent. In following Bartolus, however, Werbőczy then contradicts himself, declaring that a single act might be sufficient, providing that it proceeded from the people's tacit will.[53] Either way, once custom had emerged from its gestation, it enjoyed an equal efficacy to statute and both might be considered separate manifestations of *ius*. As Werbőczy explains, 'Hence, *ius* is the general name and a law is an aspect of *ius*. For every *ius* consists of laws and customs, that is the written and unwritten law.'[54] Although Werbőczy presumes here that customary law will be

[49] Péter Bónis, 'Bartolus in Medieval Hungary', 17–18; Bónis, 'The Commentators and the Hungarian law', 122–3.

[50] Trip., Prol. [12. 3] (DRMH 5, 37); cf. Brie, *Die Lehre vom Gewohnheitsrecht*, 135.

[51] Trip., Prol. [10]: *Vocatur autem consuetudo quasi communis suetudo & usus hominum, quia in communi est usu* (DRMH 5, 33). Cf. Gratian, D.1. *c.*5. (The word play is lost in translation). The expression ultimately derives from Isidore of Seville, *Etymologies*, 5, 3.

[52] Ibbetson, 'Custom in the *Tripartitum*', 18.

[53] Trip., Prol. [10. 5–7] (DRMH 5, 33). See Rady, 'The Prologue to Werbőczy's *Tripartitum*', 136.

[54] Trip., Prol. [2. 1] (DRMH 5, 21). For a similar construction, see György Bónis, 'Einleitung', in DRH 1301–437, 9–37 (25).

unwritten, he later concedes by reference to the Lombard *Libri feudorum* that it might also be written down.[55]

Since customary law and statute law enjoyed a similar authority, the manner of handling any contradiction between them was important. In following Bartolus, Werbőczy was able to show that the two separate sources of authority were capable of interaction and that custom might operate not only *secundum* and *praeter* but also *contra legem*.[56] First, where the precise terms of statute law were uncertain, custom might act as a guide, thus serving to interpret the published text. Secondly, being akin to law as an *imitatio legis*, custom might compensate for the absence of law, filling in the gaps where statute was silent. Thirdly, where custom and statute law were in conflict, the two might exercise a mutual abrogatory power. An existing custom might thus be voided by a new statute; likewise an older statute might be rendered null by a custom that developed after its promulgation.[57] Nevertheless, Werbőczy refused to embrace Bartolus's position that both custom and statute law emanated from the popular will, the first through the people's tacit consent, the second through their express consent, working through their inherent legislative capacity. Although aware of the civilian distinction between custom as *tacitus* and statute as *expressus*, the establishment of statute law remained for Werbőczy a right that was shared by ruler and people and did not adhere to the people alone.[58]

In moving to the main text, Werbőczy discards much of the earlier scheme that he had presented in the Prologue. The Bartolist claims in respect of the popular origins of custom and of the antiquity of the law are now superseded by reference to a different set of sources of authority that locate custom as arising out of written instruments and court practice. Reviewing 'whence originates our custom that is to be observed in court' and 'this municipal custom of ours', Werbőczy establishes four main springs. The first of these comprises 'sources in pontifical and imperial law', namely Romano-canonical law, but as it was Werbőczy's intention to describe Hungary's laws and not the European *ius commune* in general he moves speedily on. The second source consists of constitutions and public decrees, namely statute law, here exclusively understood as laws made by the ruler and diet. The third category comprised the privileges of princes. By this, Werbőczy meant not just privileges but written rights in general, given under the royal seal. Finally, Werbőczy sets as a source of authority 'the decisions of judges and letters of adjudication, passed and delivered and composed in one and the same order, manner and procedure on many occasions, and confirmed by judicial process'.[59]

The sources of Hungarian customary law elucidated in the main text are not conceived as instruments by which popular practice may be recognized or the people's consent tested. They are instead proposed as self-standing authorities

[55] Trip., Prol. [11. 1] (DRMH 5, 34). He follows here Bartolus.

[56] Walter Ullmann, 'Bartolus on Customary Law', *Juridical Review*, 52 (1940), 265–83 (280). The distinctions were developed by the glossators. See Brie, *Die Lehre vom Gewohnheitsrecht*, 118–19; also, Garré, *Consuetudo. Das Gewohnheitsrecht*, 82.

[57] Trip., Prol. [12. 2] (DRMH 5, 37).

[58] Trip., Prol. [11] (DRMH 5, 35). See also Trip., II. 12 [9] (DRMH 5, 243).

[59] Trip., II. 6 (DRMH 5, 233–5).

that operate as both the origin and foundation of Hungarian customary law. Nevertheless, the Bartolist conceptions that inform the Prologue continue to influence the main text, although they are now more muted. Statute law thus depended for its efficacy upon its adoption as custom. As Werbőczy writes, not all statutes will retain authority over time, but some may be set aside 'by the contrary use of the people [...] for real and continuous use often invalidates a law'.[60] In this way, he harks back to the Prologue and to the contention that custom might set aside an anterior statute. In much the same fashion, Werbőczy avers that practice may serve to embed the written law, renewing its suasion. The laws thus of Hungary's first kings 'have by now been almost entirely effaced due to their extreme age' but it is nonetheless acknowledged that 'through long use some element of law has flowed down from the constitutions of almost all these saintly kings'.[61] By the same token, however, statutes only retained an authority of their own for a short time, their potency thereafter depending upon the degree to which they were found good.[62] In respect of a concrete example of custom's constitutive role, Werbőczy alludes to the procedural obstruction of court judgments practised by litigants in pursuit of their suits. As he explains, the physical impeding or *repulsio* of a bailiff constitutes a 'most ancient use and long custom' to the extent that it is now recognized as a part of the kingdom's law.[63] In this way, custom as the product of popular practice is smuggled back into the main text, apparently contradicting the author's contention that custom arose out of the specific sources that he had previously identified.

All of this may be put down to intellectual laziness on the part of our author. Nevertheless, it seems more likely that the sources that Werbőczy identifies as the roots of Hungarian customary law constituted the means by which it was disclosed to him. At the time that Werbőczy was writing, there were only a few sources available to him that revealed the law. These were royal letters and other written instruments that were known from their use in court to be possessed of legal authority. Some of these were communicated in formulary books and we can track the way that their individual passages later made their way into the text of the *Tripartitum*.[64] On top of this, there were recent legislative acts, a few of which Werbőczy quoted verbatim in his text. Finally, there was his own experience as a lawyer and judge, which yielded a fund of information upon which he was able to draw. What Werbőczy proposes as the sources of Hungarian customary law were, therefore, the sources of his own knowledge. Werbőczy's confusion of the means by which the law might be known with the means of its creation is not unusual—Brutails's account of Andorran customary law partly falls into the same epistemological trap.[65]

Werbőczy's understanding of customary law's origins was thus the same as the way he understood its content to be as he said it was. Customary law arose out of a combination of written instruments, legislative acts and the decisions of courts.

[60] Trip., II. 2 [9] (DRMH 5, 229).
[61] Trip., II. 6 [9] (DRMH 5, 233–4).
[62] Trip., II. 2 [10] (DRMH 5, 229).
[63] Trip., II. 73 [2] (DRMH 5, 343).
[64] Bónis, KJE, 252–8.
[65] J.-A. Brutails, *La Coutume d'Andorre*, 2nd edition (Andorra la Vella, 1965), 47–74.

As we have seen, however, he also permitted common practice and conviction to have a role in adjusting the law's application, in the form of the people's real and continuous use. Apart from the derivative generalities given in the Prologue, Werbőczy gives no explanation in respect of how popular use and custom might impinge upon the customary law. In what follows, we will fill in the blank. As we will argue, the courts adjusted the law and determined what customs were normative in respect of the cases that came before them. The courts, however, on account of their composition did not only dispose an exclusively lawyerly law, but also acted as vehicles by which popular apprehensions of the law's content affected judgments and the law's application in concrete cases.[66] Hungarian customary law thus rested upon the formal sources of authority that Werbőczy identified, but it also drew through the activity and membership of the courts on a popular understanding of what the law was and should be. The written law, lawyerly practice and common conviction thus worked together to provide the substance of Hungarian customary law. In the two chapters that follow, we will examine their interaction.

[66] See here, Ferenc Eckhart, 'Jog- és alkotmánytörténet', in Bálint Hóman, ed., *A magyar történetirás új útjai* (Budapest, 1932), 269–320 (285).

# 3

# Customary Law, Legislation and Letters

## THE ROMANO-CANONICAL TRADITION

Theoretical accounts often set up the written statutory law in opposition to the unwritten customary law. The Prologue to the *Tripartitum* preserves this distinction. In the main part of his text, however, Werbőczy treats all law as written in the sense that it was mainly contained in written instruments. As we have argued, the stress that Werbőczy put on written instruments arose from his working methods. He knew the law to be as he said it was because it had been revealed to him in the texts of the sources that he had before him—royal legislation and letters drawn up in the course of litigation—as well as from his own experience of the courts. In what follows, we will tease out the content of these sources, indicating the ways in which they were both constitutive and declaratory of the law. Rather than impose an explanatory model of our own, we will broadly retain Werbőczy's categories, using these as the starting point for our investigation. We will, however, consider what he calls 'the privileges of princes', namely letters presented in court under the royal seal, in the more general sense of legal instruments, and accordingly review the types of record produced in the course of judicial proceedings. We will begin, however, with Werbőczy's reference to Hungarian customary law as originally deriving from Roman and Canon Law—*ex pontificii Caesareique fontibus*—an expression upon which he spends no time and which he will use only once again, in a quite different context.[1] The import of Werbőczy's remark on the contribution of these sources to Hungary's legal development is, however, considerable, for it suggests that a substantial part of the kingdom's law (by implication, all that was not otherwise contained in the main text of the *Tripartitum*) was historically founded on Romano-canonical practices.[2]

* * *

The assimilation of a Romano-canonical legal vocabulary and procedure was a gradual process in Hungary, which is closely associated with the advent and spread

[1] Trip., I. 11 [2] (DRMH 5, 61), in respect of the apostolic authority of St Stephen.

[2] See thus, János Zlinszky, 'Werbőczy jogforrástana', *Jogtudományi Közlöny*, 48, no. 10 (1993), 374–6 (376). Péter Bónis, 'The Commentators and the Hungarian law in the Middle Ages, with special regard to the Tripartitum', in Péter Antalóczy, ed., *Hagyomány és érték. Állam és jogtudományi tanulmányok a Károli Gaspar Református Egyetem fennállásának 20. évfordulójára* (Budapest, 2013), 116–26 (121). For the legal significance of the term *fons*, see Riccardo Orestano, *I fatti di normazione nell'esperienza romana arcaica* (Torino, 1967), 2.

of legal literacy and of the lettered law. The origins of this development go back to the earliest centuries of the kingdom, when the first steps were taken to textualize legal activity in Learned Latin, and its consequence was profound. Once rights and practices had been put down in writing and rendered in a lawyerly language, their meaning altered, lending a precision and legal significance that was often missing in an exclusively oral legal culture. The heightened awareness of words thus sharpened the perception of legal phenomena.[3] Speech itself changed to meet the pace set by the written word. Individual noblemen might garble their Latin, signing 'with their own goblin' (*mano propria*) or appealing to 'the pig of the law (*porcus iuris*)', but in their clumsy endeavours they sought nonetheless to lean on the language of the written law.[4] The act of writing facilitated, moreover, the conversion of facts into claims, giving a formal name to an event, or disassembling it into its parts, to which questions of law might then be attached and the appropriate procedures deployed.[5] The vocabulary of the lettered law, and the procedures that followed from its articulation, mostly derived from church practice, which drew for its part on civilian norms. Hungarian customary law was thus from the very start of the kingdom's history moulded by the juristic tradition of the *ius commune*, which blended the *utrumque ius* of Roman and Canon Law.

During the eleventh and twelfth centuries most litigation took place orally. Suits were presented in person, resolved by the king or one of his officers without recourse to written instruments, and concluded without the judgment being put in writing. Parties to an action were cited by a court official, the *pristaldus* or *pristav* (*poroszló*), who delivered the summons by voice. The suit was heard either by the king's court, by the lord of the county (*ispán*) or by an itinerant judge, who bore a pendant metal brooch as proof of his authority.[6] The evidence of neighbours or the outcome of an ordeal by fire was gathered by the pristaldus, and reported back to the court. The judgment was announced publicly, in front of the pristaldus and witnesses, and they were expected to remember it. Any written account that was made of the proceedings served not so much as a record of the case and the court's decision but as a *notitia* or aide-memoire, listing those involved in the action so that they might be subsequently called upon to render testimony. For this reason, the name of the pristaldus who had officiated at court in a land dispute was sometimes inscribed on a stone that stood at the boundary of a contested property.[7] The famous Várad Register, which lists the outcome of several hundred ordeals from the early thirteenth century, is nevertheless more typical. It itemizes the parties, the

[3] H.L.A. Hart, *The Concept of Law*, 2nd edition (Oxford, 1994), 14. See also, Jack Goody, *The Logic of Writing and the Organization of Society* (Cambridge, 1986), 127–70.

[4] István György Tóth, *Literacy and Written Culture in Early Modern Europe* (Budapest and New York, 2000), 134, 191; more generally, Walter J. Ong, 'Orality, Literacy and Medieval Textualization', *New Literary History*, 16, no. 1 (1984), 1–12 (5–6).

[5] Massimo Vallerani, *Medieval Public Justice* (Washington, D.C., 2012), 15–17, 32.

[6] András Kubinyi, 'Isten bárányát ábrázoló törvénybeidéző pecsét (billog)', *Folia Archaeologica*, 35 (1984), 139–59; Emil Jakubovich, 'I. Endre király törvénybeidéző ércbilloga', *Turul*, 47, nos. 3–4 (1933), 56–74.

[7] Martyn Rady, *Nobility, Land and Service in Medieval Hungary* (Basingstoke and New York, 2000), 66.

bare substance of the plaint and the referring judge, the outcome of the test, the witnesses and the pristaldus, together with their usual place of domicile, so that they might subsequently be found to give proof of what they knew. Hence—'Golsa of the village of Bán sued his fellow villager, Sedun, for setting fire to his house and doing six marks' worth of damage, the judge being Agya, lord of Crasna [County], the pristaldus Luca of the village of Kovácsi. Sedun carried the iron at Oradea [Várad] and was proved'.[8]

A similar regard for oral testimony also affected private business arrangements in respect of sales and purchases. A contract of sale was thus not drawn up in writing but instead drinks were bought all round, so that those who had witnessed the transaction might the better recall it. By the early fourteenth century, this procedure was sufficiently established to constitute 'an ancient custom'.[9] The ceremony survived into the modern period, with even more lavish inducements to mindfulness.[10] It was only in business involving Jews, with whom such pleasantries were impossible, that even as early as the eleventh century, recourse was had to a written instrument. The so-called *cartula sigillata*, which was sealed by the parties, noted the item purchased or the amount of a loan and the names of those who bore witness to the transaction. Although the presence of the seals lent the *cartula sigillata* special authority as an instrument, the evidence of the witnesses whose names were written upon it was still regarded as decisive in any subsequent dispute.[11]

As the examples of the Várad Register and the *cartula sigillata* suggest, the preference for oral testimony and witnessing had little to do with literacy. Personal recollection was deemed more reliable and of greater authority than ink and parchment. As Innocent IV (1243–54) explained, it seemed unnatural to trust the skin of a dead animal more than the voice of a living man.[12] It was only when oral

[8] Samu Borovszky and János Karácsonyi, eds., *Regestrum Varadiniense examinum ferri candentis* (Budapest, 1903), 163 (1213).

[9] Thus, in respect of the purchase of a vineyard, *iuxta antiqua consuetudinem comitatus Symigiensis mercipotum bibendo*, MNL OL DL, 99906 (1327). See also Trip., III. 34 [3] (DRMH 5, 422–3). The custom was hardly unique either to Somogy County or to Hungary. See Christopher McNall, '"Lytkup" in the Rural Court Books of Old-Time Poland', *Czasopismo Prawno-Historyczne*, 49 (1997), 11–25; C.G. Proll, *De iure mercipotus in contractibus, vulgo vom Weinkauf* (Marburg, 1768). The Hungarian name for *mercipotus*, *áldomás*, is a calque of the German *Trankopfer*. See Gerhard Köbler, *Deutsche Rechtsgeschichte. Ein systematischer Grundriss*, 6th edition (Munich, 2005), 15.

[10] Melinda Égető, *Hegytörvények forrásközléseinek gyűjteménye (1470–1846)* (Budapest, 2002), 68. Of course, the inducements might also promote forgetfulness. Dr Robert Gray tells me that on one occasion on the Széchényi estates in the late eighteenth century, several bibulous parties to a contract were unable on the morrow to recall the terms of their agreement. Dr Gray has also noted the practice in Hungary of tweaking the ears of youthful witnesses so that they might recall the more keenly. See R.W. Gray, 'Etching the Law on the Land: The Role of Landscape and Custom in Defining the Space of the Hungarian Village in the Eighteenth and Nineteenth Centuries', *Central Europe*, 11, no. 2 (2013), 82–101 (87). Pulling witnesses' ears (*testes per aures tracti*) was also common elsewhere. For an extravagant example of this type of physical inducement to memory, coming from eighteenth-century Transylvania, where a boy witness was beaten, see Livia Magina, *Instituția judelui sătesc în Principatul Transilvaniei (sec. XVI–XVIII)*, PhD thesis (Babeş-Bolyai University of Cluj-Napoca, 2013), 177.

[11] B.L. Kumorovitz, *Die erste Epoche der ungarischen privatrechtlichen Schriftlichkeit im Mittelalter (xi–xii. Jahrhundert)*, Studia Historica, 21 (Budapest, 1960), 11–12; 'Statutes of King Coloman Concerning the Jews [1095–1116]', DRMH $1^2$, 66.

[12] James A. Brundage, *Medieval Canon Law* (London and New York, 1995), 133.

testimony proved impossible to secure through conventional routes or where a record was needed to show who had been witnesses to an event that recourse was had to writing. Exceptionally, the written word might also be used to give proof when subsequent recollection was thought likely to be tainted. Because one could not trust the honesty of one's relatives, testaments were sometimes framed in writing and their authority enhanced by the addition of the royal seal. The fact that several of the earliest surviving Hungarian wills were composed by women (as for instance the testament composed by the Lady Colourful in 1146) suggests that they felt especially vulnerable not only to coercion but also to convenient lapses in the memory of kinsmen.[13]

The recollection of kinsmen, neighbours and witnesses was efficacious only in the context of close, stable communities. Religious foundations were, however, not only rich but their properties were also widely dispersed, in some cases over many hundreds of miles.[14] Thus, from the eleventh century, abbeys and convents began to attach worth to the written record, as a form of additional proof of ownership both in respect of an estate and of its boundaries and appurtenances. In the same fashion, kings were also law makers, but they could not trust that their ordinances would be adequately broadcast through oral dissemination. From the very first, therefore, Hungary's kings relied upon scribes, both to promote their will through written instruments as well as to respond to religious foundations and to those, like the Lady Colourful, who were desirous that their rights be reinforced in parchment.

The first scribes were foreign churchmen. Indeed, the earliest of whom we are aware, a certain 'Heribert C', who was active in Hungary at the start of the eleventh century, had previously worked in the chancellery of Otto III.[15] He was the first of many such western clerics, who were encouraged to settle in the new kingdom.[16] Nevertheless, Hungarians were not slow to acquire an education abroad, after which they returned home to put their skills into practice. For the most part, they visited the great schools in France and, later, the universities of Paris, Bologna and Padua. We know of twenty such students in attendance at the University of Paris before the thirteenth century, and thereafter there were seldom less than a dozen present at any one time.[17] England was also a destination, with students

[13] Kumorovitz, *Die erste Epoche*, 25–7; for the Lady Szines, who feared her will would be disregarded, *maxime vero de illis loquor, qui propinquitate mihi coniuncti fuerint in seculo*, see László Erdélyi and Pongrácz Sörös, eds., *A Pannonhalmi Szent-Benedek-Rend története*, 12 vols. (Budapest, 1902–16), i, 597–8 (and many other editions).

[14] See thus the distribution of properties belonging at the end of the twelfth century to the Hospitaller preceptory in Székesfehérvár, in Zsolt Hunyadi, *The Hospitallers in the Medieval Kingdom of Hungary c. 1150–1387* (Budapest, 2010), 24–9.

[15] László Solymosi, *Írásbeliség és társadalom az Árpád-korban* (Budapest, 2006), 15. The identification was first made by Harry Bresslau, 'Zu den Urkunden König Stephans von Ungarn', *Archiv für Urkundenforschung*, 6 (1918), 65–76 (70–1). He is called 'Heribert C' to distinguish him from Heriberts A, B, D, E, and F, with several or all of whom he may be identified. See Wolfgang Huschner, 'Abt Odilo von Cluny und Kaiser Otto III in Italien und in Gnesen (998–1001)', in Michael Borgotte, ed., *Polen und Deutschland vor 1000* (Berlin, 2002), 111–61 (132).

[16] László Mezey, 'A latin irás magyarországi történetéből', *Magyar Könyv-Szemle*, 82 (1966), 1–9 (6–7). On Hungary's early exposure to classical learning more generally, see Előd Nemerkényi, *Latin Classics in Medieval Hungary: Eleventh Century* (New York, 2004).

[17] István Hajnal, *L'Enseignement de l'écriture aux universités médiévales*, 2nd edition (Budapest, 1959), 195.

learning at Oxford and Lincoln, where they told others of their homeland and its institutions. Well before the celebrated comment of Humbert of Romans at the Council of Lyons in 1274 that Hungary should no longer be reckoned among the 'barbarian nations' of Europe,[18] John of Salisbury as well as the English forger of the papal bull *Dolentes* were knowledgeable of at least some aspects of Hungary's government and laws.[19] Links between Hungary and England were particularly intense at the end of the twelfth century and during the course of the Fifth Crusade (1213–21), even to the extent of Hungarians acquiring land in the Plantagenet kingdom.[20]

From the second half of the thirteenth century, Hungarian students were increasingly drawn to the North Italian universities, following in the footsteps of the distinguished Hungarian canonists, Damasus and Paulus Ungarus. There they acquired a knowledge of civil and Canon Law, trading manuscripts of the *Digest* to one another.[21] Indeed (and ironically so, in view of Humbert's observation), there were after 1265 enough Hungarian students at Bologna to constitute a *natio* at the university.[22] All in all, we can track the movement of no less than eighty Hungarians at Bologna in the century before 1300. Upon their return to Hungary, not only did the students apply what they had learnt but they also brought books home with them, which further served to disseminate knowledge of Roman and Canon Law. The will of Ladislas, a canon of the Esztergom chapter, drawn up in 1277, thus included complete copies of Justinian's *Digest* and *Codex*, Azo's *Summa*, an edition of Gratian, a collection of decretals and one of Goffredo da Trani's textbooks on church law.[23] The spread of legal education was further advanced by Hungary's cathedral schools, most notably the one at Veszprém that, according to a royal charter of 1270, promoted throughout the kingdom, 'the study of the liberal arts, as at Paris in France [...] and is foremost in its devotion to justice, thereby preserving the laws of the kingdom'.[24] From this description, it would appear that the school at Veszprém was most probably educating those

[18] Jenő Szűcs, 'Theoretical Elements in Master Simon of Kéza's *Gesta Hungarorum* (1282–1285)', in László Veszprémy and Frank Schaer, eds., *Simonis de Kéza Gesta Hungarorum* (Budapest and New York, 1999), xxix–cii (xxxiv, liii).

[19] For John of Salisbury, see W.J. Millor, H. E. Butler and C.N.L. Brooke, *The Letters of John of Salisbury*, 2 vols. (Oxford, 1955–79), ii, 377, discussed in Joseph Deér, 'Der Anspruch der Herrscher des 12. Jahrhunderts auf die apostolischen Legation', *Archivum Historiae Pontificiale*, 2 (1964), 117–86 (152–3). For the bull *Dolentes*, see Georges Digard, 'La Papauté et l'étude du droit romain au xiii$^{e}$ siècle. A propos de la fausse bulle d'Innocent IV *Dolentes*', *Bibliothèque de l'École des Chartes*, 51 (1890), 381–419 (416). The relevant text is published in György (Georgius) Fejér, *Codex Diplomaticus Hungariae ecclesiasticus et civilis*, 11 vols. in 44 parts (Buda, 1829–44), iv/2, 254–6, and Matthew Paris, *Chronica Majora*, ed. H.R. Luard, vi (Rolls Series, 1882), 293–5. For Hungarian students in England, see József Laszlovszky, 'Nicholaus clericus; A Hungarian student at Oxford University in the twelfth century', *Journal of Medieval History*, 14, no. 3 (1988), 217–31.

[20] József Laszlovszky and Zsuzsanna Papp, 'Angol-magyar kapcsolatok és a Magyarországról kialakult kép Angliában a 13. században', in Attila Bárány, Laszlovszky and Papp, *Angol-magyar kapcsolatok a középkorban*, 2 vols. (Máriabesnyő, 2008–11), i, 201–27 (219).

[21] Bónis, KJE, 22. [22] Solymosi, *Írásbeliség és társadalom*, 41.

[23] Nándor Knauz and Lajos Dedek, eds., *Monumenta Ecclesiae Strigoniensis*, 3 vols. (Esztergom, 1874–1924), ii, 71–2, noted in György Bónis, *A jogtudó értelmiség a Mohács előtti Magyarországon* (Budapest, 1971), 28.

[24] György (Georgius) Fejér, *Historia Academiae Scientiarum Pazmaniae Archi-Episcopalis* (Buda, 1835), 221; RA, no. 2747.

destined for the lower ranks of the clergy or for routine legal business. Not only was a university training in Canon Law regarded by this time as a prerequisite for major ecclesiastical advancement, but even in the countryside the higher ranks of the clergy were increasingly now filled by 'men of learning, trained in Canon and Civil Law'.[25]

* * *

The royal chapel functioned as the kingdom's foremost scriptorium and as the main repository for the legal texts gathered by students and others on their travels. Although eleventh-century materials refer to a vice-chancellor, *capellanus* and *notarius*, it is doubtful that the royal scriptorium had any dedicated staff before the middle years of the twelfth century.[26] It was probably only during the last decades of the century that the royal writing office finally separated from the chapel to constitute a properly separate chancellery.[27] The seemingly ad hoc arrangement of the royal writing office is demonstrated by the frequency with which charters were issued in the form of *Empfängerbriefe*, namely letters composed by the recipient, often on the basis of a previous charter, which were then read through and sealed by clerics of the chapel.[28] Nevertheless, the influence of foreign forms on the style of the charters published by the royal chapel is obvious. In the first decades of the kingdom, Heribert and his successors left their mark, pulling Hungarian practice in the direction of imperial. Thereafter, however, a French style tended to predominate. Most of all, however, it was the written forms of the papal Curia that determined the shape, phraseology and internal organization of Hungarian royal letters. Nor is this surprising, for the royal chapel was not just a charter-issuing and charter-sealing institution. It was also the royal letter box and organizer of the king's correspondence, and it was from Rome that most post came. More than 500 letters from Rome thus survive that were sent in the two centuries following the earliest extant papal letter to Hungary, written by Gregory VII in 1074.[29]

No royal letters survive in their original form from the eleventh century but only a handful of later transcripts that have been heavily interpolated. During the course of the following century, the number of extant royal charters registered a steady increase, rising dramatically after 1200. For the reigns of Ladislas I and Coloman, namely from 1077 to 1116, we have only six royal charters. In the ninety years from the accession of Stephen II in 1116 to the beginning of Andrew II's reign in 1205, just over 120. By contrast, 300 royal charters survive from the thirty-year rule of Andrew II and well over a thousand from the reign of his successor, Béla IV.[30] Altogether, just over 4,400 royal letters exist either in their original form

[25] Bónis, *A jogtudó értelmiség*, 29.

[26] László Fejérpataky, *A királyi kanczellária az Árpádok korában* (Budapest, 1885), 14–30.

[27] Solymosi, *Írásbeliség és társadalom*, 186; András Kubinyi, 'Királyi kancellária és udvari kápolna Magyarországon a xii. század közepén', *Levéltári Közlemények*, 46, no. 1 (1975), 59–121 (60).

[28] Kubinyi, 'Királyi kancellária és udvari kápolna', 90–2; Imre Szentpétery, *Magyar oklevéltan* (Budapest, 1930), 53.

[29] Solymosi, *Írásbeliség és társadalom*, 186.

[30] Hajnal, *L'Enseignement de l'écriture*, 196–7.

or as transcripts from the whole of the Arpad period. Of these, three-quarters derive from the last four decades of the thirteenth century.[31]

The quantity of material surviving from Hungary during the High Middle Ages is, of course, significantly less than from contemporary England or France. Nevertheless, if we compare the rate of increase, then we can establish a rough comparability between Hungarian and, for instance, French practice.[32] Behind this correlation lay a similar dynamic—a flight to the written record brought about by the disintegration in both Hungary and France of traditional 'communities of memory' as a consequence of social and political change.[33] In Hungary, this development is most clearly exemplified in the arengas of charters that from the late twelfth century hammered home for the benefit of the unwary the importance of recording rights in written form. Among these, the most conspicuous was the *memoria* and *oblivio* formula, which borrowed directly from the imperial chancellery in stressing the role of the written word in commemorating things past and in preserving them from forgetfulness.[34]

The increased use of written instruments impelled the growth and professionalization of the royal chancellery, which in its turn further encouraged the use of letters. The proper establishment of the chancellery office under Béla III was thus accompanied by his personal injunction, given in 1181, 'that I, Béla, consider it necessary that whatever is discussed before My Highness be confirmed by written testimony'.[35] It was during the same decade that the internal arrangement of royal charters stabilized in the form that they would retain over the following centuries: the *intitulatio* (originally preceded by an *invocatio*), *salutatio*, *arenga*, *narratio*, *dispositio*, *corroboratio*, date and year of issue, and a witness list (subsequently replaced, in the last years of the twelfth century, by a list of current office holders).[36] Within this scheme, which is common enough throughout Western Europe, we may detect individual influences. The *datum per manus* formula, which named the chancellery officer who had supervised the writing of the charter, is thus of imperial origin; likewise the *Dei gratia* attaching to the royal title as a mark of humility, as well as the style of the *corroboratio*. The *in perpetuum*, *salutem*, and the *eapropter* conjoining the *narratio* and *dispositio* have, by contrast, papal antecedents; similarly, the *sanctio* and *comminatio* that attached before the mid-thirteenth century to royal grants, threatening retribution for any invasion of the new owner's property.[37] Even so, we may note certain Hungarian peculiarities, attaching in par-

[31] Solymosi, *Írásbeliség és társadalom*, 206–7.

[32] Hajnal, *L'Enseignement de l'écriture*, 196–7.

[33] For analogous developments in France, see Fredric L. Cheyette, 'Suum cuique tribuere', *French Historical Studies*, 6, no. 3 (1970), 287–99 (297–9). See also Bónis, *A jogtudó értelmiség*, 20.

[34] Emil Jakubovich, 'XII. századi oklevéltöredék. Miska ispán fia István végrendelete 1164-ból', *Leveltári Közlemények*, 2 (1924), 155–62 (156); RA, 1, nos. 105, 130. Cf. MGH, DD, FI, 2, 474; MGH, DD, FI, 3, 59 (noted by Kubinyi, 'Királyi kancellária és udvari kápolna', 108).

[35] László Fejérpataky, *III. Béla király oklevelei* (Budapest, 1900), 29.

[36] Szentpétery, *Magyar oklevéltan*, 74.

[37] Ferencz Eckhart, 'A pápai és császári kanczelláriai gyakorlat hatása árpádkori királyi okleveleinek szövegezésében', *Századok*, 44 (1910), 713–24 (718–19). See also, Gábor Barabás, 'Der Einfluss der Papsturkunden auf die Schreiben der päpstlichen delegierten Richter in Ungarn in der ersten Hälfte des 13. Jahrhunderts', *Specimina Nova. Pars Prima. Sectio Mediaevalis*, 7 (2013), 19–37.

ticular to privileges, namely the lengthy *narrationes* that spelled out the services done by the recipient of a royal grant, and the elaborate royal title recorded on privileges that listed every land and realm that had ever belonged to Hungary's rulers, including distant parts of Rurikid Russia and the crowns of Bulgaria and Serbia.[38]

Contact with the west not only shaped the form and internal arrangement of charters but also provided the terminology which framed Hungary's nascent institutions and legal arrangements. The extent to which the laws of Hungary's earliest kings conformed to actual conditions in the kingdom, as opposed to being learned pastiches of Frankish and other texts, must remain uncertain.[39] Nevertheless, they mediated the vocabulary of Roman Law, thereby amplifying both the authority of the ruler and, conversely, the principle of consultation and consent: *augustus*, *lex*, *decretum*, *auctoritas*, *monarchia*, *senatus*, *communis concilium*, *regalis potentia*, *facultas*, *dominium*, and so on. By the thirteenth century, these would be combined with a more theoretical language—that it was the purpose of justice to give *suum cuique* and, more ominously, in the words of Ladislas IV, *ipse mihi sum lex*.[40] In similar fashion, the Romanist language of rank and status used in Hungary's earliest laws—*cives* or *civiles*, *servi*, *hospites*, *comites*, *milites*, *plebei*—was picked up and deployed more generally. Names were sometimes applied in a quite misleading fashion, as for instance the term *cives* used for the subject population attached to royal castles. By their application, however, these terms lent the weight of classical authority to the kingdom's social organization, emphasizing in particular the division between a martial caste of native and foreign warriors and a largely servile population that worked on royal and private estates.[41]

Education abroad, the importation of learned texts, the growth in correspondence and increased reliance upon the written record extended the kingdom's exposure to a lawyerly vocabulary, deriving in the main from the learned *ius commune* of Roman and Canon Law. The language of property holding was particularly affected, mainly after around 1100, lending increased sophistication in respect of the rights of property and security of possession. As elsewhere, the introduction of a terminology deriving from Roman Law had the consequence of making the

[38] Elemér Mályusz, *Királyi kancellária és krónikairás a középkori Magyarországon* (Budapest, 1973), 6–17; Gyula Kristó, *Középkori históriák oklevelekben (1022–1410)* (Szeged, 1992), 14–29; János M. Bak, 'Lists in the Service of Legitimation in Central European Sources', in L. Doležalová, ed., *The Charm of a List: From the Sumerians to Computerised Data Processing* (Newcastle u/T, 2009), 34–45 (42–4), reprinted in Bak, *Studying Medieval Rulers and Their Subjects* (Farnham and Burlington, VT, 2010).

[39] The literature on Hungary's eleventh-century laws is substantial, but see in particular György Bónis, 'Szent István törvényének önállósága', *Századok*, 72 (1938), 433–87; Bódog Schiller, 'Das erste ungarische Gesetzbuch und das deutsche Recht', *Festschrift Heinrich Brunner* (Weimar, 1910), 379–404; Monika Jánosi, *Törvényalkotás a korai Árpád-korban* (Szeged, 1996); DRMH $1^2$, *passim*.

[40] AUO, vii, 221; Nora Berend, *At the Gate of Christendom: Jews, Muslims and 'Pagans' in Medieval Hungary, c. 1000–1300* (Cambridge, 2001), 176; Imre Nagy, Dezső Véghely and Gyula Nagy, eds., *Zala vármegye története. Oklevéltár*, 2 vols. (Budapest, 1886–90), ii, 643.

[41] György Györffy, *Wirtschaft und Gesellschaft der Ungarn um die Jahrtausendwende* (Budapest, 1983), 111–12.

law as practised more precise and comprehensive.[42] The distinction between ownership and use was thus fully apprehended by no later than the twelfth century, permitting properties to be rented, pledged or held in trust; likewise the distinction between movable and immovable property, which was a feature of the vulgar Roman Law. Indeed, Hungarian notaries drank so fully at the well of contemporary legal jurisprudence that they borrowed its confused vocabulary of the law of property, according to which *dominium* only amounted to physical occupation as opposed to right of ownership (*ius in re*).[43] The separation of ownership from use would subsequently be amplified with such terms as *arenda*, *impignoratio*, *emphyteusis* and, in an example of how imported words might lose their original meaning, *feodum* (*pheudum*).[44]

The language of conveyance similarly built on terms current in Romano-canonical procedure. Their adoption encouraged practice within Hungary to imitate that followed elsewhere, as for instance in respect of the institution to property or *statutio*, whereby a new owner was formally introduced to an estate, or of the warranty clause in charters, known as the *evictio* or *expeditoria cautio*, that obliged a seller to guarantee the purchaser of land against subsequent legal claims 'with his own labours and expenses'.[45] The *renunciatio* clause, frequently included after the mid-thirteenth century in charters of alienation, which invalidated the written rights of the previous owner, was likewise an integral part of Romano-canonical procedure. Its inclusion in deeds was actively promoted in Hungary by churchmen as a way of buttressing ecclesiastical rights to property.[46] Even so, the *renunciatio* was invoked as early as the 1260s in a case exclusively involving laymen that had come before Béla IV for adjudication.[47] Likewise, the notion that uncontested occupation constituted a right to possession through *praescriptio* was clearly understood by the thirteenth century, although it was not until much later that specific periods of limitation stabilized in respect to different types of property (generally at thirty or thirty-two years).[48] To these terms and formulas we may add a host of others that similarly derived from the learned law and which were applied in respect of land transactions and of civil suits and procedure from no later than the thirteenth century: *testamentum*, *dos* and *dotalitium*, (*fraternalis*) *adoptio*, *mobilia* and *immobilia*, *concambium*, *hereditas*, *acquisita*, *fassio*, *proprietas*, *malae fidei possessor*, *tutor* and

[42] Winfried Trusen, *Anfänge des gelehrten Rechts in Deutschland. Ein Beitrag zur Geschichte der Frührezeption* (Wiesbaden, 1962), 3.

[43] Ernst Levy, *West Roman Vulgar Law* (Philadelphia, 1951), 32. Transylvanian Saxon writers did, however, use the term correctly. See László Nagy, *Jus Transsilvanico Saxonicum* (Cluj, 1845), 42. See also Béni Grosschmid, *Werbőczy és az angol jog* (Budapest, 1928), 391–2.

[44] László Veszprémy and Frank Schaer, eds., *Simonis de Keza Gesta Hungarorum* (Budapest and New York, 1999), 175 (ch. 94). *Feodum* survived only in the sense of a property held in pledge or leased—hence, from 1378, *in feodum seu censum annualem*: MNL OL DL, 6553. See also ZsO, i, nos. 137, 353, 378; ZsO, ii/1, nos. 372, 3188, 4898; ZsO, iii, nos. 163, 2956 etc.

[45] Bónis, KJE, 98; József Gerics, 'Arpád-kori jogintézmények és terminológia törvényhozásunk egyik keltezetlen emlékében', in Gerics, *Egyház, állam és gondolkodás Magyarországon a középkorban* (Budapest, 1995), 248–74 (257), first published in *Századok*, 103 (1969), 611–40.

[46] Bónis, KJE, 66.

[47] AUO, iii, 157.

[48] György Bónis, *Einflüsse des römischen Rechts in Ungarn* (*Ius Romanum Medii Aevi*, 5, no. 10) (Milan, 1964), 93.

*fiduciaria, fidedignum, procurator, evocatio, calumnia, iure perpetuo, sana mente, ex certa nostra scientia, salvo iure alieno, nil iuris reservando, non obstante* and so on.

Outside the law of property, Hungarian usage was less obviously influenced by Romano-canonical terms. Instead, a distorted vocabulary prevailed, with individual words acquiring a customary meaning that was often remote from their original sense. After the thirteenth century, the financial basis of composition for manslaughter changed. Instead of being based on the value of the victim's worth, it now rested on the perpetrator's, being thus the sum he paid to save his own life. Its designation accordingly changed from *compositio* to *homagium*, a term which is otherwise never used in this way outside Hungary. The word normally employed to describe a violent trespass—*potentia, actus potentiae, potentialis,* and so on—likewise acquired a specific legal meaning in Hungary.[49] *Potentia* would, indeed, be refined in the fifteenth century into 'major' and 'minor' acts of might, with the former including those most harmful to noblemen. The term, *nota infidelitatis*, which although rooted in Canon Law is otherwise rare, also had a wide currency in Hungary from the thirteenth century onwards, including not only lèse-majesté but also the most egregious crimes.[50]

In 1309, in a famous case heard before the papal legate, Cardinal Gentilis, Bishop Ladislas of Srem disputed the basis of his adversary's plaint on the grounds that, 'in Hungary cases proceed not according to Civil and Canon Law but according to the customs and statutes of the realm'.[51] This was true inasmuch as neither the laws of Justinian nor the law of the church had any formal authority in the kingdom's lay courts. Nevertheless, even by this time, a part of the vocabulary and with it some of the principles of the learned law of Europe had been implanted in Hungary. The earliest phase of reception may be detected in the laws of the eleventh century. Thereafter, Romano-canonical norms were transmitted through the chancellery, foreign study and correspondence, and accelerated by the new reliance placed upon written instruments, which in their internal form and arrangement increasingly imitated those composed elsewhere. The customary law of the realm thus by degrees became 'Romanized', picking up, embedding and disseminating a new vocabulary that lent the law greater sophistication. The process would continue into the fourteenth and fifteenth centuries, pulling procedure and legal language further in the direction of the law that was followed throughout most of Europe. In this respect, Werbőczy's unqualified assertion that the laws of Hungary 'originally evolved from sources in pontifical and imperial law' was neither empty nor rhetorical but an accurate summation of an important part of their evolution.[52]

[49] *Potentia* does, however, occur with a specific and analogous meaning in law in thirteenth-century Silesia. See G.A. Stenzel, *Liber Fundationis Claustri Sanctae Mariae Virginis in Heinrichow* (Wrocław, 1854), 42.

[50] Extrav. Comm. 1. 8. 3, in *Corpus Iuris Canonici*, eds. E.L. Richter and E. Friedberg, 2 vols. (Leipzig, 1879–81), ii, col. 1247.

[51] *Monumenta Vaticana historiam regni Hungariae illustrantia*, 9 vols. in 2 series (Budapest, 1887–1909), ser. 1, ii, 313. See Bónis, *Einflüsse des römischen Rechts in Ungarn*, 76.

[52] Cf. Károly Viszky, 'Néhány megjegyzés a hazai jogban található római hatások kutatásához', *Jogtörténeti Tanulmányok*, 4 (1980), 319–33 (320–2).

## LETTERS AND THE *LOCA CREDIBILIA*

The work of the chancellery was only one aspect of the way in which a Romanized terminology became embedded within the customary law. The dissemination of a vocabulary that derived from Romano-canonical practices, together with the procedures that interacted with the written word, was also accomplished by institutions of the church. From an early stage in the kingdom's history, these were engaged, physically, in transforming both oral plaints into written actions and judicial events into legal deeds. The most common instrument that they circulated was the *litterae relatoriae*, the 'letter of report' that communicated in a schematic fashion what churchmen had witnessed in the course of the law's performance. On account of their formulaic character, these letters of report established a uniformity of language and practice, particularly in respect of the procedural law. The homogenizing function played by monasteries and chapter houses was pre-eminently due to their role as *loca credibilia* or 'places of authentication'.

During the twelfth century, corporate bodies and individuals increasingly sought to secure their rights to property or the terms of their testaments by having the royal seal attached to a deed. The royal seal was believed to give special efficacy, on account both of its supposedly authentic character and of its symbolic association with the king's majesty. From around 1200, however, charters recording land transactions were often also issued under the seal of a convent or chapter, sometimes with a list of witnesses, but increasingly without.[53] The increased reliance upon religious houses to record transactions may have arisen as a practical response to the difficulties of travel, but it equally probably derived from practices followed at this time elsewhere in Europe, before the advent of public notaries.[54] Importantly, however, the seals of religious houses not only substituted for the royal seal but were considered, by no later than the fourteenth century, at least equal if not superior to it. Charters authenticated with the king's seal might thus be taken to one or more religious houses where they were transcribed and reissued under the seal of the relevant convent or chapter.[55] Prudent noblemen and others might, moreover, ask that chapters make additional copies lest the original be lost or its validity contested.[56] The speed with which the seals of religious houses acquired a credible authority in respect of private contracts and transactions obviated the need for public notaries, except in business that touched exclusively upon church affairs.[57] The work performed by public notaries

[53] For early examples, see AUO, i, 89, 100, 161, 170, 188, 194 etc. See also Szentpétery, *Magyar oklevéltan*, 76.

[54] Zsolt Hunyadi, 'Administering the Law: Hungary's *Loca Credibilia*', in CLCE, 25–35 (26).

[55] Franz (Ferenc) Eckhart, 'Die glaubwürdigen Orte Ungarns im Mittelalter', *Mitteilungen des Instituts für österreichische Geschichtsforschung*, Supplement 9 (1913–15), 395–558 (420).

[56] Thus in 1435 John of Széchen, canon of Arad, requested *pro iuris cautela* the Csanád chapter to transcribe and confirm earlier letters issued by an imperial notary and the archbishop of Esztergom. See Pesty-Magina, no. 33.

[57] On public notaries in medieval Hungary, see István Barta, 'Középkori közjegyzőségeink történetéhez', in Bernát L. Kumorovitz and Loránd Szilágyi, eds., *Emlékkönyv Szentpétery Imre* (Budapest, 1938), 31–46.

in Europe more generally after the thirteenth century was thus undertaken almost exclusively in Hungary by religious houses.[58] Indeed, church institutions eventually squeezed out public notaries from those few cities on the Dalmatian coast where, as a consequence of Italian influence, they had previously been working.[59]

Despite the vicissitudes of the Reformation, the destruction and migration of chapters and convents during the Turkish wars, and the 'modernization' of the kingdom's institutions in the mid-nineteenth century, the *loca credibilia* of the church survived in Hungary (but with important modifications in Transylvania) until 1874.[60] Throughout this time, they continued to perform much the same tasks—recording testaments and transactions, including where possible the performance of *statutiones*, confirming the appointment of attorneys, converting verbal recognizances and undertakings (*fassiones*) into written instruments that carried legal authority, transcribing documents and republishing them under their own seals, and providing secure conditions for the storage of important documents, often over centuries.[61] Although there were plenty of occasions in the Middle Ages when the monks and canons were alleged to have engaged in fraudulent activity—misusing their seals (or being thought to have done so)—the institution of the *loca credibilia* rested on trust. The seals of the *loca* had to be physically recognizable, for which reason the seals of smaller and less busy religious houses were deemed to be 'inauthentic' insofar as they were less easily identified. By the same token, those requesting written confirmation of a deed or transaction had also to be either personally known to the monks and canons, or, if they were not, able to give a guarantee of identity from somebody whom they could recognize. *Loca credibilia* thus tended to be fairly evenly distributed around the kingdom, seldom more than two or three days' journey from any one place. By the middle of the fourteenth century, there were thus in Hungary no less than forty-seven chapters and convents that were empowered to authenticate private transactions with their own seals.[62] We should add to their number the seals of privileged cities, as administered by their magistrates, that carried authority in respect of the business affairs of citizens and townsfolk, and the seals of the kingdom's principal judges. The seals of urban magistracies, however, had only limited authority in respect of resident noblemen and of properties owned by citizens in the countryside. Charters issued under the seals of judges were often also taken to a religious house for

[58] We may very occasionally glimpse the activity of imperial and public notaries. See Franz Zimmermann, Carl Werner et al., eds., *Urkundenbuch zur Geschichte der Deutschen in Siebenbürgen*, 7 vols. (Sibiu and Bucharest, 1892–1991), iii, 158; Pesty-Magina, no. 33; Imre Nagy, Farkas Deák and Gyula Nagy, eds., *Hazai oklevéltár* (Budapest, 1879), 455.

[59] Eckhart, 'Die glaubwürdigen Orte', 462.

[60] For the later history of the *loca credibilia*, see László Papp, *A hiteleshelyek története és működése az újkorban* (Budapest, 1936); for Transylvania, Zsolt Bogdándi, 'Az erdélyi hiteleshelyek oklevéladó tevékenysége Bocskai István idején', in János Barta (ifj) and Klára Papp, eds., *'Nincsen nekünk több hazánk ennél'. Tanulmányok a Bocskai felkelés történetéhez* (Budapest, 2004), 96–104.

[61] Eckhart, 'Die glaubwürdigen Orte', 484–5.

[62] Eckhart, 'Die glaubwürdigen Orte', 462.

republication under its own seal, even though the seal of a high judge was considered to have a complete authority.[63]

The *loca credibilia* were more, however, than charter-issuing agencies. From the thirteenth century onwards, they played an increasing role in the administration of justice. The roots of this function are commonly ascribed to their earlier role in supervising ordeals and in oath taking, where they not only supervised the event but acted as its witness, and to the impact of the law of 1231 that obliged religious houses to oversee and vouch for the activity of the pristaldus, 'because many people suffer harm from false pristaldi'.[64] During the second half of the thirteenth century, it thus became usual for individual monks or canons to accompany the pristaldus in summoning, gathering evidence and executing court judgments, and in issuing letters that reported on judicial acts which served to supplement, and eventually replace, the pristaldus's own recollection. The replacement of the pristaldus as a permanent office holder with the bailiff or *homo regius*, who was appointed by the king for the occasion out of the ranks of the noblemen of the relevant county, did not alter the function attaching to the man of the convent or chapter.[65]

* * *

Let us examine in detail how the *loca credibilia* operated in respect of the kingdom's judicial administration. We shall do so first by reference to the simplest procedure, that of a *statutio*, which was the institution to a property.[66] A local nobleman wishes to obtain title to a property from the king, either an estate that has escheated to the crown by default of heirs or, which is more common, a piece of land that he has been farming but for which he has no charter attesting to ownership. He is likely to travel to the king to obtain right, although he may use intermediaries to press his suit.[67] Reminded of the petitioner's loyal service, the king will graciously concede the title and will issue a letter through the chancellery attesting to the donation. At this stage, however, the letter will not give full right but will include in the grant of title the phrase *Dicitur nobis*, thus indicating that the king is making the grant provisionally, on the basis of what he has been told and not out of sure knowledge (*ex certa nostra scientia*), as well as the formula, *salvo iure alieno*, which allows the grant to be rescinded should it be shown to impinge on another's rights.[68] Since the grant is not yet complete, the letter is not addressed to the

63 Bernát L. Kumorovitz, *A magyar pecséthasználat története a középkorban* (Budapest, 1993), 76–80.

64 1231: 10 (DRMH 1², 38). The literature on the origins of the *loca credibilia* is summarized in Hunyadi, *The Hospitallers in the Medieval Kingdom of Hungary*, 191–6.

65 The *pristaldus* continued to survive until well into the fourteenth century in some urban jurisdictions. See M.G. Kovachich, *Formulae Solennes Styli* (Pest, 1799), 22, 37. We will very occasionally note clerics being chosen as *homines regii*. See Iusztin Zoltán, 'Oamenii Regelui. Aspecte instituţionale din prima parte a secolului al xiv-lea de pe teritoriul Transilvaniei şi al Banatului medieval', *Apulum*, 48 (2011), 65–78 (76).

66 The procedure and vocabulary derived from church practice. See J.B. Dantoine, *Les Règles du droit canon* (Brussels, 1742), 15.

67 Szentpétery, *Magyar oklevéltan*, 89–90.

68 It thus constituted the reverse of *non obstante iure alieno*, by which the king extended rights irrespective of whether they impinged upon those of a third party. For the origin of the clause, see

nobleman but to a monastery or chapter, usually close to the estate involved. Only when they have confirmed what the nobleman has told the king will the gift be confirmed. The letter to the monastery or chapter accordingly rehearses the nobleman's petition and the royal response, requiring the religious house to send out one of its members as a witness who will act in concert with any one of several noblemen named in the letter as a potential bailiff. The noblemen so listed are actually acquaintances of the petitioner, for it is he who has suggested their names to the king—rulers cannot, after all, be expected to know every nobleman in the realm or to have their clerks draw up lists in regard to their availability.[69] Bearing this correspondence, the nobleman travels to the convent or chapter, presents the letter, and a monk or canon is duly found. They are joined there by one or more of the nobles named in the letter as suitable bailiffs, who should take a solemn oath before the canons or brethren that they will execute their tasks faithfully. It is the responsibility of the noble petitioner to make sure one turns up to be sworn. The little group then repairs to the vacant estate, where after proper announcement a gathering is held of the neighbouring landowners. No great ceremony is involved; the new owner simply walks up the path of the main residence. If the house is occupied, the inhabitants may come out to block entry; or one of the neighbours may protest, declaring that the property or a part of it belongs rightfully to him. To make sure that all have an opportunity to oppose the institution, the bailiff and the cleric will remain for several days nearby. Providing no protest is made, the monk or canon repairs back to the religious house in the company of the noble bailiff. Oaths are taken anew and a letter is drawn up in the convent or chapter, although it will only be released once the petitioner has paid for the work done on his behalf by the cleric and bailiff.[70] The letter will repeat verbatim the letter originally received by the king, note that institution has taken place and that there were no objections, and be sealed as an authentic record. The nobleman duly collects the letter and takes it to the royal court, where its contents are transcribed anew and published in the form of a patent with an impressed seal. The patent letter promises that the contents will be reissued upon future demand in the form of a privilege with pendant seal. Technically, such an instrument would carry an indisputable and absolute authority, but it costs time and money, and so most noblemen are content with a patent. (Indeed, some nobles are so penny pinching that they do not even have the chapter's record of the institution confirmed by the royal court, trusting that their subsequent physical possession of the property will be proof enough of their rights.)[71]

Gerhard Baaken, 'Salvo mandato et ordinatione nostra. Zur Rechtsgeschichte des Privilegs in spätstaufischen Zeit', *Zeitschrift für Württembergische Landesgeschichte*, 40 (1989), 11–33.

[69] Pál Engel, 'Királyi emberek Valkó megyében', in Engel, *Honor, vár, ispánság. Válogatott tanulmányok* (Budapest, 2003), 578–99 (590–5), first published in *Mediaevalia Transilvanica*, 3 (1999), 71–88.

[70] The bailiff was paid for his services by the convent or chapter from the fees it collected from the petitioner. See Eckhart, 'Die glaubwürdigen Orte', 497. The fees payable are listed in 8 March 1435: 11 (DRMH 2, 71). The aliener might give the new occupant a symbolic clod of earth.

[71] See thus Kovachich, *Formulae Solennes*, 148.

Similar procedures might be invoked in respect of a range of outdoor activities—inspecting boundaries, measuring a property in advance of its division, effecting recoveries, holding inquests and views, taking the oaths of compurgators and witnesses, and so on. As a commonplace formula of the time put it in respect of the work of the places of authentication—*ad citationes, inquisitiones, prohibitiones, reambulationes et captivationes possessionum.*[72] In all of these, the bailiff will be accompanied by a monk or canon. He will act as witness to the events and his report will be transmitted by the institution to which he belongs back to whoever has instructed the matter. The example which we have given above is typical of the fourteenth or fifteenth centuries and is, indeed, modelled upon a *statutio* that took place in 1388 in Uzh County.[73] In this case, as in our own reconstruction, no objection was laid to the institution—unsurprisingly, as the petitioner's family had been in occupation (probably illegally) of the land for well over a century.[74] Had the institution been obstructed or a protest been laid before the bailiff, then this would have been duly noted in the letter that was returned to the king and those objecting told to direct their complaint to the royal presence. Until they did so (and they would normally be given a year), ownership of the estate would remain *lite pendente*, in the hands of those having physical possession.

The testimony of a man of the chapter or convent might also be required in cases of occupation and robbery. In this case, the procedure followed very much the routine of the *statutio*, with the cleric observing all that took place and compiling a report. A royal bailiff, usually appointed at the suggestion of the plaintiff, will visit the place of a trespass, illegal seizure or 'act of might' (*actus potentiae*), inspect the site, and interrogate witnesses and others. The accompanying cleric will write the findings down in a letter that will be sent under the chapter's seal to the king or instructing judge. The letter will recite the original instruction and report what has been learned. It may also record that summonses have been issued, directing the parties to attend court within a specified period, although this 'rolling up' of the parts of the case is more usually a feature of fifteenth-century procedure. At this stage, the parties will usually settle, for the king's justice is expensive and time-consuming, or they will go to arbitration, depositing a cash surety that will be forfeited in the event that they reject the decision reached. Should the parties nonetheless submit to the royal rigour, they will be called to attend court. Further evidence may then be called for, and a bailiff and cleric sent out anew to take sworn depositions. Or an oath taking may be ordered, either in the form of a decisory oath, whereby the party who has marshalled the best evidence concludes his case by solemnly swearing on the head of his adversary, or by an act of compurgation, by which fellow noblemen uphold the integrity of one or other of the suitors. The evidence of the oath taking, which usually happens at a place convenient to the parties, will be relayed back to the court, on the basis of which it will render its

[72] Eckhart, 'Die glaubwürdigen Orte', 538.

[73] MNL OL DL, 281293, reproduced in István Balogh, Géza Érszegi and Ágota Henzsel, eds., *Középkori oklevelek a Szabolcs–Szatmár–Bereg Levéltárában* (Nyiregyháza, 2000), nos. 21–3, 36.

[74] It had probably once belonged as forest or scrub to the royal lordship of Uzhgorod (Ungvár), now in Ukraine, and had been clandestinely cleared.

judgment. The final document presented to the court will often be very long, repeating the content of previous letters as well as the texts of the instructions that the bailiff and cleric have received.

This brief survey of the work played by the *loca credibilia* in Hungary is typical of the predominantly written methods that distinguish civil law jurisdictions, to which Hungary historically belongs. There is no single trial, but a sequence of episodes, initiated by interim decisions of the court. Evidence is gathered and mediated by the paperwork that the court orders to be collected on its behalf. The interrogation of witnesses and neighbours, together with the taking of oaths, usually takes place at a distance, being reported back to the court in writing. The parties will still attend court or they may appoint agents to look after their interests, but their presence is not necessary and a decision can be reached in their absence. The purpose of the proceedings is for the court to sift the dossier that has been gathered and come to a judgment based on the written statements put before it, and on what it thinks the law to be.

The strongly written element attaching to the activity of the courts explains, moreover, how the language of the chancellery came to be diffused throughout the kingdom and, indeed, so rapidly. By the end of the thirteenth century, the language of the law had obtained a remarkable uniformity across the kingdom. Vocabulary and procedures had become standardized; the style and form of letters published by the *loca credibilia* had likewise assumed a strong regularity, imitating in their phraseology the charters issuing out of the central royal offices. Explanation for this development is usually ascribed to the distribution of formularies by the chancellery that instructed monks and canons on how they were to frame and compose letters.[75] No such manuals survive, however, from before the fourteenth century and then only in small numbers. Possibly they were so well used that they fell apart or were so heavily written over and emended as to become unusable.[76] We know, however, that individual charters might be specially filed and used as exemplars of *consuetudo communis regni et stilus Curie*.[77] Nevertheless, the passage of correspondence between the centre and the *loca credibilia*, together with the habit of rewriting previous correspondence in the body of the reply in such a way as to yield a comprehensive dossier, had the consequence of impressing the chancellery's own vocabulary and style, and with it a regularity of forms and formulas.

The institution of the *loca credibilia* stood in place of public notaries, whose absence in the legal affairs of the laity was noted as unusual by contemporaries.[78] Possibly, and as has been argued, the replacement of public notaries by ecclesiastical agencies of authentication reduced the flow of civilian principles into the kingdom, but this is difficult to show either way. It is more certain that the use of clerics to frame legal instruments bent Hungarian practice towards the techniques and pre-

[75] Szentpétery, *Magyar oklevéltan*, 91.

[76] For a later example of this phenomenon, see *Formular Styli Juridici 1650–1660*, OSzK, MSS, Fol. Lat. 1852.

[77] Frigyes Pesty and Tivadar Ortvay, eds., *Oklevelek Temesvármegye és Temesvárváros történetéhez*, i (Bratislava, 1896), 102.

[78] Bónis, *Einflüsse des römischen Rechts*, 32–3.

suppositions of church courts. The large, specialized vocabulary relating to the types of letter and instruction that might be sent, along with the names attaching to procedures, thus overwhelmingly derive from ecclesiastical practice, as mediated through the chancellery and its agencies in the countryside, the *loca credibilia*.[79] In this respect, written instruments served to shape Hungary's customary law not only by providing the means whereby the chancellery style was more widely disseminated but also by tilting Hungarian practice towards some of the procedural techniques and assumptions of the Romano-canonical law of the church.

## LEGISLATION AND STATUTE

In his discussion of the written sources of Hungary's customary law, Werbőczy gives first place to 'constitutions and public decrees'. Werbőczy briefly lists the legislation of Hungary's kings, starting with the 'splendid constitutions' of St Stephen. He notes that these are concerned more with spiritual than judicial matters and that, like the other laws of the eleventh century, they 'have by now been almost entirely effaced due to their extreme age'.[80] In his discussion of Hungary's earliest laws, Werbőczy mentions neither the laws of Coloman from *c.* 1100 nor the supposed fragment of an earlier statute of Andrew I, even though this was known to his near-contemporary, Antonio Bonfini (1434–1503).[81] Moving on, he resumes his list with the legislation of Andrew II, and then of Louis the Great, Sigismund, Albert of Habsburg, Matthias Corvinus and Wladislas II.[82] Werbőczy overlooks the several laws enacted by Andrew III at the end of the thirteenth century and of Wladislas I, as well as the more meagre legislation of Charles Robert and of his granddaughter, Mary.[83]

Werbőczy's list promotes the idea that there was an established and coherent body of law in the form of measures enacted by Hungary's kings. In this respect, Werbőczy's understanding reflected the opinion more widely held at the time that there were recognizable instruments of statute law issued by Hungary's monarchs over the course of the previous centuries that continued to retain some validity and so merited collection. At the same time, however, Werbőczy stressed that the laws of the kingdom did not originate in the monarch's plenitude of power, but that legislative capacity was historically shared between ruler and estates, by virtue of an arrangement that went back to the earliest period of Hungarian kingship.[84] Neither this, nor Werbőczy's contention that the kingdom was possessed of a discrete corpus of written law can be demonstrated as true for the Hungarian Middle

[79] Iván Borsa, 'Irattipusok a középkori Magyarországon', *Levéltari Közlemények*, 64 (1993), 27–37 (30).

[80] Trip., II. 6 [4–5, 9] (DRMH 5, 233).

[81] The legislation of Andrew I is given in Bonfini's *Rerum Ungaricarum Decades*, II. II. 45 ff (Basle, 1543, and many subsequent editions). Its authenticity is disputed and so it is not included in DRMH 1.

[82] Trip., II. 6 [6–8] (DRMH 5, 233).

[83] It would indeed have been remarkable had Werbőczy mentioned Charles Robert's laws, for these only survive in a short fragment. See DRMH 2, 1–2, 155.

[84] Trip., II. 3 [3–4] (DRMH 5, 529).

Ages as a whole. Although it may be intermittently discerned in earlier periods, the notion of the people's consent to law was very much a product of the later fifteenth century. Moreover, it is probably not possible to talk of legislation in any realistic way even at this time, since it was overwhelmingly concerned with matters of fleeting concern and not with the elaboration of an enduring body of rules.

Until the fifteenth century, most Hungarian rulers eschewed law making. The exceptions were Hungary's first Christian monarchs whose published decrees were aimed as much at promoting the royal rule as at imposing a Christian and penitential order.[85] No laws survive from the twelfth century and only a handful from the thirteenth. Of Hungary's thirteenth-century laws, those published by Andrew II, Béla IV and Andrew III were the product of conditions verging on civil war through which the ruler bought support by promising to uphold the liberties of his subjects, publishing these formally as privileges. For his part, Charles Robert deliberately avoided making laws, for which he was reproved at the time.[86] As far as we are aware, his son, Louis the Great, published only a single code, in 1351.[87] From the late fourteenth century onwards, decrees of the ruler steadily mounted in number, partly in response to the Turkish threat which forced a reorganization of the kingdom's military and other resources, and partly in response to recurrent succession crises. Increasingly also, these laws dealt with matters of judicial organization and procedure, with the aim of speedier justice and of bringing to account those who had taken the opportunity of interregna to oppress others. Nevertheless, the legislation of the fifteenth and early sixteenth centuries retained an overtly political character, often reproducing the programmes of whichever baronial faction was in power and, just as frequently, overturning measures only recently agreed. Their content in respect of the substantive law was always slight.

The reluctance of Hungary's rulers to publish laws has been explained by the salience of customary law which rendered royal intrusions both unnecessary and unwelcome.[88] It is, however, equally likely that rulers considered normative instruments to be restrictive of their own authority and discretion. Their preference was for decisions that settled disputes on an individual basis, and for rights that were targeted at single beneficiaries. Laws established principles and imposed obligations. In this respect, they hemmed in the king's identity as 'the living law' and the notion that legal capacity proceeded from 'the royal authority, princely magnificence and the plenitude of power'.[89] In this respect, it is no coincidence that Louis the Great's compilation of 1351 was framed in the manner of a royal charter of donation, ceded 'out of our royal benevolence' to the kingdom's nobles on account of their meritorious deeds, 'in order to encourage them to engage with dedicated mind in similar works of faithful service'.[90]

[85] György Bónis, 'Szent István törvényének önállósága', 462–6; see more generally, Thomas Pollock Oakley, *English Penitential Discipline and Anglo-Saxon Law* (New York, 1923).

[86] György Bónis, 'Petrus de Vinea leveleskönyve Magyarországon', *Filológiai Közlöny*, 4, nos. 1–2 (1958), 1–26, 173–93 (188).

[87] DRMH 2, 8–13.

[88] Ferenc Eckhart, 'Jog- és alkotmánytörténet', in Bálint Hóman, ed., *A magyar történetirás új útjai* (Budapest, 1931), 269–320 (285–6).

[89] Bónis, 'Petrus de Vinea leveleskönyve', 189.

[90] DRMH 2, 9.

The relatively minor role occupied by royal legislation is reflected in terminology and in the manner of publication. A law of the ruler might thus be variously described as a *privilegium*, *statutum*, *decretum* or *edictum*. It might be issued as a privilege or patent, with a pendant seal or with the king's impressed privy seal. A list of current office holders might or might not be included in the eschatocol. Variations in the notarial marks attached to individual charters indicate that the way in which the law was instructed and drawn up in the chancellery changed on occasion. The manner of promulgation also differed. A law might thus be sent in manuscript form to the individual cities and counties of the realm for dissemination, or ordered to be proclaimed 'in markets and other public places, wherever'.[91] Since, however, the recipients were expected to pay for such copies of the laws as they received, their actual circulation was never certain. Much medieval legislation was thus lost and only partly recovered by the diligence of scholars working in the eighteenth and nineteenth centuries.

The efficacy of any individual law was, moreover, uncertain. A formulary from the second half of the fifteenth century thus suggests that the laws of individual kings retained cogency for the duration of their reigns, but that their subsequent authority depended upon the degree to which their provisions were embraced in customary use.[92] As we have seen, Werbőczy came close to a similar formulation. Moreover, even where the statutory law was known, it might be that courts either agreed to deliver their judgments in accordance with customary practice or were instructed by the ruler to do so.[93] Indeed, in a remarkable passage dealing with due process in law, Werbőczy affirmed that the customary rules of procedure followed in the kingdom's courts were unalterable by statute, even though that statute's provisions might subsequently acquire a customary authority of their own: 'For otherwise the rights of the whole nobility of the kingdom of Hungary would necessarily be reduced to nothing by the introduction of new laws (even though these be learned and brought into common use).'[94] As far as we can make out, however, no lawyer or jurist invoked this apparent *Ewigkeitsklausel* in opposition to Habsburg interference with the judicial process.

By the time Werbőczy was composing his account, it was generally accepted that the laws of the ruler should be promulgated with the agreement of the *communitas regni*, as embodied in the kingdom's diet.[95] This reflected the increased regularity with which diets gathered or were summoned—to decide on matters during interregna, to deliberate on the succession, or to add the semblance of consent to new arrangements of taxation and military recruitment. In less than two decades—from the accession of Wladislas I in 1440 to the election in 1458 of Matthias Corvinus—the diet convened on at least seventeen separate occasions, sometimes

[91] György Bónis, 'Einleitung', in DRH 1301–1437, 9–37 (23–4).

[92] Bónis, 'Einleitung', 25.

[93] DRH 1301–1457, 377. See also DRMH 5, 7.

[94] Trip., II. 6 [13] (DRMH 5, 235). Discussed in David Ibbetson, 'Custom in the *Tripartitum*', CLCE, 13–23 (22).

[95] See generally, János M. Bak, *Königtum und Stände in Ungarn im 14.–16. Jahrhundert* (Wiesbaden, 1976), 43–50.

twice in the same year.[96] During the thirty-two years of Matthias's reign, the diet assembled a little less frequently, but still twenty-five times; under his Jagiello successors, Wladislas II and Louis II, on forty-three occasions in thirty-six years. A notable feature of these later diets, particularly those called by the Jagiello kings, was their mass character. Instead of being attended by their representatives, noblemen turned up in person—often in their thousands—rendering assemblies of the diet rowdy, dangerous, and all too open to the type of demagoguery in which Werbőczy himself was skilled.[97]

Many of the laws published by the Jagiello kings were more political manifestos than legislative acts, aimed either at buttressing the powers of the kingdom's nobility or at promoting the interests of whichever baronial faction was currently in ascendancy. Although Wladislas II achieved some notable achievements in respect of the reorganization of the kingdom's courts and judicial procedure, the majority of laws from the Jagiello period are a hotchpotch of political programme, private bills, emergency measures affecting finance and the army, personal denunciations, and quaint recollections of a mythical Hungarian past. Many laws never received the royal assent and so languished; others were of such an ephemeral character as not to have survived. Most diets held in the later fifteenth and early sixteenth centuries thus had little legislative consequence. Indeed, of the forty-three diets that met between 1490 and 1526, only a dozen produced cogent laws that were agreed upon jointly by the ruler and the assembled noble community.[98]

Despite the deficiencies in the kingdom's legislative organization and the insufficiency of its laws, by no later than the sixteenth century two principles had been established that shaped both Werbőczy's understanding of the kingdom's statutes and the way in which law making would be understood in the centuries that followed. First, law in the sense of a royal statute was now comprehended as emerging out of agreement between the king and the political community. Secondly, the political community was understood in the sense of the noble estate, as gathered in the kingdom's diet. With the Habsburg takeover of the kingdom after 1526, the period of mass diets came gradually to an end and more tractable assemblies were generally now summoned.[99] Hungary's Habsburg monarchs would also (and controversially) impose legislation by decree, without any form of popular consultation. Nevertheless, the notion of statute law proceeding out of a dialogue or *tractatus*, in the form of a treaty between the ruler and the nation, as represented in the diet, proved impossible to efface, imposing a permanent restraint on absolutist ambitions.[100]

Notwithstanding the importance that Werbőczy ascribed to statute law and to the principle of consent, the *Tripartitum* eschews almost any mention of the diet

[96] 1440, 1441, 1442 (twice), 1444, 1445, 1446 (twice), 1447 (twice), 1448, 1451, 1452, 1453, 1454, 1455, 1456. We exclude the convocations of regional diets.

[97] For this and much of what follows, see Martyn Rady, 'Jagiello Hungary' in DRMH 4, pp. xxxiv–xliv. See also Martyn Rady, 'Rethinking Jagiello Hungary', *Central Europe*, 3, no. 1 (2005), 3–18.

[98] In 1492, 1495, 1498, 1500, 1504, 1514, 1518 (twice), 1521, 1523, 1526. See János M. Bak, 'Diets and their Decisions 1490–1526', in DRMH 4, pp. li–lvi.

[99] The last mass diet was the coronation diet of 1572. See Géza Pálffy, *The Kingdom of Hungary and the Habsburg Monarchy in the Sixteenth Century* (Boulder, CO and New York, 2009), 179.

[100] István M. Szijárto, *A diéta. A magyar rendek és az országgyűlés 1708–1792* (Budapest, 2005), 39.

and of its legislative role.[101] The most that Werbőczy gives is a discussion of the *lex regia* that permitted a residual power to the people through the royal obligation to consult, although—unlike Aquinas and Bracton—he does not explain how the original transfer of power from people to ruler might be reconciled with the people's retention of a share in law making.[102] More surprising is the way that Werbőczy's account makes such little use of statute law. In a few places, he quotes directly from previous legislation, mostly from the statutes of Wladislas II published in 1492 and 1498, but also extensively from a law of 1435 that was subsequently used in the preparation of Matthias's code of 1486.[103] Elsewhere, there are references to recent laws, most frequently to statutes passed by the diet in 1492, 1495, 1504 and 1514.[104] The impression remains that Werbőczy had at his disposal the texts of only a few statutes, mainly those promulgated in the three decades before publication of the *Tripartitum*. The small set of statutes upon which Werbőczy relied in composing the *Tripartitum* confirms his larger observation that only such written law as remained in active use was possessed of a continued and persuasive authority.[105]

* * *

As we have seen, Werbőczy had proposed in the Prologue to the *Tripartitum* that custom and statute law constituted two self-standing and independent sources of legal authority. Interacting and complementing one another, they together constituted what he called *ius*. In the main text, when considering the making of customary law in Hungary, Werbőczy abandoned this formulation, with custom taking upon itself the overarching quality that had previously belonged to *ius*. Statute law thus became a subordinate aspect of customary law, contributing to its substance, but only in respect of those of its provisions that had themselves acquired a customary character. Regardless of Werbőczy's inconsistencies, his formulation accurately conveyed the way that both that the kingdom's statutes and the written law in general acted not in a normative way, but instead reflexively with customary law. On the one hand, the sources he proposed shaped the substance of the law, but on the other their content was customized through practice and use. The written

101 There is a cursory reference in Trip., II. 20 (DRMH 5, 271).

102 Trip., II. 3 (DRMH 5, 229). See also Trip., I. 3 [6] (DRMH 5, 51). For Aquinas and Bracton, see Ernst H. Kantorowicz, *The King's Two Bodies: A Study in Medieval Political Theology* (Princeton, NJ, 1957), 150–1; Walter Ullmann, 'The Medieval Papacy, St Thomas and Beyond', in Ullmann, *Law and Jurisdiction in the Middle Ages* (London, 1988), 23.

103 Trip., I. 29 [1–4] (DRMH 5, 92–3) and 1435: 17–18 (DRMH 2, 73–4) (cf. 1486: 26: DRMH 3, 52–3); Trip., II. 67 [8–13] (DRMH 5, 331–3) and 1492: 55–6 (DRMH 4, 28–31); Trip., II. 77 [5–10] (DRMH 5, 355–7) and 1492: 51–2 (DRMH 4, 26–7); Trip., III. 19 [3–8] (DRMH 5, 399) and 1498: 38 (DRMH 4, 114–15).

104 Cf. Trip., II. 11 [1] (DRMH 5, 239) and 1492: 96 (DRMH 4, 42–3); Trip., II. 24 [5] (DRMH 5, 279) and 1486: 25 (DRMH 3, 52); Trip., II. 31 [1] (DRMH 5, 289) and 1486: 14 (DRMH 3, 47–8); Trip., II. 57 [3] (DRMH 5, 319) and 1504: 4 (DRMH 4, 164–5); Trip., II. 67 [1] (DRMH 5, 331) and 1492: 55 (DRMH 4, 28–9); Trip., II. 73–4 (DRMH 5, 343–7) and 1500: 9 (DRMH 4, 142–3); Trip., II. 75 [1–2] (DRMH 5, 347–9) and 1495: 3 (DRMH 4, 56–7); Trip., III. 25 (DRMH 5, 405) and 1514 *passim* (DRMH 4, 176ff).

105 See further on this point, Andor Csizmadia, 'Hungarian customary law before the bourgeois rebellion of 1848', *Journal of Legal History*, 4, no. 2 (1983), 3–37 (6).

law depended for its efficacy upon repeated acts of recognition, observance and compliance. Even statutes, to which Werbőczy apportions the largest normative weight, might lapse, with their individual provisions being forgotten or their texts inadequately preserved. More than three centuries before Werbőczy, Cosmas of Prague had famously observed that the law had a nose of wax, but that the ruler was possessed of an iron hand which could bend it to his will.[106] The history of its written law suggests that in Hungary it was custom's claw which did most of the twisting.

[106] Cosmas of Prague, *The Chronicle of the Czechs*, ed. Lisa Wolverton (Washington, D.C., 2009), 124 (2.8).

# 4

# Customary Law and Medieval Courts

## THE *TRIPARTITUM* AND THE DECISIONS OF JUDGES

In his discussion of the sources of the kingdom's customary law, Werbőczy includes in addition to the written law, the decisions of the judges of the royal Curia and the letters of adjudication that they composed at the conclusion of cases. No sooner has Werbőczy made this point than he moves confusingly on, from the decisions of judges to the procedure of courts and to the importance of maintaining due process and the rule of law. Despite this departure, it is clear from Werbőczy's account that he does not consider that the decisions of judges yielded a means whereby the law might be known. His point is that the customary law of the realm proceeded out of judgments repeatedly made in the court room on account of which the customary law of Hungary, or at least a part of it, constituted judge-made law.

Two immediate problems arise in respect of Werbőczy's account. The first is that the letters of adjudication of which he speaks were not themselves catalogued or retained in such a way as to constitute a physical body of jurisprudence to which judges might refer. It was only much later that any order was imposed on case records and that finding aids were drawn up to guide the courts to previous decisions. Even so, these manuals were slender in their scope, scanty in their referencing, and unsystematic in their content.[1] In the absence of a written body of previous decisions, courts relied on memory. Accordingly, as Matthias Corvinus noted in the 1480s, if a court did not meet sufficiently often, the danger arose that the death of its members would over time rob posterity of its accumulated knowledge of the law.[2] Secondly, the use that Werbőczy made of the term *iudex* and *ordinarius* rested upon a convention of Romano-canonical law that attributed the decisions of courts to their presiding officer. In fact, most Hungarian courts operated as collegiate bodies and judgments were collectively agreed. Within this structure, the influence of the ordinaries was mercifully little. Most Hungarian judges were until the eighteenth century appointed to office mainly on account of their martial reputation and as a reward for their loyalty, for they were allowed to rake off a share of the court's income from fines. Except for the judges whose offices derived historically from the chancellery, they were for the most part functionally illiterate—the

[1] See thus, MNL OL, B 53, *Index manualis in juridicis (1752–1827)*. Described in Zsolt Trócsányi, *Erdélyi Kancelláriai Levéltár. Repertórium* (Levéltári Leltárak, 68) (Budapest, 1976), 43.

[2] Bónis, KJE, 161, 225.

Latin of one sixteenth-century vice-palatine was so rudimentary as to earn him the soubriquet of 'Cicero'.[3] It is thus not conceivable that the decisions of the realm's ordinaries constituted a body of learned law upon which courts and lawyers might rely. Instead, decisions were for the most part proposed by the court officers known as the protonotaries, although the extant record preserves the illusion that they proceeded from the judges' own ruminations.

## COURTS OF THE ROYAL PRESENCE

The courts of the Curia, over which the ordinaries of the realm presided, constituted royal courts and they administered justice in the king's name. It was to these courts that noblemen took cases that involved property or violence, which could not be resolved by the counties or through arbitration. Back in the twelfth and thirteenth centuries, the king had personally overseen a good deal of the litigation that came to the royal seat for judgment. Even then, however, the king did not dispense justice alone, for he was expected to attend to the opinions of the lords and noblemen who comprised his entourage. Thus, Béla III, administering justice beneath an oak tree, still framed his decision in association with ten named lords as well as 'other ministers of the king, from near and far, whom it would take too long to name and list'.[4] The periodic assizes over which the king presided, and to which some litigation was in the twelfth and thirteenth centuries moved, likewise drew upon a constituency of lords, churchmen and others that was sufficiently numerous to merit the description of a *congregatio*. At the assizes, which were usually held in the coronation city of Székesfehérvár, the king delivered justice 'in the assembly of his realm, [. . .] held for the relief of his kingdom, sitting in judgment together with the barons and nobles of the kingdom, in order to determine the cases of litigants'.[5]

Although some fleeting attempts at its revival may be detected, the institution of the assizes did not last much beyond the thirteenth century.[6] Throughout the Middle Ages, however, cases continued to come before the monarch's own person (*propria persona*) for adjudication. On these occasions, the king judged with those high prelates and barons who were in attendance at his court and, if he was travelling, judgments were put in writing by the king's mobile privy chancellery. Many of the cases so moved either involved litigants who had the privilege to have their

[3] Dezső Szabó, *A magyar országgyűlések története II. Lajos korában* (Budapest, 1909), 80, 189, 195. See also Loránd Szilágyi, *A magyar királyi kancellária szerepe az államkormányzatban 1458–1526* (Budapest, 1930), 99.

[4] AUO, i, 69–70. See also Imre Hajnik, *A magyar birósági szervezet és perjog az Árpád- es a vegyes-házi királyok alatt* (Budapest, 1899), 9.

[5] AO, ii, 30; AUO, x, 137; HO, ii, 188. See also 1222: 1; 1231: 1; 1290: 18 (DRMH 1, 32, 36, 44); György Bónis, 'The Freedom of the Land in Medieval Hungarian Law', *Anciens Pays et assemblées d'états*, 53 (1970), 94–116 (101–3).

[6] Bónis, 'The Freedom of the Land', 103–4. See also Joseph (=József) Holub, 'La répresentation politique en Hongrie au Moyen Age', *Studies presented to the International Commission for the History of Representative and Parliamentary Institutions, Xth International Congress of Historical Sciences, Rome 1955* (Louvain and Paris, 1958), 77–121 (83).

suits determined by the king alone, or comprised acts of egregious violence.[7] Since violent crime done by noblemen frequently resulted in the confiscation of property or an act of pardon, recourse to the ruler's personal jurisdiction was inevitable insofar as he constituted the fount of grace and the root of all property in land. Matters affecting noble orphans also came before the king personally, since he was considered their ultimate guardian.[8] By virtue of the royal plenitude, decisions of the ruler might set aside the provisions of customary law on grounds of equity and conscience, thus for instance temporarily removing the ordinary rules of inheritance or abolishing established methods of tithe collection, *ex speciali gratia ac de plenitudine potestatis nostre [. . .] legibus seu consuetudinibus quibuslibet non obstantibus*.[9] The royal right to administer the law even to the extent of overturning the decisions of ordinary justice was later explained in terms of the *absoluta potentia et auctoritas* that attached to the monarch.[10] It would eventually constitute a separate branch of jurisprudence, although its application was confined to the administration of land trusts.

The clamour of petitioners assailing the royal ear obliged rulers both to establish new forums for justice that operated in their name but did not depend on their personal attention, and to institute new mechanisms to expedite business. These measures were often unwelcome. Béla IV's attempt to have all plaints put in writing—by which he meant that litigants should proceed in the first instance through the scribes of the royal chapel and not press their suits on him in person—caused friction and had eventually to be postponed.[11] As late as the 1480s, however, Matthias still complained of the many suitors 'who come forth and loudly proclaim that [rights of inheritance] have devolved to them, by which they not only deafen the ears of the royal highness with their unwelcome shouting but also detain his majesty from more important tasks'.[12] Nonetheless, from the start of the

[7] Alternatively, when the matter was so hard that a royal decision was needed. See Imre Hajnik, *A király bírósági személyes jelenléte és ennek helytartója a vegyesházakbeli királyok korszakában* (Budapest, 1892), 7.

[8] Alajos Degré, *A magyar gyámsági jog kialakulása a dualizmus korának gyámsági kódexéig* (Budapest, 1977), 10, 23.

[9] Imre Nagy, Dezső Véghely and Gyula Nagy, eds., *Zala vármegye története. Oklevéltár*, 2 vols. (Budapest, 1886–90), i, 182. See also T. Smičiklas, ed., *Codex Diplomaticus Regni Croatiae, Dalmatiae et Slavoniae*, ix (Zagreb, 1911), 239, 300. Discussed in György Bónis, *Einflüsse des römischen Rechts in Ungarn* (*Ius Romanum Medii Aevi*, 5, no. 10) (Milan, 1964), 84. The form of *derogatio* used here is papal in origin, possibly mediated through Sicily. See Erik van Mingroot, *Sapientiae immarcessibilis: A diplomatic and comparative study of the Bull of Foundation of the University of Louvain* (Leuven, 1994), 193.

[10] The claim to an *extraordinaria potestas et auctoritas* was made by Matthias in 1486 in the so-called *Articuli palatinales* (DRMH 3, 74), and is an early example of the way in which this originally theological distinction, applied to the pope's power since the thirteenth century, spilled over into the discourse of temporal rule. See Francis Oakley, 'The Absolute and Ordained Power of God in the Sixteenth and Seventeenth Centuries: Philosophy, Science, Politics, and Law', *Journal of the History of Ideas*, 59 (1998), 669–90 (681–3); also, Joseph (=József) Holub, 'Ordinaria potentia–absoluta potentia', *Revue Historique de droit français et étranger*, 27 (1950), 92–9.

[11] *Magistri Rogerii Carmen super destructione regni Hungariae per Tartaros facta*, ch. 6, in János M. Bak, Martyn Rady and László Veszprémy, eds., *Anonymus and Master Roger* (Budapest and New York, 2010), 145–7. See also 1267: 10 (DRMH 1², 41).

[12] 1486: 26 (DRMH 3, 51–2).

thirteenth century, if not earlier, most royal justice was delegated—first to the palatine who practised an itinerant justice, and secondly to the high judge (*comes curialis, iudex curiae regiae, országbiró*), who administered the king's court in the name of the ruler, acting in the capacity of the 'royal presence' whenever the king was unavailable.[13] Neither of these officers acted, however, as sole judges. The palatine dispensed justice in the localities in conjunction with the chief men of the counties while the king's judge of the 'royal presence' held court in association with members of the royal council. Matters which went directly to the king for adjudication were from the close of the thirteenth century referred to as proceeding before the king's 'special presence'.

The pattern of delegation meant, however, that the court at which the king was supposed to judge in person soon separated from the royal *propria persona*, his real self, being entrusted instead to an officer of the crown. As we have seen, the court of the 'royal presence' was in the thirteenth century mainly presided over by the high judge. In the fourteenth century, the king's court of the 'special presence', wherein the king had previously judged in person, was likewise put in the hands of the chancellor, who in turn delegated its presidency to his own deputies.[14] To begin with, judgments published by the chancellor maintained the fiction that the king had actually been in attendance at the court but that, 'on account of the absence of his seals', the letter of adjudication had to be authenticated with the chancellor's own.[15] The court of the special presence took over most of the work that had previously flowed to the high judge's court of the royal presence, while the king now judged *propria in persona* in a court of the 'personal presence'. In the 1430s the court of the personal presence was itself placed in the hands of delegated justices, while the court of the special presence was allowed to languish. It was eventually revived in 1453, thereby effectively creating two courts of the royal presence, with largely overlapping jurisdictions.[16] On top of this, the king continued throughout the later Middle Ages to maintain his own court, where he judged *propria in persona*, wherever he happened to be, often in the company of just a few of his entourage.[17] Notwithstanding the eclipse of the court of the royal presence by the court of the special presence, the high judge retained a court of his own that was mostly concerned with deciding cases of inheritance.[18] The palatine's court

[13] The title of *iudex Curiae* is impossible to translate. Judge of the Court is ambiguous, but 'Aulic Judge' (the solution deriving from 'Aulic Court' as a translation for *Hofgericht*) is surely too exotic. The title of *országbiró* (a calque of *Landesrichter*), which attached to the office after the fifteenth century, has no obvious English counterpart. We are not convinced by the occasional German expedient of *Judexkurial*.

[14] József Gerics, 'A magyar királyi kúriai biráskodás és központi igazgatás Anjou-kori történetéhez', in Gerics, *Egyház, állam és gondolkodás Magyarországon a középkorban* (Budapest, 1995), 295–318 (305), first published in *Jogtörténeti Tanulmányok*, 1 (1966), 285–306.

[15] Bernát L. Kumorovitz, *A magyar pecséthasználat története a középkorban* (Budapest, 1993), 74.

[16] György Bónis, Alajos Degré and Endre Varga, *A magyar birósági szervezet és perjog története*, 2nd edition (Zalaegerszeg, 1996), 27.

[17] ZsO, vii, no. 1484; MNL OL DL, 20249. See also András Kubinyi, 'Adatok a Mátyás-kori királyi kancellária és az 1464. évi kancelláriai reform történetéhez', in L. F. Lendvai, ed., *Tiz éves a bölcsészképzés a miskolci egyetemen* (Miskolc, 2004), 25–58 (52).

[18] Trip., I. 30 [3] (DRMH 5, 93); István Stipta, *A magyar birósági rendszer története*, 2nd edition (Debrecen, 1998), 27.

continued to receive cases transmitted from the counties, as well as to hear cases in which the king was a party, although jurisdictional boundaries were not closely defined.[19]

The apparent proliferation of courts and their recurrent changes of name should not obscure strong institutional continuities. With the exception of those occasions when the king in his movements around the realm judged *propria in persona*, all these courts were located in the Curia—in Visegrád during the Anjou period and, subsequently, in the royal palace on the Buda hill. Membership of these courts was elastic. In their composition, the courts drew mainly upon members of the royal council, which was itself a heterogeneous and varied body, but their sessions were often supplemented by assessors, drawn from the ordinary nobility, who were appointed either by the ruler or by election of the diet. The participation of noble assessors seems intended to dilute the influence of the high officers of the council over the judicial process.[20] Almost certainly, however, court sessions rarely embraced the eighty or so barons, prelates and others who had the right to attend formal meetings of the royal council, for we know of many suits that had to be postponed because of an insufficiency of adjudicators.[21] Cases were, moreover, frequently moved back and forth between the king's own personal court and the court of whichever presence functioned in his name at the time, and even assigned to the palatine or high judge, should that be deemed convenient.[22] We suspect that the rise of the *tavernicus* (*magister tavernicorum* or 'master of the provisioners'), an office otherwise redundant by the fourteenth century, to the role of appeal judge for the kingdom's nascent cities partly originated in procedural expediency of this type.[23] Nevertheless, it is probably prudent not to think in terms of a number of separate courts but of one court, the Curia, with a membership that overlapped with the royal council, and over which the realm's ordinaries either individually or in tandem dispensed justice, usually in the name of the king.[24]

Most judges of the realm were in the first place warriors, while the barons and nobles in attendance at the courts of the Curia were scarcely lettered. Matthias liked to humiliate his councillors by drawing their attention to books.[25] Moreover,

[19] Bónis, Degré, Varga, *A magyar bírósági szervezet*, 28; György Bónis, *A jogtudó értelmiség a Mohács előtti Magyarországon* (Budapest, 1971), 253.

[20] Hajnik, *A magyar bírósági szervezet*, 52. The intermittent presence of elected assessors in the royal courts may be traced back to the thirteenth century. See Gerics, 'A magyar királyi kúriai biráskodás', 297.

[21] Bódog Schiller, *Az örökös főrendiség eredete Magyarországon* (Budapest, 1900), 38–55. In following Nándor Knauz (*Az országos tanács és országgyűlések története*, Pest, 1859), Schiller conflates the day-to-day operation of the royal council, which included governmental and judicial tasks, with its more periodic function in law making, on which occasions it drew upon a broader and invited membership. For absenteeism, see Hajnik, *A magyar birosági szervezet*, 52–3; Schiller, *Az örökös főrendiség*, 122–3.

[22] Hajnik, *A király bírósági személyes jelenléte*, 11–12.

[23] Martyn Rady, *Medieval Buda: A Study of Municipal Government and Jurisdiction in the Kingdom of Hungary* (Boulder, CO and New York, 1985), 135–6.

[24] Bónis, Degré, Varga, *A magyar bírósági szervezet*, 28.

[25] Martyn Rady, 'The Corvina Library and the Lost Hungarian Royal Archive', in James Raven, ed., *Lost Libraries: The Destruction of Great Book Collections since Antiquity* (Basingstoke and New York, 2004), 91–105 (95).

those members of the council who attended court sessions as well as the ordinaries themselves could seldom be trusted to render a considered judgment, for they were often connected as leaders or servitors to factional groupings in the kingdom's politics. Accordingly, they were increasingly relegated to a minor role in the actual workings of the court, even to the extent of becoming only nominal participants in the administration of the law. Details of the precise operation of the kingdom's courts and of the role that its individual participants played are difficult to establish with any precision before the eighteenth century. Nevertheless, by interrogating the existing charters and by reading back from the later period as well as across from what we know of procedures operating elsewhere in Europe, we can arrive at a reliable reconstruction.

First, the court assembled only intermittently, at the opening stage of the proceedings when the record of the case was begun (the *Levata*) and at the conclusion, when the final decision was agreed upon and pronounced. In the intervening time, it might reconvene to consider the arrival of new paperwork or to deliver an interlocutory judgment on the basis of what had been learned. As in the church courts, therefore, sessions of the royal courts in Hungary primarily constituted 'meetings designed to receive the documents' that the court had previously sent for.[26] Sessions of the court were public in the sense that the doors of the court room were left open so that aspiring lawyers might learn the manner of proceeding in law, to which end they also hoped to be paid to perform minor judicial tasks.[27] At this time, advocacy was learned primarily by pupillage and, possibly even, by attendance at the inns, where a part of the kingdom's judicial business evidently took place.[28] We imagine that a single public meeting of the court saw several or more cases being opened and, likewise, a number of final and interlocutory judgments pronounced. Cases were thus 'bundled up', probably according to the county where individual plaintiffs were resident.[29]

Secondly, most of the routine business of the courts was undertaken by scribes and, in particular, by the more experienced clerks known as protonotarics, the origins of whose office may be traced back to the thirteenth century. These were usually not university trained, for graduates tended to seek out employment in the upper branches of the chancellery and in the offices that supported royal government.[30] As in continental Europe today, public administration was deemed a worthier vocation than a career in the court room. The clerks and protonotaries were mainly recruited, therefore, from the common nobility or burgher class and

[26] R.H. Helmholz, 'Judges and Trials in the English Ecclesiastical Courts' in Maureen Mulholland and Brian Pullan, eds., *Judicial Tribunals in England and Europe 1200–1700* (Manchester and New York, 2003), 102–16 (105).

[27] György Bónis, *A jogtudó értelmiség a Mohács előtti Magyarországon* (Budapest, 1971), 305.

[28] Hajnik, *A magyar bírósági szervezet*, 229–30.

[29] ELTE, Egyetemi Könyvtár, MSS, *Litterae et Epistolae Originales*, no. 6, 347–83; *Litterae et Epistolae Originales*, no 33, 271–86 (which is probably part of the same sequence).

[30] For the organization of the kingdom's government in the later fifteenth century, see András Kubinyi, 'A Mátyás-kori államszervezet', in Zsigmond Pál Pach, ed., *Hunyadi Mátyás. Emlékkönyv Mátyás király halálának 500. évfordulójára* (Budapest, 1990), 53–147 (81–97); Kubinyi, *Matthias Rex*, trans. Andrew T. Gane (Budapest, 2008), 47–52.

they learned the law not in the schools but through practical experience—by drafting documents, observing procedures, and performing as arbiters in disputes.[31] Successful protonotaries could, indeed, amass considerable sums both from fees and from the privileged advice that they gave *per fas et nefas* to litigants.[32] Many of the clerks and protonotaries were appointed to office through patronage, thus acting as the *familiares* of officers higher up in the realm's judicial organization. Increasingly, though, they tended towards a professional body, often remaining in office after their patrons had died or been transferred elsewhere in the royal administration.[33]

## PROTONOTARIES AND THE COMPOSITION OF COURTS

By the mid-fourteenth century, the protonotaries had charge of the seals of their respective judges, which entitled them to draft correspondence in the name of their principals.[34] A considerable amount of the paperwork that belonged to the courts was thus composed and sealed by the protonotaries, to the extent that whole cases were eventually transferred to the inns where the protonotaries frequently resided, being administered there *private in hospitio*.[35] It was also to the protonotaries that litigants (or their attorneys) turned in the first place, having them set in train the procedures by which an oral plaint was converted through the chancellery into a legal action.[36] By the middle decades of the fifteenth century, the weight of business undertaken by the protonotaries made it possible to conceive of them as judges in all but name.[37] It is, however, more profitable to consider them as case managers who handled the individual suits that came to court, collected the relevant papers and arrived at a decision that was then put for approval to the assembled lords, prelates and nobles. In this respect, the role of the protonotary was akin to that of a *rapporteur* in other continental jurisdictions, of which it has been written:

> His duty was to sift the documentary evidence, to assess in writing which articles had been proved and which remained doubtful, and finally, in the light of this detailed scrutiny, to estimate what the correct verdict should be. He was then ready to lead the final discussion on the suit which would take place in private [...] At that session, the *rapporteur* took his colleagues through the case article by article, he gave them his

31 Bónis, *A jogtudó értelmiség*, 192, 195–6, 281–6; György Bónis, 'Men Learned in the Law in Medieval Hungary', *East Central Europe/L'Europe du centre-est*, 4, no. 2 (1977), 181–91 (188–9).

32 Bónis, *A jogtudó értelmiség*, 369.

33 Bónis, *A jogtudó értelmiség*, 58, 62, 64, 175–81, 267, 279, 355, 376.

34 Bónis, *A jogtudó értelmiség*, 191.

35 1486: 20 (DRMH 3, 49–50); 1492: 69 (DRMH 4, 33). Cases continued to be heard in the inns or in private homes irrespective of prohibitions. See Hajnik, *A magyar bírósági szervezet*, 228; Bónis, *A jogtudó értelmiség*, 359. See also Iván Bertényi, *Az országbírói intézmény története a xiv. században* (Budapest, 1976), 128.

36 Imre Nagy, Dezső Véghely and Gyula Nagy, eds., *Codex diplomaticus domus senioris de Zichy*, 12 vols. (Budapest, 1871–1931), xi, 496. The royal chapel had previously undertaken this role. See Bónis, *A jogtudó értelmiség*, 32.

37 Bónis, *A jogtudó értelmiség*, 292, 353. See also 1471: 14 (DRMH 3, 25).

> opinion upon the value of the testimony offered by the witnesses, supporting his view with quotations from the various depositions; and he provided them with any further information that was required.[38]

We doubt that this description of the work of a *rapporteur* in the sophisticated sixteenth-century Paris Parlement applies in its entirety to the activity of a protonotary in Hungary's royal courts in the later Middle Ages. Nevertheless, it indicates by analogy why the protonotaries should have been considered at that time *vicegerentes in iudicatu*, *legum tractatores*, *magistri iudicantes*, and in the contemporary vernacular, 'the masters of judging' (*ítélőmesterek*).[39] Their presence in the court room was, indeed, considered so vital that in the event of their absence cases might be prorogued.[40]

The protonotaries only become visible in the extant record from the middle of the fourteenth century, after which their presence in the court is regularly noted in letters of adjudication.[41] Their rise to prominence depended not only, however, upon the need for professional officers who might through their experience and learning administer court proceedings in accordance with the law. The protonotaries also directed proceedings by lending their recommendations and advice, thus reducing the extent to which politics and partisanship affected the judicial process. The court having thus been opened publicly, with the judges, lords, prelates and nobles in attendance, adjourned after the *Levata*, leaving business in the hands of the protonotaries. Upon its reassembly, the protonotaries gave their opinions, to which we imagine the court usually gave its assent, and an interlocutory decision or the final judgment was duly announced. Under these circumstances, it was possible to dispense entirely with the formal convening of a court, reducing procedures and personnel to a minimum. This is certainly what Matthias intended when, in 1458, he reorganized the court of the special presence, assigning its presidency to a protonotary, to be assisted by just six 'prudent noblemen'.[42] The purpose of the reformed court of the special presence was to deal with cases of violence that would otherwise have been heard by the king in council, on which account the court was empowered to issue summonses requiring the parties to present themselves before it within the space of a month.[43]

During the second half of the fifteenth century, court procedures became complicated by the introduction of new phases after the *Contestatio litis*, the point at

[38] J.H. Shennan, *The Parlement of Paris*, 2nd edition (Stroud, 1998), 64–5. Thus also R. Naz, 'Rapporteur' in *Dictionnaire de droit canonique*, 7 vols. (Paris, 1935–65), vii, col 453: 'Son rôle est d'exposer, devant les juges reéunis, les faits de la cause; d'analyser les preuves produites; de présenter les causes incidents qui ont pu surgir et la solution qu'elles ont reçue; de donner enfin son avis sur le fond de procès.'

[39] Bónis, *A jogtudó értelmiség*, 47, 82, 199, 201. See also 1439: 23 (DRMH 2, 83); Ferenc Kovács, *A magyar jogi terminológia kialakulása* (Budapest, 1964), 144–5.

[40] Hence, from 1503: *causa propter arduitatem et absentiam magistrorum prothonotariorum prorogata est* (MNL OL DL, 56340). See Bónis, *A jogtudó értelmiség*, 393.

[41] Hajnik, *A magyar birósági szervezet*, 49.

[42] There is no evidence that these were elected by the diet, as suggested by István Stipta, *A magyar birósági rendszer története*, 2nd edition (Debrecen, 1998), 31.

[43] 1458: 27 (DRMH 3, 5).

which the case was formally joined. In assessing the claims of the parties, the protonotaries had hitherto borne the burden of business, privately weighing up the various proofs and measuring the content of the plaint against what the law was understood to be, and then reporting back to the court with their recommendations. Possibly under South Italian influence, this episode now saw the formal submission of paperwork between the parties (the *parium*), followed by exchanges between their advocates, most notably motions for dismissal (*exceptiones*) and the rebuttal and counter-rebuttal of individual charges in the plaint (*allegationes*).[44] Some of this activity might be performed in writing but a part was plainly supported by oral explanation, delivered in the main before the court by attorneys. It might also be that at this stage in the case the court sought outside advice, for instance from canon lawyers when matters affecting the law of the church were discussed.[45] The new complexity attaching to proceedings after the suit had been joined, served to prolong cases as well as to force the court to reconvene more often in order to give interlocutory judgments either on individual points of law or to launch a further stage of out-of-court procedures. As the court became more demanding both of time and of expertise, so its composition had to be specified more closely as well as the aptitude of its members.

To meet this new circumstance, a reform of court organization was put in train by Matthias in 1464. By this time, two overlapping courts of the royal presence were in existence—the court of the special presence that Matthias had reorganized six years previously, and the court of the personal presence. The second of these had by this time stabilized from an ad hoc body representing the king, under the presidency of a delegated royal officer, to a more formal body that was headed by a permanent judge of the *personalis praesentia*, who was now usually recruited from the staff of the chancellery. Matthias accordingly conjoined the two courts, assigning its presidency to the *personalis* judge, and he attached to the combined court the two protonotaries who had previously officiated separately in the courts of the special and personal presence. The *personalis* court took over the adjudication of major cases of violence that had previously belonged to the court of the special presence, issuing short summonses and holding special sessions for offences of this type.[46] The judge of the new *personalis* court was for the first few decades of its existence headed by a leading churchman, thereafter by a lay officer. Until the appointment of Werbőczy in 1516, none of the *personalis* judges had any practical knowledge of the law, although they could at least read.[47]

As early as the 1440s, attempts had been made to specify who might attend court sessions, but the measures enacted had not endured.[48] Following the establishment of the new *personalis* court, the tradition that members of the council might attend its sessions was replaced by selection. In the first place, it was laid down that the barons and prelates who attended the court should be chosen by

[44] Bónis, *A jogtudó értelmiség*, 269, 288.
[45] Hajnik, *A magyar bírósági szervezet*, 55.
[46] Bónis, *A jogtudó értelmiség*, 262.
[47] Bónis, *A jogtudó értelmiség*, 339–40. The earliest reference to Werbőczy as *personalis* is 11 August 1516. See MNL OL DL, 72171.
[48] 1446: 7 (DRMH 3, 114).

their fellows; to their number were now formally added assessors, drawn from the common nobility. The terms of the assessors' appointment varied, since in some years they were selected by the diet and in others chosen by the king, although generally the electoral principle prevailed. The number of assessors varied from fourteen to sixteen, elected for a term of three years, and they were generously paid for their labours.[49] Although it was laid down that the assessors be *jurisperiti*, knowledgeable in the laws of the kingdom, we should not imagine that this extended to literacy, since the protonotaries were instructed to explain the content of letters of judgment 'in the vernacular to those who do not understand'.[50] Nevertheless, the assessors seem for the most part to have had some practical experience of the law. Most came from the better-off members of the common nobility and were thus used to private litigation, while not a few had held judicial office in the local administration of the realm, either as magistrates or as deputy lords of counties.[51] Only one assessor can be shown to have received a university education.[52]

In the wake of its reorganization, the *personalis* court now began to sit as a fully collegiate court that brought together the ordinaries and protonotaries of the several other courts of the Curia, who joined together with the *personalis* judge in hearing cases.[53] The new forum acquired around this time the name by which it would be known in the following centuries, the Royal Table or *tabula regia iudiciaria* (*Királyi Itélőtábla*). Its designation as a *tabula* rather than a *bancus* or bench is indicative of the way in which the *personalis* court mainly conducted its business, mostly by moving paperwork across the table rather than by attending to oral testimony and arguments. The court might, however, still function in several capacities. Business that belonged to the individual courts of the palatine and high judge was thus put before it for adjudication, although on these occasions the presidency of the court was given, as appropriate, to the palatine or high judge, and their respective protonotaries took charge of presenting the case and sealing the letters of adjudication.[54]

The Royal Table was crowded. Its membership included besides the barons, prelates and assessors, the ordinaries and their deputies, four protonotaries and other notarial staff—more than forty persons in all. Although some members of the court might be absent for individual sessions, one meeting held in 1498 under the presidency of the palatine listed twenty-nine participants by name, to which we should probably add a dozen or more unnamed assessors and others.[55] The

[49] 1498: 2 (DRMH 4, 89); 1500: 10 (DRMH 4, 145); Hajnik, *A magyar bírósági szervezet*, 56.

[50] 1500: 11 (DRMH 4, 145).

[51] Bónis, *A jogtudó értelmiség*, 350; András Kubinyi, 'Die Beisitzer des königlichen Rates aus dem mittleren Adel unter den Jagiellonen', in Kubinyi, *Stände und Ständestaat in spätmittelalterlichen Ungarn* (Herne, 2011), 232–51 (243). Also published in Hungarian in *Mályusz Elemér Emlékkönyv* (Budapest, 1984), 257–68.

[52] Bónis, *A jogtudó értelmiség*, 351.

[53] 1486: 68 (DRMH 3, 66); 1492: 10 (DRMH 4, 9).

[54] The composition of the courts of the palatine, high judge and *personalis* were thus largely identical. See Bónis, *A jogtudó értelmiség*, 345–6.

[55] Bónis, *A jogtudó értelmiség*, 345–6.

apportionment of responsibilities within the court cannot be determined with any precision, although the way in which its members were listed in surviving materials suggests a formal gradation of influence. Plainly though, the preparation of written materials and of the legal argumentation remained with the protonotaries.[56] The tendency remained for these to determine the more straightforward cases either in private in the inns or in abbreviated sessions, wherein only they and a few others actually heard the case and gave judgment.[57]

The Royal Table remained institutionally close to the king's council, thus reflecting the historical origin of the Curia courts. Accordingly, the assessors elected by the diet were entitled to attend meetings of the council, although as parvenus they were expected to take an oath that they would handle the business of the realm discretely, and were only individually required to attend for six months of the year.[58] Moreover, it remained possible for cases to be referred up from the Royal Table to the council, where the king gave a judgment *propria in persona*. On these occasions, the ordinaries, protonotaries and assessors might attend the council (the ordinaries and at least some of the assessors would have been there ex officio anyway), but their right to participate in further discussion was curtailed. If the council overturned the judgment, it remitted the case back to the Royal Table, leaving it to complete the paperwork and see to execution.[59] In broad outline, therefore, the structure of Hungary's higher courts on the eve of Mohács anticipated the form which Curia justice would assume in the early modern period, with the Royal Table adjudicating cases in the first instance and a higher tribunal exercising a largely supervisory jurisdiction.

The royal courts of medieval Hungary did not administer a scholarly law that was driven by texts and treatises. Membership of the courts consisted overwhelmingly of judges, assessors and others who had had no legal training and they were directed by protonotaries whose expertise derived from practical experience. Among these, Werbőczy was an outstanding but, nevertheless, typical representative, not having received a formal education in the law but having learned its content and ways from service in the courts. Although plainly familiar with some civilian texts, his understanding of the law did not depend upon these but was based upon observation of court practice, of the procedures followed in the courts and of the decisions rendered there by judges and protonotaries. In this respect, Werbőczy's assertion that the customs of the kingdom flowed from the repeated judgments of ordinaries was not a learned opinion on the role of *exempla* in the Hungarian legal system. It was instead a statement about how personal experience had shaped both his own knowledge of the law and thus by extension the contents of the *Tripartitum*.

* * *

Around the middle years of the fourteenth century, the compiler of a formulary book, who had received his education abroad, lamented how in Hungary it was the fashion that 'lay judges are not taught how to render judgments by doctors, but

[56] Bónis, *A jogtudó értelmiség*, 345–6. [57] Bónis, *A jogtudó értelmiség*, 353, 359, 389.
[58] 1500: 10 (DRMH 4, 143). [59] 1500: 7 (DRMH 4, 143).

learn from one another, and they work out how they should judge from what they hear, the younger from the older, and one to another.'[60] In this brief observation, many of the characteristics of Hungarian judicial practice are laid bare. The customary law, to which the judges deferred, was not in origin the learned law, as taught in the universities, even though its vocabulary and procedures comported with the larger Romano-canonical tradition. It was instead the law that had been historically observed, or was thought to have been observed, and it was communicated by the practice of the courts. The written law, in the form of legal instruments and statutes, might alter its content, but only to the degree that these were actually followed. By this measure, Hungarian customary law was, if not made by judges, then at least made by the protonotaries, who over generations passed on among themselves their special knowledge and techniques.

Nevertheless, it is not possible to conceive of customary law as developing only among a small group of practitioners, whose routines and presumptions were self-reinforcing. The protonotaries may well have directed the proceedings of the courts, but these courts were crowded. Traditions of collective justice prevailed, to such an extent that attempts to administer justice without the requisite number of adjudicators being present and behind closed doors met with immediate protests.[61] In letter after letter, therefore, the judgment delivered in the king's name spelled out that not only was it in accordance with ancient custom, however ill defined, but that it had also been reached 'together with the prelates, barons and noblemen of this our kingdom'.[62] The urgency with which the diet pressed that elected assessors be allowed to attend court sessions, and the vigour with which the realm's principal office holders resisted this demand or proposed that their own representatives join with the assessors, suggests that such statements were not entirely rhetorical. Plainly, the composition of the court was thought to influence the outcome of the proceedings, notwithstanding the direction given to it by the protonotaries.[63]

The protonotaries were, however, knowledgeable not only of the law that was administered in the Curia courts but also of procedures and practices observed more generally within the kingdom. In this way, they provided a link between the Curia and the agencies of justice in the countryside, which retained even at the level of the fortnightly assizes a strongly communal element. Typical biographies suggest that apprenticeship as a notary in the chancellery was often followed by service in a place of authentication, or as a magistrate in one of the counties, or as an attorney, after which a successful lawyer might return to the Curia as a protonotary or deputy to one of the ordinaries. Even a career spent entirely in the royal service might be interrupted by the requirement to supervise out-of-court proceedings in the countryside, to preside over the assembly of a county when criminal cases were discussed, or to adjudicate a particularly tricky dispute.[64] On top of this, protonotaries regularly supplemented their income by

[60] Kovachich, *Formulae Solennes Styli* (Buda, 1799), 29.
[61] Bónis, KJE, 192. [62] Hajnik, *A magyar birósági szervezet*, 152.
[63] Kubinyi, 'Die Beisitzer des königlichen Rates', 237–50; Hajnik, *A magyar birósági szervezet*, 55.
[64] Bónis, *A jogtudó értelmiség*, 249–51, 256, 265–75, 282–6, 384–8.

taking on private legal work, for which they received gifts of land from grateful patrons. In this respect, Werbőczy was not alone in acquiring a considerable body of property.[65]

Nor were the courts of the Curia institutionally remote from the passage of litigation in the countryside. Even after the return of the palatine's itinerant court to the Curia in the mid-fourteenth century, either the palatine or another judge (often the lord of the county) appointed on his behalf continued to preside over the periodic assemblies of the counties. They passed judgment there in concert with the local magistrates and a self-informing jury of noblemen, who communicated their understanding of the law and of its appropriate application. Cases might also be opened at the assembly and transferred thence to the Curia.[66] The county assemblies were populous, if only for the reason that noblemen attended in order to make sure that no action was launched against them in their absence. Having determined that none were, they usually returned home after a few days, appointing proxies to see to their interests.[67] The more routine business of the county was overseen by the *sedria* (*sedes iudiciaria*), headed by the deputy lord (*alispán*) and attended by other magistrates and noblemen. The sedria met frequently, often weekly or fortnightly. Cases opened in the sedria might be transferred to the Curia for adjudication.[68] There was also a regular flow of mandates from the Curia to the sedria, mostly instructing the holding of inquests.[69] Particularly egregious acts of violence were often investigated through an ad hoc assembly of local landowners and others, the so-called *congregatio proclamata*. During the fourteenth century, assemblies of this type were usually held under the presidency of the palatine; thereafter, by the lord and officers of the county, acting on a royal mandate. Once the evidence had been gathered, often in considerable detail, with individual statements included, it was relayed back to the Curia and the relevant summonses issued. Although ostensibly abolished in 1486 on account of the tumults to which they gave rise, these ad hoc gatherings continued to be called, only petering out at the beginning of the sixteenth century.[70] We should imagine that there were besides these judicial assemblies gatherings of the county for the purpose of electing magistrates and delegates to the diet, welcoming a newly appointed lord of the county, reading out new statutes and

65 György Bónis, 'Egy Jagelló-kori magyar jogász', in Emil Schultheisz, ed., *A szegedi tudományegyetem állam- és jogtudományi karának évkönyve* (Budapest, 1953), 5–24 (15–18); Tibor Neumann, 'Werbőczy István származása és pályakezdése', in Gábor Máthé, ed., *A magyar jog fejlődésének fél évezrede. Werbőczy és a Hármaskönyv 500 esztendő múltán* (Budapest, 2014), 31–57 (49–52).

66 Géza Istványi 'A generalis congregatio', *Levéltári Közlemények*, 17 (1939), 50–83, and *Levéltári Közlemények*, 18–19 (1940–1), 179–207 (61, 69, 182–3).

67 József Holub, *Zala megye története a középkorban* (Pécs, 1929), 175–6.

68 Holub, *Zala megye*, 269–73; Ferenc Piti, Tibor Neumann and Norbert C. Tóth, eds., *Szatmár megye hatóságának oklevelei (1284–1524)* (Nyiregyháza, 2010), nos. 309, 357, 366, 368.

69 Piti, Neumann and Tóth, *Szatmár megye*, nos. 391, 395, 400, 403, 404, 408, 411, 412 etc.; Norbert C. Tóth, ed., *Szabolcs megye működése a Zsigmond-korban* (Nyiregyháza, 2008), 93–8.

70 Istványi, 'A generalis congregatio', 190; István Tringli, 'Megyék a középkori Magyarországon', in Tibor Neumann and György Racz, eds., *Honoris causa. Tanulmányok Engel Pál tiszteletére* (Budapest and Piliscsaba, 2009), 487–518 (507); Viktor Vadász, 'A tanúbizonyítás rendszere a középkori magyar büntetőeljárásban', *Iustum Aequum Salutare*, 7, no. 3 (2011), 143–57 (152).

commencing certain types of legal action. Evidence for these is, however, scanty before the sixteenth century.[71]

As these examples suggest, there were not two separate judicial organizations in medieval Hungary—on the one hand the institutions of royal justice in the palace and, on the other, the county courts that gave justice in the countryside. The two spheres overlapped, with officers from the centre administering local activities and with cases passing to and fro between the counties and the judicial hub of the realm. Certainly, procedures followed in the counties were often crude. Meetings of the magistracy might thus take place in an intimidatory atmosphere of violence and of strong words. Until the end of the fifteenth century, the courts of the county paid little regard to the written word, their determinations being at best recorded in 'slipshod texts, with muddled phrases, in a criminally barbaric Latin and an indecipherable hand'.[72] Nonetheless, the flow of business together with the frequent appearance of royal officers at judicial events in the localities served to bind judicial practices followed in the countryside to those observed in the principal royal courts, thus contributing to the consistency of the kingdom's legal arrangements. In this respect, Hungary's local jurisdictions were no more 'little commonwealths' than their English counterparts.[73] By the same token, moreover, a channel was opened whereby the legal presumptions of Hungarian noble society more generally might be brought to bear on decisions of the courts, thus impeding the judicialization of the customary law and its reduction to 'the common learning in our books'.[74]

Communal apprehensions of the law, conveyed through the lay membership of the courts, were thus amplified. Academic lawyers might well distinguish between the *stylus* of the court, being the manner of its proceeding—its *ordinatio loquendi, scribendi et procedendi*—and its *decisiones* or judgments, which rested on the customary law.[75] In practice, however, the procedures of the courts shaped the judgments given, with the consequence that Hungarian customary law did not separate from popular observance and become entirely a matter of court practice. The legal knowledge that belonged to the professional law men and protonotaries was adjusted, augmented and even superseded as a consequence of the composition of the courts and of their procedural inter-action with noble society. On account of this, the administration of justice in Hungary never acquired the character of a Common Law system, in the sense of resting on 'a body of ideas received by a caste of lawyers, these ideas being used by them as providing guidance in what is

[71] Tóth, *Szabolcs megye működése*, 138.

[72] Gyula Gábor, *A megyei intézmény alakulása és működése Nagy Lajos alatt* (Budapest, 1908), 103, 111. See also Antal Főglein, 'A vármegyei jegyzőkönyv', *Levéltári Közlemények*, 16 (1938), 142–67 (143).

[73] See thus R.H. Helmholz, 'Independence and uniformity in England's manorial courts', in Lloyd Bonfield, ed., *Seigneurial Jurisdiction* (Berlin, 2000), 213–36 (213), citing the seventeenth-century cartographer, John Norden.

[74] J.H. Baker, *The Law's Two Bodies: Some Evidential Problems in English Legal History* (Oxford, 2001), 81–2, citing Coke and Walmsley.

[75] Roy Garré, *Consuetudo. Das Gewohnheitsrecht in der Rechtsquellen- und Methodenlehre des späten ius commune in Italien (16.–18. Jahrhundert)* (Frankfurt a/M, 2005), 256.

conceived to be a rational determination of disputes litigated before them'.[76] Instead, it retained a hybrid form, its content emerging from the interplay of judicial reasoning and a more general understanding of the law. In this respect, the composition of the kingdom's courts contributed to the ambiguity of the Hungarian customary law, with its roots in both lawyerly practice and lay conviction.

[76] A.W.B. Simpson, 'The Common Law and Legal Theory', in Simpson, *Legal Theory and Legal History: Essays on the Common Law* (London and Ronceverte, 1987), 359–82 (376).

# 5

# King and Nobility

## CLASSIFICATION AND LEGAL POSITIVISM

From the nineteenth century onwards, Hungarian legal history has been dominated by two overlapping approaches.[1] The first of these has been the pandectist, which has sought to press the content of the law into a modern civilian classification, breaking its aspects down into increasingly narrow divisions and sub-divisions. The consequence has been 'to smash to pieces the history of [...] law for the sake of a consistent modern legal doctrine'.[2] It is, nevertheless, a methodology that survives, sometimes with the explanation that this is how law students should have their textbooks arranged.[3] The second has been the legal positivist school, which considers the historic content of the kingdom's law to be both organized and fixed, comprising a body of substantive principles that may be known from a close reading of the sources. Hungarian legal positivism obtained cogency through the work of the Hungarian school of historical law, which sought to establish structures and continuities in the law, ascribing these to the unfolding over time of the national spirit. Nevertheless, while students of legal positivism managed to relate a part of the kingdom's medieval law, as for instance in regard to the early law of contract, none managed a comprehensive account. The most that was achieved was a description of the legal procedures of the kingdom's courts, not the substance of the law by which they judged.[4] As one of the shrewdest exponents of the historical law school observed, criticizing the axiomatic approach of his colleagues, the facts of history were too contingent to permit the sort of fixity to which they aspired.[5] In confirmation of this, more recent accounts have shown how the courts were inconsistent in explaining their judgments by reference to custom of the realm. Tendentious decisions might thus be justified as being in accordance with customary law, while well-established principles of adjudication were never so explicitly grounded.[6]

[1] For these developments, see generally Barna Mezey, ed., *Magyar jogtörténet*, 2nd edition (Budapest, 1999), 47–8, 55–7.

[2] Karl von Amira in 1875, quoted in Reinhard Zimmermann, *Roman Law, Contemporary Law, European Law: The Civilian Tradition Today* (Oxford, 2001), 39.

[3] Jozef Beňa and Tomáš Gábriš, *History of Law in Slovakia I. (Until 1918)* (Bratislava, 2008), 10.

[4] Imre Hajnik, *A magyar bírósági szervezet és perjog az Árpád- és a vegyes-házi királyok alatt* (Budapest, 1899); János Vinkler, *A magyar igaszágszolgáltatási szervezet és polgári peres eljárás a mohácsi vésztől 1848-ig*, 2 vols. (Pécs, 1921–7).

[5] Ferenc Eckhart, 'Jog- és alkotmánytörténet', in Bálint Hóman, ed., *A magyar történetirás új útjai* (Budapest, 1932), 269–320 (271).

[6] Bónis, KJE, 193–209; István Tringli, 'A magyar szokásjog a malomépitésről', in Tibor Neumann, ed., *Analecta Mediaevalia 1* (Budapest, 2001), 251–68 (260).

These upsets are not unexpected. Customary law is unlike modern law and its application in concrete instances will often be uncertain. The decisions of courts that adjudicated by customary law were moulded by circumstance and shaped by an apprehension of what the law should be and, in particular, that it comported with truth and justice. There might be some recollection of past judgments, but they were not considered binding, for each case embodied a different truth to which the courts inclined to defer.[7] In a phrase that went back to the age of the Fathers, and received new currency from Ivo of Chartres, Gratian, Gregory VII and Urban II, 'Our Lord Christ has called himself truth, not custom.'[8] The interest of the courts in seeking remedies rather than in adjudicating according to the law's content additionally hindered the establishment of a body of substantive propositions, which might otherwise have served to straitjacket the law.

Medieval theorists were familiar with this aspect of customary law. First, they regarded the customary law after the manner of a 'work in progress', which arose in gradual fashion from popular practices that were by their very nature inconstant. Attempts to impose consistency upon customary law by such recourses as writing it down or attending to previous judgments were thus contrary to its nature.[9] The idea of the law as emerging out of a popular but fluctuating conviction subsequently fed into the work of Savigny and of the historical law school, underpinning the belief that the law's codification was both impossible and undesirable. Secondly, commentators considered that customary law should be reasonable or *rationabilis* in its application. Since what was reasonable intersected with divine law and natural law, established principles might be set aside in the interest of higher commands.[10] Uncertainty and unpredictability are not, of course, unique to customary law, but are inherent within all legal systems. They are, however, more embedded in customary law, even to the extent (as Savigny saw) of reducing its substantive content to a common conduct and belief that alters over time.[11]

Notwithstanding these objections, historians of Hungarian customary law have generally sought to establish fixed principles. Their working method has been to proceed from royal legislation and the text of the *Tripartitum*, treating these as reliable indications of the law, to be fleshed out by the information given in charters.[12] Where this evidence is equivocal, the *Tripartitum* is often invoked as proof of the correct legal solution. The understanding of Hungarian legal positivism towards the kingdom's law and the contents of the *Tripartitum* is amply summed up in the otherwise incomprehensible formulation of one of its principal exponents: 'Before

[7] See thus Alice Rio, 'Introduction', in Rio, ed., *Law, Custom and Justice in Late Antiquity and the Middle Ages* (London, 2011), 1–22 (9).

[8] Gerhart Ladner, *The Idea of Reform: Its Impact on Christian Thought and Action in the Age of the Fathers* (Cambridge, MA, 1959), 138–9.

[9] Roy Garré, *Consuetudo. Das Gewohnheitsrecht in der Rechtsquellen- und Methodenlehre des späten ius commune in Italien* (*16.–18. Jahrhundert*) (Frankfurt a/M, 2005), 224–5.

[10] Garré, *Consuetudo. Das Gewohnheitsrecht*, 170–1.

[11] Friedrich Carl von Savigny, *Vom Beruf unserer Zeit für Gesetzgebung und Rechtswissenschaft* (Heidelberg, 1814), 14.

[12] The limitations of this technique are noted by Eckhart, 'Jog- és alkotmánytörténet', 286.

Werbőczy, we know only Werbőczy; and after Werbőczy we largely only see Werbőczy.'[13] However ingeniously stated, this approach is flawed. First, Werbőczy's *Tripartitum* provides only a partial snapshot of the law, as Werbőczy understood it to be at the time that he was writing. Certainly, a part of what he wrote broadly conformed to what the courts and legislation described as *consuetudo regni.*[14] Other parts were in marked contrast, for the customary law was never stable. In view of this instability, it is also not helpful to consider legal terms as possessing a single historic meaning, for their substantive content was also fluid.[15] Secondly, Werbőczy imposed his own scheme on the customary law, describing it as he thought it should be rather than as it was. In particular, he over-emphasized the claims of the kindred over property, overlooking arrangements that served to diminish the structure of rights adhering to *aviticitas*. Likewise, his description of the kingdom's public law and of the rights of the nobility in respect of the ruler was partly propagandistic, with little basis in the historic record. On other occasions, Werbőczy imposed symmetries that did not exist in order to lend the law greater coherence, or *faute de mieux* copied arrangements described in the *Summa Legum*. Some of what Werbőczy wrote was subsequently picked up by the courts and entered into common practice, but other aspects were ignored, being recognized as fanciful.

Werbőczy's *Tripartitum* cannot thus be made the unqualified starting-point for an investigation into the content of Hungarian customary law. Like any other legal text of its time, it may not be interrogated in such a way as to disclose a set of enduring rules. Instead, his work should be considered as a statement of what Werbőczy thought the law to be at the moment of the *Tripartitum*'s composition, as an expression of what he believed the law should be, and as an exercise that both built on customary practices and was in turn customized and adapted through use. By critically reviewing his text and measuring it against practice and court judgments, we will in the following four chapters expose the dissonant propositions and presumptions that stood in the way of the customary law's substantiation as an integrated body of stable propositions.

## ORIGIN AND MEANING OF NOBILITY

The relationship of monarch and nobility is the subject of the earliest chapters of the *Tripartitum*'s main text. In describing the historic origins of the Hungarian nation, Werbőczy starts by establishing the mutual bond that drew together the ruler and the nobility. His account rests upon a version of the *lex regia*, by which the

[13] József Illés, *A magyar házassági vagyonjog az Árpádok korában* (Budapest, 1900), 4; repeated verbatim in Illés, *Bevezetés a magyar jog történetébe. A források története* (Budapest, 1910), 17. Restated approvingly in György Bónis, 'Törveny és szokás a Hármaskönyvben', *Acta Juridico-Politica*, 2 (1942), offprint, 3.

[14] László Blazovich, 'A Tripartitum és forrásai', *Századok*, 141 (2007), 1011–23 (1017–21).

[15] The point is well made by Péter Banyó, 'Válasz Homoki-Nagy Mária birálatára', *Aetas*, (2001, nos. 2–4), 308–10 (308).

people gave their power to the ruler. In consequence of this transfer, the monarch was vested with the right to create noblemen, mostly by assigning to them the landed property that was the mark of their status. It is possible to read into his description an explanation for the prevailing system of landed relations, whereby all noblemen were deemed to hold property by virtue of an original act of royal donation. Plainly though, the link between the two parties was more intimate than a history of property conveyance. On the one hand, it drew the parties into 'a mutual bond' so close 'that neither can be separated nor removed from the other and neither can exist without the other', on account of which all nobles might be deemed metaphorically to partake in the king's symbolic majesty as members of the Holy Crown.[16] On the other, it permitted the nobleman unlimited access to the king's justice, and thus 'to be subject to the power of none other than the lawfully crowned prince'.[17]

Werbőczy's account of the *lex regia* is historically misconceived, culled from the most popular chronicle of his day.[18] Nevertheless, in his description of the intimacy of the bond between king and noblemen he accurately summarized the way in which their relationship was understood. The Hungarian nobleman stood in an immediate and personal relationship to the ruler. The land he held was, at least ostensibly, the king's reward for the service and loyalty that his forbears had shown the monarch, the continued possession of which was intended to spur him to further acts of valorous endeavour on the royal behalf. The king, for his part, was expected to nurture the nobleman, to welcome him to his court, and as a paterfamilias to care for his children in the event of his untimely death. Kings took these responsibilities seriously, not least by their apparent attentiveness to suits involving orphans and by their endless sojourns around the kingdom.[19] The practice of the courts that we described in the last chapter reflects the closeness of these relations. The nobleman was thus entitled to plead before the royal presence and so to receive justice from the king's fictive person. Likewise, all noblemen were entitled, at least in theory, to join together in the king's company to administer the law and give counsel. All this is true enough and we will expose in the section that follows the historic roots of Werbőczy's formulation. From it, however, Werbőczy deduced two propositions that had little basis in Hungarian customary law, but which subsequently became two of its most contentious aspects—the elective nature of Hungarian kingship and the nobility's right to resist the monarch.

* * *

[16] Trip., I. 3 [6]; I. 4 [1] (DRMH 5, 51–3). The literature on the Holy Crown is vast, but is conveniently summarized in László Péter, 'The Holy Crown of Hungary, Visible and Invisible', SEER, 81, no. 3 (2003), 421–510. See also, Kees Teszelszky, *Az ismeretlen korona. Jelentések, szimbólumok és nemzeti identitás* (Pannonhalma, 2009), 18–59.

[17] Trip., I. 9 [4] (DRMH 5, 57).

[18] Johannes de Thurocz, *Chronica Hungarorum. Textus*, eds. Erzsébet Galántai and Gyula Kristó (Budapest, 1985), 33–4 (ch. 12).

[19] The extraordinary extent of the royal ambit of the realm is shown in Pál Engel and Norbert C. Tóth, *Itineraria Regum et Reginarum (1382–1438)* (Budapest, 2005), 55–131. For orphans, see Hajnik, *A magyar bírósági szervezet*, 55.

The intimacy of the connection between ruler and nobleman had its origins in the thirteenth and fourteenth centuries and in the creation of the noble estate. Originally, the title of noble was mainly honorific, applied with little discrimination to various types of freemen and warriors, being thus broadly analogous to such terms as *honestus*, *verus* and *altior*.[20] Within the hierarchy of the better-off in Árpád Hungary, the primary distinction lay in regard to membership of the royal retinue. Members of the retinue, whether attending the king in person or representing his rule in the countryside, were known as lords or *comites*, in Hungarian *ispánok* (sing. *ispán*), although they might also be called *magnates*, *principes*, *optimates* and so on.[21] During the late twelfth and early thirteenth century, members of the class of *comites* began to consolidate their territorial power, partly to compensate for a decline in the royal largesse that had hitherto sustained their own munificence and wealth. Hungary's kings hastened this process by giving away chunks of the royal estate to the *comites*. Although associated with the 'new institutions' of Andrew II and his attempt to shift the royal resources from a domain-based economy to one resting on monetary foundations, it is plain that the alienation of royal lands had been proceeding apace over several or more decades.[22]

The consequences of alienation were most immediately felt by the warriors (*iobagiones castri*) attached to the realm's network of earthen forts.[23] These warriors constituted the *proceres castri*, superior to the rank-and-file who made up the bulk of the army, and they were sustained by the large parcels of land that they held of the king.[24] There were generally between forty and sixty of these warriors in each county, but their number varied considerably.[25] Although the warriors had the right to plead before the king or palatine in certain matters, they were subject to the jurisdiction of the lord of the county and thus obliged to follow him in war and perform other duties at his behest.[26] Nevertheless, their historic connection to the ruler and their status as hereditary officers were made plain in the titles that they often adopted, *iobagiones* (retainers) 'of the holy king', *iobagiones naturales* and *filii iobagionum*.[27] We should at this point note that the title of *iobagio*, although later denoting a peasant (*jobbágy*) and roughly

[20] János Varga, *A királyi serviens* (Budapest, 2006), 21–3 (published as a supplement to *Levéltári Közlemények*); Attila Zsoldos, *A szent király szabadjai. Fejezetek a várjobbágyság történetéből* (Budapest, 1999), 33.

[21] The literature on the origins of the Hungarian nobility, with a review of the terminology commonly used in the sources, is discussed by Zsolt Hunyadi, '*Maiores*, *Optimates*, *Nobiles*. Semantischen Fragen zur Frühgeschichte des ungarischen Adels', *East Central Europe/L'Europe du Centre-Est*, 29, nos. 1–2 (2002), 134–43 (137).

[22] Gyula Kristó, *Histoire de la Hongrie Médiévale. Tome 1. Le temps des Árpáds* (Rennes, 2000), 129–30. The alienation of warrior property is evident from as early as the reigns of St Ladislas and Coloman. See György Györffy, ed., *Diplomata Hungariae antiquissima* (Budapest, 1992), 268, 276–7.

[23] Described with aerial photographs, József Dénes, 'Várak és erődítmények a középkori Magyarországon', *Rubicon* (2011, no. 1), 36–41.

[24] Zsoldos, *A szent király szabadjai*, 33, 48–9, 65, 93.

[25] Zsoldos, *A szent király szabadjai*, 103, 108–10.

[26] Zsoldos, *A szent király szabadjai*, 15.

[27] Zsoldos, *A szent király szabadjai*, 32.

translatable as servant, was in origin a term of honour that also attached to the king's high dignitaries.[28]

In order to preserve their status, warriors sought to confirm both their lands and their persons as directly subordinate to the ruler. By this route they might be lifted out of the 'burden', 'service and obligation' of the castle, freed of its 'blemish' and 'stain', and able to enter into a new relationship with the ruler.[29] By the first decades of the thirteenth century, such recipients of the royal grace were known as *servientes regis*, to which the designation of *nobilis* may even at this early stage have been attached.[30] The title of *serviens regis* was plainly a meritorious one, implying a connection to the ruler that was sufficiently intense to permit permanent membership of the royal household, *familia* and *aula*. Newly created *servientes* might be expected to continue to perform military duties, but from now on as part of the king's own retinue, in token of which they received other rewards.[31] In an early example of the benefits and duties that derived from royal service, a certain Johannes Latinus of Transylvania was on account of his many services to the king granted the privilege in 1204 that, 'he and his heirs shall have complete right to keep company in the royal palace, and in respect of the goods and properties, homes and otherwise that he has acquired or will acquire, he shall not pay anyone any impost or tax, nor shall he and his heirs be obliged to contribute anything, except in respect of military matters, in which they are expected to serve us and the kingdom according to the liberty granted them.'[32] Some twenty years later, a prominent warrior and his family from Turopolje in Slavonia were 'released from their obligations to the castle of Zagreb, sundered from the chains of lower office [...] and introduced in glory through the gift of liberty to membership of the royal home, to enjoy the virtuous company of the servants of the king (*servientium regis*)'.[33] Unsurprisingly, others pressed for a similar status, adopting in token of their aspiration the title of royal *servientes*, even though the king had not formally extended this right to them. During the second and third decades of the thirteenth century, so-called royal *servientes* appear throughout the kingdom, too numerous for each to have been the recipient of the king's special pleasure.[34] The Golden Bull of 1222 is an early indication of their political weight and sense of collective identity, but also of the royal interest in promoting their rights and

[28] The word is of Turkic origin and conceals the title of *beg* or chieftain, rendered as bäg or bäglär on the Orkhon inscription. See *Encyclopaedia of Islam* (London and Leiden, 1960), i, 1159. The first reference to a high officer of the king holding the title of *iobagio* is from 1172. See László Erdélyi and Pongrácz Sörös, eds., *A Pannonhalmi Szent-Benedek-Rend története*, 12 vols. (Budapest, 1902–16), i, 604.

[29] Zsoldos, *A szent király szabadjai*, 12, 13.

[30] Varga, *A királyi serviens*, 25–6. Not one of the early references on which Varga relies is, however, without its difficulties. The association of *serviens* with *nobilis* is almost certainly a mid-thirteenth-century development.

[31] Attila Zsoldos, 'II. András Aranybullája', *Történelmi Szemle*, 53 (2011), 1–38 (13).

[32] AUO, i, 91–2.

[33] Joannes Kukuljević, ed., *Jura Regni Croatiae, Dalmatiae et Slavoniae*, 2 vols. (Zagreb, 1861–2), i, 51.

[34] Zsoldos, 'II. András Aranybullája', 12.

fostering their allegiance.[35] By the middle years of the thirteenth century, the *servientes* had generally assumed the title of *nobiles*, which became the conventional term of description.

The transition from warriors of the castle to nobles was a lengthy process, extending over almost two centuries. In the process, some *iobagiones castri* failed to make the leap, either being pulled into a servile relationship with a local landowner or, as was widespread in Slavonia, never managing to escape the service of the lord of the county. Status disputes involving the claims of still remaining castle warriors to the dignity of noblemen would indeed continue to pass before the courts until the end of the fourteenth century.[36] By the same token, others of humbler origin, as for instance a valiant fisherman or stonemason, some servants of churchmen and labourers previously tied to royal castles, were able to effect the transition, sometimes by deception.[37] Nevertheless, irrespective of their routes to preferment, the marks of new noblemen were the same. They held the title of *serviens* and, later, of nobleman by the king's grace and might pass it onto their descendants; they fought in the royal army under the king's standard, shared in the privileges of rank as part of the *collegium*, *societas* and *coetus* of the kingdom's nobility; and they were possessed of their own property, held directly of the king. In most cases, these properties were the same packages of land that they had previously occupied as warriors of the castle, but if insufficient they were permitted to petition the ruler for additional villages. It was in the ruler's interest to ensure that his *servientes* were possessed of sufficient land to discharge a military function as mounted warriors, which in the context of the thirteenth century meant an estate of three to six *aratra* (roughly two or three square kilometres).[38]

To begin with, the nobleman's connection to the ruler was signified by his descent from an ancestor who had first acquired from the king the status of a royal *serviens* and nobleman. Members of the emerging noble class thus tended to style themselves in the form *de genere*, followed by the name of the founder of their line, after the manner of the established *comites* class.[39] In this respect, the contemporary Hungarian name for noble and nobleman, *nemes*, being roughly the equivalent of the German *Geschlecht* (lineage), reflects the importance of descent as a mark of privileged status.[40] Over the course of the later thirteenth and fourteenth centuries, however, the sign of nobility shifted from descent to land possession. Noblemen tended now to call themselves after a toponym, chosen by reference to their family's premier property. Likewise, they no longer called their relatives *fratres generationales* but instead *condivisionales*, the kinsmen with whom they shared legal entitlement to the family's landed assets. Increasingly too, nobles were defined as *possessionati* and, by the same token, those without land categorized as *ignobiles* and

[35] DRMH $1^2$, 32–5.

[36] ZsO, i, nos. 985, 2413; *Történelmi Tár* (1902), 209, 227. See also László Bártfai Szabó, *A körösszegi és adorjáni gróf Csáky család története*, i (no more published) (Budapest, 1919), 10–11.

[37] Varga, *A királyi serviens*, 66–7, 77; *Történelmi Tár* (1902), 201, 217.

[38] *Történelmi Tár* (1902), 199, 207, 211, 213, 217, 218.

[39] Hunyadi, '*Maiores, Optimates, Nobiles*', 137.

[40] *Magyar nyelv történeti-etimológiai szótára*, 4 vols. (Budapest, 1967–84), ii, 1011.

*rustici*, even though there long remained an intermediate category of non-nobles who were in fact *possessionati*.[41] By the early fourteenth century (if not before), the possession of property given (at least in name) by the king had become the sign of status and the *manifestum indicium* of noble rank.[42] Its significance and origin in an act of royal donation are epitomized in a later ditty:

> When by way of reward, the king, our lord,
> Gives to anyone, for services done,
> A village or just a small plot,
> Then he becomes noble, on the spot![43]

Landownership was, however, only a sign of noble rank and did not constitute its substance, which derived instead from the intimacy of the bond between man and king. As Werbőczy made clear, in a passage often overlooked by historians who would make nobility a product of land holding,

> It should be known, furthermore, that one can become or be created a true noble in another way, without the donation of property rights: namely, when our prince separates and frees common people from servility and ignobility, placing and assigning them in the society, rank and number of the true nobles of the realm. Such men are regarded as true nobles even without the grant of an estate, and these nobles, howsoever created, and all their heirs who descend legitimately in the male line must always be regarded as true nobles, even if they do not possess a noble coat of arms or letters describing the coat of arms and its grant.[44]

By including coats of arms, Werbőczy complicates his account, for most nobles had unilaterally adopted their own devices, not holding these by letter or grant.[45] Nevertheless, his observation that true nobility was acquired by the ruler's promotion of men into the *coetum, collegium numerumque* of the realm's nobility indicates the degree to which the original idea and language of ennoblement still carried meaning in the sixteenth century.

To some extent, the association of land with noble status 'objectified' the relationship between king and nobleman, subverting the immediacy of their connection and rendering the original idea of the personal bond that arose from membership

[41] György Bónis, *Hűbériség és rendiség a középkori magyar jogban*, 2nd edition (Budapest, 2003), 319–21.

[42] Bónis, *Hűbériség és rendiség*, 319; thus, from 1283, *nobiles in Hungaria existentes tenere seu possedere possessiones suas proprias consueverunt.* See Marija Karbić, 'Dioba posjeda i plemićki rod: primjeri iz Slavonije', *Scrinia Slavonica*, 10 (2010), 70–86 (70).

[43] Ferenc Szentpáli Nagy, *Verbötzi István törvény könyvének compendiuma* (Cluj, 1798), 2 (first published in 1701). In fact, we know of a case from the 1370s when the beneficiaries of an earlier royal grant were denied noble status. See *Magyar Történelmi Tár* (1861), 123.

[44] Trip., I. 6 (DRMH 5, 53). Cf. László Péter, 'In the *Tripartitum*, it is not the nobility as a whole who are called members of the Holy Crown but only those who benefited from royal donation of land, a minority within the nobility.' Given in Péter, 'The Holy Crown of Hungary, Visible and Invisible', SEER, 81, no. 3 (2003), 421–510 (451), citing further literature. See also László Péter, *The Antecedents of the 19th Century Hungarian State Concept: An Historical Analysis. The Background and Creation of the Doctrine of the Holy Crown*, unpublished D.Phil thesis (Oxford, 1965), 14.

[45] Iván Bertényi, 'Középkori cimerjogunk néhány kérdése', in Bertényi, *A cimertan reneszánsza. Tanulmányok* (Budapest, 2010), 163–78 (173), first published in *Levéltari Szemle*, 36, no. 2 (1986), 21–36.

of the royal retinue into a more formal one that derived from the structure of land tenure.[46] Nevertheless, the intimacy of the relationship of nobleman to king persisted not just as a fiction but also as one of the underlying suppositions of Hungarian noble society. First, even though the Hungarian nobleman increasingly understood his rank to derive from the land he held, his obligations to the ruler arose from the personal bond to the ruler that possession of this land signified. As elsewhere in Europe, they derived from *amor* rather than being more meanly based on a material transaction.[47] Holders of estate, therefore, on which conditions were laid in respect of the service that they owed the ruler—as, for instance, the lancers of Spiš and various other clusters of warriors who possessed land conditionally in return for specified services—were never considered full nobles, nor the so-called *praediales* who held land of other (mainly ecclesiastical) landowners.[48] Secondly, since the mark of noble status and the royal relationship that stood behind it, were identical in respect of every nobleman, it was possible to conceive of all noblemen as being possessed of the same rights or, in the language made famous by Werbőczy, as enjoying *una eademque libertas*. As Werbőczy explains, 'all [...] barons, and other magnates, nobles and notables (*proceres*) of this kingdom of Hungary enjoy [...] by reason of their nobility and temporal goods one and the same prerogative of liberty, exemption and immunity; nor has any lord more or any nobleman less liberty. For this reason they live under one and the same law and custom, and follow one and the same legal procedure in court, and they differ from one another only in the amount of their man price (*homagium*).'[49]

As the last line of Werbőczy's account suggests, there had by the last years of the fifteenth century arisen a distinction within the nobility, between the common nobility and a hereditary aristocracy, made up of the *barones naturales*—so called to distinguish them from those barons who held their title by virtue of the high royal office that they discharged.[50] These 'barons by birth' were permitted several marks of special status, not just the higher price that they paid for their lives but also the privilege of using a red wax seal and the title of *magnificus*. They also enjoyed hereditary rights to attend the royal council when it convened on the occasion of the diet and to field military units, under their own flags.[51] Since the emergence of this new class threatened his assumption of an equality of noble rights, Werbőczy

[46] As argued in Péter Váczy, *A szimbolikus államszemlélet kora Magyarországon*, 2nd edition (Máriabesnyő–Gödöllő, 2004), 52–3.

[47] Hence Guillelmus de Cuneo, *Super Codice* (1513), for whom the grant of a fief arose *propter amorem magis quam propter lucrum*. See Magnus Ryan, 'Succession to Fiefs: A Ius Commune feudorum?', in John W. Cairns and Paul J. du Plessis, eds., *The Creation of the Ius Commune: From Casus to Regula* (Edinburgh, 2010), 143–58 (149). See also, Frederic L. Cheyette, *Ermengard of Narbonne and the World of the Troubadours* (New York, 2001), 233–4.

[48] Martyn Rady, *Nobility, Land and Service in Medieval Hungary* (Basingstoke and New York, 2000), 79–95.

[49] Trip., I. 2 [1] (DRMH 5, 47–9).

[50] The term *barones naturales* goes back to the 1480s. See Pál Engel, 'Nagy Lajos bárói', *Történelmi Szemle*, 28, no. 3 (1985), 393–413 (398). See also Engel, 'Vár és hatalom. Az uralom territoriális alapjai a középkori Magyarországon', in Engel, *Honor, vár, ispánság. Válogatott tanulmányok* (Budapest, 2003), 162–97 (192), first published in *Világosság*, 25 (1984).

[51] Martyn Rady, 'Jagiello Hungary', in DRMH 4, pp. xi–xlvii (pp. xxx–xxxi).

disparaged the new-found title of hereditary baron as *solo nomine*, unlike the title belonging to the 'true barons', which derived from office.[52] He was, however, powerless to check the political weight of the hereditary baronage which later acquired an absolute majority in the upper house of the Hungarian diet, stabilizing in the seventeenth century at about fifty great families.[53]

Since all nobles were identical in their rights, sharing an equal liberty, it followed that they might have an equal share in the business of the realm. One of the outstanding features of medieval Central European society as a whole is that its nobility stood for the most part in a direct relationship to the king, not holding their property at one or several removes from the ruler by process of subinfeudation and thus not dividing their fealty. As a consequence, all nobles might be deemed to have the right to attend the ruler and have their counsel heard, although this privilege was in practice reserved to the better-off noblemen, the so-called *proceres*, and later exercised through deputies. Nevertheless, during the succession crises of the mid-fifteenth century, when it became expedient to enlarge the practice of consultation in order to capture a wider share of opinion, the right of all nobles to give counsel became increasingly entrenched in the kingdom's politics. Diets thus not only became more numerous but also began to acquire the character of mass assemblies. By the beginning of the sixteenth century, diets of the kingdom were often attended by several thousand or more noblemen, possibly by as many as 10,000 in the case of the Hatvan diet of 1525.[54] As in contemporary Poland, Bohemia and, indeed, elsewhere in Europe, where there were as a consequence of their immediacy to the ruler many 'tenants-in-chief', participation in the kingdom's affairs was likely to be equally populous.[55]

Werbőczy does not discuss the kingdom's diets, except obliquely in the context of law making, for it was not his purpose to describe the kingdom's arrangements of public law. He does, however, slip into his account two statements regarding the rights of the nobility in respect of the ruler, which he presents as flowing quite naturally from the immediacy of their relations. These affected the royal succession and the so-called right of resistance. Because the inferences he drew were so closely bound up with the notions of a historic connection between ruler and nobility and of established noble privilege, they became embedded within the kingdom's customary law as almost incontrovertible elements. Both could be, and in time were, rescinded, but only with great difficulty. Indeed, notwithstanding their repudiation by ruler and diet, both continued to linger on in a

[52] Trip., I. 93 [4] (DRMH 5, 175).

[53] Jean Bérenger and Charles Kecskeméti, *Parlement et vie parlementaire en Hongrie 1608–1918* (Paris, 2005), 28–9.

[54] For the Hungarian diets at the close of the Middle Ages, see Rady, 'Jagiello Hungary', pp. xxxiv–xl; Martyn Rady, 'Rethinking Jagiello Hungary', *Central Europe*, 3, no. 1 (2005), 3–18 (10–13).

[55] The Polish example is notorious. Dr Christopher Nicholson tells me that in Bohemia the right to attend the diet belonged to a thousand or so noblemen, but that most of them stayed away. The cases of Croatia and England are less appreciated, but see Géza Pálffy, 'Jedan od temeljnih izvora hrvatske povijesti: pozivnica zajedničkog hrvatsko-slavonskog sabora iz 1558. godine', *Zbornik Odsjeka za povijesne znanosti Zavoda za povijesne i društvene znanosti Hrvatske akademije znanosti i umjetnosti*, 23 (2005), 47–61 (59); J.C. Holt, *Magna Carta*, 2nd edition (Cambridge, 1992), 322.

form of legal half-life, being imagined as aspects of noble privilege that could never be effaced by the simple act of legislative will.

## ELECTION AND SUCCESSION

The royal succession was defined throughout most of medieval Europe according to principles of primogeniture, seniority, suitability and election. The balance between these elements, and indeed the way that these elements were themselves understood, was not governed by normative laws but shifted according to circumstance.[56] In the context of medieval Hungary, we may, however, observe that the period of the Árpád kings saw a general trend away from seniority to primogeniture, although the passage between the two was marked by bloodshed and insurrection.[57] The vicissitudes attending the expiry of the Árpád line and the advent of Hungary's 'mixed dynasties' (variously the Angevin, Luxemburg and Jagiello lines, along with Albert of Habsburg, Albert's son, Ladislas V, and Matthias Corvinus) saw an additional stress put on expediency, whereby the holder of effective power or the one deemed the most suitable to wield it was granted the status of ruler. This was cloaked with the principle that whosoever wore the Holy Crown and went through the proper ceremony of coronation (at Székesfehérvár, with the Archbishop of Esztergom presiding) was the rightful king, even should an ox, by some accident, be chosen for this role.[58] Where biological claims were missing, the mysteries of coronation and of St Stephen's diadem were invoked to fill the void.[59] Even so, when the young Louis the Great was crowned in July 1342, the leading royal chronicle described the event as having taken place at Székesfehérvár, with the indubitable heir, the son of the recently buried Charles Robert, and 'with the consent and unanimous will of all the barons and of the entire nobility of the whole realm of Hungary, and with the Holy Crown' as well as with the robes and insignia of St Stephen.[60] Plainly, the chronicler considered it worth reporting that besides the correct crown and regalia having been used, the baronage and the whole political nation were agreed upon Louis's succession as the late king's biological heir, although he did not grade these elements in any order.[61] Later interpretations would, however, seek to dissect accounts of Louis I's coronation, using the individual

56 See thus Ralph E. Giesey, 'The Juristic Basis of Dynastic Right to the French Throne', *Transactions of the American Philosophical Society*, NS, 51 (1961), 3–47 (3–4).

57 Martyn Rady, 'Election and Descent in Medieval Hungarian Kingship', in Corinne Péneau, ed., *Élections et pouvoirs politiques du VII^e au XVI^e siècle* (Paris, 2008), 383–90 (384–5).

58 Martyn Rady, '"They brought in an ox as king: they elected and installed him": The royal succession in later medieval Hungary', in Frédérique Lachaud and Michael Penman, eds., *Making and breaking the rules: succession in medieval Europe, c. 1000–c. 1600* (Turnhout, 2008), 61–9 (63); Erik Fügedi, 'Coronation in medieval Hungary', *Studies in Medieval and Renaissance History*, NS, 3 (1980), 159–89 (175), reprinted in Fügedi, *Kings, Bishops, Nobles and Burghers in Medieval Hungary* (London, 1986). See also, Maya Bijvoet Williamson, ed., *The Memoirs of Helene Kottanner (1439–40)* (Cambridge, 1998), 43 (ch. 3).

59 The Holy Crown was not St Stephen's but a late-thirteenth-century confection.

60 Imre Szentpétery, ed., *Scriptores rerum Hungaricarum*, 2 vols. (Budapest, 1937–8), i, 503–5.

61 Rady, '"They brought in an ox as king..."', 62.

episodes in the narrative of the event as justification for either a hereditary or elective scheme of monarchy.[62]

Notwithstanding the importance ascribed by the chronicler to descent, coronation, acclamation and the express regard of the realm, some additional mechanism might be required to identify whom to crown and thus to promote to the supreme office. The principle of primogeniture that had by the first decades of the twelfth century largely governed the succession in Árpád Hungary was renewed by Hungary's Angevin rulers, who sought to extend the order of inheritance to daughters. Nevertheless, the claims of Louis's heir, Mary, were generally considered weak and she depended for political survival upon her husband, Sigismund of Luxemburg. Thereafter, however, daughters were the best that Hungary's rulers could manage, with most kings dying prematurely, not siring a male heir. To begin with, the way round the problem was for the king or royal council to nominate a suitable successor. It was by this route that Sigismund's son-in-law, Albert of Habsburg, acquired the throne in 1437. Thereafter, however, the diet assumed the initiative in determining the succession. Where the identity of the next ruler was disputed, it plainly made sense to broaden the principle of consultation in order to achieve and bind political consensus. In 1440, therefore, upon Albert's death, the diet appointed Wladislas I of Poland as king, without waiting to see whether Albert's pregnant widow would be delivered of a boy. Four years later, upon the death of Wladislas, without heir, the diet elected governors and later a single governor, John Hunyadi, to rule during the minority of Albert's infant, Ladislas V, who was now acknowledged as the rightful heir. When in 1457 Ladislas himself died childless, the diet elected Hunyadi's son, Matthias Corvinus, although he had no royal blood in him. Upon Corvinus's own death, again without legitimate heir, the diet chose the king of Bohemia, Wladislas II, even though his claim to the throne was more remote than that of Ladislas's uncle, Frederick III. Wladislas did eventually manage at the age of fifty to produce a male heir. Although the baby Louis was born prematurely and spent his first days in an incubator made of the carcases of freshly slain pigs, he survived, only to die himself without heir on the field of Mohács.[63]

During the fifteenth century, therefore, the right of election moved to the foreground, eclipsing biological succession, but only because it might not be asserted. The test came with the illness of Wladislas II in 1505, at that time still without a male heir. Fearful lest several previous compacts with the Habsburgs be invoked and the Emperor Maximilian thus accede to the throne by way of a private dynastic arrangement, a packed diet meeting on the field of Rákos beside Pest proclaimed its right to elect a 'national king' as Wladislas's heir, but only in the event that 'there be no male heirs who by the law and custom of this kingdom should succeed'.[64] The moving spirit behind the Rákos declaration was most

[62] *Monumenta Comitialia*, v, 469, 476. [63] Rady, 'Jagiello Hungary', p. xiv.

[64] The full text of the Rákos declaration is given in Henrik Marczali, *A magyar történet kútfőinek kézikönyve* (Budapest, 1901), 317–20, and in János M. Bak, *Königtum und Stände in Ungarn im 14.–16. Jahrhundert* (Wiesbaden, 1973), 158–9.

probably Werbőczy, who was rewarded by the diet with a slice of tax revenue.[65] Three years later, however, following the improbable birth of the future Louis II, Wladislas thought it prudent to obtain the diet's consent to have the child crowned in his own lifetime. The event which took place in 1508 was accompanied by a ceremony in which the assembled nobility were expressly asked by the palatine whether they accepted Louis as king, the first occasion upon which this so-called 'old custom' was in fact invoked.[66] Upon Wladislas's death in 1516, Louis succeeded immediately—there was no second coronation, nor was the renewed agreement of the diet sought.

Despite the invocation in 1508 of the 'old custom' of obtaining the nobility's consent, it is clear from the sequence given above that the royal succession rested on descent in the male line. Only when there was no indubitable male heir did the identity of the new king depend upon election. Nevertheless, even though the Rákos declaration recognized primogeniture as the natural means of royal succession, the *Tripartitum* maintained the opposite. In describing the immediacy of king and nobility in terms of 'some reciprocal transfer and mutual bond' (*quondam translationem reciprocam reflexibilemque connexionem*), Werbőczy slipped into his text the following maxim: 'For the prince is elected only by the nobles, and nobles are created and adorned with the dignity of nobility only by the prince.' It seems extraordinary that Werbőczy should have written this, particularly since he was most likely the author of the earlier Rákos declaration that had previously affirmed the priority of the hereditary principle.[67] It seems equally remarkable that Wladislas II should have sanctioned this passage. We might aver that, as in France, there was in late medieval Hungary no single body of integrated norms capable of guiding the succession but 'in reality a congeries of different ideas coming from the different legal systems of medieval times'.[68] Nevertheless, the *Tripartitum* does not present election as just one ingredient determining the succession, but as the deciding principle.

In 1526, Louis died without heir on the field of Mohács. Two diets subsequently met that in short order elected two different kings, both of whom were crowned with the sacred diadem in Székesfehérvár, by the hand of the same bishop of Nitra (the archbishops of Esztergom and Kalocsa having fallen at Mohács). The claims, however, of the rivals rested upon different principles. John I Zápolya, the voivode of Transylvania, rested his claim upon the Rákos declaration of 1505—the king had died without heir and so it fell to the diet to appoint a 'national king'. By contrast, Ferdinand of Habsburg emphasized his family's recent marriages into the Hungarian royal house and thus his hereditary claim to the throne, albeit operating at one remove and, as critics put it, in the manner of a dowry.[69] According thus to Ferdinand's sister, Mary, who was also the widow of the late King Louis, election was not the constitutive act of kingship but the token of its recognition, which derived through right of inheritance.[70]

[65] DRMH 5, pp. xxxi–xxxii. [66] Bak, *Königtum und Stände*, 68–9.
[67] Bak, *Königtum und Stände*, 67. [68] Giesey, 'The juristic basis of dynastic right', 4.
[69] István Schlett, *A magyar politikai gondolkodás története* (Budapest, 1996), 111.
[70] Rady, ' "They brought in an ox as king…" ', 61.

The two competing conceptions of the succession would be teased out over the succeeding centuries. Hungary's Habsburg rulers continued thus to affirm the hereditary nature of their rule, while still making nods in the direction of the electoral principle. Thus, Ferdinand I, having had the diet agree in 1547 to recognize his heirs as Hungary's kings, and having received formal invitation of the estates to crown his son, Maximilian, as his successor, thought it yet worthwhile to convene a diet in 1563 to have Maximilian elected. Similar circumstances attended the coronation of Rudolf in 1572 and, with rather more discussion, the coronation of Ferdinand II in 1618.[71] Indeed, until the second half of the seventeenth century, the convocation of an electoral diet was considered the necessary prelude to coronation. Although subject to heavy-handed manipulation, the negotiations preceding election reinforced the notion of a contract between ruler and the political nation and of the presence within the kingdom's public law of two mutually opposing subjects of right.[72]

Although both the law of 1547 and the unbroken succession of Habsburg rulers suggests that the principles of inheritance and primogeniture now trumped the principle of election, rendering it a mere formality prior to coronation, the idea that the identity of the monarch was for the diet to dispose remained embedded within legal and political consciousness. At times of crisis, therefore, Werbőczy's account of the elective nature of Hungarian kingship was apt to be revived, even to the extent of pitting the future Maximilian II and the son of John I, John II Sigismund, as potential candidates in a vote for the throne.[73] Election by the diet might thus be proposed as a way of promoting a new king to power or, more ingeniously, used to deny an existing ruler the right to office on the grounds that he had been improperly appointed. The Bocskai rebellion at the start of the seventeenth century, Gábor Bethlen's revolt that began in 1619 with his own election as king, the magnates' conspiracy of the 1660s, and Ferenc Rákóczi's *Recrudescunt* manifesto of 1703, thus took their stand by elective rule, 'which custom was maintained for centuries unimpaired', melding it into programmes that variously combined confessional tolerance, Calvinist messianism, resentment of Viennese rule and an emerging sense of Hungarian nationhood.[74] These rebellions against Habsburg rule did not only, however, look for legal sustenance to the idea of elective monarchy but also combined this with another right promoted in the *Tripartitum*, the right of resistance.

## THE RIGHT OF RESISTANCE

The Golden Bull of 1222 was issued by Andrew II on behalf of the royal *servientes*. It was extracted from the king at a time of political turmoil, amidst what appears

[71] 1547: 5; Rezső Hazslinszky, *Magyarországon a királyi szék betöltése a xvi. században* (Békéscsaba, 1893), 11–13; György Bónis, *Révay Péter* (Budapest, 1981), 35.

[72] István M. Szijártó, *A diéta. A magyar rendek és az országgyűlés 1708–1792* (Budapest, 2005), 196–200.

[73] *Monumenta Comitialia*, v, 460.

[74] The quotation is from *Recrudescunt*. See László Péter, '*Ius resistendi* in Hungary', in Péter and Martyn Rady, eds., *Resistance, Rebellion and Revolution in Hungary and Central Europe: Commemorating 1956* (London, 2008), 41–55 (48).

to have been the complete collapse of the king's government. Although frequently compared to Magna Carta and to other contemporary instruments that sought to constrain the royal power, it was not underpinned by notions of 'fealty' or of the mutuality of obligations that arose from fidelity.[75] The interest of the *servientes* was at this stage to bind their fate to the ruler's by developing a bond of *fidelitas* with him, not to elaborate the political and legal implications that followed from this bond. For this reason, teasing out personal links between Hungarian noblemen and their counterparts in other, more highly developed monarchies is tantalizing but probably not worthwhile.[76]

In its concluding part, the privilege included the famous resistance clause, which is conventionally recorded as its thirty-first article:

> We have also decreed that if we or any of our successors at any time should seek to oppose the terms of this settlement, both the bishops and other *iobagiones* (high royal dignitaries) as well as the nobles of the realm, singularly and in common, both present and future, shall by this authority have the right in perpetuity to resist and speak against us and our successors without the charge of perfidy.[77]

The use of the term *nobiles*, which was not yet a synonym for *servientes*, suggests that this clause was intended to benefit the king's leading men, some of whom had recently risen against him, and not the *servientes* on whose behalf the Golden Bull was composed. Nevertheless, once the *servientes* had taken on the name of *nobiles*, the right that had been granted to the leading men to oppose the ruler was considered to belong automatically to them.

The resistance clause given in the Golden Bull was weak. It fell short of permitting insurrection, still less the right given in Magna Carta 'to distrain and distress us in every way [...], namely by seizing castles, lands and possessions'. Nor did it establish an institutional mechanism for ensuring the ruler's compliance, in the manner of Magna Carta's council of twenty-five barons.[78] The impression thus remains that the resistance clause was included to avoid something that was from the king's point of view rather worse. This is most likely to have been the sanction of *comminatio*, supervised by the kingdom's leading churchmen, in the manner of an ecclesiastical anathema, which was the usual device included at this time in charters in order to strengthen their power. Indeed, upon the reissue of the Golden Bull in 1231, the resistance clause was replaced by this more fearsome instrument—'We agree of our free will that if we, our sons, or our successors attempt to infringe upon this liberty which we have granted, the archbishop of Esztergom

[75] Cf. Holt, *Magna Carta*, 75–81; László Péter, '*Ius resistendi* in Hungary', in Péter and Rady, *Resistance, Rebellion and Revolution*, 41–55 (41–2).

[76] For a brief historiographical review of these putative links, see István Petrovics, 'Aranybulla', in Gyula Kristó, Pál Engel and Ferenc Makk, eds., *Korai magyar történeti lexikon (9–14. század)* (Budapest, 1994), 55–6. See also Pál Engel, *The Realm of St Stephen: A History of Medieval Hungary, 895–1526* (London and New York, 2001), 95; Martyn Rady, 'Hungary and the Golden Bull of 1222', *Banatica*, 24, part 2 (2014), 87–108.

[77] 1222: 31 (DRMH 1, 35). The numbering of the articles is an eighteenth-century innovation.

[78] Holt, *Magna Carta*, 471.

shall have the authority, after proper warning, to bind us or them, in the chains of excommunication'.[79]

Although originally distributed in seven copies, each with a hollow golden seal, recollection of the Golden Bull faded after its reissue in 1231. Although we may detect its influence, the privileges issued for the nobles by Béla IV in 1267 and Andrew III in 1290 and 1298 make no explicit reference to the Golden Bull. Only in 1318 was the text of the original Golden Bull recovered and deployed by the kingdom's bishops at a meeting of the diet (or in anticipation of one) in the hope of bridling the extensive royal powers claimed by Charles Robert over the disposal of ecclesiastical property. The text of the 1222 bull, with its resistance clause, suited their purpose more than the 1231 reissue, since it was unlikely in view of Charles Robert's good relations with Pope John XXII that the threat of excommunication would carry any leverage with the ruler.[80] It is this copy of the Golden Bull, composed in 1318 and sealed only with lumps of wax, that disappointed schoolchildren now inspect in the museum of Esztergom cathedral, and beside which the judges of Hungary's constitutional court currently take their oaths of office.

As it turned out, however, Charles Robert did not confirm the Golden Bull. His son, however, did so, republishing the Golden Bull on the occasion of a diet that met over several weeks in the last months of 1351.[81] Republication of the Golden Bull formed part of a much larger programme undertaken by Louis of rewarding his followers in the aftermath of his Neapolitan campaign and of generally enhancing the power of the nobility in the countryside in the wake of the Black Death.[82] In much the same manner as the Magna Carta, the Golden Bull had plainly acquired by this time a certain mythic quality, even though many of its provisions were obsolete. In 1384 and again in 1397, the Golden Bull was republished, on the first occasion through the reissue of Louis's charter of 1351, and on the second in a revised form that sought to update its contents.[83] The 1397 version omitted, however, the resistance clause. It is uncertain whether this arose by neglect or design, although we may generally observe Sigismund's opposition at this time to other constraints on his authority.[84] In 1440, the Golden Bull was included in a *libellus*, which otherwise contained the texts of the laws of 1298 and 1351 as well as a short compendium of customary regulations. These were confirmed by Wladislas I several days after his coronation.[85]

From 1387 onwards, it was usual for Hungary's medieval rulers to commit themselves to 'electoral capitulations' in advance of their coronation, the contents of which might later be published in the form of laws (or, as in the case of the 1490

[79] 1231: 22 (DRMH 1, 39). 'Proper warning' was by this time a canonical requirement for excommunication.

[80] Alajos Degré, 'Az ellenállási jog története Magyarországon', *Jogtudományi Közlöny*, 35 (1980), 366–71 (368). It was commonplace by this time for excommunicates to petition Rome or a papal legate to have their sentence lifted.

[81] The text is given in DRMH 2, 8–13.

[82] Pál Engel, Gyula Kristó and András Kubinyi, *Histoire de la Hongrie médiévale. Tome 2. Des Angevins aux Habsbourgs* (Rennes, 2008), 80–3.

[83] DRMH 2, 14–15, 21–4. [84] Bak, *Königtum und Stände*, 31.

[85] DRMH 2, 90, 218; DRMH 1, 71–5.

capitulation be subsequently deemed a law).[86] As far as we know, however, none of these made explicit reference to the Golden Bull, notwithstanding their general statements with regard to preserving the kingdom's noblemen in their rights and privileges. Nor did the ruler's coronation oath, which was usually delivered midway through the ceremony, make reference to the Golden Bull, ranging instead around the maintenance of peace and of the faith, the exercise of royal justice, care for widows and orphans, and the preservation of regalian rights and of the territory of the kingdom.[87] Extraordinarily, however, Werbőczy claimed otherwise. In the ninth chapter of the first part of the *Tripartitum*, Werbőczy enumerated the cardinal privileges of the nobility, which he drew from the text of the Golden Bull—the nobleman's freedom from arrest; his right to be impleaded only before the king; and his exemption from taxation. To these, he added as the nobility's fourth and final liberty:

> If any of our princes and kings should venture to act contrary to the liberties of the nobles, then, as stated and expressed in the general decree of the most illustrious prince, our former Lord King Andrew the Second, called 'of Jerusalem' (which decree every Hungarian king is wont to swear on oath to observe before the Holy Crown is placed on his head), they have for ever more the liberty to resist and oppose him without taint of infidelity.[88]

Later on in the *Tripartitum*, Werbőczy renewed his description of Andrew II's achievement and listed his Golden Bull as one of those statutes that 'the Hungarian people to the present day exalt to the stars as if they were holy decrees.'[89]

It is uncertain whether Werbőczy was confused or mischievous in asserting that Hungary's rulers swore expressly at their coronation to uphold the Golden Bull. They never had and they never indeed would do so, although later commentators, reading Werbőczy, often presumed that this was a vital part of the ritual of coronation.[90] From 1526, Hungary's rulers frequently included reference to the Golden Bull either in the electoral capitulations that preceded the coronation or in the inaugural diploma, published after the ceremony but negotiated previously in concert with the diet.[91] After 1687, however, oblique reference was included in the actual coronation oath to the Golden Bull, in the context of the clause stating that its resistance clause no longer applied. It was in this paradoxical and roundabout

[86] Its text is given in Bak, *Königtum und Stände*, 152–4. From 1584 the text of the 'Farkashida' capitulation was included in the *Corpus Juris Hungarici*. See András Kubinyi, 'Die Wahlkapitulationen Wladislaws II. in Ungarn', in Rudolf Vierhaus, ed., *Herrschaftsverträge, Wahlkapitulationen, Fundamentalgesetze* (Göttingen, 1977), 140–62 (141).

[87] Emma Bartoniek, 'A koronázási eskü fejlődése 1526-ig', *Századok*, 51 (1917), 5–44 (12–14); Michaela Bodnárová, 'Iuxta morem patrium. Ungarische Krönungen der Jagiellonen 1490/1508 und Ferdinands I. von Habsburg 1527', in Florin Ardelean, Christopher Nicholson and Johannes Preiser-Kapeller, eds., *Between Worlds: The Age of the Jagiellonians* (Frankfurt a/M, 2013), 21–36 (28). There is a handy guide to the ritual of coronation in Bak, *Königtum und Stände*, 165–76.

[88] Trip., I, 9 [6] (DRMH 5, 57). The description 'of Jerusalem' refers to Andrew II's brief participation in the Fifth Crusade in 1217–18.

[89] Trip., II, 6 [6] (DRMH 5, 233).

[90] Teszelszky, *Az ismeretlen korona*, 250.

[91] Thus, Ferdinand I's electoral capitulation of 20 November 1526, given in Bak, *Königtum und Stände*, 163.

way that recollection of the Golden Bull remained within the coronation ceremony until the end of the monarchy.

* * *

By including the right of resistance among the nobility's four cardinal liberties, Werbőczy promoted it to an inalienable right, included within a document upon which Hungary's rulers were alleged to swear during the ceremony of coronation.[92] We have no evidence that any insurrection against the Hungarian ruler was ever justified in the Middle Ages by reference to the resistance clause, notwithstanding the inventiveness with which some rebels explained their actions. From the beginning of the seventeenth century, however, the *ius resistendi* was regularly invoked as an excuse for rebellion, but now in the context of a 'national' right rather than just a right of the nobility. The diet of Szerencs of 1605, which elected Stephen Bocskai prince of Hungary in opposition to Emperor Rudolf II, thus referred to the content of the right, 'according to which we may take arms against His Majesty in our defence for our lives and liberty'. In the same year, the diet of Krupina expressly footnoted the *Tripartitum*, 'For if the king goes against the laws and decrees of the kingdom, it is possible to resist him without the taint of infidelity, Part 1, Chapter 9.'[93] On the occasion of his own rebellion, Imre Thököly averred in 1684 that the right of resistance constituted 'the spirit of Hungarian freedom, the true regulator of government, the judge and avenger of subjects, which may completely and entirely erase the stain of rebellion.'[94] Rákóczi's *Recrudescunt* manifesto, besides affirming the elective character of Hungarian monarchy, likewise paid heed to Andrew II's 'great law' that conferred 'never ceasing power to resist the king whenever he degrades the laws'.[95]

The resistance clause was along with the idea of elective monarchy declared void in 1687 by a cowed diet. The notion that the ruler might be legitimately resisted in the event of his disparaging the kingdom's laws persisted, however, along with the belief that the political nation was still possessed of the right to choose the monarch. Both principles were invoked during the course of Rákóczi's rebellion, were part of the arsenal deployed against the government of Joseph II in the late 1780s, and formed a little of the intellectual underpinning behind the deposition of the house of Habsburg in 1849. The right of resistance was, moreover, tacitly assumed by Hungary's county governments, expressing itself in the nineteenth century in the *vis inertiae* (the 'respectfully putting aside' of royal instructions), in breaking the seats of commissars appointed over them, and in the sealing up committee rooms.[96] Like the right to elect the ruler, the right of resistance was deemed

[92] Péter, '*Ius resistendi* in Hungary', 46.

[93] *Monumenta Comitialia*, xi, 154, 242. See also, Martyn Rady, 'Bocskai, Rebellion and Resistance in Early Modern Hungary', in Péter and Rady, *Resistance, Rebellion and Revolution in Hungary*, 57–66 (65–6); Graeme Murdock, *Beyond Calvin: The Intellectual, Political and Cultural World of Europe's Reformed Churches, c. 1540–1620* (Basingstoke and New York, 2004), 74.

[94] Degré, 'Az ellenállási jog', 369.

[95] Péter, '*Ius resistendi* in Hungary', 48.

[96] Péter, '*Ius resistendi* in Hungary', 50–3; Elemér Balogh, 'The Place of the Golden Bull in Hungarian Constitutional History', in Lajos Besenyei, Géza Érszegi and Maurizio Pedrazza Gorlero, eds., *De Bulla Aurea Andreae Regis Hungariae MCCXXII* (Verona, 1999), 203–24 (223).

not only a noble prerogative, but also a privilege of the nation that was so rooted in history as to be impossible to revoke.

For the salience and continued cogency in Hungarian public life of the two principles of election and resistance, Werbőczy's *Tripartitum* bears significant responsibility. It is, nevertheless, also a telling illustration of the way that Werbőczy implanted ideas of his own into his text, lending the title of custom to principles that comported with his personal conviction of what the law should be. Werbőczy's exposition of the relationship between king and nobility, and of their mutual interdependence, was neatly crafted and it may be supported by what we know of the historical roots and retained meaning of nobility in Hungary. From his account, he nevertheless drew inferences that had little support in the customary law of the kingdom. Werbőczy was both a lawyer and a politician, who inclined towards the type of noble republicanism that looked for sustenance to the diet and John Zápolya. His brief foray into the kingdom's public law had, however, the more enduring legacy of souring political life in Hungary in the centuries to come.

# 6

# The Nobleman and His Land

## *AVITICITAS* AND ALIENABILITY

The landed wealth of the kingdom's nobility rested upon a double foundation and was famously subject to a 'twofold restriction'.[1] On the one hand, all land was held of the ruler, originating in an act of donation and ennoblement. Thus, upon the expiry of the nobleman's line or his condemnation for perfidy, his property reverted to the ruler. On the other hand, however, the nobleman held his land conjointly with his relatives, and indeed with all those kinsmen who were descended from the original beneficiary of the royal grace. This joint-ownership was not only expressed through such mechanisms as inheritance and rights of pre-emption, but was also translated into a panoply of interconnecting and concurrent rights. Because the kinsmen had a legal interest in the nobleman's land, since they might acquire a part of it should he die without sons, they were deemed to have a right of veto in respect of its alienation. The notion of *aviticitas*, that is of the concurrent rights of all those descended from a single *avus* (technically grandfather, but meaning ancestor), formed an integral part of the Hungarian system of landholding until 1848. The consequence was that the Hungarian nobleman did not really own his land at all. He held it of the ruler, to whom it might eventually revert, and at the same time as a trust on behalf of his sons, heirs and kinsmen.

This system lies at the heart of Werbőczy's discussion of noble landholding, which occupies most of the first part of the *Tripartitum*. Much of what Werbőczy writes can be supported by the evidence of charters. Werbőczy did, however, give stresses and interpretations of his own, the purpose of which was to lend coherence to the arrangements he described. Moreover, he tended to overlook trends in the customary law that weakened *aviticitas* and he over-emphasized the legal solidarity of the kindred, which even at the time he was writing was experiencing a partial dissolution. To this end, he even introduced a new crime, the betrayal of a kinsman (*proditio sanguinis*), advertising it as the most awful of acts, although the penalty he prescribed was purely rhetorical.[2] The *Tripartitum* thus had the consequence of preserving the structure of *aviticitas*, contributing thereby to the immobility of Hungary's relations of landed property and impeding the kingdom's development

[1] Ákos Timon, *Ungarische Verfassungs- und Rechtsgeschichte* (Berlin, 1904), 508.
[2] Trip., I. 34 (DRMH 5, 105).

in respect of its commercial law. By the early nineteenth century, the *Tripartitum*'s responsibility for the retardation of Hungary and for the primitiveness of its economic institutions was established and the abolition of *aviticitas* accordingly became a goal of reformers. Until this time, however, *aviticitas* constituted the bedrock of Hungarian landholding and was the source of most litigation over property.

* * *

Except for the royal house of Árpád, no continuities can be established between the families that led the Hungarians at the time of the conquest and those which emerge into the light of the historical record in the thirteenth century.[3] Nevertheless, almost four centuries after the arrival of the Hungarians in Pannonia, some land was still held as *descensualis*, that is by an alleged right of first occupation.[4] Recalling this, Simon of Kéza's chronicle from the late thirteenth century described how at the time of the conquest Hungary's captains 'chose for themselves places to settle [. . .], and the other kindreds settled wherever they liked'.[5] *Descensualis* rights were from the very first, however, challenged by the *ius regium* which posited that the whole of the kingdom's territory belonged by right to the ruler.[6] This permitted the royal fisc to absorb all those lands in the kingdom that had not yet been occupied by the conquering Hungarians and affirmed the principle that first occupation depended upon the royal consent. By the end of the eleventh century, the fiction had thus taken root that *descensualis* land was in fact property granted by St Stephen, all other land constituting 'possessions given by other kings'.[7] In contrast to Simon of Kéza, Hungary's earliest chronicler generally affirmed this position, imagining that at the time of the conquest all property was conveyed to the chief men of the realm by express grant of the ruler.[8]

*Descensualis* property was held jointly by all members of the kindred. Thus the laws of King Coloman specified that this type of property passed to 'successors or heirs', whereas land acquired by royal donation went 'to the son'. In respect of the latter, the other members of the kindred only had a right to the estate in the event of its owner having no direct heir.[9] Thus, two systems of inheritance operated, with *descensualis* estates passing down through the kindred, who worked it communally,

[3] The literature on the continuity of the leading families after the conquest is summarized in Erik Fügedi, *The Elefánthy: The Hungarian Nobleman and his Kindred* (Budapest and New York, 1998), 5.

[4] Eszter Waldapfel, 'Nemesi birtokjogunk kialakulása a középkorban', *Századok*, 65 (1931), 134–67, 259–72 (151).

[5] László Veszprémy and Frank Schaer, eds., *Simonis de Kéza Gesta Hungarorum* (Budapest and New York, 1999), 86–7 (ch. 33).

[6] The term *descensualis* had several other meanings. It might also refer to the royal right of supply for officials or to pastureland, being thus the equivalent of *szállás*.

[7] Coloman: 20 (DRMH 1, 26).

[8] *Anonymi Bele Regis notarii Gesta Hungarorum*, ch 15, 17, 18, 30, 32, 37 etc., in János M. Bak, Martyn Rady and László Veszprémy, eds., *Anonymus and Master Roger* (Budapest and New York, 2010), 43, 49, 69, 71, 81 etc. See thus Péter Váczy, *A szimbolikus államszemlélet kora Magyarországon*, 2nd edition (Máriabesnyő–Gödöllő, 2004), 48.

[9] Coloman: 20 (DRMH $1^2$, 26). See also Martyn Rady, *Nobility, Land and Service in Medieval Hungary* (Basingstoke and New York, 2000), 25–6. Coloman's provision is partly anticipated in St Stephen II: 2 (DRMH $1^2$, 9).

and donated property being inherited in the first instance by sons. This twofold arrangement is hardly unusual, and bears comparison with the Anglo-Saxon distinction between 'folkland' that was inherited by the kin, and 'bookland' that passed down through sons.[10] During the twelfth and thirteenth centuries, however, it became increasingly common for *descensualis* estates to be broken up and allocated to the kindred's constituent family groups, after which the several parts of the now divided property were treated as if royally donated, thus passing to sons. The break-up of royal castle estates and the allocation of their parts both to the *comites* and to the emerging class of *servientes* nobles further increased the proportion of donated property and the predominance of land that passed down through direct male heirs. The Golden Bull of 1222 affirmed the principle that sons should inherit, no longer making a distinction between *descensualis* and donated land. In the event of the nobleman having no sons, the Golden Bull permitted a right of free disposition, which was a measure probably aimed against the royal right of escheat in default of heirs.[11]

With the break-up of communally worked and owned properties, noblemen started to describe themselves not by reference to the *genus* to which they belonged but instead to their family's estate. With the passage of each generation, however, the family property was usually redivided to accommodate the latest layer of heirs. The heirs often renamed themselves accordingly, although individual families might still retain a toponym that recalled their ancestral estate, particularly if it was their usual place of burial. The practice of what anthropologists call 'perpetual segmentation' was indeed regarded as part of the customary order as early as the first decades of the thirteenth century.[12] Division of the estate did not, however, extinguish the collective legal rights of the nobleman's larger extended family and of the kindred to which he belonged. In the event of a nobleman dying without direct heirs, the right of inheritance was tracked back and his estate apportioned to his closest relatives, even if the line of consanguinity had been interrupted by a division.[13] Accordingly, the members of the kindred were still deemed to have a concurrent legal interest in the estate, unless a privilege was had from the ruler specifically excluding their rights.[14] This right was not limited (as elsewhere) to the fifth or seventh degree, but involved all those who could adequately prove their descent.[15] The rights of the kindred in respect of the property of its members did not sit easily with the principle of free disposition in the event of death without direct heir, as adumbrated in the Golden Bull.

10 The literature on Anglo-Saxon land holding is immense. I rely principally here on Julie Mumby, 'The descent of family land in later Anglo-Saxon England', *Historical Research*, 84, no. 225 (2011), 399–415.

11 1222: 4 (DRMH $1^2$, 32).

12 Ilona Bolla, 'A közszabadság lehanyatlása a xiii. században', *Történelmi Szemle*, 17, no. 1 (1974), 1–23 (6); Martyn Rady, 'Erik Fügedi and the Elefánthy Kindred', SEER, 77, no. 2 (1999), 295–308 (299).

13 AUO, v, 74.

14 HO, ii, 83; AO, v, 34. See also Martyn Rady, 'The "Title of New Donation" in Medieval Hungarian Law', SEER, 79, no. 4 (2001), 638–52 (642).

15 Antal Murarik, *Az ősiség alapintézményeinek eredete* (Budapest, 1938), 97–100.

We will look in vain for established rules of succession before the fourteenth century, and even during the Angevin period we will find sufficient anomalies to suggest that the norms of inheritance were fluid. Such is indeed exactly what one would expect to find in a customary system. Where practices changed, so did the rules. Generally, disputes over property which could not be settled by arbitration came before the king and were thus decided on the basis of whatever policy was paramount at the time. In the first years of Béla IV's reign, therefore, the king plainly preferred to limit inheritance to direct heirs, with the fisc sweeping up the estates of noblemen who had died without the solace of sons. After the Mongol invasion of 1241, however, policy altered, with the king more likely to affirm the right of free disposition.[16] When, therefore, in 1258 Béla IV donated land to a warrior in Zala County with a reversion clause in favour of the ban of Slavonia, he felt it necessary to spell out that this unusual legal arrangement meant that neither the warrior nor his heirs had the right *donandi seu legandi in vita vel in morte*.[17] As the terms of this privilege suggest, rulers were at this time also reluctant to obstruct grants of property to the church, since 'what has been given to God should be holy and irrevocable.'[18] The right of heirless townsmen to give their land to the church *pro remedio anime* is a frequent feature of the urban privileges granted by Hungary's thirteenth-century kings.[19]

In contrast to thirteenth-century royal practice, Hungary's Angevin rulers adopted a more restrictive approach to inheritance, enlarging thereby the royal right of escheat in default of heirs.[20] By no later than the 1330s, the principle of the royal succession to all noble land that had no direct or indirect heir was regarded as customary.[21] In respect of gifts in mortmain, however, no consensus obtained except that donations to the church should not be made at the expense of kinsmen's rights of inheritance.[22] Most gifts in mortmain were made with the royal consent, but this may have been aimed less against the royal right of escheat as against the claims of distant relatives.[23] In 1498, it was laid down by the diet that churches were forbidden to petition for lands of the crown or to purchase estates, which was subsequently understood as also preventing laymen from giving away property to religious bodies.[24] It was only, however, in 1647 that it was unequivocally laid down that churches should not be in receipt of secular property, either by gift or by any other form of alienation.[25]

16 Waldapfel, 'Nemesi birtokjogunk', 152–3.

17 AUO, vii, 484–5.

18 AUO, i, 141.

19 Murarik, *Az ősiség*, 126–41.

20 Pál Engel, 'Nagy Lajos ismeretlen adományreformja', *Történelmi Szemle*, 39, no. 2 (1997), 137–57.

21 László Blazovich, 'A Tripartitum és forrásai', *Századok*, 141 (2007), 1011–23 (1019).

22 1351: proemium (DRMH 2, 9).

23 See thus Pesty-Magina, nos. 253–4. Although childless, the testator did have kinsmen. See Pesty-Magina, nos 198, 261. As far as may be ascertained, the royal consent did not on this occasion include the *Quod si* formula setting aside any latent royal rights, which suggests that the consent was not primarily obtained with the aim of preventing escheat to the crown on grounds of an insufficiency of heirs.

24 1498: 55 (DRMH 4, 125). The article should be read in conjunction with its title, which is contemporary. See MNL OL DL, 26361. See also Károly Csemegi, *Az egyházi holtkéz a magyar törvények szerint* (Budapest, 1897), 31.

25 1647: 17; MJL, iv, 175–6.

Irrespective of royal policy and the legal gap in respect of gifts in mortmain, a more stable customary regime was in the making, which blended the existing traditions of landholding and inheritance. By the second half of the fourteenth century, its terms were clear. Possessors of estate might not dispose of their property by will, even if they lacked direct heirs, but upon death their land went to their sons and, if there were none, to cousins and uncles. By the same token, the consent of kinsmen was required for any alienation since they also retained a legal interest in the property.[26] Even in the event of a landholder dying without any living relative, the property might not be willed by testament, but it returned to the crown.[27] The exception to this rule was land defined as *acquisita*, namely property which had not been inherited but acquired by the current holder. *Acquisita* land that had been purchased was freely disposable by the owner, but once it had been passed onto an heir its status changed to inherited estate, and thus constraints applied to its alienation.[28]

The customary rules of inheritance were acknowledged in 1351, on the occasion of Louis the Great's reissue of the Golden Bull. The 1351 privilege affirmed the content of the Golden Bull with one exception, 'namely, that contrary to the clause according to which noblemen dying without heirs should be able and allowed in life and death to give, grant, sell or alienate their estates to churches or to others whom they wish, they should in fact have no right at all to do so, but the properties of these same nobles should devolve (*devolvantur*) to brothers, collateral relatives and kinsmen (*in fratres, proximos et generationes*) by right and according to law, pure and simple, without anyone's objection'.[29] At the same time, the crown began a pursuit of its rights to property, with the aim of uncovering lands that had been settled and cultivated by noblemen, without any instrument conferring right of possession. The land that they had taken, although usually unoccupied, was deemed to belong by default to the ruler, by royal right, and so, by extension, those who had settled on it were the 'concealers of royal rights' (*celatores iurium regium*). The ensuing investigation involved much of the territory of modern-day Slovakia, where Hungarian noblemen had over generations been clearing woodland valleys and making assarts. It resulted most spectacularly in a flood of petitioners to the royal court, claiming that they had lost their original charters of donation and requesting their reissue, 'by title of new donation'.[30] The fourteenth century thus saw the entrenchment of the double foundation of Hungarian landholding—on the one hand, the embedding of the rights of the kindred in respect of all inherited estate, and, on the other, the notion that noble property was held as a consequence of an original act of royal donation, and thus ultimately revertible to the crown.

The principle that the legal ownership of noble property was vested in the kindred benefited the individual nobleman, giving him a stake in the property of

[26] Waldapfel, 'Nemesi birtokjogunk', 150–1. [27] HO, ii, 64.

[28] Péter Banyó, 'Birtoköröklés és leánynegyed. Kísérlet egy középkori jogintézmény értelmezésére', *Aetas* (2000, no. 3), 76–92 (79).

[29] 1351: proemium (DRMH 2, 9).

[30] Rady, 'The "Title of New Donation" in Medieval Hungarian Law', 639–40.

his kinsmen and thus the prospect of access to wealth through the biological misfortune of others. Although partible inheritance sometimes resulted in a proliferation of successors and thus the partition of estates into dwarf-holdings, it was often also insufficient to prevent the expiry of heirs. Even after the passage of half-a-dozen generations, a cluster of inter-related families might still have difficulties producing a male successor.[31] Noblemen were all too apt to play the system, using ingenious devices in order to enhance their chances of a windfall inheritance. The most frequent of these was the 'fraternal adoption' or, simply, *contractus*, whereby a nobleman, with the consent of his kinsmen, adopted another nobleman as his brother. If the lines of either nobleman expired, then the other adopted brother or his descendants succeeded to the inheritance. Since this arrangement was ostensibly damaging to the royal fisc, which would otherwise have taken possession of the heirless estate, it required the royal consent. This was usually given, for mutual inheritance pacts were less harmful to the fisc than might be thought, since the king was generally expected to re-donate property that escheated to the crown by default of heirs. In order to advance their cause with the king, noblemen entering into an inheritance pact might, nevertheless, allege a convenient common ancestor.[32] The device of fraternal adoption, which as a form of 'spread betting' could involve several or more interlocking contracts of inheritance, was also employed by Werbőczy, who over his lifetime entered into at least four separate agreements of this type.[33] Mutual inheritance agreements might, moreover, be passed onto heirs, with the consequence that a property was saved from escheat even several centuries after the original act of adoption.[34]

Property holding in medieval Hungary was not especially cruel to women. On marriage, the wife negotiated a dower or *Morgengabe* from her husband and received from her own kinsmen a bridal gift that might include, besides the paraphernalia of movables, property in land (the *contrados* or *allatura, hozomány*).[35] Although the land she received at marriage was usually worked as part of her husband's estate, it remained her own. Should the union be childless, it reverted to her kinsmen in accordance with the civilian formula of *materna maternis, paterna paternis*, although her husband's kinsmen often instead bought her out.[36] Upon her spouse's death, the widow might continue to reside in the family home until either

[31] See thus the case of Kalocsa family and the two Kamarás families of Pest County, all of which were inter-related. Five generations after the original donation of property to them in the late seventeenth century, the three families were left with eight female descendants but only two male, thus standing on the edge of extinction. RL, C/67 Sárközy család levéltára, Bundle 3, no. 15.

[32] Pesty-Magina, nos. 241, 245.

[33] Vilmos Fraknói, *Werbőczi István életrajza* (Budapest, 1899), 354, 359–60, 362.

[34] As occurred in the 1770s in respect of the Apafi estates, which passed to the Bethlen family on the basis of a mutual inheritance agreement concluded in 1584. See SJAN Sibiu, Colecţia Brukenthal, Q1–4, no. 338 (1722–72).

[35] József Illés, *A magyar házassági vagyonjog az Árpádok korában* (Budapest, 1900), 19, 28–32, 42–5. Werbőczy conflates the *paraphernalia* with the *allatura*, which is not unusual in accounts of this type. See D. B. Walters, *The Comparative Legal Method: Marriage, Divorce and Spouses' Property Rights in Early Medieval European Law and Cyfraith Hywel* (Aberystwyth, 1982), 44.

[36] Benő Zsögöd, *Öröklött s szerzett vagyon* (Budapest, 1897), 9, 59. Curiously, Zsögöd (Béni Grosschmid) regards the *paterna-materna* formula as a mark of Hungarian national genius.

her own death or remarriage. She and her daughters might receive by will the movables of the dead man and any property that he had acquired by purchase. Daughters, if they married beneath them, might not only retain their noble status, but also pass it on to their children.[37]

The rights of daughters to landed property were, however, far less certain. The principles governing female inheritance were laid down in a succession of statutes, starting with the Golden Bull of 1222, and were adumbrated by Werbőczy at some length.[38] All of these pointed in the same direction. Daughters should not receive their inheritance in land, but be given a cash settlement amounting to a quarter of the value of the father's landed estate, to be shared out between them. The principal exception lay in regard to daughters who were single or who had married propertiless men, to whom land might be given as a way of maintaining their status.[39] All this is obvious enough, for to have routinely granted land to daughters would upon their marriage diminish the family's stock of property, transferring it to outsiders. It is in this respect telling that where local customary arrangements, such as that prevailing among the castle warriors of Turopolje in Slavonia, preferred that daughters be given their inheritance in land, marital strategies should have been distinguished by a strong tendency towards endogamy.[40]

Many uncertainties attended the precise calculation of the quarter. It was unclear whether land that the father had personally received by royal donation should be included in the equation. Nor was it evident whether the daughters having received their share had to be given additional cash in the event that more land came into their immediate family on account of the expiry of a more distant branch. These issues were still the subject of court judgments in the eighteenth century and, even then, no consensus was reached.[41] Moreover, the requirement that daughters receive cash in lieu of land was so frequently overlooked as to suggest that customary practices followed quite different rules to the ones laid down in normative instruments. Charters issued in the course of litigation during the fourteenth and fifteenth century, suggest that somewhere around a half of all cessions of the daughters' quarter were given not in money, but in land.[42] On many occasions, the grant was made following arbitration, but there were also occasions on which courts either confirmed or proceeded from the assumption that the daughters received their inheritance in landed goods. At times, it was indicated that this was a temporary measure. The family had insufficient cash to pay off the girls, so land

[37] Martyn Rady, 'The Filial Quarter and Female Inheritance in Medieval Hungarian Law', in Balázs Nagy and Marcell Sebők, eds., *Festschrift in Honor of János M. Bak* (Budapest and New York, 1999), 422–31 (425).

[38] For the relevant statutes, see the glossary entry on 'Filial Quarter' in DRMH 4, 312–13; for courts and arbitration, see Banyó, 'Birtoköröklés és leánynegyed', 85; Trip., I. 27 [2], 88–90 (DRMH 5, 87, 171–3).

[39] Trip., I. 29 [5–7] (DRMH 5, 91); 8 March 1435: 18 (DRMH 2, 74).

[40] Marija Karbić, 'Heiratsstrategien des Kleinadels von Turopolje (Slawonien) im späten Mittelalter', *East Central Europe/L'Europe du Centre-Est*, 29, nos. 1–2 (2002), 167–76.

[41] Mária Homoki-Nagy, *Az 1795. évi magánjogi tervezetek* (Szeged, 2004), 58–60; Mária Homoki-Nagy, *A magyar magánjog történetének vázlata 1848*-ig (Szeged, 2010), 82. See also Ignác Frank, *A közigazság törvenye Magyarhonban* (Buda, 1845), 494.

[42] Péter Banyó, 'Birtoköröklés és leánynegyed', 83–4.

was given in the expectation that it might later be redeemed. Sometimes, indeed, the land so distributed was formally recorded as a pledge.[43] On other occasions, however, no such commitment to redemption was understood. The daughters received a tract of land that they possessed in seemingly perpetual right, to be passed onto their heirs. In order to obtain it for themselves, kinsmen had to sue, pitting the customary laws of male inheritance against the rights of daughters to a share in their father's patrimony.[44] In Transylvania, it was so common for the quarter to be given in land as to constitute the usual form of female inheritance, with the consequence that many family estates were over time dangerously depleted.[45]

Where noblemen had only daughters and wished to convey the entirety of their estate upon them, other remedies were sought. In some cases, they succeeded in extracting from the ruler the privilege of cognatic inheritance, by the terms of which the property descended through the female line should there be no sons to inherit. The consequence of this was the confusing description found in the surviving legal material of 'men of the female line', namely the descendants of a female forbear who had acquired her property by right of cognatic inheritance.[46] The privilege of cognatic succession was not generally, however, granted to land already in the nobleman's possession, for that would have been prejudicial to his kinsmen, but only to estates that he had himself received by donation of the ruler. Since individual estates might over time be split up among heirs and conjoined with other lands, it could also happen that parts of a single inheritance were deemed to proceed by cognatic succession, the remainder by agnatic. In this respect, the right of female inheritance was deemed both to reside in the family and to adhere to the property.[47]

As an alternative to obtaining the right of cognatic succession, noblemen without sons might petition the ruler to convert a daughter into a male heir, thus preserving the agnatic descent with the fiction that the woman was now legally a man. Privileges recording the 'prefection' of a daughter (*prefectio in filium in heredem masculinum*) commonly included reference to the right of the monarch to set aside customary arrangements. Indeed the royal prerogative was seldom more keenly expressed than in charters of this type.[48] Altogether over 100 grants of prefection are known to have been made in the two centuries following the earliest use of this device in 1332.[49] Although the right of prefection derived from the ruler's *plenitudo potestatis*, its exercise nevertheless acquired its own customary character.

[43] Zsigmond Jakó, ed., *A kolozsmonostori konvent jegyzőkönyvei*, 2 vols. (Budapest, 1990), ii, no. 5272.

[44] Ioan-Aurel Pop, ed., *Diplome Maramureșene din secolele xvi–xviii, provenite din colecția lui Ioan Mihalyi de Apșa*, 2nd edition (Cluj, 2012), 78–80.

[45] András W. Kovács, *The History of the Wass de Czege Family* (Hamburg, 2005), 73–5. For the sixteenth century, see also Jakó, *A kolozsmonostori konvent jegyzőkönyvei*, ii, nos. 4207, 4370, 4783, 4858, 4911.

[46] The description was later acknowledged to be an 'idiocy'. See János Szegedi, *Tripartitum Juris Hungarici Tyrocinium* (Košice, 1764), 155 (I: 67) (first published in 1734).

[47] RL, C/67 Sárközy család levéltára, Bundle 2, no. 31; SJAN Sibiu, Colecția Brukenthal, Q1–4, no. 209 (*In causa Halleriana*, 1741–66).

[48] Erik Fügedi, *The Elefánthy: The Hungarian Nobleman and his Kindred* (Budapest and New York, 1998), 54.

[49] Rady, 'The Filial Quarter and Female Inheritance', 427. The figure is surely an under-estimate.

During the later fourteenth century, therefore, it became the practice that acts of prefection depended upon there being no male relative alive within the fourth degree, and towards the end of his reign Louis the Great revoked all prefections which harmed the interests of collateral heirs.[50] The Timişoara diet of 1397 gave additional force to these arrangements by restricting grant of prefection while any kinsman survived within the fifth degree, although it was often difficult to prove consanguinity.[51] Closer kinsmen might, however, set aside their rights and agree to a prefection, even though it was potentially injurious to their interests, or a reversionary clause be included in the charter of prefection to take into account the rights of any future male heirs that the father might sire.[52] It was sometimes also understood that a grant of prefection should take account of whether the daughter stood in financial need. In 1370, therefore, Louis the Great revoked a grant of prefection since 'according to the trustworthy report of very many of our faithful men, Our Majesty has learned that the noble lady is not so greatly burdened by poverty as was reported to Our Majesty and that she has been joined in matrimony to a nobleman who has sufficient property.'[53] Plainly, however, this requirement was subsequently overlooked in subsequent centuries.[54]

The limits that the collective rights of the kindred imposed upon what the individual nobleman might do with property affected more than just inheritance. The concurrent interest retained by kinsmen in the estate meant that they could block the alienation of any part of it. Sales, exchanges and (less certainly) pledges of land required, therefore, the consent of all those kinsmen who might be considered potential heirs. Accordingly, their names were often added to contracts of sale or pledge which barred them from subsequent protest. If their consent was not forthcoming, the alienation might be challenged or, if they were not informed of it, they and their heirs might launch a retrospective action for recovery, even centuries after the event. Likewise, children conceived but not yet born retained the right to void the alienation of an estate upon their coming of age. Although a limitation (*praescriptio*) of thirty or thirty-two years normally worked in respect of most property transactions, it carried no weight in cases involving kinsmen. As Werbőczy himself noted, 'Among kinsmen [...] no prescription is ever applied regarding their property rights [...] and the payment by them of the dower and quarter.'[55]

## THE *ASSUMPTIO* AND USURIOUS CONTRACTS

There were many occasions when noblemen had to alienate land, if only to raise the necessary sum to pay the quarter share due to one or more sisters upon the

[50] DRH 1301–457, 141.
[51] 1397: 54 (DRMH 2, 25, 181); Fügedi, *The Elefánthy*, 58.
[52] Pesty-Magina, no. 293.
[53] MNL OL DL, 29706. See also Fügedi, *The Elefánthy*, 56, 153.
[54] See thus Ferencz Bethlenfalvi Balázsi and Nándor Szederkényi, eds., *Heves vármegye története*, 4 vols. (Heves, 1890–7), ii, 333.
[55] Trip., I. 78 [5] (DRMH 5, 156).

death of the father. The need to obtain the complete consent of relatives rendered this an undertaking that could never be concluded with complete certainty, notwithstanding the pressure that might be applied on them or the diligence of *loca credibilia* in hunting down lost relatives, interrogating clergymen in respect of marriages they had performed, and negotiating 'the most dangerous and hazardous roads' in pursuit of a deposition.[56] Although alienees were usually warranted by the alienor, often with the promise that if the alienation was contested, a property of the same value would be given in recompense, this was an uncertain instrument. Warrantors might fail to discharge their obligations or pass the duty on to whoever had warranted them when they had first acquired the property. Warrantying might thus involve protracted proceedings, with previous owners having to be chased up, who might be less than dutiful in responding to a court summons—particularly if they had acquired the land in the first place by unscrupulous means.[57] Some warranty clauses in charters thus contained a moral injunction, declaring that a subsequent failure to uphold the vendor's rights would amount to a breach of Christian faith.[58]

From the 1340s, however, we will find increasing reference in land sales to alienors giving a new type of surety, known as the *assumptio oneris*.[59] According to the terms of this clause, the alienor acknowledged that there might be relatives or unborn children who could object to the transaction, but he assumed their 'burdens and complaints' (*onera et gravamina*: the expression probably derives from a Hungarism, *tehérvállalás*), committing himself to repay the alienee out of his own wealth in the event of the transaction being voided.[60] This personal commitment was considered a more effective guarantee than a warranty. Frequently also, alienors not only promised to compensate the alienee in the event of the transaction's failure but also to pay a cash penalty in addition. The *vinculum* was normally set at the value of the nobleman's *homagium*, namely 200 florins, which was roughly the equivalent of 400 sheep or fifty peasant households.[61] Significantly, however, the *vinculum* was laid not only on the alienor but also on the kinsmen whose burdens he had assumed, even if they were not mentioned by name in the contract.

The import of the *assumptio oneris* was thus clear. By imposing a financial penalty for protesting the alienation of a property, the kinsmen were effectively barred from so doing, except in cases where they were severely prejudiced and thus the *vinculum* worth paying. Accordingly, much noble property was effectively lifted

[56] Martyn Rady, 'Warranty and Surety in Medieval Hungarian Land Law', *Journal of Legal History*, 23, no. 1 (2002), 23–36 (28). Kinsmen approving an alienation might thus note that their consent had not been obtained under duress. See MNL OL DL, 279535.

[57] Frigyes Pesty, *Krassó vármegye története*, 4 vols. (Budapest, 1883–4), iii, 136–51. See also Rady, 'Warranty and Surety', 25–6.

[58] Pesty-Magina, no. 175.

[59] For the *assumptio oneris*, see Rady, 'Warranty and Surety', 29–34; Béla Händel, 'A tehérvállalás középkori jogrendünkben', *Századok*, 78 (1944), 373–418. György Bónis's important study, 'Les sûrétés personnelles en Hongrie du XIIIe au XVIIIe siècle', *Recueils de la Société Jean Bodin pour l'histoire comparative des institutions*, 29 (1971), 725–65, does not discuss this clause.

[60] The *assumptio* formula was generally applied to sales; its use in pledges was less consistent.

[61] The value put on a peasant household, as the equivalent of eight sheep, is surely suggestive of just how little profit obtained from the peasant economy.

out of the constraints of *aviticitas* and rendered freely disposable. No longer was the agreement of relatives needed for land to be alienated. By the terms of the *assumptio oneris*, their consent was presumed and, were it to be subsequently denied, the *vinculum* became payable. By the fifteenth century, the legal conditions attending alienation had thus altered to the disadvantage of the kindred and in the direction of a free market in land. Although the constraints of *aviticitas* still held, a way had been found to evade them.

The significance of the *assumptio* clause was plainly apprehended by Werbőczy who accordingly devoted space to its discussion. His account is complicated and the distinctions that he makes are his own, unsupported in the legal records of the time. He starts off with a definition: '"Assuming the burdens" means to give an assurance that a father or kinsman's recognizance to a purchaser will be observed'.[62] Thereafter, he categorizes alienations made under the *assumptio* in three ways. First, alienations might be made *simpliciter*, 'not for reasonable cause [...] but out of ill will or gluttony (*gulose*) or even to do deliberate harm'. Secondly, they might be made for reasonable cause, to redeem *Morgengabe* or pay the daughters' quarter, or to make general improvements to the estate. Thirdly, they might be made out of extreme need, for instance to redeem a capital sentence or discharge a ransom. As Werbőczy explains, in the last of these cases, the *assumptio* should always stand and might not be reversed, even by the son deprived of his inheritance. In the first, where the *assumptio* was made *simpliciter*, it might immediately be revoked by the kinsmen and was considered to have no legal force. In the intermediate case, where the *assumptio* was made on reasonable grounds, it might still be revoked but only upon condition that the *homagium* was paid and the purchasers recompensed to the value of the property. We should note here that the usual *vinculum* specified was, as it turned out, responsive to inflation, rising to 1,000 florins in the eighteenth century.[63]

Werbőczy's account seemingly endorsed the *assumptio*, clarifying its use. Nevertheless, his account was not embraced in customary practice. First, Hungary's courts preferred to consider property matters passing before them according to the principle of *salvo iure alieno*, thus judging not by the test of reasonableness but on the basis of whether anyone's rights had been prejudiced.[64] In order that this be properly tested, it was generally required by the courts that proper notice of the alienation be given at an assembly of the county and thus relatives allowed an opportunity to protest it in advance.[65] Secondly, the circumstances under which an alienation might be lawfully made were limited in Werbőczy's account to the payment of the filial quarter, redemption of the *Morgengabe* or other pledges in land, and to transactions that benefited the estate: 'to create, if necessary, fishing ponds, build mills, houses and residences or to buy another and perhaps better

[62] Trip., I. 59 (DRMH 5, 129–31).
[63] RL, C/71 Sigray család levéltára, I–1f (1784).
[64] Rady, 'Warranty and Surety', 33.
[65] *Observationes in Tripartitum*, OSzK, MSS, Quart. Lat. 2378, fol. 27 (I. 59). The courts thus applied the terms of Trip., I. 60 to the *assumptio*.

estate for the price of the sold estates or portion, or to exchange estates'.[66] Apart from satisfying the claims of daughters and wives, in respect of which kinsmen had in any case a contingent liability, the use of the *assumptio* was thus principally confined to matters of estate improvement. After the sixteenth century, however, the economic management of properties fell increasingly within the purview of 'family conferences', the purpose of which was formally to reconcile the interests of kinsmen in matters where they had a concurrent legal interest, imposing on them (even in their absence) binding agreements that retained a fully legal character.[67] Although the *assumptio* continued to be used right through until the eighteenth century, its value thus declined, having been superseded by an alternative institutional remedy.[68]

* * *

Besides the *assumptio oneris*, there was a further device to which noblemen might have resort in order to avoid the constraints of *aviticitas*. This was the usurious contract, entered into with Jews. It is uncertain whether Werbőczy was even aware of the use to which this instrument was put. At several points in the *Tripartitum*, Werbőczy inveighs against usury, which he understood in its broadest sense, even to the extent of including the commercial gain made from land held in pledge. In the third part of the *Tripartitum*, he gives nonetheless the verbatim text of the oath that Jews should give in court, 'because it frequently happens that Jews are judged and required to swear [it] against Christians', which could only have arisen as a consequence of their usurious dealings with noblemen.[69] It should be noted here that there is little exceptional about the text that Werbőczy gives. Indeed, in the performance of the oath it was far less insulting to Jews than other rituals of oath-taking prevalent in Central Europe at the time.[70]

By the late fifteenth century, the financial operations of many Hungarian Jews were more akin to banking than to pawn-broking, particularly in the capital city, where there was a Jewish community of about 500 persons (roughly 5–10 per cent of the city's population).[71] The interest charges payable on loans were high—in the region of 35–50 per cent or more per annum—but mainly because the risks of default or of the debt's cancellation were so high.[72] Surviving accounts give the impression that most Jewish loans were made to townsfolk, either because they were more likely to need commercial capital or as a consequence of the towns

[66] Trip., I. 59 [3] (DRMH 5, 129).

[67] István Kállay, 'A családülés', *Levéltári Közlemények*, 43, no. 1 (1972), 3–32 (6, 24).

[68] OSzK, MSS, Fol. Lat. 4388, fol. 23 (*c.* 1750); RL, C/71 Sigray család levéltára, I–1f (1784).

[69] Trip., III. 36 (DRMH 5, 425).

[70] See 'Oath more judaico', in the 1906 *Jewish Encyclopedia* (internet version). For a contemporary Hungarian oath to be taken by Jews, see MZsO, v/1, 97. See also, Géza Komoróczy, ed., *Jewish Budapest* (Budapest, 1999), 21. The oath given in the *Tripartitum* seems modelled on the one laid down by Archbishop Conrad I of Mainz in the late twelfth century. See Péter Újvári, *Magyar zsidó lexikon* (Budapest, 1929), 962.

[71] László Zolnay, *Buda középkori zsidósága* (Budapest, 1968), 23.

[72] The Buda *Stadtrecht* of *c.* 1400 inveighed against usury, but reserved its penalty to the Day of Judgement. See Karl (Károly) Mollay, ed., *Das Ofner Stadtrecht. Eine deutschsprachige Rechtssammlung des 15. Jahrhunderts aus Ungarn* (Budapest, 1959), 126 (ch. 192).

themselves keeping better records. Nevertheless, there is evidence not only of nobles but also of peasants taking out loans from Jews.[73] The mechanisms by which debts were contracted demonstrate some sophistication. The terms of the debt were recorded in special letters of credit (*litterae obligatoriae*) that might be witnessed by the local town magistracy or by a place of authentication. These specified the interest on the loan and additional penalties for late repayment—often 'the duplication and reduplication' of the capital sum.[74] The debt itself might, however, be sold on, in the manner of a bill of exchange and was, in this sense, a negotiable instrument.[75] Upon repayment, the letters were cancelled. Although urban magistracies sometimes kept a record of the debts that individual citizens had incurred, there was no formal system of registration before the eighteenth century.[76]

Loans taken from Jews were invariably collateralized, either against movables, usually jewellery, or against landed property. Movables were usually lodged with the lender until such a time as the debt was discharged. Land, however, was not administered in the usual manner of a pledge, whereby the property was retained by the lender until the loan was repaid. It remained instead with the borrower, although the borrower might at the time of the contract be obliged to hand over to the lender his deeds to the land. Only in the event of the debt not being repaid or of the deadlines on instalments being missed was the land physically possessed by the lender.[77] In respect of land that was put up as collateral, the debt was thus secured in the manner of what might also be known as a *hypotheca* or mortgage loan, and not in the manner of a pledge.

There is nothing particularly exceptional about this arrangement. The *hypotheca* was a familiar institution in Roman Law and was commented upon by Azo, Accursius and Baldus.[78] It had, moreover, been in use in the Austrian lands since the thirteenth century, where it was generally known as the *jüngere Satzung* (to distinguish it from the *altere*, which was the loan raised on a pledge given in pawn).[79] Hungary is not supposed to have had the mortgage loan before the 1770s.[80] Plainly, however, it was familiar with this form of capital-raising by no later than the close of the Middle Ages and noblemen were ready to contract debts by mortgaging parts of their estate to Jews. It was, indeed, easy for them to do so; since they were not obviously surrendering the physical possession of the land at the time of the contract, they did not require the consent of their kinsmen in the manner of a sale or pledge. Should the land be forfeit on account of non-payment of the debt, the lender had the letters of credit with which to pursue his suit, and the courts

[73] MZsO, i, 132–3; MZsO, v/1, 59. [74] MZsO, i, 271; MZsO, v/1, 48–9, 118.

[75] MZsO, v/1, 67, 107.

[76] 1723: 107. The *Ofner Stadtrecht* laid down that all loans should be recorded on letters issued by the city magistracy (ch. 201). See Mollay, 129.

[77] MZsO, i, 264, 267; MZsO, v/1, 48–53, 87, 118; MZsO, ix, 71.

[78] Paul J. du Plessis, 'Towards the Medieval Law of Hypothec', in John W. Cairns and Paul J. du Plessis, eds., *The Creation of the Ius Commune: From Casus to Regula* (Edinburgh, 2010), 159–74 (165–72).

[79] Ursula Flossmann, *Österreichische Privatrechtsgeschichte*, 5th edition (Vienna, 2005), 173.

[80] See thus, János Botos, *Reformkori és 1848-as kisérlet földhitelintézet létrehozására* (Budapest, 1998), 10–11; Botos, *A magyarországi jelzálog-hitelezés másfél évszázada* (Budapest, 2002), 8.

generally regarded these as outweighing the rights of relatives. Nobles also sometimes included in letters of contract a statement of urgent need that might, as we have seen in respect of the *assumptio*, have the legal consequence of setting aside the usual norms in respect to the alienation of landed estate—*pro quibusdam suis et magnis et arduis necessitatibus*, and so on.[81] Should the courts be reluctant to enforce the terms of letters of credit, the king might intervene by instructing officials and magistrates to pursue the debt, and the collateral upon which it rested, on the lender's behalf.[82] Equally, however, the ruler often acted on behalf of noble and other debtors, obliging Jewish financiers to cancel interest payments or even to forego a portion of the capital sum originally lent.[83] Petitions to the ruler for cancellation were usually accompanied by a statement of distress or by a description of the way in which a small debt had escalated through interest and late-payment charges, from 25 to 250 florins and so on. The frequency, with which petitions of this type were approved by the ruler, sometimes expressly by way of his *plenitudo potestatis*, is demonstrated not only by the extant record but also by the inclusion in chancellery formularies of titles specifically dedicated to the royal *relaxatio usurae*.[84]

We can well understand Werbőczy's reluctance to discuss usurious relationships. However much they may have offended his moral sensitivities, they even more disturbed the order of noble property-holding in the Hungarian countryside. In much the same manner as the *assumptio oneris*, the mortgage tilted relations of property towards the alienability of land, to the disadvantage of the noble kindred. Whereas, however, Werbőczy had earlier sought to hem in the use of the *assumptio* with the test of reasonableness, in respect of the mortgage loan he said nothing at all, either because it was so repugnant to him or on account of his own ignorance of this type of commercial instrument. By saying nothing, however, Werbőczy left the mortgage loan in a legal void, which served to diminish its subsequent use. It continued thus to be relied upon in the cities as a means of obtaining commercial credit, but in the countryside fell into desuetude until its revival in the late eighteenth century.[85]

## GUARDIANSHIP AND WARDSHIP

Until the *Tripartitum*, there were no legal norms attaching to wardship, even though wardship had ever since the fourteenth century been overseen by Hungary's secular courts.[86] Generally, if the father died, the mother was presumed to fulfil the role of

[81] MZsO, v/1, 121. [82] MZsO, i, 148, 155–6, 212–14, 236, 321.

[83] MZsO, iv, 86. See also Újvári, *Magyar zsidó lexikon*, 693.

[84] MZsO, i, 173, 177, 194–5, 209, 267, 295, 321; MZsO, iv, 86; MZsO, v/1, 59, 87; MZsO, viii, 73. For formularies, see MZsO, v/1, 113, 129. See also, Komoróczy, *Jewish Budapest*, 13.

[85] György Bónis, *Buda és Pest bírósági gyakorlata a török kiűzése után 1686–1708* (Budapest, 1962), 207.

[86] Alajos Degré, *A magyar gyámsági jog kialakulása a dualizmus korának gyámsági kódexéig* (Budapest, 1977), 9.

guardian (*tutor*), for which reason widows generally acted on behalf of underage sons in respect both of their care and of legal actions.[87] As an alternative, fathers might assign guardians in advance of their death, in much the same way as they appointed *procuratores* from among their fellow noblemen to look after their legal interests when they were abroad.[88] Testamentary conveyances of guardianship carried, however, little legal weight and might be contested if there were male relatives who could discharge the duty. The king was by the fifteenth century regarded as the guardian-in-chief of all orphans, the earliest instance of this royal role being in 1377. His involvement was usually limited to issuing letters of protection, releasing wards from legal actions aimed against them, or to instructing officers of the county to desist from harrying them.[89] In towns, the council took over in this regard the role of the ruler, assigning guardians to wards in the absence of testamentary provision. Their role in this regard persisted into the nineteenth century.[90]

Where male relatives were, by will of the father or by appointment of the ruler, entrusted with guardianship, it was all too frequent for them to abuse their vocation, seizing the ward's property as their own, or alienating it, sometimes through use of the *assumptio oneris* formula.[91] Alternatively, they might retain the income of the estate as their own, neglecting the interests of the ward. Indeed, right through until the eighteenth century, guardianship was partly understood as an office that brought with it revenues, which might be bestowed by the ruler in the manner of a gift. The only right that belonged to the ward was to dismiss the guardian, but this could only be done upon their reaching the age of fourteen and even then might be contested by reference to the instructions of the deceased father. It was also impossible under these circumstances to sue for compensation for the property and revenues that had been squandered.[92] We should note that although guardianship normally came to an end at twelve years, it might be prolonged by the terms of the testament, or even at the request of the ward, for up to twelve more years.[93] In 1421, therefore, an orphan 'on account of his continued study of the liberal arts in various schools' appointed his uncle as his guardian, assigning him the income of his property in return for his uncle's protection of the estate.[94]

It was Werbőczy's achievement to give order to the system of guardianship in Hungary, employing a threefold classification. The scheme he followed, although rooted in Roman Law, was provided by Raymundus's *Summa Legum*, in respect of which there is an obvious textual link:

[87] ZsO, ix, nos. 18, 179, 189, 234, 238, 273, 326, 335, 463, 538, 738 etc.

[88] Rady, *Nobility, Land and Service*, 177.

[89] Gábor Béli, 'Degré Alajos és a régi gyámsági jog', in András Molnár, ed., *Levéltáros Elődeink. Degré Alajos és Szabó Béla munkassága* (Zalaegerszeg, 2006), 25–39 (31); ZsO, ix, no. 610.

[90] ZsO, xi, no. 431.

[91] Degré, *A magyar gyámsági jog kialakulása*, 8.

[92] Alajos Degré, *Feudális gyámsági jog Magyarországon. Kandidátusi Értekezés Tézisei* (Budapest, 1955), 6.

[93] Degré, *Feudális gyámsági jog*, 7.

[94] ZsO, viii, no. 1080.

> Ubi notandum quod triplex est tutela scilicet Legitima, Testamentaria & Dativa (Trip., I. 112 [2]).[95]
>
> Tria sunt genera tutorum, videlicet testamentarii, legitimi et dativa. (*Summa Legum*, 1. 34).[96]

Conceivably, and as has been argued, both the *Tripartitum* and the *Summa Legum* were borrowing here from the same civilian source.[97] In respect, however, of the excuses that guardians might make in order to avoid this duty and of the reasons for considering a potential guardian to be ineligible, the *Tripartitum* followed the *Summa Legum* verbatim, in respect not only of its vocabulary and phraseology but also of the ordering of its points.[98] Werbőczy's account, deriving from Raymundus's, thus contains not only a terminology that is unusual for him, for instance *capitalem inimicitiam* ('mortal enmity') and *curator*, a term not otherwise known at this time in Hungarian legal literature, but also illiteracy (*litterarum inscientiam*) as a reason for refusing guardianship—grounds that would have surely disqualified most of the Hungarian nobility.[99] Nevertheless, the *Tripartitum* interspersed the borrowed text with additional observations that interrupt and explicate its content. Moreover, Werbőczy's treatment of guardianship is substantially fuller than the account given in the *Summa Legum*, altogether ten times its length. Unlike, therefore, other parts of the *Tripartitum*, where Werbőczy copied the *Summa Legum* regardless of its applicability and to the confusion of his readers, in this portion of his text he uses the *Summa Legum* critically, amplifying its otherwise slender content.

Werbőczy followed Raymundus's scheme and vocabulary of statutory, testamentary and appointed or 'dative' guardianship. At the same time, however, he sought to marry these categories with the structure of noble inheritance, even to the extent of disregarding the rights that widows had hitherto enjoyed. As a consequence, the *Tripartitum* effectively wrote women out of the structure of guardianship unless they were possessed in their own right of hereditary property (presumably because they were the heirs of estate that was passed down through the female as well as the male line, that is by cognatic descent, or were in possession of an *allatura* or quarter in land). Hence: 'should the [orphaned] son have kinsmen, upon whom his paternal goods and rights should devolve and pass, then the guardianship and maintenance of these paternal goods shall be exercised not by the mother but by the kinsmen closest by birth'.[100]

Testamentary guardianship, by will of the deceased father, was also circumscribed, being allowed only when the testator knew his closest kinsman to be an inappropriate guardian and, even then, paradoxically, the appointment might be

[95] DRMH 5, 194.

[96] Alexander Gál, ed., *Die Summa Legum brevis levis et utilis*, 2 vols. (Weimar, 1926), i, 195. See further, Ádám Tóth, 'A gyámság intézménye a római jogban és Werbőczy', in Gábor Hamza, ed., *Tanulmányok Werbőczy Istvánról* (Budapest, 2001), 153–65 (161).

[97] Discussed in Béli, 'Degré Alajos és a régi gyámsági jog', 32–7.

[98] Cf. Trip., I. 101–2 (DRMH 5, 105–7) and Gál, *Summa Legum*, I, 198–200.

[99] Trip., I. 122 [5–6], and Trip., 124 [3] (DRMH 5, 204, 207). Werbőczy's assertion that poverty might also be a disqualification for guardianship further indicates his immediate debt to the *Summa Legum* rather than to other civilian sources. See Degré, *A magyar gyámsági jog*, 15.

[100] Trip., I. 113 [5] (DRMH 5, 195).

overturned by the objections of his widow and kinsmen.[101] Providing, however, that no objections were sustained, so Werbőczy averred, testamentary guardianship generally trumped statutory.[102] In respect of the third mode of guardianship, by appointment of the ruler, this only occurred when there were no kinsmen and no testamentary guardian had been appointed.[103] The *Tripartitum* also required that guardians appointed by the ruler render to the county magistrates full accounts in respect of the property of wards, but this practice was not normal until the eighteenth century and, even then, was seldom enforced.[104]

The largest portion of Werbőczy's account is, however, devoted to statutory guardianship, in particular to the identity of those who should normally act as guardians when there was no testamentary provision. His premise is that in cases where no suitable guardians had been previously assigned, 'the office of guardianship passes and devolves to the deceased person's brothers and kinsmen who would inherit his goods were he to die in default of heirs.' Thus the father's kinsmen took precedence over the mother's since they were the ones who had claim to the estate. In cases, however, where the mother had land of her own, then the selection of the guardian might be made from either group of kinsmen. The choice should nevertheless pay heed to maturity and so the eldest member of the two groups should be appointed to the guardianship. Nevertheless, the guardian so appointed should be taken from among those 'closer and nearer to the orphans in the line of consanguinity', thus preserving the connection between guardianship and inheritance.[105] We can imagine only with difficulty circumstances in which the oldest and closest kinsman would not also be the next in line of inheritance, so in this respect Werbőczy's scheme might be said to work.

Werbőczy's account benefited the land of the kindred rather than the orphan. The closest in line to the orphan was less likely to destroy his ward's inheritance since the property might in time revert to him and his heirs. Consanguinity was hardly a bar, however, to the plundering of revenues, which remained a frequent complaint of heirs right through to the nineteenth century.[106] Certainly, in amplifying the *Summa Legum* Werbőczy did not fail to mention the various grounds for disqualifying a guardian, either before or after he had assumed office (dishonesty, plunder, maltreatment, immorality and so on). By removing, however, the rights of statutory guardianship from widows, Werbőczy left the ward exposed to the depredations of his kinsmen, thus exacerbating their plight. In this respect, Werbőczy's interest in advancing the rights of the kindred and in entrenching *aviticitas* comported with the self-interest of noble guardians.

Notwithstanding its inventiveness, Werbőczy's account was taken up in actual practice and his threefold categorization of guardianship was subsequently accepted as normative.[107] So also was his stress on consanguinity and statutory guardianship,

[101] Trip., I. 114 (DRMH 5, 197).
[102] Trip., I. 119 (DRMH 5, 201).
[103] Trip., I.115 (DRMH 5, 197).
[104] Degré, *Feudális gyámsági jog*, 11–13.
[105] Trip., I.117 [3] (DRMH 5, 201).
[106] Degré, *A magyar gyámsági jog kialakulása*, 21.
[107] Gusztáv Wenzel, *Visszapillantás az előbbi magyar királyi curiának 1724–1769-iki működésére* (Budapest, 1875), 93.

even though it worked to the disadvantage of wards, who had in the past been legally sheltered by their widowed mothers. The increased use of testamentary provision, which only became common from the end of the sixteenth century, went some way towards restoring the practice of female guardianship, although the appointment of widows might be contested by the ward's male kinsmen.[108] In similar fashion, Werbőczy's introduction of the term of *curator* subsequently passed into lay use, as a way of describing a someone who had been granted power of attorney on account of the legal incompetence or physical absence of another, who was of full age.[109]

## THE PEASANTRY

The *Tripartitum* was presented to the diet in the immediate wake of the Peasants Revolt of 1514 and it includes in both its first and third parts reference to the legislation passed by the diet in the wake of its suppression, which clamped down on the free movement of peasants, tying them to the land. The 1514 diet thus put an end to the complex arrangements of licensing the movement of tenants between lords as well as closing off emigration to the growing market towns and the centres of the Hungarian cattle trade.[110] The laws of 1514 also enacted a list of additional obligations on the peasantry, ranging from compulsory labour services of a day per week and an annual *census* of one florin, to charges on produce and a periodic levy of chickens, geese, and pigs. Most notoriously, the diet specified the collective fate that now befell the peasantry on account of their faithlessness, coupling this to the restrictions now imposed on their movement:

> In memory of this betrayal of theirs and in order that their present punishment should extend and be transmitted to their descendants and that it be known for all time what an enormous sin it is to rebel against the lords, all peasants living anywhere in this country [...] shall henceforth because of this taint of infidelity of theirs lose their liberty that allowed them to move from one place to another, and they shall be subject to the lords of the land in full and perpetual *rusticitas*, nor in future may they have the right to move from one place to another to settle there without the will and agreement of their lords.[111]

We will hunt in vain, however, for any definition of *rusticitas* or of 'perpetual' for these were not legal terms but literary ones. Their origin goes back to the thirteenth-century *Gesta Hungarorum* that described how the ancient Scythians

108 Gábor Béli, *Magyar jogtörténet. A tradicionális jog* (Budapest and Pécs, 2009), 63.

109 OSzK, MSS, Fol. Lat. 1852, fol. 45 (1650–60).

110 László Makkai, *Agrarian Landscapes of Historical Hungary in Feudal Times* (Budapest, 1980), 12. On the continued (and unexpected) development of some Hungarian towns in the sixteenth century, see Jaroslav Miller, *Urban Societies in East-Central Europe, 1500–1700* (Aldershot and Burlington, VT, 2008), 20–2; Balázs A. Szelényi, 'The Dynamics of Urban Development: Towns in Sixteenth and Seventeenth-Century Hungary', *The American Historical Review*, 109, no. 2 (2004), 360–86 (379, 382–4).

111 1514: 14 (DRMH 4, 184–5).

had condemned to common servitude (*in communium servitutem*) those who failed to attend the meetings of the community, and this account was retained in the royal chronicles of the fourteenth century.[112] In Thuróczy's *Gesta*, published in 1488, however, 'servitude' was augmented by *perpetuam rusticitatem*.[113] The law of 1514 clearly borrowed from this source, picking up its terminology and applying it in a new context. Werbőczy's own account demonstrates the sleight that has taken place. In the third part of the *Tripartitum*, Werbőczy thus recalls that the peasants had lost on account of their rebellion their *libertas* 'to betake themselves from their place of residence as and when they wanted' and were as a consequence now subject to their lords in 'full and perpetual *rusticitas*'.[114] In the first part of the *Tripartitum*, however, where he discusses ancient Hungarian and Hunnish history, Werbőczy anticipates this later description, anchoring it in its literary background. Borrowing from Thuróczy, he explains that it was their failure to attend the ancient communal gathering that had resulted in many Huns being reduced to 'perpetual rusticity' (*perpetuam rusticitatem*), a term which he alternated with 'common and perpetual servitude (*communem & perpetuam in servitutem*)'.[115] He then went on to explain the origin of the estate of peasants, again following Thuróczy:

> This sanction is said to have reduced great numbers of Hungarians to the status of common people. Otherwise it could not have happened that one of them became a lord and the other a servant, one a noble and the other ignoble and a peasant (*ignobilis et rusticus*), since they are all descended from one and the same lineage, that is from Hunor and Magor.[116]

In this way, Werbőczy amplified the meaning of the legislation of 1514, explaining its metaphorical content by reference to an ancient division within the Hungarian people that had been confirmed and renewed as a consequence of the peasants' insurrection. For his description of 'perpetual rusticity' Werbőczy has of course been roundly condemned, even though he was later to advise that free movement be restored to the kingdom's peasantry.[117]

With the exceptions of *rusticitas* and the abolition of free movement, Werbőczy disregarded the substance of the laws passed in 1514. Labour services, fixed in 1514 at one day per week, are thus passed over in silence, not to mention the

[112] László Veszprémy and Frank Schaer, eds., *Simonis de Kéza Gesta Hungarorum* (Budapest and New York, 1999), 30–1 (ch. 7); Imre Szentpétery, *Scriptores Rerum Hungaricarum*, 2 vols. (Budapest, 1937), i, 257.

[113] Johannes de Thurocz, *Chronica Hungarorum. Textus*, eds. Erzsébet Galántai and Gyula Kristó (Budapest, 1985), 34 (ch. 12).

[114] Trip., III. 25 [2] (DRMH 5, 405).

[115] Trip., I. 3 [2–5] (DRMH 5, 48–51).

[116] Trip., I. 3 [5] (DRMH 5, 50–1). Hunor and Magor were the putative progenitors of the Hungarians. Their names respectively conceal Hungarian and Magyar.

[117] See thus Endre Ady's poem, 'Új törvényt, Werbőczi', given in *Társadalmi Szemle*, 7 (1952), 1293; Gyula Szekfű, in Bálint Hóman and Szekfű, *Magyar történet*, 3rd edition, 5 vols. (Budapest, 1935–6), ii, 587, 591, and most accounts composed under the communists—thus, for instance, György Bónis, 'Men Learned in the Law in Medieval Hungary', *East Central Europe/L'Europe du centre-est*, 4, no. 2 (1977), 181–91 (191). For Werbőczy's subsequent advice, see István Csekey, *Werbőczy és a magyar alkotmányjog*, Acta Juridico-Politica 2 (Cluj, 1942), 20; Ferenc Kubinyi, 'János király budai országgyűlése az 1530-ik év végén', *Századok*, 10 (1876), 581–3 (582–3).

chicken, geese, and bacon that should now periodically furnish the nobleman's table. Most strikingly, Werbőczy overlooked the requirement of 'the ninth', which was the tithe payable to the lord (thus constituting the 'ninth tenth', which was due after the tenth or tithe had been paid to the church), even though it had long been a source of contention among the nobility, with some landlords choosing by way of enticement not to levy it, to the *grande preiudicium et desolacionem possessionum* of their fellows.[118] Instead, Werbőczy gives some general rules of procedure to be followed in the event of disputes conjointly involving noblemen and peasants, and a short account of the rules of inheritance and guardianship as they touched upon peasant tenancies. Incredibly, he suggests that sons and unmarried daughters should succeed equally to the plot as well as to the movables of a dead father.[119] Although causing difficulties for historians, this does not seem to have been the custom either at the time Werbőczy was writing or subsequently.[120] Peasant rules of inheritance were, however, notably diverse, with some communities favouring the partition of the plot among the sons and others practising parental disposition, primogeniture or even the allocation of the holding by lot.[121]

Werbőczy's reluctance to treat in any detail upon the laws and customs of the peasantry is explained during the course of his discussion in the third part. In a remark that hardly squared with his account of Hungary's peasants descending from the fallen sons of Hunor and Magor, he noted that their condition was *multiplex*, for some were Germans, and others Czechs, Serbs, Romanians or Bulgarians, both Catholics and Orthodox.[122] Returning to this point a few chapters later, he observes that, just as the condition of the kingdom's peasants was *multiplex* (the same adjective is used), 'so are the legal customs that have to be kept according to the ancient usage of the place'.[123] Werbőczy's explanation that the laws and customs of the peasantry were so varied that they might not be described normatively is, however, disingenuous, for the condition and obligations of the peasantry had been supposedly standardized in the legislation of 1514. It was not, however, in Werbőczy's interest to disclose the gulf between legislative provision and practice, for such might expose the extent to which statute was ignored in everyday observance. Indeed, it was at this time in the interests of the nobility that peasant obligations not be fastened too tightly.

Peasant justice was largely overseen by village courts, which adjudicated lesser crimes, mostly of the type that led to public shaming, and minor disputes over property. The competence of the village court partly depended upon the powers

118 MNL OL DL, 38106. See thus István Szabó, *Jobbágyok–Parasztok* (Budapest, 1976), 152–6. The distinction between 'ninth' and 'tenth' was misunderstood even by those who had to pay it. See Péter Takács and István Udvari, *Szlovák nyelvű paraszti vallomások Mária Terézia korából* (Nyiregyháza, 1992), 60, 73.

119 Trip., III. 29 (DRMH 5, 417).

120 István Kállay, *Úriszéki bíráskodás a xviii–xix. században* (Budapest, 1985), 413, 430–2; Endre Varga, *Úriszék. xvi–xvii. századi perszövegek* (Budapest, 1958), 789–90, 1023.

121 Ernő Tárkány Szűcs, 'Öröklési jogi szokások', in *Magyar Néprajzi Lexikon*, 5 vols. (Budapest, 1977–82), iv, 134.

122 Trip., III. 25 [1] (DRMH 5, 404–5).

123 Trip., III. 30 [6] (DRMH 5, 418–19).

which the landlord chose to delegate to it.[124] Matters of weight were usually heard by manor courts, but contentious business might be referred to the magistrates of the county for adjudication. Most litigation, however, got no further than the landlord's court, where it was judged by the lord's appointee, in the company of village elders, local dignitaries and representatives of the county administration. Disputes were handled by negotiation, according to what seemed the most appropriate solutions at the time. In their litigation, however, peasants tended to follow the procedural norms adopted among the nobility, making *prohibitiones* before the village or landlord's court, being introduced to their plots in formal acts of *statutio*, giving warranties on conveyances, and so on. In similar fashion, the substantive law of the peasantry recognized a distinction between inherited and acquired land, making the first inalienable (although recognizing the landlord's ultimate right of ownership), and it adopted the terminology of female rights to land that were current among the nobility—*paraphernales* (movables given at marriage), *allatura*, the daughters' quarter and the *Morgengabe*.[125] As a consequence, peasant justice obtained a relatively high degree of sophistication, in terms both of the content of the law and of its administration, increasingly mimicking the customary practices of the nobility.

Despite Werbőczy's demonstration that cases might be moved from manor courts to the county and thence to the courts of the Curia, the jurisdiction that landlords exercised over their peasant tenants was understood in terms of a private right that followed from the nobleman's possession of the land. In most cases, this included the right to adjudicate serious crimes, although it was only a minority of lords that had the right to impose the death penalty. Nevertheless, landlords were reluctant to cede oversight of their courts to representatives of the county administration, preferring instead to dispense an independent and unsupervised justice. It was their conviction that their jurisdictional rights over the peasantry were complete, notwithstanding previous legislation that had served to limit their authority.[126] By the seventeenth century, and probably before, cases that we might otherwise have expected to pass before the manor court were regularly taken up instead by appointees of the lord, most usually his estate managers or overseers. These met in closed session, often using village headmen to gather evidence and hold inquests on the basis of whose testimony they arrived at a collective judgment on the landlord's behalf.[127] The jurisdiction of estate managers persisted into the twentieth

124 György Komoróczy, *Helytörténeti források 1848-ig* (Debrecen, 1972), 352–3.

125 Kállay, *Úriszéki bíráskodás*, 328–40, 383, 388–99. See also Alajos Degré, 'Elemente des römischen Rechtes im Vermögensrecht der ungarischen Leibeigenen', in György Antalffy, ed., *Einzelne Probleme der Rechtsgeschichte und des römischen Rechts*, Acta Juridica et Politica, 17 (Szeged, 1970), 27–35 (31–2).

126 The view was accordingly put to the Staatsrat by Egidius Borié in 1761 that the rights of Hungarian noblemen had long been constrained by legislation and thus could not be considered private. See Győző Ember, 'Mária Terézia urbérrendezés és az államtanács', *A Gróf Klebelsberg Kunó Magyar Történetkutató Intézet Évkönyve*, 5 (1935), 103–49 (117); also, Dezső Szabó, *A magyarországi úrbérrendezés története Mária Terézia korában* (Budapest, 1933), 7–8.

127 István Kállay, *Management of Big Estates in Hungary between 1711 and 1848* (Budapest, 1980), 18–20.

century, although it was by this time confined to peasants who worked as indentured labourers on the lord's home farm.[128]

In much the same fashion, noblemen regarded the dues and services that the peasants owed to them as an extension of their private property, to be allocated and apportioned as they deemed fit. In support of their rights, they looked towards the *Tripartitum* and the privilege it afforded the nobility that they might 'freely use and enjoy as they will their just rights and all revenues within the boundaries of their estates at all times'.[129] Clearly, however, it was not in the interest of landlords to squeeze their tenants, demanding the full range of payments and services to which they were entitled. Notwithstanding the provisions of 1514, peasants might still flee the estate, often with the connivance of neighbouring proprietors who had empty plots to fill. Indeed, this sort of competition for peasants forced in 1547 repeal of the prohibition on their movement. Individual counties, however, enacted bans of their own—Uzh County in 1555, Zala in 1558, and so on—and their right to legislate in this matter was recognized in 1608.[130] Even so, most landlords did not at this time demand labour services, except at harvest time, and in most places they did not exact the ninth. Other dues were often commuted to lump sum payments, payable by the individual peasant or the community as a whole. Surveys of the obligations laid on the peasants in individual lordships from the sixteenth and early seventeenth centuries thus frequently include such remarks as 'they pay no census,' 'they give no *muneralia*,' (i.e. pigs and fowl) 'they do no service but pay instead 40 florins collectively,' 'they should harvest two days a year, gather and transport hay,' and so on.[131] In the majority of cases, however, commitments of this type were not specified in writing but were agreed orally. When after 1767, therefore, commissars appointed by the Queen Empress toured the Hungarian countryside to establish the obligations that were laid on peasant communities they most commonly reported that no written evidence of these could be found.[132]

By not rehearsing the legislation of 1514 in all its details, Werbőczy permitted landlords to negotiate separate arrangements with their peasants. Werbőczy's

[128] Gyula Illyés, *People of the Puszta*, trans. G.F. Cushing, 2nd edition (Budapest, 1979), 122–38, first published in Hungarian in 1936.

[129] Trip., I. 9 [5] (DRMH 5, 57). See also Ember, 'Mária Terézia urbérrendezés és az államtanács', 115.

[130] *Corp. Stat.*, ii/1, 1; 1608 (*post. cor.*): 13; Mária Homoki-Nagy, 'A szabad költözködési jog biztositása Magyarországon', *Tanulmányok Dr Veres József 70. születésnapjára*, Acta Juridica et Politica 55 (Szeged, 1999), 122–31 (123–6).

[131] Ferenc Maksay, *Urbáriumok. XVI.–XVII. század* (Budapest, 1959), 133, 244–5, 251–2, 254, 281–2, 405, 787.

[132] Peasant responses to the commissars' nine-point questionnaire are available in Péter Takács and István Udvari, *Szlovák nyelvű paraszti vallomások Mária Terézia korából* (Nyiregyháza, 1992); Péter Takács and István Udvari, *Zemplén megyei jobbágy-vallomások az úrbérrendezés korából*, 2 vols. (Nyiregyháza, 1995–6); Péter Tóth and József Tirnitz, *A Mária-Terézia úrbérendezés kilenc kerdőpontos vizsgálatai Sopron vármegyében–Antworten auf die Neun Fragepunkte der Maria Theresianischen Urburialregulierung im Komitat Sopron*, 2 vols. (Sopron, 1998–9); Zita Horváth, *Paraszti vallomások Zalában*, 2 vols. (Zalaegerszeg, 2001–6). See in particular the responses to Question One ('Does this place currently have an *urbarium*?') and Question Seven ('Do the inhabitants here pay the ninth to their landlord?').

approach certainly benefited the peasantry for much of the sixteenth century, sparing them the full rigour of the laws enacted in the wake of the peasant uprising. By the same token, however, the sparseness of his account later permitted landlords to increase the burdens falling on the peasantry, particularly in respect of compulsory labour services. From the end of the sixteenth century, landlords expanded their home farms to take advantage of the rise in agricultural prices.[133] In so doing, they increasingly relied upon the corvée as a means of estate cultivation, with the consequence that in some places services eventually exceeded the one day per week specified in the laws of 1514.[134] Indeed, by the mid-eighteenth century, it was reckoned that a return to the provisions of 1514 would actually serve to lighten the load imposed upon the peasantry.[135] Only in the last decades of the eighteenth century were the rights and duties of the Hungarian peasantry formally specified in a way that lent them an enduring legal character. Even so large areas (relating in particular to vineyards, cleared land and common pastures) continued to be defined by reference to local agreements and practices.[136]

* * *

The structure of rights belonging to the nobility has been described as Werbőczian and as 'his system'.[137] It was to the extent that the *Tripartitum* lent some coherence to what was otherwise a kaleidoscope of changing principles and divergent practices. Werbőczy was the political spokesman of the kingdom's common noblemen and as a lawyer he looked towards their interests. *Aviticitas* benefited them, for it gave them the greatest chance of augmenting their land through their kinsfolk's adversity. Larger landowners had less need for windfalls. Their concern lay instead with preserving the integrity of their estates against partition between heirs, which might over time diminish their families' status and political influence. From the second half of the seventeenth century, therefore, the greatest noble houses sought to convert their possessions into trusts that were indivisible. Since the establishment of trusts was a right that belonged to the crown, there developed over time a branch of chancellery jurisprudence that elaborated how such trusts should be formed and administered. Over time, the chancellery developed its own set of customary practices, which differed from those observed in the kingdom's courts.[138] Nevertheless, the majority of Hungarian noblemen eschewed land trusts, looking instead to *aviticitas* as the best guarantee of their material prosperity.

133 Maksay, *Urbáriumok*, 20, 29–33, 47.

134 R.W.B. Gray, *Land Reform and the Hungarian Peasantry c. 1700–1848*, unpublished PhD thesis (University College London, 2009), 78–9, 89–90; Eva H. Balázs, Lilla Krász and György Kurucz, *Hétköznapi élet a Habsburgok korában 1740–1815* (Budapest, 2007), 146–7.

135 Ember, 'Mária Terézia urbérrendezés és az államtanács', 118.

136 Robert W. Gray, 'Bringing the Law Back In: Land, Law and the Hungarian Peasantry before 1848', SEER, 91, no. 3 (2013), 511–34 (523–7).

137 See thus Erik Fügedi, *The Elefánthy: The Hungarian Nobleman and his Kindred* (Budapest, 1998), 20.

138 These partly derived from Philipp Knipschildt, *De fidei commissis familiarum nobilium*, first published in Strasbourg in 1626 (with twelve subsequent editions). See also Mór Katona, *A magyar családi hitbizomány* (Budapest, 1894), 23.

Werbőczy twisted his account of property holding in the direction of inalienability. He endeavoured, therefore, to hem in practices that worked towards the dissolution of estates or that might have served to restrict the concurrent legal rights of kinsmen. He thus skirted over the cession of the daughters' quarter in land. Likewise, he hemmed in the use of the *assumptio* and he either did not know or did not care to know of usurious contracts. Unlike, however, his invention of a new order of guardianship that worked in kinsmen's favour, his schematization of the *assumptio* was not embraced in practice. In respect of the peasantry, he said strikingly little, even though their condition had been extensively addressed in the most recent legislation. By not repeating the harsh regime outlined in the statute of 1514 and retreating into rhetorical generalities, he left the way open for noblemen to administer their tenants in the way that best suited their economic needs. Nevertheless, at the heart of the structure of rights that Werbőczy proposed stood the crime that he had invented: the betrayal of a kinsman (*proditio sanguinis*), which was 'the deceitful, sly and fraudulent deprivation or disinheritance of a brother or sister from their lawful rights by their brother or sister'.[139] Although never becoming a part of the kingdom's law, the *proditio* stood as Werbőczy's metaphor for *aviticitas* as not only a network of legal relations but also as a moral principle governing noble conduct. By giving *aviticitas* an ethical underpinning in this way, Werbőczy contributed to its continued salience until the nineteenth century as the most important aspect of noble landholding in Hungary.

[139] Trip., I. 34 (DRMH 5, 105).

# 7

# Crime and Prosecution

## CRIMINAL CASES

Werbőczy devotes little space to criminal justice. Where he does treat upon the subject, it is almost entirely with respect to the implications of crime for the nobleman's estate and, in particular, to the modes of compensation and of redemption. Werbőczy's reticence may be explained in several ways. First, the civilian tradition was not much concerned with criminal actions, these being confined to just a few books of Justinian's *Digest* or considered mostly from the point of view of procedure, as in Durandus's *Speculum judiciale*.[1] Secondly, Werbőczy himself was a judge trained in the Curia courts, which dealt mostly with actions over land rather than matters of crime. Even where cases involving egregious violence came before the Curia courts, they were mainly understood and treated as suits over property, for land was invariably at the heart of the case and the confiscation of land was the usual consequence of a guilty verdict. Werbőczy's account is, however, not only unsatisfactorily brief but also misleading. At the time he was writing, the criminal law in Hungary was being recast, with the manner of its prosecution changing. By not discussing the criminal law in any detail, Werbőczy left the way open for its subsequent development and, as it turned out, for the enlargement of 'public power' in the legal process.

The laws of the eleventh century had made theft, murder, robbery, violent entry and rape punishable by death, the codes of St Ladislas being particularly bloody. Throughout the Middle Ages and, indeed, subsequently, crimes of violence attracted the death penalty. These were commonly defined as 'acts of might', *actus potentiae* or simply *potentia*, although their definition was uncertain and a distinction was later made between 'minor' and 'major' infringements. Generally, the category of major crimes included the invasion of homes, the beating, wounding or killing of noblemen, the theft of charters, plunder, arson, the violation of virgins and matrons, and so on.[2] Werbőczy himself defined the more serious acts of might as 'the breaking into houses of nobles without just cause, the seizing of their estates and the appurtenances thereof, the arrest of nobles without just cause, or the beating, wounding or slaying of nobles'.[3] In fact, however, and as Werbőczy's

[1] Peter Stein, *Roman Law in European History* (Cambridge, 1999), 58–9, 106.

[2] 8 March 1435: 3 (DRMH 2, 65); 1462: 1 (DRMH 3, 15); 1486: 15 (DRMH 3, 48); for minor, see 1439: 32 (DRMH 2, 86).

[3] Trip., II. 67 [9] (DRMH 5, 333). See also Trip., II. 42 [5], II. 67 (DRMH 5, 301, 331).

account makes clear, the harsh penalties laid down for even egregious crimes of violence were by the time he was writing seldom, if ever, enforced.

Even as late as the thirteenth century, we will find noblemen and others being executed, usually then by hanging, upon their conviction for murder or robbery, or occasionally disfigured through the slicing of the nose.[4] Clearly, the notion that there was a public interest in crime and its punishment was no less present in Hungary than elsewhere.[5] In practice, however, most acts of violence carried no penalty, providing an agreement between the parties was obtained. Thus, for instance, the kidnapping of a villager's wife, together with the seizure of his goods, was settled in 1213 between the adversaries, without the exaction of any penalty.[6] In the same year, a charge of robbery and assault was dropped by the plaintiff in return for a cash consideration, on condition that if the sum be not paid then the matter would be referred to the royal court. The terms of the agreement suggest that the justice of the king's court was only sought in cases where the private negotiation of differences had failed.[7]

As these examples (and many others) suggest, recourse to the judgment of courts was very much a last resort, with matters otherwise being resolved by arbitration and agreed compensation. Indeed, even after the case had been opened in court, it remained possible to proceed to arbitration, with the court often pressing the parties to come to a settlement. In 1327, for instance, the nobleman Thomas complained to the high judge that his kinsman, Andrew, had broken into his estate, said shameful words to one of his peasants, and wounded a woman. Andrew denied the charge and was accordingly required to purge himself with twenty-five noble compurgators before the Vác chapter. He failed to attend the oath-taking, on the basis of which his guilt was presumed. Andrew was duly sentenced to death and the confiscation of his estate ordered, in letters drawn up by the court. In view of their blood relationship, however, the court recommended that the two parties meet and come to terms, which they did. Andrew accordingly assigned to Thomas's son and nephew a portion of his property and the letters previously issued authorizing his punishment were cancelled.[8] In similar fashion, a case of murder coming in the same year before the high judge, which was to have been resolved by champions, was at the last moment settled by the parties in exchange for cash compensation.[9]

[4] AUO, i, 168–9; AUO, vii, 77–8, 100–2, 351–2, 484–5; AUO, xi, 105–8. See also Tomáš Gábriš, *Maintaining Peace and Justice in Árpádian Hungary: Punishment and Settlement of Disputes*, MA thesis (Central European University, Dept of Medieval Studies, 2007) (online CEU eTD Collection), 21–2, 26–7.

[5] Susan Reynolds, *Kingdoms and Communities in Western Europe, 900–1300*, 2nd edition (Oxford, 1997), 21.

[6] János Karácsonyi and Samu Borovszky, eds., *Regestrum Varadiniense Ordine Chronologico Digestum* (Budapest, 1903), 160.

[7] Karácsonyi and Borovszky, *Regestrum Varadiniense*, 158.

[8] Gyula Kristó, László Blazovich, Tibor Almási et al., *Anjou-kori oklevéltár*, 31 vols. (in progress) (Budapest and Szeged, 1990–2007), xi, nos. 114, 176.

[9] *Anjou-kori oklevéltár*, xi, nos. 309, 313. For further examples, see Karácsonyi and Borovszky, *Regestrum Varadiniense*, 160, 179, 184–5, 205–6, 222, 286–7, 305 etc. See also Gábriš, *Maintaining Peace and Justice in Árpádian Hungary*, 61–74.

In the second of these cases, compensation was determined by reference to the *homagium* or man price. As Werbőczy later took pains to explain, the *homagium* was not a wergild, but was instead the price of the guilty man's head, 'for the dead cannot at any price be redeemed and raised from the dead'.[10] (It should be noted that at one place Werbőczy himself falls into the same error of which he accuses others, namely imagining the *homagium* to be based on the victim's worth.)[11] The *homagium* itself was a product of the fourteenth century, and may be related to the *succubitus duelli*, which was the payment made by the loser of a judicial combat in order to save his life.[12] *Homagium* and *succubitus* are often conflated in contemporary accounts.[13] The *homagium* as the value of a man varied according to status, with the *homagium* of a baron or prelate put at 400 florins, the man price of a nobleman and burgher at 200 florins, and a peasant's head at only a few score.[14] The *homagium* was not, however, an upper limit in respect of compensation, but the starting point, for major crimes of violence might be deemed to merit the additional confiscation of goods, including the guilty man's entire property.

The idea that violence constituted a wrong that might be settled by compensation partly had its origins in procedure. When matters involving violence came before the courts, they were handled in the manner of private suits launched by one party against another.[15] The process followed was largely identical. The action was commenced by the plaintiff, with the court gathering information and proof through an inquest, ordeal, purgation and compurgation, and on the basis of the evidence deciding whether compensation should be paid. The principal exceptions were crimes of violence perpetrated by 'public malefactors' who, by refusing to submit to arbitration or to judgment of the courts, were often outlawed, or cases where a party acted in contempt of the court's ruling or through forged letters.[16] We should at this point note that the distinction between a civil suit and an action for affray was uncertain in later medieval Hungary. Hungarian procedural law permitted ritualized violence as a means of introducing stages in actions over property, most notably in respect of the *repulsio* or armed obstruction of a bailiff seeking execution of a court order, and of the right of forcible *reoccupatio* of an estate unjustly seized. Additionally, symbolic acts of physical force might serve to speed

10 Trip., III. 5 [3] (DRMH 5, 385). 11 Trip., II. 35 [1] (DRMH 5, 295).

12 József Gerics, 'Árpád-kori jogintézmények és terminológia törvényhozásunk egyik keltezetlen emlékében', in Gerics, *Egyház, állam és gondolkodás Magyarországon a középkorban* (Budapest, 1995), 248–74 (265). Also published in *Századok*, 103 (1969), 611–40.

13 Martyn Rady, 'Warranty and Surety in Medieval Hungarian Land Law', *Journal of Legal History*, 23, no. 1 (2002), 23–36 (31).

14 Trip., I. 2 [2]; III. 9; III, 26 [16] (DRMH 5, 49, 389, 411). By the eighteenth century, if not before, the courts were flexible in their estimation, reducing the *homagium* for minor offences. See RL, C/67, Sárközy család levéltára, Bundle 2, no. 42.

15 There is nothing unusual in this. See Jeremy Hayhoe, *Enlightened Feudalism: Seigneurial Justice and Village Society in Eighteenth-Century Northern Burgundy* (Rochester, NY, 2008), 62.

16 Thus a case of 1299, when for forgery and violent occupation the culprits were condemned to be burnt, *iuxta statuta Regni* (although we know of no statute to this effect!): AUO, v, 239. See also AUO, i, 168–9.

an action through the courts, moving them higher up the order of hearing and obviating procedural delays.[17]

Beyond this, however, negotiation was a recourse that was specifically urged in the kingdom's laws. Louis I's legislation of 1351 is emphatic in this respect. A nobleman condemned to death for a major crime should thus be held by the judge for three days, during which period peace should be obtained with the plaintiff. If a deal could not be struck between the two, then the guilty man should be handed over to his adversary, who might accordingly kill him. Should he do so, however, that was the end of the matter and the plaintiff could expect no compensation. The sons and relatives of the dead man might keep the property due to them, safe and undisturbed. Should, however, the culprit refuse to come to terms with his victim, he might expect his whole property to be seized.[18] There was thus a clear incentive for both wrongdoers and victims to come to terms, on the one hand to avoid death or the complete loss of goods, on the other to ensure that at least some compensation was received. The laws of Sigismund might well pronounce that 'the ancient and laudable custom of our realm prescribes and allows a settlement to be freely made in all cases of violence' but procedures and penalties pointed all the same in the direction of compromise.[19]

## PERFIDY (*NOTA INFIDELITATIS*)

The crimes described under the heading of *nota infidelitatis* were broader than treason, which is how it is sometimes translated.[20] Certainly, the *nota* included crimes against the royal person, as well as offences against the body politic and thus what might be understood as *Landesverrat*.[21] The *nota*, however, also extended to crimes that were thought to be especially repugnant and not just those involving accroachment on the commonwealth or the king's majesty. For this reason, we will use in place of treason the terms 'perfidy' and 'perfidious', which avoid the implication of an offence exclusively directed against king or country, while preserving the idea that the crime involved in some way a breach of *fides*. We regard this as more satisfactory than retaining the original Latin term, if only because the *nota* was not technically the crime, but the blemish that attached to the criminal on account of his misdeed.

The list of perfidious offences, first compiled in 1462, was long: rebellion; forgery; counterfeiting; arson; murdering a kinsman or spouse; pillage; disregarding

[17] Martyn Rady, 'Justice Delayed? Litigation and Dispute Settlement in Fifteenth-Century Hungary', *Central Europe*, 2, no. 1 (2004), 3–14 (10–13). Available in Hungarian as Rady, 'Késedelmes igazságszolgáltatás? Pereskedés és perlezárás a 15. századi Magyarországon', *Aetas*, (2008, no. 1), 167–77.

[18] Imre Hajnik, *A magyar birósági szervezet és perjog az Árpád- és a vegyes-házi királyok alatt* (Budapest, 1899), 390.

[19] 8 March 1435: 4 (DRMH 2, 65).

[20] As in DRMH 1–3, subsequently adjusted. See DRMH 4, 333.

[21] For *Landesverrat*, see J.G. Bellamy, *The Law of Treason in England in the Later Middle Ages* (Cambridge, 1970), 5.

letters of judgment; killing a judge or a litigant in the courtroom; betraying a castle; heresy and incest.[22] The 1462 list was republished in 1495, with one minor addition, and Werbőczy follows this, overlooking other offences which had been pronounced as perfidious in intervening legislation.[23] Even disregarding these later laws, the schedule was clearly unstable, with some offences, such as the illegal occupation of royal land, losing over time their perfidious character and others, such as forgery and the violation of a stepmother, acquiring it.[24]

Political considerations also served to amplify the law of perfidy, with Hungary's rulers often using accusations of faithlessness as a way of disadvantaging malcontents, of forcing political compliance, or of sequestrating property. Ladislas V thus proposed to indict John Hunyadi posthumously (!) on grounds of thwarting royal policy, probably with a view to capturing the huge Hunyadi patrimony.[25] Werbőczy himself was charged with perfidy for holding an illegal diet and usurping the office of palatine, neither of which had been previously listed as perfidious offences (although conceivably they might have been considered acts *contra statum publicum, regis & corone*).[26] Likewise, in the most notorious of Rudolf II's 'fiscal trials', the aim of which was to seize for the crown the assets of those declared guilty of perfidy, István Illésházy was originally condemned on account of his questioning the royal right of urban incorporation, an action deemed to infringe the royal *Macht, Jus und Autorität*.[27] In all three examples, not only were the charges politically motivated, but they also lacked substance in statute law. Acts were described as perfidious on grounds of expediency, according to the royal will.

Not only was the list of perfidious crimes uncertain but also their penalty, the manner of their pardon, and the procedures to be followed in respect of their prosecution. Werbőczy attempted to give order to these arrangements, but his ingenuity resulted in compromises that deviated from actual practice. First, he attempted to bring the law of perfidy into line with procedures followed in respect of crimes of violence. Accordingly, he averred that should the supreme penalty be imposed for perfidy, the king might not seize the lands of the slain man: 'By capital sentence, however, the ownership and right of inheritance of goods and property rights is not lost, but if a condemned person has suffered the ultimate sanction by sentence, then all his goods and property rights devolve directly upon his sons (if he has any) or closer kinsman or other lawful successors.'[28] In fact, there is plenty of evidence

22 1462: 2 (DRMH 3, 16, 89).

23 1495: 4. See thus 1498: 18, 19, 32, 72 (DRMH 4, 57, 99, 111, 133–5). The performance of two *repulsiones* as grounds for perfidy is given in 1504: 4 (DRMH 4, 165). It is not included in Werbőczy's main list, given in Trip., I. 14 (DRMH 5, 67–9), but is discussed in Trip., II. 75 (DRMH 5, 349–51).

24 *Anjou-kori oklevéltár*, xxiv, no. 407; AUO, i, 221; Alexander Húščava, *Ján Literát a liptovské falzá* (Bratislava, 1936) (with German summary), 181. For the violation of stepmothers, I am indebted to Dr Christopher Nicholson, 'Writing the Law in Bohemia and Hungary in the Later Middle Ages', unpublished conference paper, Leeds International Medieval Congress, July 2012.

25 Henrik Marczali, 'Záh Felicián pöre', *Budapesti Szemle*, 100, no. 276 (1899), 379–90.

26 István Horvát, *Verbötzi István emlékezete*, ii (Pest, 1819), 242–50; Trip., I. 14 [2] (DRMH 5, 66–7).

27 Árpád Károlyi, *Illésházy István hűtlenségi pöre* (Budapest, 1883), 39.

28 Trip., I. 16 [3] (DRMH 5, 71).

to suggest that those guilty of perfidy were apt to lose both their heads and their lands.[29] Secondly, perfidy might *in extremis* be understood to implicate not only the perfidious man but also his whole family. The example of Felicián Záh, whose attempted murder of Charles Robert and of the royal family in 1330 resulted in the extirpation of his entire kindred, was recalled in the chronicle literature and yielded a precedent that was to be later deployed by Ladislas V against Hunyadi's sons.[30] Werbőczy includes oblique reference to the notion of blood guilt in his account of how the royal pardon for perfidy restored the pardoned man to his estate but still served to disinherit his kindred and heirs, although his proposition has no support in the extant sources.[31]

The charge of perfidy was one of the most effective weapons in the royal arsenal. It was often used to satisfy wider opinion or as a signal that a political actor had stepped out of line. Pardon might thus speedily follow conviction or, indeed, be intimated in the original sentence of condemnation. When Werbőczy was charged with perfidy, his lands were ordered to be confiscated, with the concession by the king's grace that the rights of his wife and children were unaffected, which effectively meant that much of the estate remained intact.[32] Plainly, a deal was expected. Likewise, although the property of perfidious men was usually grabbed quickly, for the most part they went into a not very distant exile, where they waited upon events. Sentenced upon demand of the diet to death and confiscation of goods for their part in the loss of Belgrade in 1521, Bálint Török and Francis Héderváry moved to the court of John Zápolya in Transylvania in the expectation of a royal pardon. They were not to be disappointed.[33]

The advantage to the king of the charge of perfidy was that it was extra-judicial and thus did not depend upon the uncertainty of the legal process. Upon denunciation or mere *fama*, the king in concert with the royal council published an *edictum* that declared the nobleman guilty.[34] Immediately, his estates were either sequestrated by the crown or given away by royal donation. The perfidious man was usually allowed the right to come before the council to explain himself. More usually, however, he launched a legal action either against the new possessor or

[29] AO, ii, 280–4; Húščava, *Ján Literát*, 184; György Székely, 'Hunyadi László kivégzése', *Jogtörténeti Szemle*, (1986, no. 1), 33–43 (40). Following the revolt of the Transylvanian voivodes in 1467, those not pardoned by Matthias lost both their lives and their possessions. I am grateful for this information to András W. Kovács.

[30] Marczali, 'Záh Felicián pöre', 379. For Záh, see also Tibor Almási, 'Záh Felicián ítéletlevele', *Aetas*, (2000 nos. 1–2), 191–7; M.G. Kovachich, *Supplementum ad Vestigia Comitiorum*, 3 vols. (Buda, 1798–1801), i, 268–75.

[31] Trip., I. 16 (DRMH 5, 69–71).

[32] Horvát, *Verbötzi István emlékezete*, ii, 249–50 (*iuribus uxorum et liberorum eorundem ex speciali gratia Regia salvis remanentibus*).

[33] Béla Radvánszky and Levente Závodszky, eds., *A Héderváry család oklevéltár*, 2 vols. (Budapest, 1909–22), ii, lii–v; József Bessenyei, *Enyingi Török Bálint* (Budapest, 1994), viii. See also 1521: 40 (DRMH 4, 253).

[34] AO, ii, 281; Gusztáv Wenzel, 'A Hédervári Ferenc jószágai fölötti per és itélet 1523-ban', *Magyar Történelmi Tár* (1859), 1–80 (78); Dani Králik, 'A királyi kincstár képviselője a perben', in *Emlékkönyv Grosschmid Béni* (Budapest, 1912), 223–57 (237). Similar procedures applied in England until their abolition by Henry VIII. See Kenneth Minogue, 'Treason and the Early Modern State', in Roman Schur, ed., *Die Rolle der Juristen bei der Entstehung des modernen Staates* (Berlin, 1986), 420–35 (427).

against the king, proceeding through the court of the palatine. He was entitled, moreover, to refuse entry to his estate until such a time as the matter was resolved in law, although in the case of scattered estates this recourse often only saved a part of the property. In the meantime, his wife, relatives and neighbours might launch separate actions of their own, claiming a share of the estate as dower or as their own property, previously given in pledge to the condemned man. Adjudication of the condemned man's guilt thus took place in the context of the legal actions launched in defence of the estate. Normally, the courts were satisfied if it could be shown that proper procedures had been followed, although investigation might disclose that the alleged offence had been invented, in which case a pardon might follow.[35]

During the 1490s, the diet claimed the right to pronounce sentences of perfidy in place of the council.[36] Although acknowledged by the ruler, the diet's right of attaint was only occasionally allowed, normally when it suited the royal purpose. The diet was too uncertain an instrument and, as later occasions made clear, it could use the opportunity to embarrass the ruler, either by indicting royal officers or (as was feared might happen with Illésházy) by forcing charges to be dropped.[37] Werbőczy recognized the role of the diet in regard to pronouncing upon perfidy, and the arrangement of his text certainly suggests that this was the usual procedural manner. Nevertheless, he also acknowledged the persistence of the older procedural form whereby perfidy was established, 'by the judicial decision and sentence passed by justices ordinary of the realm, *arising from and following a royal donation* made to any person on the grounds of [...] such acts that bring about the taint of infidelity'.[38]

In a notorious case arising just two years after publication of the *Tripartitum*, the procedure described by Werbőczy was followed exactly. In this example, the Lady Benigna had recently arranged the murder of her third husband, Gregory Kereky, upon word of which the royal council ordered the confiscation of her estate, for the killing of a spouse fell within the law of perfidy.[39] Benigna had already given over her main property to the voivode, so the bailiffs had to be content with the outlying estates. Benigna then sued for their recovery through an attorney, avoiding her own attendance at court on grounds of ill health. The matter came before the council, with the king's procurator (*director causarum regiarum*) urging that Benigna's absence was tantamount to an admission of guilt, for the palatine himself was sick but could still manage to travel to Buda! Unconvinced by this argument, the council remitted the case to the palatine's court, which was the usual forum for cases wherein the king was an interested party. The palatine judged Benigna guilty of perfidy and thus the confiscation to have been legal. As it turned out, however,

35 ZsO, iii, nos. 1033, 1248; Pesty-Magina, no. 90.

36 See thus 1495: 3, which reversed 1492: 13 (DRMH 4, 9, 57). See also Martyn Rady, 'Jagiello Hungary', in DRMH 4, p. xxxvi.

37 Károlyi, *Illésházy István hűtlenségi pöre*, 50–5; *Monumenta Comitialia*, vii, 344; *Acta Comitialia Hungarica Soproniensia 1681*, pamphlet (no place of publication, no date), 204.

38 Trip., II. 75 [4] (DRMH 5, 349). My italics.

39 For an analogous case of the murder of a husband being considered, along with incest, as perfidious, see HO, vii, 455–6.

the king pardoned Benigna shortly afterwards and she seemingly regained full possession of her property.[40]

* * *

It is precisely because of the procedural ambiguities attending the law of perfidy that we should regard it from the point of view of the growth of the idea of the state. Whereas crimes of violence were still considered after the manner of private litigation, perfidy was held to be an offence that could be neither negotiated nor redeemed. It demanded the loss of the condemned man's head and lands, even though in practice the supreme penalty was seldom invoked and a pardon often obtained. Moreover, the manner in which perfidy was proclaimed and property confiscated did not follow the ordinary practices of the courts, but proceeded by way of decree, through the edict of the royal council or by the decision of the diet. Only subsequently might the courts be involved, in determining whether a case had been properly made to allow the confiscation of goods. The growing number of offences included within the law of perfidy additionally points to the expansion of what was understood to be public power, which now captured a greater role in the adjudication of crime. It is in this respect that the law of perfidy touches directly upon the growth of the office of public prosecutor and upon the development of inquisitorial practice in Hungary.[41]

## PUBLIC PROSECUTION AND WITCHCRAFT

Kings had in the past been party to legal actions, usually in matters affecting the monarch's private estates. In the thirteenth and fourteenth centuries, the ruler was in such cases represented on an ad hoc basis by *speciales notarii*. In the 1380s, a greater stability arose in respect of the royal representative with the appointment of a *procurator causarum domini regis* or, as he was later known, the *director (et procurator) causarum Suae Majestatis* (or *regiarum*).[42] The task of the royal director was to uphold the royal interest, particularly in matters where the fisc might be involved. We will thus find individual *directores* at county and other assemblies, chasing up the fate of royal properties or, more unusually, acting on behalf of orphans and others over whom the king had a special responsibility.[43] In view of his association with the royal financial interest, the director was by the sixteenth century also

[40] Gábor Döbrentei, *Régi magyar nyelvemlékek*, 5 vols. (Buda and Budapest, 1838–88), ii, pp. vi–vii; Sándor Lázs, 'Kinizsiné Magyar Benigna könyveinek sorsa', *Magyar Könyvszemle*, 126, no. 1 (2010), 100–2; Králik, 'A királyi kincstár képviselője a perben', 237–8. The relevant part of the council's discussion is also given in Géza Szendrei, ed., *Emlékképek az ugyészség történetéből* (Budapest, 1996), 69–78.

[41] László Kosztolányi, 'Az első magyar ügyészi szervezeti törvény állam- és jogtörténeti előzményei európai kitekintésben', in Géza Szendrei, ed., *Emlékképek az ugyészség történetéből* (Budapest, 1996), 5–45 (8).

[42] László Nánási, 'Ügyészek a rendi Magyarországon', *Jogtörténeti Szemle*, (2009, no. 3), 34–41 (35); also *diffinitor causarum regiarum*, ZsO, ix, no. 740. See also, György Bónis, *A jogtudó értelmiség a Mohács előtti Magyarországon* (Budapest, 1971), 131.

[43] ZsO, ii/1, no. 7725; ZsO, ix, nos. 1153, 740; ZsO, xi, nos. 1288, 1304, 1332, 1348, 1489.

known as the *fiscalis* of the crown and he would indeed later become the legal administrator of the royal treasury (although technically falling under the authority of the palatine).[44]

Of particular interest to the *fiscalis* were crimes of perfidy, precisely because they yielded a windfall to the treasury in the form of confiscated property. Accordingly, the *fiscalis* increasingly assumed the function of a public prosecutor, gathering the evidence of crime or of an estate being owed to the crown for any other reason. He might thus instruct inquests, gather testimony and authorize arrests for purposes of interrogation.[45] The evidence so gathered would then be put before the court or council, forming the basis of the indictment. When procedural difficulties arose, he might be expected to intervene in order to rescue the crown's case, as he sought to do in the case of the Lady Benigna by disparaging her excuse of ill health. The powers of the royal *fiscalis* were such that even as early as the 1430s there were attempts to hem him in, by in particular refusing him both a seat among the court's judges and the opportunity to scrutinize the paperwork produced in the course of litigation.[46] Perhaps not surprisingly, one *fiscalis* was on the eve of Mohács described as 'the most litigious and argumentative man of his time'.[47] Nevertheless, the emergence of the office of the *fiscalis* is testimony to the interrelationship of the crime of perfidy with the developing notion of public prosecution.

Although Werbőczy fleetingly acknowledged a distinction between civil and criminal cases, he does not discuss the role of public prosecution.[48] His understanding of court procedure was rooted in adversarial practice, on account of which he portrays the royal director as only the king's surrogate in cases moved against the ruler.[49] Notwithstanding Werbőczy's silence, public prosecution gathered ground, being adopted by degrees in the counties. During the 1540s, county magistrates took the lead in launching plaints on behalf of the county, particularly in respect of local malefactors. By the beginning of the seventeenth century, most counties had their own *fiscales* who took over the role of prosecution from the magistrates. The authority belonging to county *fiscales* extended by degrees to all manner of crime, including moral offences, as well as to representing the county in matters wherein it also was a party. Royal instructions enlarged the scope of the new class of public prosecutors by making them responsible for protecting the peasantry against unjust burdens. Thus, over time the Hungarian *fiscalis* might be celebrated as 'the guardian of the laws, of lawful customs, and of the rights of the estates and the avenger of the harmed'. In similar fashion, manor courts appointed during the seventeenth century their own prosecutors, usually trained lawyers, who prepared indictments against wrongdoers and represented the lordship in matters coming before the county.[50] The development

44 Nánási, 'Ügyészek a rendi Magyarországon', 35–7. The origin of the term *fiscalis* bears some comparison with its Scottish counterpart. See Henry H. Brown, 'Evolution of the Procurator-Fiscal', *Scottish Review*, 34 (July 1899), 101–10.

45 Nánási, 'Ügyészek a rendi Magyarországon', 37.

46 1439: 23 (DRMH 2, 84).

47 Ferenc Zay, *Az Lándorfejirvár elveszésének oka e vót, es igy esött*, ed. István Kovács (Budapest, 1980), 15.

48 Trip., III. 11 [7–8] (DRMH 5, 393).

49 Trip., II. 39 (DRMH 5, 297–9).

50 Nánási, 'Ügyészek a rendi Magyarországon', 37–8.

of public prosecution made possible the application of torture, which was otherwise inconceivable when suits were moved as private actions. Nevertheless, a large body of offences continued to be prosecuted by litigants. Even though an ostensibly 'public crime', such as robbery or assault might be involved, the victim pursued his case as a private litigant, with the *fiscalis* only being involved in respect of the execution of sentence. Such prosecutions remained commonplace until the nineteenth century.[51]

We may certainly regard public prosecution as a cumulative development that spilled over from royal practice to affect Hungary's courts more generally. The adoption by counties, cities and lordships of the term of *fiscalis* indicates as much. Nevertheless, the process of institutional adoption was hastened by the identification of new types of offence that required special methods in their prosecution. Already in the fifteenth century, cities of the kingdom had begun to expand the ambit of public prosecution to include a range of moral crimes—bad language, dicing, adultery, prognostication and so on.[52] The 'citified' theology of Protestantism enlarged the notion that certain activities offended the sacral community.[53] Essentially victimless, and thus not easily comprehended within an adversarial framework, begging, promiscuity and gossiping were henceforth prosecuted by indictment of the authorities. There was, however, one crime in particular that obliged a major alteration in the way that crime was managed. This was the crime of witchcraft.

Before the first decades of the sixteenth century, cases of witchcraft had been treated relatively lightly by the courts, often only incurring compensation for damages. Subsequently, however, penalties became more severe, sometimes as a consequence of the pressure exerted on courts by pressure from below. In an illustration of this trend, in 1528 two women found guilty of sorcery by the city magistracy of Sopron were freed on payment of a fine, much to the dissatisfaction of the citizens. Plainly responding to popular discontent, the magistracy adopted a tougher approach, the next year passing the death sentence on a conjuror, after which it treated all cases of witchcraft as capital offences.[54]

Like perfidy, witchcraft was considered an exceptional crime.[55] Irregular procedures were adopted in its prosecution, most notably indictment by denunciation, while torture and special tests were routinely employed in its investigation. From the sixteenth century, the only penalty upon conviction was death, without possibility of extenuation. In respect of witchcraft, Hungary was not particularly crazed. In the 250 years preceding formal abolition of the crime in 1768, altogether fewer

[51] István Kállay, *A magyarországi nagybirtok kormányzata 1711–1848* (Budapest, 1980), 262–3.

[52] See thus Karl (Károly) Mollay, ed., *Das Ofner Stadtrecht. Eine deutschsprachige Rechtssammlung des 15. Jahrhunderts aus Ungarn* (Budapest, 1959), 126, 155–6, 169, 173 (ch. 190, 288, 290, 331, 345).

[53] Steven Ozment, *The Reformation in the Cities: The Appeal of Protestantism to Sixteenth-Century Germany and Switzerland* (New Haven and London, 1975), 6–7.

[54] Ildikó Németh, 'Boszorkányperek Sopronban', *Rubicon* (2012, no. 1), 39.

[55] On the relationship of treason to witchcraft more generally, see Christoph Gerst, *Hexenverfolgung als juristischer Prozess. Das Fürstentum Braunschweig-Wolfenbüttel im 17. Jahrhundert* (Göttingen, 2012), 38–9.

than about 1,600 cases came before the courts, only a third of which resulted in the death penalty.[56] Even so, the crime of witchcraft served to influence the manner of prosecution in Hungary's lower courts, enhancing the role of the public prosecutor. Right through until the eighteenth century, accusations of witchcraft were often made by a plaintiff, in the manner of a private suit, sometimes in the context of damages suffered as a consequence of spells.[57] Thereafter, however, and unlike most other cases pursued as a 'private wrong', the case was normally taken over by the local magistracy, which either assumed the role of the plaintiff or appointed a special prosecutor to conduct the action. What had originally been a private plaint was thus converted into a public prosecution. In place of the original petitioner, there now stepped in the *magistratus et actor* or the *dominus judex veluti magistratus*, or, if a special prosecutor was appointed, the *fiscalis* (alternatively, *actor director* or *ordinarius*).[58]

Once appointed, the prosecutor was responsible for the case against the accused. The action thus proceeded to court with the charge laid in his name—hence, *Levata causa magistratus ut actoris*, *Causa fisci levata*, and so on.[59] The prosecutor assembled the evidence, the witnesses thus being summoned on his behalf, and at his request the accused might be subjected to torture or the water test. Although torture and the test required the consent of the court, their outcome provided part of the evidence on which the prosecutor subsequently relied. If the evidence that he gathered proved insufficient or compromised, the prosecutor might abandon the case.[60] In the event of the case being brought to a conclusion, the court weighed the case and declared on the guilt of the accused. The accused might, however, be tortured again prior to execution, either to set an example or with the aim of extracting the names of accomplices.

* * *

During the sixteenth and seventeenth centuries, prosecutors took on an increasing share of the tasks that had hitherto been considered from the point of view of private litigation, launching actions against malefactors that had hitherto been brought by their victims. Once the principle of public prosecution was established in practice, it became over time applied to a wide range of misdeeds that had hitherto been considered private wrongs, negotiable between the parties.[61] These were accordingly redefined as criminal cases and adjudicated at separate

[56] Ferenc Schram, *Magyarországi boszorkányperek 1529–1768*, 3 vols. (Budapest, 1970–82), iii, 91. A higher figure of 2147 cases, involving 3866 persons, is given by Péter G. Tóth, 'Bűbajosok és boszorkányok a bíróságon', *Rubicon* (2012, no. 1), 32–8 (33). More generally on Hungarian witches, see Éva Pócs, *Between the Living and the Dead: Perspectives on Witches and Seers in the Early Modern Age* (Budapest, 1999).

[57] Andor Komáromy, *Magyarországi boszorkányperek oklevéltára* (Budapest, 1910), 1–6, 101, 105–8, 270, 617.

[58] Komáromy, *Magyarországi boszorkányperek*, 75, 83, 88, 89, 91, 101, 103, 116–17, 260, 263, 278 etc.

[59] Komáromy, *Magyarországi boszorkányperek*, 274, 278, 282, 284–5.

[60] Komáromy, *Magyarországi boszorkányperek*, 104.

[61] See thus, László Pakó, 'The Inquisitors in the Judicial Practice of Cluj at the end of the sixteenth century', *Transylvanian Review*, 21, Supplement no. 2 (2012), 181–97 (188–92).

court sessions.[62] Accordingly, the older view preserved in the *Tripartitum*, that crimes of violence might be resolved by negotiation without recourse to the courts, was replaced by the belief that infractions had a public character. In respect of the criminal law, the *Tripartitum* was thus by degrees superseded by the extravagant penal codes borrowed from the German lands, which by their comprehensive character and emphasis on punishment further extended the public power that the courts now administered.[63]

[62] Gábor Béli, 'Strafrechtspraxis und Strafrechtswissenschaft in Ungarn im 18. Jh.', in Barna Mezey, ed., *Strafrechtsgeschichte an der Grenze des nächsten Jahrtausendes* (Budapest, 2003), 110–21 (110).
[63] Béli, 'Strafrechtspraxis und Strafrechtswissenschaft', 113–14.

# 8

# Medieval Procedure and Judicial Decision Making

## SOURCES OF PROCEDURAL LAW

Werbőczy's account of Hungarian judicial procedure is all that remains from the Middle Ages on this subject. There is little, however, that is exceptional in his description. Notwithstanding the minor variations that arose out of the operation or *stylus curiae* of Hungary's courts, Hungarian procedural law broadly conformed to the *ordo iudiciarius* followed throughout most of Western Christendom.[1] Much of the activity of the courts involved the gathering of proof, not only by the examination of charters but also by inquests and oaths. A large part of court business was thus performed at a distance, out in the countryside where the inquests and oath takings were held, with the paperwork being sent back to the court. Because the courts assembled only periodically—usually in the weeks following the octaves of St George's, St James's, Epiphany and Michaelmas—cases were regularly held over from one session to the next, in between which the next tranche of documents was gathered.[2] Most cases were accordingly 'protracted', proceeding episodically from one octave to the next, and often taking a year or more to come to conclusion. Thereafter, however, they might be reheard, for the retrial was built into the practice of Hungary's courts as the principal remedy in law.

Because of its chronological treatment of the stages of an action, the description given in the *Tripartitum* resembles at first glance any one of the many *ordines judiciarii* that were published in Europe as guides to procedure in ecclesiastical courts. Whereas, however, the *ordines judiciarii* usually aimed at a comprehensive review of procedures, Werbőczy's account is selective and it leaves out large chunks of the judicial process.[3] Instead, therefore, of taking us through the various stages of an action, Werbőczy moves briskly from the summons to the proof, and thence to the judgment and remedies. Although there are indications in the text with respect to the procedures to be followed in the courtroom, these are not discussed by

[1] See thus R.H. Helmholz, *The Canon Law and Ecclesiastical Jurisdiction from 597 to the 1640s* (*Oxford History of the Laws of England*, 1) (Oxford, 2004), 313.

[2] For the meaning and use of the octaves, see Márta Kondor, 'A királyi kúria biróságaitól a kancelláriáig. A központi kormányzat és adminisztrácio Zsigmond-kori történetéhez', *Századok*, 142 (2008), 403–36 (411–14).

[3] For the *ordines*, see A.-M. Stickler, 'Ordines judiciarii', in *Dictionnaire de droit canonique*, 7 vols. (Paris 1924–65), vi, cols. 1132–43; Helmholz, *The Canon Law and Ecclesiastical Jurisdiction*, 312–13.

Werbőczy in any detail but are only alluded to. Moreover, unlike later commentators, Werbőczy discusses neither the personnel who might be present in court, nor even which of the several courts in the Curia were the most appropriate for specific types of action. Elsewhere, as for instance in his discussion of inquests, Werbőczy presumes his audience to be familiar with the institutions which he describes.

The explanation for Werbőczy's abbreviated treatment of procedure lies in respect of his audience. From the fourteenth century onwards, legal actions in the Curia courts were not only determined for the most part by written instruments but also mainly conducted by attorneys acting on behalf of the individual litigants. The attorneys attended court furnished with letters of authority from a place of authentication that gave them full power to act on their clients' behalf. Although most lawyers were locally recruited by their clients, litigants in a hurry might enlist the jobbing attorneys who, as we know from later evidence, busied around the doors of courtrooms.[4] Accordingly, there was no need for the parties to attend court at all, and there was certainly no compulsion, not even in respect of the most serious charges.[5] In many cases, the whole business might even be wrapped up in discussions in the inn between the lawyers and the protonotaries who were handling the case.[6] (On the whole, however, parties in joint-actions usually appointed one of their number to attend court, the remainder being represented by their attorneys.) Under these circumstances, Werbőczy evidently saw little point in discussing procedural matters which would normally be handled on a nobleman's behalf by his agents. Instead, he confined his account to what he regarded as the most important parts of the action where the noble litigant was most likely to be directly involved. Indeed, towards the end of his account, Werbőczy provided his noble audience with a 'check list', itemizing those matters which should be attended to in order to prevent a suit from failing.[7] In short, Werbőczy's account is addressed to noblemen who are presumed to understand the broad outlines and vocabulary of procedure, and not to the attorneys who managed their suits.

In order, thus, to reconstruct Hungarian procedure as followed in the early years of the sixteenth century, we must look beyond Werbőczy's account. Fortunately, there are other sources on which we may rely, most notably formularies and the various types of record issued during the course and at the conclusion of cases passing through the courts. Although the *litterae judiciales* and *sententionales* issued by the courts are themselves terse and abbreviated, the *signaturae* or notes that are often entered on the dorse of charters yield important clues with regard to the

[4] MNL OL, N 105, *Deputatio Regnicolaris in Juridicis*, Lad. MMM, fasc. 5, fol. 180. These would obtain their letters from the Curia. See Joannes Kitonich, *Directio Methodica Processus Judiciarii Juris Consuetudinarii inclyti regni Hungariae* (Trnava, 1619), Book 10, ch. 26. Given on page 494 of the 2004 Zagreb edition, edited by Branko Smerdel, and published by the Law Faculty of Zagreb University. We henceforth rely on this edition.

[5] 1500: 13 [3] (DRMH 4, 147).

[6] See thus 1486: 20 (DRMH 3, 50); 1492: 69 (DRMH 4, 33); Kitonich, *Directio Methodica*, 4. 2, 8. 9 (2004 edition, 108, 314). See also Imre Hajnik, *A magyar bírósági szervezet és perjog az Árpád- és a vegyes-házi királyok alatt,* (Budapest, 1899), 229–30.

[7] Trip., II. 82 (DRMH 5, 361–5).

stages of an action.[8] We may also work backwards from later records and court manuals which survive in large quantities from the seventeenth and eighteenth centuries, as well as from the mid-sixteenth century *Quadripartitum*, which was originally intended to replace the *Tripartitum*. A particularly valuable source for procedural law is the extensive handbook published in 1619 by János (Ivan) Kosztaniczai Kitonich, the *Directio methodica processus judiciarii Juris consuetudinarii Inclyti Regni Hungariae*, which was subsequently incorporated in an amended form in the fourth edition of the *Corpus Juris Hungarici* (1742–51).[9]

## THE SUMMONS

Despite the range of material on which we may rely, the precise method of commencing a suit is seldom elaborated in the extant record. Even Kitonich is no help here. The surviving charters imply that the action was begun by verbal petition to the ruler or to one of his principal judges: hence the formulae in letters introducing an action, *exponitur nobis* [i.e: *regi, iudici*], *expositum est nobis, dicitur nobis,* and so on. In view of the importance attaching to the written record, it is implausible that most petitions brought before the central courts of the realm were delivered orally.[10] It seems more likely that plaints were made in the form of what would later be called a *Klageschrift* or *libellus*, drawn up by an attorney. The attorney put his client's oral statement into writing, identifying the substantive issues on which the court should rule and which the action turned. In subsequent practice, the *libellus* was as its name suggests 'a little book', being a folio folded lengthways, on the first side of which was written the names of the plaintiff and defendant, the charge, the circumstances of the dispute, as well as any relevant dates and places. Indeed, the earliest extant Hungarian case file, dating from 1588, refers unmistakably to information, now lost, which had been previously entered *in papiro in modum libelli.*[11] We will, moreover, occasionally find the *libellus* appearing in the text of the *Tripartitum* under quite different names: most notably as the *actio, declaratio actionis, series actionis* or *acquisitio* (although these terms are not consistently applied).[12]

Once received and read by the protonotaries of the Curia, the petition was recast in the fashion of a letter of summons, to which the protonotaries appended the

[8] MNL OL DL, 63239; MNL OL DL, 20424; MNL OL DL, 20425; MNL OL DL, 27322; MNL OL DL, 10008, fol. 18.

[9] For Kitonich, see Valentin Putanec, 'Kajkavski pisac Ivan Pergošić kao Varaždinac', *Varaždinski Zbornik* (1983), 333–7 (I am grateful to Nataša Štefanec for giving me a copy of this article); Gusztáv Wenzel, *Tanulmányok a magyar jogtudomány köréből. Kitonich János 'Directio Methodica Processus Judiciarii Juris Consuetudinarii inclyti regni Hungariae' czimű munkájának jogtudományi méltatására* (Pest, 1851); Wenzel, 'Kitonich János xvii. századi magyar jogtudósról és munkáiról', *Új Magyar Múzeum*, 2, no. 2 (1851–2), 14–37.

[10] Kovachich, *Formulae Solennes Styli* (Pest, 1799), 166. See also Martyn Rady, 'Hungarian Procedural Law and Part Two of the *Tripartitum*', in CLCE, 47–70 (55); Alajos Degré, *A Négyeskönyv perjogi anyaga* (Budapest, 1935), 119–21.

[11] MNL OL, O 1, *Processus octavales*, Bundle 4, no. 183.

[12] Trip., II. 26; II. 82 [1] and [4] (DRMH 5, 281, 361).

judge's seal. At this point, the *libellus* had served its function, which doubtless explains why they are frequently missing from later case files. The *libellus* was certainly not passed on to the defendant. Instead, the defendant responded to the information and charges that were communicated to him in the letter of summons. Accordingly, when the suit eventually came to court, the charges and circumstances laid in the letter of summons provided the substance of the claim. They could not be emended or added to without the case collapsing.[13]

The importance attaching to the summons explains Werbőczy's insistent advice that it must be drawn up carefully.[14] If composed ambiguously, then it could all too easily result in the action being lost. Indeed, in order to ensure that the right vocabulary and information were included, one mid-sixteenth century Transylvanian formulary gave for the benefit of clerks no less than 34 different versions of a summons—summons by reason of the non-fulfilment of an obligation, summons on account of the kidnapping of a nobleman, summons for beating a royal bailiff, and so on.[15] Moreover, the plaintiff had to take care that all the respondents named were legally capable, for a summons addressed to a dead man, minor or lunatic misjoined the action and might have the result of rendering it void.[16] The letter of summons did more, however, than just give notice to the respondent that a suit had being brought against him. It also determined the speed with which the case would be heard for it laid down when the matter in hand might be expected to come to court. Cases involving violence or where an urgent solution was thought expedient on account of the vulnerability of one of the parties were hurried through the courts, to be commenced within a matter of weeks. Other litigation proceeded at a more leisurely pace and it might, indeed, take several years before a less urgent case was heard at one of the standard octave sessions of the courts.[17]

By the second half of the fifteenth century there were two principal types of summons employed in Hungary. They are known to historians as the *evocatio* and the *insinuatio.* The *evocatio* was usually delivered in respect of property actions where the descent of the estate or the lie of its boundaries was contested.[18] Normally, three summonses, each setting a time to appear in court, were issued, the last of which involved the summons being read aloud at three markets. For every occasion on which the respondent failed to attend court he would be fined and, eventually, the case would be heard in his absence. After 1486, the proclamation at three markets was replaced by the *insinuatio* ('terminal summons'), which formally notified the respondent in writing that the case would be heard irrespective of his own

[13] Degré, *A Négyeskönyv perjogi anyaga*, 134–6.

[14] Trip., II. 82 (DRMH 5, 363). For the importance more generally in Romano-canonical procedure of casting the *libellus* accurately, see Robert Maranta, *Praxis, sive de ordine iudiciorum (Speculum Aureum)* (Cologne, 1598), 272.

[15] Anna Pécsy, 'Az erdélyi fejedelmi kancellária első formulariumos kézirata', in Bernát L. Kumorovitz and Loránd Szilágyi, eds., *Emlékkönyv Szentpétery Imre* (Budapest, 1938), 385–95 (391–3).

[16] Misjoined cases might, however, on occasions proceed to court. See Pesty-Magina, no. 158, which records a prorogation given to several parties who were deceased, the case still proceeding.

[17] Hajnik, *A magyar bírósági szervezet*, 208–13.

[18] Trip., II. 18 [4] (DRMH 5, 271).

attendance.[19] Cases introduced by the *evocatio* were usually 'protracted'. Since their resolution was not considered pressing, they were invariably commenced only at the next octave session, at which they were usually postponed to allow time for the paperwork to arrive.

In cases where violence was involved or where a speedy resolution of property claims was thought appropriate, an *insinuatio* might be issued on the first occasion of summons. This would usually be combined with the setting of a date for a hearing which was only a fortnight or month distant: the so-called *evocatio brevis* or *sine procrastione.* Indeed, Werbőczy understands the *insinuatio* automatically to involve a *brevis* date.[20] The use of the *brevis* necessitated the Curia courts sitting in virtually permanent session, i.e. outside the standard octave terms.[21] When the courts were in regular session, *brevis* cases might be heard out of sequence, at the first available opportunity.[22] Almost certainly, the speed with which the *brevis* forced actions to court explains why litigants should often allege minor acts of violence in their plaint. For a claim that violence had been done had the automatic consequence of hurrying the matter to trial.[23] By the same token, those summoned at short notice were often obliged to attend court unprepared and at great personal inconvenience. Indeed, they might not receive the summons until it was too late. It might, therefore, be the case that the first business of the court was to determine whether an act of violence had been done and thus that the action fell within its competence.[24]

* * *

The letter of summons might not be delivered personally by the plaintiff to his adversary. Instead, the plaintiff was obliged to convey it to the place of authentication, chapter or convent, named in the letter.[25] The chapter or convent appointed one of the handful of royal bailiffs specified in the letter of summons as well as one of its own number who was charged with witnessing the bailiff and completing the relevant letters. The bailiff was, as we have noted, usually chosen from a list of candidates proposed by the plaintiff—an unsatisfactory arrangement that Matthias sought in vain to improve.[26] It was the bailiff's responsibility to have the summons delivered properly to the defendant. Failure to present the summons properly had

[19] Trip., II. 18 [7] (DRMH 5, 271). See also 1486: 17 (DRMH 3, 49, and note on 109 on the background to this article); 1495: 7 (DRMH 4, 59).

[20] Trip., II. 18 [3] (DRMH 5, 269–71).

[21] 1500: 13; 1518 (Bács): 41; 1526: 20 (DRMH 4, 147, 233–5, 269).

[22] Letters of judgment in *brevis* cases were also distributed out of sequence. See 'Registrum litterarum judicialium extradatarum anno 1507 in octavis Sancti Michaelis', ELTE, Egyetemi Könyvtár, MSS, *Litterae et Epistolae Originales*, no. 6, 375.

[23] See here Martyn Rady, 'Justice Delayed? Litigation and Dispute Settlement in Fifteenth-Century Hungary', *Central Europe*, 2, no. 1 (2004), 3–14 (9–11); republished as 'Késedelmes igazságszolgáltatás? Pereskedés és perlezárás a 15. századi Magyarországon', *Aetas* (2008, no. 1), 167–77.

[24] MNL OL DL, 83891, discussed in István Tringli, 'A magyar szokásjog a malomépitésről', in Tibor Neumann, ed., *Analecta Mediaevalia 1* (Budapest, 2001), 251–68 (252). I am most grateful to István Tringli for sending me a copy of this article.

[25] Trip., II. 21 (DRMH 5, 275).

[26] 1486: 8 (DRMH 3, 45); reversed in 1492: 53 (DRMH 4, 27–9).

the automatic consequence of halting the suit.[27] The letter of summons might be read by the defendant, but he could not retain it. He was, however, permitted to make a copy.[28]

In the majority of cases, the letter of summons also instructed the bailiff and cleric to perform additional tasks which were related to the business of the summons. The two most common instructions of this type were to hold an inquest or to deliver notice. The first of these (given in *litterae inquisitoriae*) ordered the bailiff and cleric to hold a preliminary inquest (*inquisitio simplex*) which would determine whether the plaint had any substance.[29] This type of investigation was most usually employed in cases where it was alleged that land had been illegally occupied or where the boundaries of an estate were disputed.[30] The inquest took evidence of neighbours, abutters and local noblemen in respect of the claims laid in the summons. Should the inquest establish that other parties were involved in the dispute that had not been named, the bailiff and cleric were empowered to issue out additional summonses. Upon completing the inquest, the cleric who had performed the inquest reported back in writing to the court which had delivered the mandate, commenting briefly on the outcome of the inquiry and naming those who had been summoned (*cum nominibus evocatorum*).[31] The report of the inquest constituted evidence that might be relied upon in court. Nevertheless, it was often the case that two, three or even more inquests might be separately sent to take evidence.[32] This might be because the plaintiff had opened the case simultaneously in several courts or because the suit involved properties in more than one county, but it was also a device favoured by the courts.[33] All too often, inquests were performed sloppily, the evidence of the witnesses being led to the point of absurdity by the *De eo utrum* (*Deutrum*), which was the sheet of questions formally put to them.[34] For the same reason, the respondent might petition to have an inquest held separately on his behalf (a *contrainquisitio*), over which he had some control in the selection of the bailiff. In this respect, it is probably helpful to consider the inquest as the gathering of proof on behalf of the plaintiff and not as an impartial investigation mounted to establish the truth of contending positions. For this reason, the letters of report sent back to the court after the inquest had been completed were often endorsed *Pro X contra Y*.[35]

[27] Trip., II. 19 (DRMH 5, 271). See also Trip., II. 82 (DRMH 5, 361–3).

[28] Degré, *A Négyeskönyv perjogi anyaga*, 124–5.

[29] For this and what follows, see Imre Hajnik, *A perdöntő eskü és az előzetes tanúbizonyitás a középkori magyar jogban* (Budapest, 1881), 11–21; Hajnik, *A magyar birósági szervezet*, 286–92.

[30] The earliest example of this type of inquest is from 1249. See AUO, vii, 290–1.

[31] Elemér Varjú and Béla Iványi, eds., *A Tomaj nemzetségbeli Losonczi Bánffy története. Oklevéltár*, 2 vols. (Budapest, 1908–28), ii, 323.

[32] Hajnik, *A perdöntő eskü és az előzetes tanúbizonyitás*, 21. Altogether, as many as six inquests might be held. See Iván Borsa, ed., *A Justh család levéltára 1274–1525* (Budapest, 1991), no. 601.

[33] HO, i, 356. See also Katalin Péter, *A csejtei várúrnő: Báthory Erzsébet* (Budapest, 1985), 32.

[34] Most notoriously in the prosecutions of Countess Erzsébet Báthory in 1610 and of László Listi in 1659. See Irma Szádeczky-Kardoss, 'A Báthory Erzsébet elleni koncepciós eljárás egyes történeti forrásainak értelmezésére', *Levéltári Közlemények*, 65, nos. 1–2 (1994), 65–87 (66, 83), and András Komáromy, *Listi László munkái* (Budapest, 1891), 48, 56–7, where the *Deutra* added in questions regarding black masses, necromancy, wizardry and lèse-majesté. For Báthory, the subject of much amateur speculation, see now Susanne Kord, *Murderesses in German Writing, 1720–1860: Heroines of Horror* (Cambridge, 2009), 54–62.

[35] See thus Imre Nagy, Farkas Deák and Gyula Nagy, eds., *Hazai oklevéltár* (Budapest, 1879), 413, 424.

From the sixteenth century onwards, the cleric was often replaced by a county officer, since few religious houses survived and, in any case, the local population was most often Protestant.[36]

Letters of notice (*litterae ammonitoriae*) served largely as a catch-all for almost all other business—as a form of notice and warning in respect of impending legal business or as an injunction.[37] The nobleman would explain in his *libellus* that he wished to engage in a transaction or to prevent parties infringing his legal rights. His *libellus* was accordingly recast in the form of a letter that mandated a bailiff and cleric to notify all parties affected. These most typically included neighbours and relatives who might be considered to have concurrent rights in respect of the transaction. It was the task of the bailiff and cleric to hunt these out. Should they object to the transaction, they were summoned to court as respondents to explain their position. Likewise, those served with an injunction, most typically to vacate a property or to hand over deeds in their possession, but who objected that this was unjust were also summoned to court.[38] Similar procedures accompanied institutions to properties and reviews of boundaries. If the institution or boundaries were contested, then summonses were duly issued by the bailiff and cleric. Summonses involving institutions and boundaries were invariably simple *evocationes* rather than *insinuationes* as the matters arising were considered insufficiently pressing to justify an early hearing.

These out-of-court procedures allowed exceptional discretionary powers to the bailiff and cleric. Not only were they responsible for leading the investigation into the facts but they were also charged with establishing the identity of all parties who might have an interest in any subsequent transaction or litigation. Moreover, they were expected to decide whom to summon and to ensure that the summons so issued was both accurately phrased and correctly delivered. In view of these functions and responsibilities, it is not surprising that Werbőczy should consider the bailiff to be *tanquam iudex*.[39] By the same token, it was perhaps inevitable that bailiffs and their supervising clerics should on occasions be violently attacked by aggrieved parties and even murdered.[40]

## TRIAL AND RETRIAL

Let us imagine that the defendant, having received the summons, actually attended the court. We add 'actually' because all too frequently the summons was ignored or not received in time. In such cases, the action was either postponed to the next octave or tried anyway on grounds of *nonvenientia*, a circumstance that gave

[36] László Papp, *A hiteles helyek története és működése az újkorban* (Budapest, 1936), 7–12.

[37] For the *admonitio* / *ammonitio* as a *notitia*, see *Commissio Systematica. Observationes in Tripartitum*, OSzK, MSS, Quart. Lat., 2378, fol. 27*v*.

[38] Trip., II. 24 (DRMH 5, 277–9). The instruction to hand over deeds was usually given in *litterae ammonitoriae et exhibitoriae*.

[39] Trip., II. 22 [2] (DRMH 5, 275–7).

[40] József Vagner, *Adalékok a nyitrai székeskáptalan történetéhez* (Nyitra, 1896), 120–3; László Papp, 'A birtokba-iktatás (statutio) lefolyása', in *Emlékkönyv Szentpétery Imre*, 372–84 (379–80); *Monumenta Comitialia*, ii, 561.

grounds for the absent party to force a retrial should the matter go against him.[41] In advance of the case opening, much time might be spent anxiously waiting for the other party to attend. In the event of an *evocatio*, the summons specified only the octave term at which the case would be heard. It was thus entirely possible to spend several weeks or even months waiting for one's opponent or his lawyer to turn up.[42] The cost of temporary accommodation in the capital might in the early sixteenth century amount to as much as 1,500 florins per suit.[43] The call to court took place in stages, with the names of the parties being shouted out from the court building at a given hour, usually after lunch. The first *proclamatio* was intended to establish who was present and thus what cases could be listed. The roll call was made on the basis of the register in which were listed the summonses that the court, or more properly the protonotaries, had previously given out, an extract of which was pinned to the door of the court.[44] Providing they responded to the call, the attendees were then assigned a division within the octave term, depending upon the date of summons, but the internal arrangement of the divisions may also have been by county.[45] The second *proclamatio* was for the distribution of paperwork between the parties (the so-called *parium*). It was the responsibility of the notaries to make copies of all documents relevant to the case so that both parties were able to see the evidence in advance of going to court. The third *proclamatio* called the parties into the court room.[46]

With both parties now in court, the case was officially *Levata*. The text of the summons was entered into the court record and the attorneys made to swear that they would not proffer false documents or engage in too much quibbling.[47] At this point, however, the case was frequently adjourned to permit the defendant to recover documents relevant to his case or to summon warrantors. It was only at the next octave session that the case was resumed and, even then, it might be delayed further, particularly if the suit was joined by new parties (or *ingerentes*) who also needed time to prepare their cases.[48] It was, indeed, possible for these to intervene in the case at any point before the letter of judgment was given out, even after the judgment had been delivered orally in court.[49] The proceedings which followed were conventionally divided into two parts. The first of these, the *pars*

[41] See thus MNL OL DL, 13318, recording three adjournments on account of the failure of one of the parties to attend.

[42] MNL OL DL, 66970; MNL OL DL, 124705; MNL OL DL, 172171; MNL OL DL, 84907, recording a wait of seventy days.

[43] György Bónis, *A jogtudó értelmiség a Mohács előtti Magyarországon* (Budapest, 1971), 397.

[44] 1498: 5; 1500: 4 (DRMH 4, 91, 141). See Degré, *A Négyeskönyv perjogi anyaga*, 124, 134.

[45] See thus the arrangement of the 'Registrum litterarum judicialium extradatarum anno 1507 in octavis Sancti Michaelis', ELTE, Egyetemi Könyvtár, MSS, *Litterae et Epistolae Originales*, no. 6, 347–83; further, *Litterae et Epistolae Originales* no 33, 271–86 (which is probably part of the same sequence).

[46] Kitonich, *Directio Methodica*, 3. 7 (2004 edition, 98).

[47] Degré, *A Négyeskönyv perjogi anyaga*, 136.

[48] In order to expedite cases, the rights of *ingerentes* might be disregarded. See Livia Magina, 'O dispută pentru locul de vad de la Mureş (1543)', *Analele Banatului, S.N., Arheologie–Istorie*, 21 (2013), 295–8 (298).

[49] Hence 1500: 12 (DRMH 4, 147): 'in future the master protonotaries when handing out the letters of judgment, have to record the handing out with these words: "handed out provided there is no third party [*Extradata, si tercia non est*]".'

*exceptiva*, usually involved the defendant's lawyer delivering reasons as to why the action should be abandoned. *Exceptiones* were later divided into two categories—*dilatoriae* that forced a delay in proceedings, for instance to recover deeds or repeat an inquest; and *peremptoriae* that, if proven, had the effect of collapsing the case, for instance demanding an opponent demonstrate his noble status or that the summons included a lunatic, which rendered it misjoined.[50] Doubtless many of these were, as Werbőczy indicates, *exceptiones frivolae* and might include many tiresome claims all of which had to be disproved by the plaintiff.[51] One fifteenth-century formulary suggests additional ruses which good lawyers were expected to use—that the incorrect seal was impressed on the summons, that a scribe had made a mistake, or even that the judge himself was partisan. On each of these points, the court was expected to rule, delivering interlocutory judgments.[52] The opportunity, however, for debate was restricted, with neither side able to give more than a set number of challenges on individual points of law.[53]

Once the case had moved beyond the phase of *exceptiones*, it entered the *pars allegativa.* At this point, the instruments of proof were submitted. In property cases, these usually involved the deeds belonging to one or both parties. Invariably, the authenticity of the instruments became the object of scrutiny and debate, and might involve the examination of deeds which were several centuries old. In one case from the 1340s, a charter was produced that had been supposedly issued by King Coloman at the beginning of the twelfth century; in another, a royal privilege that was over a century old but had had part of its text clumsily erased.[54] In the production of documents before the court, litigants were apt to confuse physical with legal weight, submitting charters that had little relevance to the suit. On the other hand, claims to property that were based on ancestral descent often required extensive documentation to prove a right of inheritance—over thirty in one case from the 1430s and in excess of 200 in the 1770s.[55] *Aviticitas* certainly merited criticism, but at least it encouraged noblemen to care for the mummies of their old deeds and for their worm-eaten muniments.[56]

In disputes over land, it was possible for the court to come to a decision on the basis alone of the charters submitted by the parties—that they were forged, had outrun the period of prescription, or were simply irrelevant to the suit.[57] A single case might yield documents in all these categories.[58] In cases of violence, however, a different route had to be followed, for it could not usually be proved by the examination of deeds. It was possible even in the later fifteenth century for the

[50] See János Szegedi, *Tripartitum Juris Hungarici Tyrocinium*, Košice, 1764 (first published in 1734), 611–12 (2. 82). For lunatics, see Degré, *A Négyeskönyv perjogi anyaga*, 96–7.

[51] Trip., II. 83 [6] (DRMH 5, 369).

[52] M.G. Kovachich, *Formulae Solennes Styli* (Pest, 1799), 408–9.

[53] Kovachich, *Formulae Solennes*, 399.

[54] MNL OL DL, 3852; Imre Nagy, *A Pécz nemzetségbeliek öröködési pere. 1425–1433* (Budapest, 1892), 45–7.

[55] The earlier case is the subject of Nagy, *A Pécz nemzetségbeliek öröködési pere*. The relevant text is given on 28–49. See also MNL OL, O 39, *Decisiones Curiales*, 39, part 2 (1773), 759–78.

[56] Our description comes from Mór (Maurus) Jókai, *A Hungarian Nabob*, trans. R. Nisbet Bain, London, 1898, 155 (first published in Hungary 1853–4).

[57] Degré, *A Négyeskönyv perjogi anyaga*, 167.

[58] Nagy, *A Pécz nemzetségbeliek*, 16–19.

parties at this point to settle the suit in battle, *de capite ad caput*, although they usually employed champions.[59] More usually, however, the extremes of adversarial combat were avoided. Instead, the court made investigations of its own in respect both of the plaint and of the integrity of the parties, assuming thereby a more investigatory role.

With the consent of the parties, court proceedings would be temporarily interrupted and a 'common inquest' (*inquisitio communis*) be performed under the supervision of a bailiff and cleric in the locality where the alleged wrong had taken place.[60] This was a more thorough version of the preliminary inquest. In order to maintain impartiality, the inquest was attended by representatives of both sides. The inquest took evidence of witnesses under oath, often recording their individual testimonies in considerable detail together with their names and status.[61] As many as 130 witnesses might be interviewed and named in the letter recording the event.[62] Normally, the inquest was held at the county seat and the lord of the county and his deputy made responsible for enforcing attendance. As an alternative, an inquest might be appointed to hold a view (*oculata revisio*), the primary purpose of which was to ascertain who was in physical occupation of a contested estate.[63] Once the record of the inquest was submitted to the court, it was possible to challenge its findings, particularly by disputing the status of witnesses and thus the value of their evidence. If the challenge was upheld, then—depending on whether the challenge had been made by the defendant or plaintiff—either a fine was payable or the case lost.[64] In subsequent centuries, challenges of this type might prompt the inquest to be reheard.[65]

With the inquest complete and its record submitted to the court, the case moved to its final stage, which was the oath taking. (As an alternative, the case might move straight to an oath taking, without going through a common inquest.)[66] By this time, the balance of proof was generally clear, which in itself favoured a private settlement between the parties. In Werbőczy's account, should the evidence be in favour of the plaintiff, then he should swear along with compurgators; should it go the other way, then the oath taking fell to the respondent and his oath helpers.[67] Within this overall scheme, however, there were a number of equations that had to be satisfied to which Werbőczy only alludes. The compurgators were not witnesses after the fact, but after the character of the man on whose behalf they swore. Accordingly, the regard in which the compurgators' supporting oaths were

[59] HO, i, 357; Pesty-Magina, nos. 136, 140.

[60] Hajnik, *A perdöntő eskü és az előzetes tanúbizonyitás*, 22–8; Hajnik, *A magyar birósági szervezet*, 295–300.

[61] See thus MNL OL DL, 56983, summarized in Bálint Ila and Iván Borsa, eds., *Az Abaffy család levéltára 1247–1515. A Dancs család levéltára 1232–1525. A Hanvay család levéltára 1216–1525* (Budapest, 1993), no. H215.

[62] MNL OL DL, 15807.

[63] Trip., II. 41 (DRMH 5, 299–301).

[64] Trip., II. 36 (DRMH 5, 295).

[65] MNL OL, O 18, *Processus tabulares*, Bundle 4, no. 19 (1732), but see Trip., II. 31 (DRMH 5, 287).

[66] Kálmán Géresi, ed., *Codex diplomaticus Comitum Károlyi de Nagy-Károly*, 5 vols. (Budapest, 1882–97), iii, 57. See also 1492: 56 (DRMH 4, 29–31).

[67] Trip., II. 32 (DRMH 5, 289).

held depended upon their individual status, which was in its turn converted into a monetary value—a bishop being worth forty florins, an ordinary nobleman and an abbess four florins, a peasant one, and so on. This was set against the worth of a disputed property or the *homagium* of a man accused of violence, and the number of oath helpers determined by reference to their quality. At the same time, multiple misdeeds might require the doubling or tripling of the compurgators, while some crimes required for their exculpation a set number of compurgators.[68] In an attempt to impose order, Werbőczy sought to link the number of compurgators to the number of inquests, the evidence of which needed to be overturned, but his scheme was not found convincing.[69]

The oath taking was not performed in court but close to a place of authentication convenient for the compurgators. Alternatively, a mobile chapel and altar might be used.[70] The oath taking was preceded by celebration of the Mass, on account of which the compurgators might be deemed not only *conjuratores* but also *consacramentales*.[71] The oath was usually taken upon the head of the defeated party, in what must have been a demanding ceremony that could stretch over several days.[72] In cases where the suit was over the ownership of landed estate, the oath might be made while ungirt and unshod, holding aloft a clod of the disputed soil.[73] Once the oath taking had been completed and the case so finally proved, the winning party might ask the court to uphold his plaint and issue letters of adjudication.[74] In cases of violence, the court would apportion damages to the plaintiff, usually according to his own inflated estimation, and impose the death sentence on his adversary, which was (as we have seen) invariably commuted into payment of the *homagium*. If the plaint was not proven, the case was deemed lost, although the court might impose perpetual silence on the plaintiff in respect of the suit, possibly also exacting a penalty for deception.[75]

Hungarian procedural law allowed a variety of legal remedies, all of which had the consequence of prolonging the legal process. The number of remedies available in Hungarian law was a consequence of three factors. In the first place, Hungarian procedural law rested to a large degree on practices followed in the ecclesiastical courts where legal delays were seen as 'an essential device to protect all concerned'.[76] Accordingly, it allowed the retrial as a matter of course, to such an extent that the retrial or *novum* should properly be seen as an episode belonging to the original action and not a separate legal stage. In this respect, it is perhaps no accident that Kitonich's account of procedure put discussion of the retrial and other remedies in law before his section on the final judgment of the court. As the 1492 law put it,

68 Hajnik, *A perdöntő eskü és az előzetes tanúbizonyitás*, 42–52; Hajnik, *A magyar birósági szervezet*, 311–28.

69 Trip., II. 32 (DRMH 5, 289–91); Kitonich, 6. 13 (2004 edition, 232).

70 József Holub, *Zala megye története a középkorban* (Pécs, 1929), 177.

71 Hajnik, *A perdöntő eskü és az előzetes tanúbizonyitás*, 42.

72 Géresi, *Codex diplomaticus Comitum Károlyi de Nagy-Károly*, iii, 57, 62.

73 György (Georgius) Fejér, *Codex Diplomaticus Hungariae ecclesiasticus et civilis*, 11 vols. in 44 parts (Buda, 1829–44), ix/6, 183.

74 MNL OL DL, 92869.

75 Hajnik, *A magyar birósági szervezet*, 387–400.

76 Jane E. Sayers, *Papal Judges Delegate in the Province of Canterbury, 1198–1254* (London, 1971), 99.

'Let them obtain a new trial, whenever they wish.'[77] Indeed, by the mid-sixteenth century, the readiness of Hungarian law to allow the retrial was considered to be one of its most signal marks.[78] Secondly, there was the problem of enforcement which meant that methods of obstruction became institutionalized and accommodated within procedural law. This was particularly the case, as we will see, in respect of the legal device known as the *repulsio.* Finally, the many errors that crept into the conduct of the trial—as, for instance, an attorney misunderstanding instructions or a failure to receive instruments on time—required a mechanism for redress that often had the consequence either of forcing a delay in the process or obliging the case to be retried in its entirety.

The principal instrument used to force a halt in judicial proceedings was the *prohibitio.* The term *prohibitio* was, however, a broad one and covered a range of legal devices.[79] By the early seventeenth century, the *prohibitio* had been broken down into the separate remedies of the *prohibitio*, the *prohibita* and the *inhibitio*, all of which had different meanings to those current at the time Werbőczy was writing.[80] In respect of a retrial, the most obvious use of the *prohibitio* (called an *inhibitio* by Kitonich) lay in relation to the summons. Defendants frequently failed to receive these in good time or else were delayed in their journey to the court. In their absence, they might be found guilty of contempt and the case go against them. Under these circumstances, the unlucky defendant was allowed to protest the *litterae judiciales* issued by the court and, if his *prohibitio* was accepted by the court, the case would be retried with him in attendance. A *prohibitio* (Kitonich's *prohibita*) might additionally be made during the trial by either party if they disagreed with an interlocutory ruling, up to a maximum of three times, which had the consequence of moving the proceedings back a stage. From the middle of the sixteenth century, a *prohibitio* (called as such by Kitonich) might also be used to block a common inquest or compurgation on the grounds that the relevant party wished to revise the statement that was being put to the test.[81] Since this effectively meant that a new trial had to take place, the *prohibitio* had to be accompanied by a new summons to court.[82]

Although cases proceeding before the Curia courts were handled by attorneys, it was advantageous to the litigant to be present, for it permitted use of a device borrowed from ecclesiastical law known as the *revocatio procuratorum.*[83] The *revocatio* worked in two ways. It might be used either to countermand a statement made by the lawyer, even to the extent of revoking an entire legal argument if this appeared to be going against the litigant's interest. Secondly, in cases which were brought *brevi termino* to the court, it was possible to dismiss the lawyer after the court's delivery of the judgment and thus reopen the case anew.

[77] 1492: 51 (DRMH 4, 27).

[78] *Quadripartitum Opus Juris Consuetudinarii Regni Hungariae* (Zagreb, 1798), p. iv.

[79] Trip., II. 20 (DRMH 5, 273); Kitonich, *Directio Methodica*, 5 (2004 edition, 168–205); see also Martyn Rady, 'Hungarian Procedural Law and Part Two of the *Tripartitum*', in CLCE, 47–70 (66).

[80] See further, Degré, *A Négyeskönyv perjogi anyaga*, 217.

[81] 1550: 54.

[82] Kitonich, *Directio Methodica*, 5. 14 (2004 edition, 184).

[83] The *revocatio* could not obviously be used unless the party was in court, but doubtless was. See 1500: 13 [3] (DRMH 4, 147).

Depending upon the stage which the action had reached, *revocatio* carried no penalty at all, a six-florin fine or a 200-florin fine. The last of these was reserved for cases of *revocatio* which involved reopening the case well after it had been concluded, or else forced the abandonment of an *inquisitio communis*, oath-taking or search for documents. As an alternative, the plaintiff, if he felt the case to be going badly, could simply demand that it be abandoned and recommence the action at a later date.[84]

The execution of judgments provided an opportunity for further remedy. Where the defendant in an action was proved in court to be holding a property unlawfully, the procedure for enforcement always involved a *(re)statutio* or (re-) institution. A cleric and bailiff were instructed by the court to visit the property and to see that the new owner took up his rightful possession. The cleric and bailiff might also record protests to the institution made by those who considered that they had a superior claim to the property. The defendant was usually forbidden from making a protest at his own eviction and thus from launching an action against the new owner. Instead, though, he had the option of simply refusing to leave. In this case, the defendant had to follow a quite specific procedure, brandishing a drawn sword before the cleric and bailiff and refusing them leave to enter the property. From Werbőczy's own account, it is clear that the *repulsio* by sword was intended to proceduralize more casual acts of violence aimed at impeding the legal process that had been expressly forbidden in previous legislation, but evidently in vain.[85] The act of *repulsio* had the consequence of forcing the action back to court. According to Werbőczy and to several royal decrees, the *repulsio* could only be used once. If it was repeated, the defendant incurred the charge of perfidy, and was liable to lose all his estate.[86] It is plain, however, that in the succeeding centuries defendants often performed the *repulsio* on several occasions, forcing the case to be reopened, apparently without penalty.[87] Of course, it might well be that, with all remedies exhausted, the defendant still refused to leave the property. In this case, he had to be physically ejected by a posse of the local nobility or by military force. Even so, he might subsequently descend upon the property and reoccupy it. For this he would, according to the law of 1507, be summoned to court on charges of perfidy.[88] Over the course of the succeeding centuries, however, the *reoccupatio* was increasingly proceduralized. Although for its performance a fine of 200 florins was payable as well as compensation for any damage done, the *reoccupatio* had, nevertheless, the consequence of forcing a retrial.[89]

84 Trip., II. 82 [22] (DRMH 5, 365).

85 1486: 16 (DRMH 3, 48–9); repeated in 1492: 57 (DRMH 4, 31).

86 Trip., II. 73–4 (DRMH 5, 343–7). See also 1500: 19 and 1504: 4 (DRMH 4, 149–51, 165).

87 Endre Varga, 'Polgári peres eljárás a királyi curián 1724–1848/49', *Levéltári Közlemények*, 39, no. 2 (1968), 269–309 (288–300); MNL OL, N 105, *Deputatio Regnicolaris in Juridicis*, Lad. MMM, Bundle 5, fols. 209–10.

88 1507: 2.

89 Varga, 'Polgári peres eljárás', 303–4. The 200-florin penalty remained, despite inflation. See MNL OL, O 8, *Protocolla tabulae septemviralis*, 10, fol. 5 (1800); MNL OL, O 116, *Protocollum inclytae tabulae districtualis judiciariae transdanubianae*, 15, fol. 6 (1799).

The examples of the *repulsio* and *reoccupatio* indicate the practical difficulties accompanying enforcement which provided a spur to negotiating a compromise rather than imposing a court judgment. Werbőczy knew this only too well from personal experience. In 1511, Werbőczy had been granted by Wladislas II lands in Bihar County which had previously belonged to Francis Jakó, but which had been confiscated by royal order on account of Francis's bigamous marriage. Werbőczy was never able, however, to take up secure occupation of Francis's properties, for his entry to the estate was consistently obstructed by Francis's kinsmen, who were members of the powerful Thordai and Bajoni families. After six years, during the course of which Francis died, Werbőczy was obliged to strike a deal. He resigned his immediate rights to Francis's estate, accepting instead only the right of reversion in the (improbable) event of the expiry of the Bajoni and Thordai lines. In return, he asked simply that the kinsmen accept that Francis had contracted an illegal marriage and, thus, by implication, that they accepted the terms of the estate's original confiscation.[90] Although couched about in the language of the law, the arrangement which Werbőczy made with Francis's relatives spells out only too clearly the limits of the law and of enforceability. Unable to make good his rights to the estate, Werbőczy was obliged to conclude a much inferior arrangement.

The extent of legal remedies available had the consequence of prolonging cases, sometimes over many decades. We know of one case from the later fifteenth century that dragged on for more than sixty years and Werbőczy himself remarked that some suits might be protracted for 'more than a human lifetime'.[91] As far as Werbőczy was concerned, the problem was not that cases might take a long time to reach any conclusion but that the judgments reached should be fair and just. Without there being a sufficient raft of remedies, it was all too easy for just cases to fail and for guilty parties to prosper, even at the expense of their own salvation. In Werbőczy's words, justice denied 'is the two-edged sword which pierces the hearts of orphans and widows and of other poor people. This is the grief which robs the spirits of the oppressed. This is the snare which drags many into the pit of eternal damnation. Many are the reasons for suits failing unjustly which, as the tinderbox of sin, are always to be avoided'.[92]

## JUDICIAL DECISIONS AND DECISION MAKING

The stress laid in Hungarian legal practice upon the formulaic measurement of proof encourages us to suppose that the role of the kingdom's courts lay somewhere

[90] Géresi, *Codex diplomaticus Comitum Károlyi de Nagy-Károly*, iii, 78–82, 91, 105–9; Dezső Csánki, *Magyarország történelmi földrajza a Hunyadiak korában*, 5 vols. (Budapest, 1890–1913), i, 629, 641.

[91] Trip., II. 71 [5] (DRMH 5, 341). See also Kovachich, *Formulae Solennes*, 158.

[92] Trip., II. 83 [8] (DRMH 5, 369). The *gladius* and *dolor* that pierces the heart is also found in Rogerius's *Epistola in miserabile Carmen* (ch. 5), written in the 1240s. See János M. Bak, Martyn Rady and László Veszprémy, eds., *Anonymus and Master Roger* (Budapest and New York, 2010), 144–5.

between umpire and abacist. In many cases, we can indeed track the way that the procedures followed by the courts resulted in mechanical outcomes. The justice of the suit was plain, supported by charters, the evidence of inquests or the oaths of helpers; or else, it was shown to be empty. In either case, the eventual decision of the court was predictable. Where more complex considerations were involved, however, courts often inclined to judgments that were expedient or contingent rather than principled or mechanically driven. They might thus come to a decision that was a compromise or else render a judgment that was equitable rather than in conformity with established practices. The lay membership of the courts contributed to this trend by favouring solutions that were not lawyerly, while the episodic movement of cases before the courts and the frequency of retrial worked in favour of negotiated outcomes. As a consequence, Hungary's courts tended to give decisions which aimed at reconciling the parties or which depended upon what the court believed to be right on the occasion. In so doing, the courts might in their judgments disregard settled norms and they deliberately eschewed statements of principle that would otherwise have contributed to the law's substantive content. The customary law of the kingdom thus continued to be distinguished by its non-normative character, which itself partly arose from the practices and composition of the kingdom's courts. In this way, the manner of the court's 'adjectival' proceedings worked against consistency in respect of the law's content and its application.[93]

Many cases proceeding before the courts involved intricate matters or touched upon issues where the customary law was uncertain. These cases often arose from the complexity with which noblemen conducted their affairs, making increasingly convoluted arrangements of assignment and pledge that outpaced the law's own development. Others involved properties that had been disputed for generations, where neither party was ready to forego their claims, particularly the one that was in physical occupation. Under these circumstances, the courts tended in their judgments to rearrange the law's content, case by case, to fit with what they deemed to be the most appropriate outcome, which was often a midway position between rival claims. So, for instance, in respect of a long-contested property over which the occupant had no proven right of possession, the court awarded it to the plaintiff, while still apportioning a slice of the land to the ousted party. Similarly, in the case of an estate whose owner had sought to sell it off without his kinsmen's consent, the court instructed that the relatives be given the right of pre-emption at a generous price. And again, in a suit that involved a long-running dispute, wherein the plaintiff had incurred a cash penalty for ignoring a previous judicial ruling, the court resolved the affair by judging anew in the respondent's favour in exchange for him not collecting the fine that the plaintiff owed him.[94]

The interest of the courts was by this measure to balance principle with expediency. Within a customary arrangement of law, however, the principles of adjudication

[93] We borrow here from Jeremy Bentham's vocabulary. See Christopher Allen, *The Law of Evidence in Victorian England* (Cambridge, 1997), 8–9.

[94] ZsO, i, no. 1017; Rady, 'Justice Delayed? Litigation and Dispute Settlement', 10–12, gives several examples.

are themselves often uncertain. New customs may be invoked that set aside existing conventions, rendering them obsolete on the occasion, or contradictory customs may be posited. Moreover, strictly adhering to what is thought to be customary may be repugnant to the court, and a decision given that conformed to what was thought to be right rather than to what was known to be proper. These circumstances meant that even the most basic assumptions might be set aside and decisions made that turned every expectation on their head. In what follows, we will look at two such judgments that affected what was understood to lie at the very heart of the system of the noble ownership of land in Hungary—the right of kinsmen to succeed to the property of one of their number who had died without direct heirs, and the supposedly undisputed royal right of escheat in the event of an estate being without a legitimate male successor. The first of these judgments was delivered in the fifteenth century, when the content of the law was for the most part unwritten. The second, however, is from the eighteenth century and stands thus as testimony to the continued instability of customary arrangements, even after their partial consolidation in the *Tripartitum*.

* * *

It was at the heart of *aviticitas* that the descendants of a single *avus* retained a concurrent interest in the land that had once belonged to him. A nobleman without the solace of sons could not give or will the land that he had inherited; nor, upon his death, might the king claim it if he had kinsmen still living. Unless the nobleman had contrived to alienate his property either by obtaining right of prefection (saving the rights of his relatives within the fifth degree), or by using the device of the *assumptio*, or by contracting an indecent mortgage loan with a Jew, his land tracked back to those collaterals who had proof of their common descent. During the 1460s, therefore, Nicholas Bánffy of Alsólendva received from King Matthias the estate of the late Paul Chuna, whose property in the county had escheated to the crown on account of a supposed insufficiency of heirs. Bánffy was soon assailed, however, by a dozen inter-related noblemen, who claimed that they were the kinsmen of Paul, and they were able to produce charters that were almost 200 years old in support of the connection. Recognizing them to be men related to Paul's line, Bánffy acknowledged their superior rights and conceded the estate to them. In so doing, he expressly referred to the principle that kinsmen were the rightful heirs of a man who had died without sons.[95] At around the same time, in an analogous case that proceeded before the high judge concerning the rights of a nobleman to land seized by his relatives, the court determined that the plaintiff had acquired the estate by a ruse, being not a direct descendant in the male line. The court accordingly apportioned the property to his kinsmen, even though their claims relied upon the identity of a great-great grandfather, who had lived a century before.[96]

[95] Imre Nagy, Farkas Deák and Gyula Nagy, eds., *Hazai okleveltár* (Budapest, 1879), 430–1.

[96] Rady, 'Justice Delayed? Litigation and Dispute Settlement', 10–11. For a further illustration, see Erik Fügedi, *The Elefánthy: The Hungarian Nobleman and his Kindred* (Budapest and New York, 1998), 84–5, 161.

Now let us compare these two examples with another that occurred only a few years before. Andrew, the dean of Pécs chapter, was a wealthy but lonely man. He had inherited substantial properties in Győr County that formed a part of the ancestral estate of the Pécz kindred, to which he belonged, but his immediate relatives had predeceased him.[97] In 1402, he made over his entire estate to noblemen from the Marczali and Berzenczei families. These were related to him by a common *avus*, Andrew's great-great-great-great grandfather, who had died about a century before. Andrew's grant acknowledged the Marczali and Berzenczei as his kinsmen, left him in occupation of the estate until his death, and imposed upon the future owners certain conditions in respect of the repayment of loans and other obligations that Andrew had contracted. Andrew reiterated the agreement in 1411 in respect of some further properties that had since fallen to him. Plainly, though, Andrew soon thought better of the arrangement, possibly (as he later claimed) because the Marczali and Berzenczei had not discharged the duties that he had previously laid upon them. He now made over his property directly to his principal creditors, adopting them as his brothers. The new agreement was confirmed by Sigismund in 1415. Upon Andrew's death, which must have occurred in the early 1420s, the newly adopted kinsmen made entry to the estate, but objection was raised by the Marczali and Berzenczei. The matter thus ended up in the court of the palatine in 1425.

We will not deal with the details of all that took place over the next eight years. The case was delayed by the deaths of some of the litigants, by searches for documents, by the appearance of allegedly long-lost relatives who needed their own claims to be assessed, and by the discovery of an ancient charter, the text of which had been amateurishly altered. The claims, however, of the Marczali and Berzenczei were good. Although their earlier agreement with Andrew was properly considered void, they were able to demonstrate a common descent going back over 100 years and thus by implication their rights to his inheritance. The palatine's court, nevertheless, threw out their case, imposing upon them perpetual silence. The court in its judgment argued that common descent was insufficient, for there had with the passage of each generation to be redistributions of property between the lines of the kindred in order for the right of inheritance to remain concurrent.[98] Since that had not taken place, the Marczali and Berzenczei should be considered as if 'men of a quite other kindred' (*veluti homines alterius generationis*) and thus had forfeited their right of succession.[99]

The court's judgment was remarkable and it might be deemed frivolous were it not that its membership on this occasion included, beside the palatine, no less than three prelates, the tavernicus, the high judge, the royal treasurer, the vice-chancellor, several barons, four protonotaries and an unnamed number of noblemen who, we are assured, were also experienced in the law (*jurisperiti*).[100] We can certainly

[97] The case is the subject of Imre Nagy, *A Pécz nemzetségbeliek*. The text of the case is given on 28–49.

[98] The court ingeniously linked the passage of generations to the time limit of the *praescriptio*.

[99] The judgment is given in Nagy, *A Pécz nemzetségbeliek*, 47–8.

[100] Nagy, *A Pécz nemzetségbeliek*, 48.

sympathize with the decision that they reached. Andrew had made all sorts of arrangements in respect of his property that would have had to be unpicked, to the detriment of his newly adopted brothers and creditors. The Marczali and Berzenczei were remote and distant kinsmen and their suit was plainly opportunistic. Nevertheless, in finding against them, the palatine's court demonstrated the malleability of the customary law and the way in which doubts might arise in matters that were otherwise thought to be governed by strongly normative rules.

Our second case also impacts directly upon the nature of the customary law. The royal right of escheat in the event of death without heirs arose from the supposed origin of all noble property in the royal gift. As custom of the realm, the royal right was supposed to take precedence over local customary arrangements, unless a royal privilege was obtained setting the customary law aside. Plainly, however, the courts did not always see it this way. Some judgments recognized that a *usus*, practised only by a few, could have the consequence of overriding the normal conventions of customary law, including even the royal right of escheat. Accordingly, a Hungarian court in the early eighteenth century set aside the principle that the land of a kinless man reverted to the crown, acknowledging that there were exceptions deriving from actual use. On this occasion, the Royal Table upheld the right of the Tybold family, which was defunct in the male line, to inheritance on the distaff side, even though this right had not been ceded by royal charter. In its judgment, the court considered the right of female succession to have been 'continuously applied and confirmed by use' in the family's past conduct. The suit for escheat launched by the crown *fiscus* was accordingly dismissed.[101] This was not an isolated case of a court affirming the efficacy of *usus* over custom, for we know of other examples that point in the same direction.[102]

Similar uncertainties persisted in other areas of the law, affecting matters that were no less significant. Some of these are highlighted in a record of early sixteenth-century judgments, which were collected with the aim of giving clarity—whether, for instance, someone needed to have been found guilty of perjury or fraud to be called a perjurer or fraudster (an early instance in Hungary's developing law of *infamia*);[103] whether someone convicted to 'fine of the tongue' (a penalty for certain procedural errors in court) could still appear in court in other actions while the fine remained unpaid; whether an action should fail if all the kinsmen who held property in common were not summoned in an action involving that land; whether the period of limitation applied to acts of violence, and so on.[104] Publication of the *Tripartitum* hardly put an end to uncertainties of this type, for as a statement of customary law its provisions might be superseded

[101] MNL OL, E 14 *Acta Hungarica*, 4. 365–406, esp. 383 (1720). The property thus passed through marriage to the Szepessy, Majthényi and Almássy families.

[102] András W. Kovács, *The History of the Wass de Czege Family* (Hamburg, 2005), 103; MNL OL, O 39, *Decisiones Curiales*, 39, part 2 (1774), 7. Use similarly trumped custom in respect of some Andorran practices of inheritance. See J.-A. Brutails, *La Coutume d'Andorre*, 2nd edition (Andorra la Vella, 1965), 63.

[103] See here Kitonich, *Directio Methodica*, 6. 27–31 (2004 edition, 258–8).

[104] *Codex Ilosvay*, OSzK, MSS, Fol. Lat. 4023, fol. 122–4*v*. A garbled version is published in J. N. Kovachich, *Notitiae Praeliminares ad Syllogen Decretorum Comitialium* (Pest, 1820), 400–6.

by new customary arrangements. Moreover, even in areas wherein certainty might be expected, imprecision attended the deliberations of the courts, which oscillated between competing norms. We have already identified in an earlier chapter contradictory approaches towards the daughters' quarter, which, as we have seen, might or might not be given only in movables. In similar fashion, the definition of acquired land, of *acquisita* as opposed to *hereditaria*, was vague and differed over time. This particularly affected royal grants of land, which might on the one hand be treated as freely disposable in much the same fashion as bought land, and yet on the other be regarded as passing only to male heirs, unless a clause to the contrary was written into the original charter of donation. This confusion, apparently clarified in the fourteenth century, subsequently returned to lend inconsistency to court judgments right through to the nineteenth century.[105] Likewise, if a nobleman had little inherited land but plenty of acquired land, was it possible for him to exclude his sons by testament from a share of the *acquisita*? There were at least two schools of thought on this and so contradictory rulings.[106] In respect of pledges of land, the rights of relatives who had been harmed by the transaction were equally imprecise, in particular whether they had the right to retake the land by paying its value or whether they were obliged to redeem the pledge in full, even though the cost of redemption often carried a hidden interest charge.[107] Similarly, was noble land inalienable in all cases? Might not a fraudster who had contracted debts to tradesmen which she had no intention of repaying, have her dower seized? A Transylvanian court certainly thought she might, notwithstanding her high noble birth.[108] And, to go back to a previous chapter, was the equation of landownership with noble status as complete as Werbőczy maintained? It was only in the eighteenth century that courts began to act consistently as if this was the case, dispossessing ignobles on the grounds that only noblemen might hold land in the countryside that was other than leasehold or peasant tenures. Until this time, however, large tracts of land, particularly in the south-east of the kingdom, constituted freehold property that was held unconditionally and on which no services were laid.[109]

* * *

[105] József Holub, 'A vásárolt fekvő jószág jogi természete régi jogunkban', *Emlékkönyv Károlyi Árpád* (Budapest, 1933), 246–54; Mária Homoki-Nagy, 'Megjegyezések Banyó Péter: Birtoköröklés és leánynegyed cimű tanulmányára', *Aetas*, (2001, no. 2), 189–93 (191). MNL OL, O 30, *Büntető perkivonatok fogalmazványai*, Bundle 3, fol. 590*r*, records a definitive statement of the Curia preventing the alteration of succession. MNL OL, O 39, *Decisiones Curiales*, 39, part 2 (1774), 154, contrastingly affirmed the nobleman's unlimited freedom to dispose of all *acquisita* by will. See also MNL OL, O 39, *Decisiones Curiales*, 13 (1750), 559.

[106] Jakab Pólya, 'A magyar birtok- és örökösödési jognak fejlődése', *Magyar Gazdaságtörténelmi Szemle*, 1 (1894), 60–5, 136–45 (142). For further difficulties involving *acquisita*, see Mária Homoki-Nagy, 'A törvényes öroklés jogi szabályozása Magyarországon 1861-ig', *Acta Juridica et Politica*, 59 (2000), 211–31 (219).

[107] Pólya, 'A magyar birtok', 140–2.

[108] SJAN–CJ, Prefectura judeţului Cluj, Fond 3, nr 126, *Protocollum inclyti Comitatus Colosiensis Generale (1731–61)*, 135.

[109] Gusztáv Wenzel, *Visszapillantás az előbbi magyar királyi curiának 1724–1769-iki működésére* (Budapest, 1875), 14–27.

The procedures of the courts were stable and they developed over time an increased sophistication. The manner of their proceeding was intended to ensure that justice was done, that the various obstacles which litigants might put in the way of their operation were accommodated, and that a practical solution was found to the cases that came before the courts. The substance of the law was, by contrast, far less apparent. Because courts eschewed fixed principles, preferring just or expedient solutions to abstract rules, the content of the law was made malleable. It was open, therefore to practices that might go against what was otherwise considered to be normative, even to the extent of permitting several, competing normative practices.[110] Even established principles of customary law might be set aside entirely in the interest of an equitable solution, subverting some of the basic propositions on which Hungarian noble society rested.

Certainly, there were in medieval Hungary and later, legal presumptions that may be shown to have exercised a particularly persuasive influence on court judgments. We have identified a number of these in the preceding chapters and showed the manner of their historical development. Litigants understood that the courts would generally defer to these, on account of which they trusted the courts sufficiently to take cases to them. These presumptions were far removed, however, from the sort of unyielding propositions that historians have sought to detect and to arrange into categories. The substance of the law thus remained fluctuating, sometimes subject to contrary court judgments but on others left in a legal void of continued indeterminacy. Notwithstanding the authority that the *Tripartitum* subsequently obtained in the practice of the courts and in Hungarian noble society more generally, its publication only partly overcame the instability inherent within Hungarian customary law. Since the authority of the *Tripartitum* rested on use, its contents might also be superseded by practices as actually followed or its individual provisions found inapplicable in specific cases. There was plenty, moreover, that the *Tripartitum* did not consider, which would need to be filled in by the courts and legislation. Later attempts, however, to mould a jurisprudence that was sure and made up for the deficiencies of Werbőczy's text foundered. The *Tripartitum* was too embedded to be easily set aside, yet the customary character of the law denied its content fixity. As a consequence, the law of the kingdom continued to rely on a customary text and on observances that might themselves be customized through practice and use.

[110] As may also have been the case in respect of watercourses that left their bed, where several opposing solutions were taken up in court practice. See Tringli, 'A magyar szokásjog a malomépitésről', 262–3.

# 9

# Early Modern Legal Institutions

## THE DIVISION OF THE KINGDOM

In 1526 the Hungarian army was defeated by the Turks on the field of Mohács and Hungary's young king was slain. Having plundered the capital, Suleiman withdrew from Hungary. It was only several campaigns later, in 1541, that Suleiman made the decision to occupy permanently the central portion of the kingdom. In the intervening years, Hungary disintegrated. The unresolved nature of the Hungarian royal succession, that is whether it was founded on election or descent, resulted in the appointment of two kings. On the one side stood Ferdinand of Habsburg who rested his claim to the throne on his relationship through marriage to the dead king's sister. Although Ferdinand went through an election, he regarded this not as a constitutive act but as recognition of his superior, hereditary right to the throne. On the other side was John Zápolya, the voivode of Transylvania, who based his right of succession on election by the diet and the Rákos decision of 1505. King John, although seeking to restore the medieval kingdom, relied increasingly upon Transylvania, which after his death in 1540 was transformed by degrees into an independent principality, under Ottoman protection. After the death in 1571 of John's son and successor, John II Sigismund, the ruler of Transylvania was determined by election of its diet, notwithstanding John Sigismund's previous nomination of a successor as prince.[1]

Hungary was thus divided into three parts—an area under Turkish occupation, the principality of Transylvania and its western dependencies (the so-called Partium), and a swathe of territory under Habsburg control, the so-called Royal Hungary, that reached in an elongated crescent from the Croatian coast to what is now north-western Romania and Ukraine.[2] Although its princes disputed the superior rights claimed by Hungary's Habsburg kings, Transylvania remained a part of the Hungarian crown lands, even to the extent that legislation of the Hungarian diet retained a persuasive authority in the principality.[3] Transylvania nevertheless

[1] Graeme Murdock, '"Freely Elected in Fear": Princely Elections and Political Power in Early Modern Transylvania', *Journal of Early Modern History*, 7, nos. 3–4 (2003), 213–44 (220).

[2] The process of Hungary's division is succinctly described in László Makkai, 'The Crown and the Diets of Hungary and Transylvania in the Sixteenth Century', in R.J.W. Evans and T.V. Thomas, eds., *Crown, Church and Estates: Central European Politics in the Sixteenth and Seventeenth Centuries* (Basingstoke and London, 1991), 80–91.

[3] SJAN-CJ, Fond 4, Comitatul Alba de Sus, no. 1, *Protocollum Marchalium Congregationum 1790–1802*, fol. 2*v*.

developed its own legal practices that set it apart from the rest of the kingdom. These were codified in the seventeenth century and published in two collections, the *Constitutiones Approbatae* (1653) and the *Constitutiones Compilatae* (1669). Different protonotaries handled cases proceeding before the prince, depending upon whether they emerged from Transylvania or from the parts of the kingdom that had been conjoined to it.[4] From the 1540s, representatives of the counties that had been attached to Transylvania also attended the principality's diet.

The larger contest between Habsburgs and Ottomans was marked by warfare that often drew in Transylvania's rulers. During the course of the sixteenth and seventeenth centuries, the contest for mastery over the kingdom was sharpened by confessional difference. By the middle decades of the sixteenth century, most of Hungary's population had converted to Protestantism, predominantly to Calvinism.[5] Along with the reformed faith came the doctrine of resistance conveyed in Calvin's *Institutes* and, therewith, the right to avenge the sort of tyrannical rule with which the Habsburgs were associated.[6] Notwithstanding a few wobbles, the Habsburg rulers were committed to the Catholic faith and to the cause of the Counter-Reformation, which they often promoted in defiance of accepted rights and freedoms. The heavy-handedness of Habsburg rule prompted a succession of conspiracies and revolts that by turns drew in the Turks, Transylvania's princes and disaffected religious communities. Territorial division and warfare thus combined with political and religious conflict to render Hungary for long periods ungovernable. It was only in 1686–7 that the main part of the Hungarian territory under Turkish occupation was liberated by the Habsburg armies, and not until 1711 that Transylvania effectively came under Habsburg control, following the defeat of Ferenc Rákóczi's insurrection. Even so, Transylvania continued to be administered separately from Hungary, having its own government and diet.

The division of the kingdom was not only territorial and confessional but also political. Hungary's Habsburg rulers imported an approach towards government and the law that was both centralizing and inspired by Romanist traditions of princely authority. The reforms that they sought to impose were resisted by large swathes of the nobility, who nestled behind their traditional institutions of self-rule—assemblies of the diet and counties. In the struggle to resist Habsburg authority, they looked for sustenance to the *Tripartitum*, both because it was thought to convey the historic law of the country and on account of its public law clauses, which yielded several means of political resistance. The *Tripartitum* became

[4] Zsolt Bogdándi, 'Wesselényi Miklós. Egy itélőmester életútja a 16. század végi Erdélyben', in Emese Egyed, László Pakó and Attila Weisz, eds., *Certamen I. Előadások a magyar tudomány napján az Erdélyi Múzeum Egyesület I. szakosztályban* (Cluj, 2013), 236–50 (242).

[5] On the progress of the Reformation in Hungary, see Robert J.W. Evans, 'Calvinism in East Central Europe: Hungary and her Neighbours', in Menna Prestwich, ed., *International Calvinism, 1541–1715* (Oxford, 1985), 167–97; Graeme Murdock, *Calvinism on the Frontier 1600–1660: International Calvinism and the Reformed Church in Hungary and Transylvania* (Oxford, 2000), 10–45.

[6] Martyn Rady, 'Bocskai, Rebellion and Resistance in Early Modern Hungary', in László Péter and Rady, eds., *Resistance, Rebellion and Revolution in Hungary and Central Europe: Commemorating 1956* (London, 2008), 57–66 (63–4); Graeme Murdock, *Beyond Calvin: The Intellectual, Political and Cultural World of Europe's Reformed Churches, c. 1540–1620* (Basingstoke and New York, 2004), 74.

thus conceived by Hungarian noblemen as the sign and bulwark of their rights, and any alteration of its text as an assault on their privileges. It was thus held to embody 'the full strength of the law' against the illegalities of Viennese rule, the content of which (as one Hungarian politician later explained) the Holy Spirit had been enjoined to preserve in unblemished integrity.[7]

Unsurprisingly, therefore, attempts by the ruler to replace the *Tripartitum* with a more manageable text, most notably the draft produced in the 1550s that is known as the *Quadripartitum*, failed. The customary law, as communicated by a text, the authority of which rested on customary use, thus endured. Likewise, successive codifications of the kingdom's statute law, published from the sixteenth century in the form of what would become the *Corpus Juris Hungarici* (CJH), rested similarly upon a notion of legal authority as deriving from practice and use, not from the precise terms of statutory legislation. Thus, even their errors and omissions garnered a customary authority of their own. The consequence was that Hungary retained the character of a customary law jurisdiction, notwithstanding Habsburg attempts to modernize and improve its legal institutions.

## THE ORGANIZATION OF JUSTICE

It is a commonplace that under the impact of war and division Hungary's legal institutions withered, surviving only in attenuated and misshapen forms. In the vacuum caused, so it is argued, Hungary's Habsburg rulers intervened, practising a despotic legal power. The 'fiscal trials' of the late sixteenth and seventeenth centuries and the intrusions of the treasury into the administration of both justice and the county administration are by this measure emblematic of Habsburg contempt for the law and of its manipulation of Hungary's institutions. As part of this process, the chancellery was reduced to an office or *expeditio* in either Vienna or Prague, headed by a secretary, with the office of chancellor becoming honorific.[8] The control over Hungarian business exercised by Austrian officials who had little sympathy for the kingdom's traditions was a frequent complaint of the diet. It was only in the 1690s that the chancellery was restored as an effective agency of government, with a membership that largely overlapped with the newly appointed Transylvanian court chancellery, which also now met in Vienna. The former royal council was, for its part, side-lined in much the same way as the chancellery. Following the Habsburg takeover of the kingdom, the royal council ceased to assemble, except on ceremonial occasions. Its place was taken by the regency council, which convened in Bratislava, but with a smaller membership and an authority that was largely confined to judicial administration. For much of the sixteenth century, the regency council was headed by a royally appointed regent or *locumtenens*, usually a prelate, and not by the palatine, whose selection depended upon the diet's

[7] György Bónis, *A birósági szervezet megújitása III. Károly korában (Systematica Commissio)* (Budapest, 1935), 74, 169.

[8] Loránd Szilágyi, 'A királyi secretariusok intézménye és az újkori magyar állam', *Emlékkönyv Domanovszky Sándor* (Budapest, 1937), 547–61 (552–61).

agreement.[9] The business of the regency council was expedited by a privy chancellery that also resided in Bratislava.[10]

While it cannot be denied that Hungary's Habsburg rulers often interfered in the work of the kingdom's courts, it was not so much their disregard for the kingdom's laws as the precision with which they sought to apply the laws that most aroused opposition. The Habsburg rulers of Hungary and their principal advisors had been schooled in the strict legality of Roman Law. They retained a respect for the written word, explicated by reference to civilian principles, in respect of which loose customary arrangements retained little authority. The misgivings which this approach engendered were typical of the resentments to which the *Verwissenschaftlichung* of the law gave rise more generally in sixteenth-century Europe.[11] Not for the first time, a lawyerly understanding of the law was confused with the law's perversion.

Nor were Hungary's Habsburg rulers at all chary about bringing prominent noblemen to account, should they be suspected of crime. During the sixteenth century, a succession of leading nobles were thus taken before the courts and their properties declared forfeit as a consequence of their guilt—Ferenc Petheő, for the alleged crime of castrating a fellow nobleman; Tamás Nádasdy, for having incestuously married his niece; András Balassa, for seizing a relative's property, and so on.[12] In an earlier period, crimes of this sort had most frequently been either overlooked or resolved by negotiation. In respect of the crime of lèse-majesté, the Habsburg rulers of Hungary considered this an offence that was directed at them personally, on account of which they might refer judgment to a court of their own choosing, even one that was located outside the kingdom. Cases of rebellion and sedition were, from the 1560s onwards, usually heard by 'delegated tribunals' that judged without reference to Hungarian law. Many of those arraigned before these courts had opposed Habsburg rule precisely on account of its apparent disregard for the kingdom's liberties (Ferenc Dobó, János Balassa, István Illésházy, Ferenc Nádasdy, Ferenc Rákóczi and so on), thus giving credence to the accusation that the special tribunals administered a partisan and political justice. Most notoriously, in 1687 a delegated court was established at the behest of the imperial commander, Antonio de Caraffa, to investigate allegations of perfidy in Prešov. The 'bloody assizes' over which Caraffa presided, claimed the lives of twenty-two noblemen and citizens (a further two died under torture) for crimes that were plainly fictitious.[13] Notwithstanding previous

[9] Győző Ember, *Az újkori magyar közigazgatás története. Mohácstól a török kiűzéséig* (Budapest, 1946), 75–119; less satisfactorily, Andor Csizmadia, ed., *Magyar állam- és jogtörténet* (Budapest, 1978), 179–81. For the diet's historic right to select the palatine, see now Norbert C. Tóth, 'Az ország nádora', *Középkortörténeti Tanulmányok*, 7 (2012), 439–50.

[10] Szilágyi, 'A királyi secretariusok intézménye', 553–4.

[11] See more generally, Gerald Strauss, *Law, Resistance and the State: The Opposition to Roman Law in Reformation Germany* (Princeton, NJ, 1986), 56–95.

[12] Ignácz Acsády, *A pozsonyi és szepesi kamarák 1565–1604* (Budapest, 1894), 19.

[13] Győző Ember and Gusztáv Heckenast, eds., *Magyarorszag története tiz kötetben, 1686–1790*, 2 vols. (Budapest, 1989), i, 84–5. For the composition of the court, which was hardly stuffed by stooges as is commonly alleged, see Miklós K. Papp, *Caraffa és az eperjesi vér-törvényszék*, 2 vols. (Pest, 1863), ii, 16. Biographies of the victims are given in J. Rezik, *Prešovská jatka z roku 1687 (Theatrum Eperiense*

commitments, it was only in the 1790s that cases of lèse-majesté were returned to the jurisdiction of Hungary's own courts.[14]

The Hungarian treasury was complicit in the work of the special tribunals since it was the royal fisc that benefited from the confiscations that followed upon a guilty verdict. Its officers were accordingly involved in the prosecution of offenders, helping to draw up the charges as well as representing the interests of the ruler in the proceedings. They were on this account criticized as the witting agents of Viennese centralization, both at the time and in subsequent historical literature.[15] The Hungarian treasury (*Ungarische Kammer*, *Magyar Kamara*) had been founded by Ferdinand in Buda in 1528, but moved the next year to Bratislava. After 1567, a separate branch known as the Spiš treasury operated in Prešov, later in Košice.[16] Although theoretically subordinate to the Hofkammer in Vienna, the Hungarian treasury took most of its instructions directly from the imperial chancellery.[17] Its purpose was to gather and administer the royal revenues—money from tolls, mining, minting, the salt trade and church vacancies as well as from the taxes voted by the diet. The treasury was additionally responsible for maintaining the network of royal castle lordships, which were the concentrations of villages that supported the kingdom's garrisons. Beyond this, the treasury was charged with supervising the properties belonging to the royal fisc and with their enlargement. To this end, it was specifically mandated to recover royal estates that had been pledged out. In fact, the treasury often did the very reverse, recovering property and then re-pledging it on more advantageous terms. By the 1580s, it had gathered almost a million florins through this recourse.[18] It also leased the right to collect church tithes, subsequently farming these out to yield an effortless profit.[19] From the toll collectors and estate managers who worked on behalf of the treasury, Hungary's Habsburg rulers received detailed news reports on conditions and developments deep in the countryside.[20] In view of its manifold activities, it is appropriate to consider the treasury administration as the effective government of the kingdom for much of the sixteenth and seventeenth centuries.

A principal task of the treasury was the sequestration of estates that fell to the royal fisc as a consequence not only of perfidy but also of death without heirs. Once possessed by the treasury, estates of this type were usually pledged out or

*seu Laniena)* (Liptovský Sv. Mikuláš, 1931). Most of those killed would appear to be either Protestants or business rivals of Caraffa.

[14] 1622: 20; Endre Varga, *A királyi Curia 1780–1850* (Budapest, 1974), 97; MJL, v, 629–31. Still in the 1550s, Ferenc and György Bebek were summoned before the diet on the charge of *nota infidelitatis* on account of their conspiring with John II Sigismund. See Pál Zsigmond Pach, ed., *Magyarország története tiz kötetben, 1526–1686*, 2 vols. (Budapest, 1987), i, 414.

[15] See thus, Acsády, *A pozsonyi és szepesi kamarák 1565–1604*, 4–5.

[16] Neither Prešov nor Košice were in Spiš County. The Spiš treasury was technically subordinate to the Hungarian treasury in Bratislava, but took most of its instructions from the Hofkammer in Vienna.

[17] These survive for the period 1531–1722 in MNL OL, E 21, *Benignae Resolutiones* and amount to no less than 534 bundles and 111 volumes.

[18] Ignácz Acsády, *Régi magyar birtokviszonyok 1494–1598* (Budapest, 1894), 64.

[19] István Nagy and Erzsébet F. Kiss, *A magyar kamara és egyéb kincstári szervek* (Budapest, 1995), 13.

[20] See, for example, MNL OL, E 137, *Relationes Commissariorum Regiorum*, Box 1, fasc. 1 etc.

sold. Unlike their medieval counterparts, Hungary's Habsburg rulers only rarely gave away land outright as a 'pure donation'.[21] In the business of sequestration, treasury officers worked with the royal *director causarum* and the other fiscals, to whose advice they were obliged to defer in all judicial matters.[22] By the eighteenth century, if not before, the treasury was retaining the opinions so given for future reference in analogous cases.[23] In the course of litigation, the treasury was tough—demanding to see full evidence of descents and questioning all arrangements that could not be grounded on the law or in written documentation. An issue that they often confronted was whether land descended through the female line, which was the claim normally alleged in court to prevent escheat on grounds of death without male heirs.[24] Later evidence suggests that where the law was uncertain, the treasury and the fiscals were apt to presume in favour of the crown and to argue that the burden of proving otherwise rested upon the respondents. The courts, however, were alert to these ruses and by no means automatically inclined to the treasury's side.[25] In respect of cases arising from the territories newly captured from the Turks, officers of the treasury were for several decades after 1686 entitled to adjudicate in criminal matters and to hear appeals arising out of civil cases. In these instances, treasury administrators tended to follow procedures practised in Lower Austrian courts.[26] With this important exception, however, the treasury was otherwise bound to proceed through the established courts and in accordance with Hungarian law.

Despite their reputation, neither the treasury nor its lawyers were particularly unscrupulous. Indeed, the list of directors for the sixteenth and seventeenth centuries included some of the kingdom's most celebrated practitioners—among others, Mózes Cziráky, Péter Alvinczi and János Kitonich.[27] In reviewing the resources more generally available within the kingdom, officers of the treasury were aware of the extent to which the pattern of exemptions had shifted the burden onto the peasants and they pressed for measures aimed at their relief. Even as early as the 1550s, therefore, they advocated a reform of taxation that would put an end to the inequalities which were so offensive to the divine order.[28] More specifically, the treasury took steps to prevent the enclosure of common land, on account of the pauperization that followed, and recommended that judges not take a portion of the fines handed out by courts but receive instead a fixed salary.[29] In respect of the kingdom's cities, over which it exercised a general right of supervision, the treasury required the magistrates to fulfil their obligations towards widows and orphans,

21 Acsády, *Régi magyar birtokviszonyok*, 60.

22 Nagy and Kiss, *A magyar kamara*, 166.

23 Nagy and Kiss, *A magyar kamara*, 167–8.

24 MNL OL, O 2, *Processus Delegatorii*, Bundle 1, no. 2 (1692–9); MNL OL, E 14, *Acta Hungarica*, vol. 4, 365–406 (1720).

25 MNL OL, O 39, *Decisiones Curiales*, 13 (1750), 554–92 (esp. 558, 561, 567, 577, 579).

26 György Bónis, *Buda és Pest bírósági gyakorlata a török kiűzése után 1686–1708* (Budapest, 1962), 300–15.

27 Ember, *Az újkori magyar közigazgatás története*, 146–7. Alvinczi (Alvinczy) was the nephew of the famous Calvinist pastor of the same name.

28 *Monumenta Comitialia*, iv, 41.

29 Ibolya Felhő, 'A szabad királyi városok és a magyar kamara a xvii. században', *Levéltári Közlemények*, 24, no. 1 (1946), 208–67 (226); *Monumenta Comitialia*, iv, 45.

take measures to improve sanitation, and improve judicial procedures. Treasury officers might also put pressure on individual councils to remove Protestants from public positions and to initiate proceedings for such outrages as breaking church windows and upsetting religious processions. In view of the authority it discharged, it is not surprising that the treasury was the frequent recipient of petitions for the redress of local grievances, in responding to which the ambit of its influence was correspondingly enlarged.[30]

Notwithstanding the inroads made by special tribunals and the treasury into the administration of justice, Hungary's courts fared rather better than most commentators have allowed. A good deal of the work that had previously gone to the courts of the Curia was now taken up by the counties, thus compensating for the failures of justice at the higher level. Indeed, in those areas under Turkish occupation, the surviving institutions of county justice provided almost the only forums for redress. Some cases were evidently adjudicated, however, by the pasha in Buda or referred across the frontier for decision to the royal courts, while criminal matters might be dealt with at special sessions of manor courts held at a distance. The *loca credibilia* were surely strained by the need to witness noble institutions to property deep in the Turkish-occupied countryside![31] In Royal Hungary and Transylvania, the judicial organization of the counties became increasingly sophisticated, with most counties being divided up into ridings where subordinate offices of the magistracy, headed by elected *szolgabirák* (sing: *szolgabiró*; *iudices nobilium*), judged minor crimes and disputes. The local offices of the *szolgabirák* drew increasingly upon a core of deputies and sworn assessors. At the same time, the institutions of county justice began to establish their own physical presence, moving their sessions from fields, barns and private homes into more appropriate buildings. It was not, however, until the eighteenth century that their accommodation became truly palatial, and even then poorer counties had to make do with arrangements that were much inferior.[32] Upper Alba County in southern Transylvania was without a house of its own as late as the 1790s, its sessions being still itinerant.[33] Nevertheless, the fact that so much judicial and other material survives from the counties after the sixteenth century is testimony to the increased professionalization of justice and administration at a local level, not least through the establishment of proper scribal offices.

As cases that had previously been taken to the courts of the Curia were now increasingly brought before the counties, the limitations that had previously applied to their jurisdiction were relaxed. During the sixteenth century, county courts generally observed an earlier restriction on judging disputes that involved damages or

[30] Ember, *Az újkori magyar közigazgatás*, 146–7; Ibolya Felhő, 'A szabad királyi városok és a magyar kamara', 226–47.

[31] Ferenc Szakály, *Magyar intézmények a török hódoltságban* (Budapest, 1997), 87–91, 127.

[32] Most spectacularly at Zalaegerszeg. See László Vándor ed., *Zala megye ezer éve* (Szombathely, 2001), 114. Pest County had its own *domus Curialis* by 1736. See RL, Sigray család levéltára, 1. 2.

[33] SJAN-CJ, Fond 4, Comitatul Alba de Sus, no. 1, *Protocollum Marchalium Congregationum*, 1790–1802, fol. 46.

property over 100 florins, but there were evidently some exceptions.[34] Thereafter, the counties assumed an increased competence, adjudicating matters of several or more thousand florins and apportioning damages and fines that far exceeded the older limit, even taking inflation into account.[35] In the 1660s, the diet acknowledged the link between the decline of the Curia courts and the need to enhance the authority of the county courts, raising the upper limit to 1,200 florins.[36] This was plainly inadequate. In the first decades of the eighteenth century, the limit was thus raised to 12,000 florins at full sessions of county courts, with cases up to a value of 3,000 florins falling within the competence of the magistrates in the ridings.[37] At the same time, the counties played an increasing role in the maintenance of order, not only ordering the periodic 'rounding up' of notorious malefactors but also taking action on instruction or even of their own volition against violent occupiers.[38] The extension of the authority of the counties to include all actions of violence was championed by the diet as one solution to the problem of disorder in the countryside.[39]

It was a frequent complaint of the diet that the Curia courts had ceased to function and that as a consequence cases remained unheard, often for decades. As the deputies complained at the 1574 Bratislava diet, cases half-a-century old had still not been settled by the courts.[40] Despite the diet's rhetoric, the central institutions of justice survived, notwithstanding their evacuation from Buda to Bratislava in the 1530s. The most active institution was the council of regency that sat under the presidency of the palatine or the *locumtenens*. The principal task of the council was to pass judgment in matters of violence and of the seizure of property, in cases involving women and orphans, and in actions transmitted from lower courts.[41] The regency council acted in much the same way as the former royal council, its judicial sessions being attended not only by its members but also by various barons, leading church men and protonotaries. By the middle years of the sixteenth century, the judicial business of the regency council was consuming roughly 200 days a year, but even this was considered too little by the diet.[42] Additional sessions under a succession of different names were subsequently mandated in order to speed up the passage of litigation, particularly in cases where a manifest injustice

[34] Péter Tóth, *Borsod vármegye közgyűlési és törvényszéki jegyzőkönyvei 1569–1578* (Miskolc, 2008), nos. 240, 320, 456, 504, 519, 580, 585, 1266, 1529, 1538, 1578, 1688, 1890, 1894; exceptions are given in Tóth, *Borsod vármegye*, nos. 903, 2081.

[35] Teréz Oborni, *Nógrád vármegye nemesi közgyűlési jegyzőkönyveinek regesztái (1597–1603)* (Salgótarján, 2001), nos. 597, 798, 931, 935, 957, 958; Zoltán Hegedűs and Zoltán Szabó, *Győr vármegye nemesi közgyűlési és törvénykezési jegyzőkönyveinek regesztái, 1638–1650* (Győr, 2007), no. 147. Prices roughly rose four to fivefold in the sixteenth century.

[36] Jean Bérenger, *Les 'Gravamina'. Remontrances des diètes de Hongrie de 1655 à 1681* (Paris, 1973), 253.

[37] István Stipta, *A magyar bírósági rendszer története*, 2nd edition (Debrecen, 1998), 76.

[38] István R. Kiss, *A magyar helytartótanács I. Ferdinand korában és 1549–1551. évi leveleskönyve* (Budapest, 1908), p. cxxii.

[39] *Monumenta Comitialia*, v, 363. [40] *Monumenta Comitialia*, vi, 44, 119.

[41] Stipta, *A magyar bírósági rendszer története*, 58–9; Ember, *Az újkori magyar közigazgatás története*, 102.

[42] Kiss, *A magyar helytartótanács*, pp. cxviii–xix; *Monumenta Comitialia*, ii, 14–15, 128, 562, 667.

was apprehended.[43] Despite its diligence, the council still moved actions of weight or particular complexity to the ruler for his personal decision, which to the consternation of the diet was usually made without Hungarian assessors being in attendance and without reference to Hungarian law.[44] Attempts to replace the king with a special judge of appeal proved, however, unsuccessful.[45]

'Protracted cases', namely those that involved disputes over descents of property, were more difficult. These largely fell outside the remit of the council and so were frequently denied a hearing for this reason.[46] During the sixteenth century, the court of the Royal Table that adjudicated suits over title met irregularly. At best, only two octave courts were held, each supposedly at a different location within the kingdom, although the judges were often too old and sick to undertake the necessary travel.[47] Accordingly, the octave sessions of the Royal Table became more of an event than of an institution, marked by celebration on account of their rarity.[48] For much of the seventeenth century, no octave courts were held at all and the Royal Table thus went into suspension for long periods. Between 1650 and 1700, the court assembled on only one occasion, in 1676, but in the fortnight during which it sat, hardly made any impression on the backlog.[49] Under these circumstances, the established routine of moving cases from one octave to the next in order to allow time for the paperwork to be gathered, had to be abandoned. Cases were thus either adjourned indefinitely, often never to be resolved, or rushed through, with the consequence that the losing party invariably petitioned for a retrial.

There were several remedies to which the court of the Royal Table had recourse. Where matters of particular weight were concerned, it was always possible for a special tribunal to be instituted on a mandate of the chancellery. On account of their associations, however, courts of this type might be shunned by litigants as 'contrary to the order and law of the country'.[50] Nevertheless, it was sometimes the case that the parties requested a special tribunal in the interests of speeding up a resolution of their differences. Delegated courts of this type were usually presided over by a senior judge (often the *personalis* or another member of the Royal Table) and attended by protonotaries, county and city magistrates, treasury officials and local military commanders.[51] It was more common, however, for the principal judges of the realm to instruct their protonotaries to hear cases and to hold an itinerant court (*iudicium ambulatorium*) on their behalf in the countryside. Often the protonotaries received a general mandate empowering them to judge all such

[43] The *iudicia brevia, brevia brevium, iudicia octavalia minores,* which were authorized by the palatine or *locumtenens,* and the *iudicia extraordinaria,* which were an extension of the palatine's court. See Bónis, *A bírósági szervezet megújítása,* 18–22.

[44] Kiss, *A magyar helytartótanács,* p. cxxiii.

[45] Kiss, *A magyar helytartótanács,* pp. cxxi–ii; *Monumenta Comitialia,* ii, 445.

[46] Bónis, *A bírósági szervezet megújítása,* 18.

[47] *Monumenta Comitialia,* iii, 509, 524; *Monumenta Comitialia,* iv, 132, 388; *Monumenta Comitialia,* v, 149; *Monumenta Comitialia,* vi, 44, 278.

[48] Ignácz Acsády, *Magyarország Budavár visszafoglalása korában* (Budapest, 1886), 74.

[49] Acsády, *Magyarország Budavár visszafoglalása korában,* 75.

[50] MNL OL, O 2, *Processus Delegatorii,* Bundle 1, no. 2 (1692–9).

[51] Endre Varga and Miklós Veres, *Bírósági levéltárak 1526–1869* (Budapest, 1989), 40–1.

cases as were presented to them and it might be several years before they completed their work in any one place. The protonotaries generally held court with local magistrates and officials, reporting back their judgments which were then sealed by the instructing judges as binding decisions.[52] The reputation of these courts was, however, low on account of the supposed openness of the protonotaries to bribery.[53]

A further remedy lay within the structure of civil law adjudication itself. The practice of the Hungarian courts was episodic, with individual cases being moved by interlocutory judgments and adjournments from one court session to the next. It was a paper-driven process that relied upon the court's collective examination of deeds, titles, records of inquests and reports of oath-takings. It did not depend upon the cross-examination of witnesses and the drama of the courtroom was largely reduced to the formalized parrying of *exceptiones* and *allegationes*. Under these circumstances, it was entirely possible to disconnect the stages in the action and have them settled at a distance through correspondence. Thus, a plaintiff would commence an action by notifying the palatine, high judge, *personalis* or, more usually, their protonotaries that a wrong had been done to him. The plaint would be recast as a mandate and the respondent required to desist from a course of conduct or to make amends. If the respondent did not do so, then a mandate of execution (*mandatum praeceptorium-executorium*) might be issued. The respondent could, however, obtain from the instructing judge a mandate of his own that forbade the execution, a *mandatum inhibitorium*, on the grounds that the first mandate was unjust (or delivered without due notice). There would then be further exchanges between the parties and the judge and fresh mandates given out—a *mandatum relaxatorium, dilatorium, moratorium, superinhibitorium, reexecutorium* and so on. It is easy to understand the contemporary complaint that 'for every hundred *praeceptoria* there was scarcely one that wasn't met by an *inhibitorium*'. Nevertheless, the pattern of exchanges had the purpose of gradually exposing the facts of the case and determining the most appropriate solution in law. It was also a more reliable and rapid expedient than waiting over several decades for the Royal Table to reassemble.[54]

Contemporaries had much to complain about—the delays, the cost of justice, the ruses and loquaciousness of the lawyers, the avarice of the treasury as well as, in the words of the 1651 diet, 'the wrongful occupations, seizures, daily murders and the thousand other crimes and offences that cry to heaven' as a consequence of the law's neglect.[55] Nevertheless, the structure of the kingdom's courts survived into the eighteenth century, withstanding warfare and political division. In the reform of justice undertaken by Charles III in the 1720s, the judicial organization as it had developed over the preceding period was broadly retained. At the head of the realm's structure of courts was the successor to the regency

[52] MNL OL, O 3, *Mandata Judiciaria*, Box 1, 1654, fols. 350–84; MNL OL, O 3, *Mandata Judiciaria*, Box 1,1656, no. 23.

[53] János J. Varga, 'Berendezési tervezetek Magyarországon a török kiűzésének időszakában', *Századok*, 125, nos. 5–6 (1991), 449–88 (462).

[54] Bónis, *A bírósági szervezet megújitása*, 37–8.

[55] 1655: 51.

council, reconstituted under the (theoretical) presidency of the palatine and renamed the Table of the Seven or court of the Septemviralis.[56] (Its late seventeenth century predecessor had indeed once had seven members, but its membership was soon inflated.) Beneath the Septemviralis lay the Royal Table, under the presidency of the *personalis*, which became the principal forum for the adjudication of major crimes, including most crimes of perfidy, the more difficult disputes over landed property, and cases involving the treasury. In place of the ad hoc courts of the itinerant protonotaries, four district branches of the Royal Table were established in order to expedite the less weighty civil suits that might be more conveniently heard at a local level—disputes over wardship, debt, breach of contract, and property actions that did not involve descents. Meanwhile, the county courts were retained, with a generally enhanced authority that included hearing actions arising from the manor courts.

The structure of the courts was linked, however, by what was a relatively new device in Hungarian procedural law, namely the appeal.[57] Until the second half of the seventeenth century, there were generally two ways by which cases might be moved for revision. The first was the retrial which involved the case being reheard in its entirety. Retrials were a commonplace and, indeed, were regarded as so integral to the proper administration of justice that they were almost automatically granted at the request of a disappointed suitor, 'because according to the law and custom of the realm, in all ordinary cases one retrial is allowed'.[58] The second was the transmission, whereby the case was moved in its entirety to a higher court, often because it was found in the course of the opening stages that it was beyond the competence of the original forum. Many cases were, nonetheless, opened by nobles at county courts in the expectation that they would be referred up to a higher tribunal. Transmissions often proceeded under the fiction of prorogation, with the case being adjourned halfway through the trial, to be resumed at a session of the higher court. Transmissions might also be made after judgment and the higher court review the facts of the case. Transmissions of this sort were, however, made by the courts rather than at the request of the litigants. It was only in respect of the central royal courts that cases might be moved specifically by appeal from the Royal Table to the council, largely on account of their proximity and the overlap of their membership.

During the second half of the seventeenth century, it became increasingly common for the Royal Table to review the judgments of lower courts, principally of the counties and of the protonotaries, at special sessions of the regency council (later of the Septemviralis court). These oversaw both actions transmitted before final judgment and cases that been already determined but where a petition for revision had been received. The name accorded to these special sessions indicates the double function that they discharged—*terminus celebrationis et revisionis*

[56] The palatine was usually represented by the high judge.

[57] Appeals made at the request of one of the parties to a higher forum were employed in urban jurisdictions from the thirteenth century, but their use was limited in the Hungarian countryside. See Gyula Gábor, *A megyei intézmény alakulása és működése Nagy Lajos alatt* (Budapest, 1908), 170–1.

[58] Kitonich, *Directio Methodica*, 8. 10 (2004 edition), 316–18.

*extraordinariorum iudiciorum et transmissionalium causarum.*[59] During the first decades of the eighteenth century, appeals after an initial judgment proved, however, increasingly common and were handled separately from transmissions. Appeals generally required the agreement of the lower court, which was obliged to hand over the relevant paperwork, but might also be moved through a mandate of the chancellery or a superior judge. The reforms of the early eighteenth century permitted a hierarchy of appeals, with it being possible to dispute the judgments of lower courts at the court of the Royal Table and, thereafter, at the court of the Septemviralis. Superior courts might variously uphold or reject the decisions made, modify them, or oblige the lower court to retry the case. Appeals normally involved only the examination of the paperwork and were frequently given perfunctory treatment, with the appeal court's usual written decision being only an unmotivated *Deliberatum est, quod etc.* The decision of the higher court was then remitted back, with the instruction that either the court of the first instance or the relevant county authorities implement its judgment.

The development of a structure of appeal courts that moved cases from the provincial branches of the Royal Table, up to the Royal Table itself and thence to the Septemviralis, and then back again for execution of the revised judgment, contributed to the increased integration not only of the kingdom's judicial administration but also of its law. Lower courts were increasingly constrained by the centre and obliged to administer decisions in conformity with its interpretation, irrespective of local customary arrangements. The leading textbook, published in many editions after 1734, János Szegedi's *Tyrocinium*—its title betrays its intended audience—thus acknowledged that the opinions of Curia courts did not constitute laws to be followed, but served an exemplary purpose. Nevertheless, since appeals to the Curia from lower courts were now commonplace, it was incumbent upon inferior tribunals to bend to the Curia's decisions and to frame their judgments accordingly. As Szegedi conceded, in view of the structure of appeal courts, the decisions of the Curia should be considered as if they were legislation.[60] Institutional mechanisms of revision and review established as part of the kingdom's judicial reorganization thus contributed to Hungary's reintegration after the many decades of dislocation and division.

## ROMAN LAW AND THE TRANSYLVANIAN SAXONS

Hungary was familiar with Roman Law, which shaped its vocabulary, determined the broad outline of its judicial procedures, and provided the learned literature to which scholars referred, albeit usually in a mediated form. The gradualness of the process whereby Roman Law influenced Hungary's law and institutions was typical of the experience of the German lands and of Central and Northern Europe

[59] Bónis, *A bírósági szervezet megújitása*, 13, 22–3.
[60] János Szegedi, *Tripartitum Juris Hungarici Tyrocinium* (Košice, 1764), 237 (II. 2).

more generally.[61] Unlike, however, the German lands to the west, Hungary did not have a Roman Law reception in the late fifteenth and sixteenth centuries, for the same conditions did not apply. Hungary already had its own body of law and practices and stood in no need of a Romanist solution to the problems of particularism.[62] Nor was it possessed of independently minded princes and cities, anxious to keep pace with a Romanizing imperial court.[63] In Hungary, therefore, legal codification and the standardization of the law did not result in the adoption or superimposing of civilian texts but instead in the publication of the kingdom's own customs and in the assembling of its written statutes.

The Roman Law reception in Europe involved more, however, than the wholesale adoption of Romanist texts. Throughout the sixteenth and seventeenth centuries, scholars and jurists engaged with the Roman Law, albeit critically and often with the purpose of adjusting its content to fit local traditions. In so doing, they gave birth to Roman-Dutch, Roman-Scots, Roman-Hispanic and Roman-Saxon law.[64] The process of harmonization did not, however, take place at the expense of Roman legal method—the movement from a set of substantive principles, through reasoning by analogy and deduction to a logical (or even syllogistic) conclusion. The increasingly general practice of giving motivated decisions, which required an exposition of the general principles that lay behind an individual judgment, served to bind Roman Law scholarship to the practice of the courts. *Aktenversendung*, whereby tribunals sought the opinion of law faculties on individual points of law, had a similar consequence.[65] Of all this, however, Hungarian law and lawyers knew little and, indeed, cared less. By holding firm to the *Tripartitum* and to the published and customary laws of the realm, Hungary became akin in its legal development to those German statelets that stuck until the nineteenth century to the text of the *Sachsenspiegel*—except that they did at least use its Romanized glosses.

One part of the territory of the Hungarian crown did, however, experience a comprehensive Roman Law reception analogous to developments in the German lands. This was not surprisingly in a German land, the home of the Transylvanian Saxons. The Saxon land comprised a cluster of four areas of settlement set on the south-eastern edge of the kingdom, all of which were distinguished by their high degree of urbanization and administrative decentralization. Within the area of Saxon settlement, the Hungarian nobility were increasingly squeezed out by the purchase of their properties and by more violent means.[66] In 1486, the community, which had for much of the previous period been mainly governed by royal

[61] The point is made at length by Winfried Trusen, *Anfänge des gelehrten Rechts in Deutschland. Ein Beitrag zur Geschichte der Frührezeption* (Wiesbaden, 1962).

[62] Gábor Hamza, *Wege der Entwicklung des Privatrechts in Europa* (Passau, 2007), 120.

[63] Wolfgang Kunkel, 'The Reception of Roman Law in Germany: An Interpretation', in Gerald Strauss, ed., *Pre-Reformation Germany* (London and Basingstoke, 1972), 262–81 (270–6).

[64] Reinhard Zimmermann, *Roman Law, Contemporary Law, European Law: The Civilian Tradition Today* (Oxford, 2001), 1–2.

[65] David Ibbetson and Andrew Lewis, 'The Roman law tradition', in Lewis and Ibbetson, *The Roman Law Tradition* (Cambridge, 1994), 1–14 (6–7).

[66] SJAN Sibiu, Colecţia de Documente Medievale, U-IV, no. 153; SJAN Sibiu, Colecţia Brukenthal, RS, no. 493.

appointees, was converted into a single legal jurisdiction or *universitas* under the leadership of the mayor of Sibiu. The law followed at this time by the Saxon community was largely customary, but also included elements taken from the *Schwabenspiegel*, the Magdeburg *Weichbild*, and the code of Iglau-Jihlava.[67]

Most Transylvanian Saxons had by the 1540s embraced Lutheranism, thereby obtaining a renewed sense of communal identity that was reinforced by burgeoning contact with the German centres of Protestantism, most notably with the University of Wittenberg. The consequences for Saxon legal development were contradictory. On the one hand, Protestantism inspired calls for the 'godly reformation' that would bring the law into conformity with divine justice. Although this was more a feature of Calvinist teaching, it found expression in the passage of Saxon legislation forbidding concubinage (under pain of death), card games and night-time revelry.[68] On the other, the German centredness of much Lutheran teaching encouraged an interest among Saxon scholars in the historic law of the German people. In this respect, the association of *deutsches Recht* with *Kaiserrecht* argued in favour of Roman Law, which might also be perceived as being closest chronologically to the pure law of early Christianity. The perception of Saxon Lutherans that they constituted a *colonia Germanici Imperii in Transsilvania* summed up the ambiguities that would subsequently attend the course of their legal history.[69]

These separate strands were pulled together by Johannes Honterus (1498–1549), who was elected in 1544 the first Protestant priest of the city of Braşov. Honterus had previously studied at Vienna, Cracow and Basle, and upon his return to Transylvania in the early 1530s set up in Braşov his own printing press and high school. The one turned out editions of Plato, Aristotle, Seneca and Cicero; the other, graduates in the *litterae humaniores*, law and medicine. In order to advance his students' legal understanding, Honterus edited a collection of almost 800 *loci communes* taken from the *Digest*.[70] In 1544, Honterus published what he alleged to be a compilation of the customary laws of the Saxon community in Transylvania, the *Compendium iuris civilis in usum Civitatum et Sedium Saxonicarum*. His intention was to provide a common code for the Transylvanian Saxons that was free of 'barbarism' and 'the old legal knowledge', rested on the principles of natural law as revealed in the Roman Law, but was adapted to local circumstances and habits. In fact, the *Compendium* owed little to Saxon legal traditions, being built up largely from the *Digest*. Its arrangement was, however, masterful, breaking down the law into four books that dealt respectively with

[67] Or so we should understand from the contents of the 1481 *Altenberger Codex*. See Gusztáv Lindner, 'A Svábtükör az erdélyi szászoknál', *Erdélyi Múzeum*, 1884, 178–82.

[68] László Makkai, 'Péter Melius, the Hungarian Reformer', *Études Historiques hongroises*, 2 vols. (Budapest, 1985), i, 1–19 (12–13); Géza Kathona, 'Méliusz Péter és életműve', in Tibor Bartha, ed., *A második helvét hitvallás Magyarországon és Méliusz életmüve* (Budapest, 1967), 105–92 (159–60); *Corp. Stat.*, i, 514, 525. Much has been made of Melius's observation that, 'Now it is the Decree of Werbőczy that is loudly proclaimed while the decree of God is under the bench.' In fact, as the career of Ferenc Németi demonstrates, a strong Calvinist conviction did not automatically lead to rejection of the *Tripartitum*. See Kathona, 'Méliusz Péter és életműve', 226, 314.

[69] Karl Kurt Klein, *Der Humanist und Reformator Johannes Honter* (Sibiu, 1935), 83.

[70] Béla P. Szabó, 'A jogtudós Honterus–Az európai 'ius commune' közvetitője', in Ágnes W. Salgó and Ágnes Stemler, eds., *Honterus Emlékkönyv* (Budapest, 2001), 28–56 (39–41).

general principles and judicial procedures; marriage, wills, inheritance and wardship; the law of obligations, contracts and commercial partnerships; and property, plaints and the criminal law.[71]

It had been Honterus's hope that the *Compendium* would be adopted as law by the Saxon *universitas*, but it was not. The leaders of the Saxon community were still hoping at the time of its publication to reconcile Saxon customary law with the text of the *Tripartitum*, on account of which they instructed a German translation.[72] When this was not forthcoming, they turned to the idea of stabilizing their own customary law in written form, to which end they commissioned several projects over the succeeding decades.[73] In fact, the fruits of this activity largely took the form of reworking Honterus's text to make it more satisfactory to a Saxon audience, while preserving his arrangement. The authors of the *Statuta iurium municipalium in Transsilvania*, eventually published in 1583 (and bankrupting the printer), thus boasted that their work rested upon 'laws and customs acquired by long use and observance', but its civilian roots were plain.[74] This was particularly evident not only in regard to the commercial law and law of obligations, but also in respect of the criminal law where it borrowed extensively from the thoroughly Romanist *Carolina* of 1532.[75] Indeed, the text of the *Statuta* specifically appealed to the Roman Law, for, as it explained, what was not in its pages could be ascertained by reference 'to the ancient decrees, statutes and rules comprehended in imperial law'.[76]

The *Statuta iurium* was confirmed by Stephen Báthory, prince of Transylvania, in the year of its publication, for the Saxons and their heirs, 'as their perpetual laws and customs'. The terms of the confirmation were prescient. Republished in both Latin and German editions, the *Statuta iurium* provided the basis of Transylvanian Saxon law for almost three centuries.[77] It was supplemented by the codes published by the Transylvanian diet for the principality as a whole (the *Approbatae Constitutiones* of 1653 and the *Compilatae* of 1669), by Benedict Carpzow's manual of criminal law, intended for use in Ducal Saxony, and—as the *Statuta iurium* had recommended—where necessary by reference to Justinian's *Novels* and the *Regulae Juris* of the *Digest*. The *Tripartitum* was used in practice to provide additional guidance, as for instance in respect of the rights of peasants or of the recurrent problem of river courses and boundaries. Interestingly, the high court of Sibiu also referred matters for guidance to the law faculties of Vienna and Dresden, thus engaging in the *Aktenversendung* that was typical of civilian jurisdictions in much of Central Europe during the early modern period, although not otherwise in the lands of the

[71] Szabó, 'A jogtudós Honterus', 44–5.

[72] The first German translation of the *Tripartitum* was published in 1599 by Formica in Vienna. No German edition of the *Tripartitum* was ever published in Transylvania.

[73] Szabó, 'A jogtudós Honterus', 52–3.

[74] Friedrich Schuler von Libloy, ed., *Statuta jurium municipalium Saxonum in Transsilvania* (Sibiu, 1853), 18.

[75] Libloy, *Statuta jurium*, 140, 252.

[76] Szabó, 'A jogtudós Honterus', 53.

[77] Libloy, *Statuta jurium*, 18. For subsequent editions, see MJL, vi, 356. The efficacy of the *Statuta* was legislated away by the Hungarian parliament in 1868. The *universitas* was abolished except as a cultural foundation in 1876.

Hungarian crown.[78] We should, nevertheless, note that Transylvanian Saxon law did not develop in isolation from legal practices observed elsewhere in the kingdom and principality. Since cases in the Saxon countryside (the *fundus regius*), which were initially decided by village courts, might be referred to the court at Sibiu for advice or transferred there for a final judgment, aspects of Saxon law began to be adjusted to accommodate the legal arrangements and language more commonly found in the Hungarian and Transylvanian countryside.[79]

## JURISTS AND LEGAL EDUCATION

The example of the Transylvanian Saxons contrasts markedly with the experience of the kingdom as a whole, where the Roman Law encountered no comparable reception. Certainly, we will notice the occasional influence—in respect of wardship, for example, where Werbőczy's own borrowing from the *Summa Legum* resulted in the widespread embrace of civilian norms; or in the occasional piece of statute law where a Romanist vocabulary or solution was adopted.[80] Likewise, we may note the activity of a few scholars who sought to bend Hungarian law to fit civilian categories, in the hope of rendering the law 'straighter, more certain and more complete' by the admission of substantive categories.[81] As in the case of the late sixteenth-century János Baranyai Decsi, the outcome might indeed be the reverse—some 900 pages of quotations, tabellations and scholastic exercises that, in the words of a later commentator, were 'for practical purposes and for court use worth absolutely nothing'.[82] The effort of the canon of Bratislava, Imre Papóczi, writing shortly after Mohács, to elaborate a law of commercial obligations on civilian principles was of comparable inconsequence.[83]

The endeavours of Decsi and Papóczi carried such little resonance because most Hungarian lawyers and jurists were either opposed to permitting Roman Law's influence or conceived it to be of only peripheral significance. As in England,

[78] Heinrich Herbert, 'Die Rechtspflege in Hermannstadt zur Zeit Karls VI', *Archiv des Vereins für siebenbürgische Landeskunde*, NF, 27 (1896), 39–161 (62, 125, 128, 141, 146); László Nagy, *Jus Transsilvanico Saxonicum*, (Cluj, 1845), 8, 65, 110.

[79] Livia Magina, *Instituția judelui sătesc în Principatul Transilvaniei* (Cluj, 2014), 275–6. See also a petition for advice addressed to Sibiu by the magistrate of Odorhei (!), SJAN Sibiu, Colecția Brukenthal, RS, no. 301 (1541). For the extent to which Transylvanian Saxon law had by the nineteenth century bent to accommodate customary practices observed in the countryside, see Nagy, *Jus Transsilvanico Saxonicum*, 76 (*fratres condivisionales*), 111 (*defectus seminis*), 213 (*homagium*).

[80] Hamza, *Wege der Entwicklung*, 126.

[81] Ioannes Decius Barovius (János Baranyai Decsi), *Syntagma Institutionum Iuris Imperialis ac Ungarici* (Cluj, 1593), *praefatio* (unpaginated).

[82] The quotation is from Martin Schmeizel (1679–1747). See János Zlinszky, 'Ein Versuch zur Rezeption des römischen Rechts in Ungarn', in Franz Horak and Wolfgang Waldstein, eds., *Festgabe für Arnold Herdlitczka* (Munich and Salzburg, 1972), 315–26 (325). See also, János Zlinszky, 'Legal Studies and works of János Baranyai Decsi', in *'Igniculi Sapientiae'. János-Baranyai-Decsi-Festschrift* (Budapest, 2004), 104–18. On tabellation and its relation to legal scholarship, see Harald J. Berman and Charles J. Reid, Jr, 'Roman Law in Europe and the *Jus Commune*', in *Scintillae iuris. Studi in memoria di Gino Gorla*, 3 vols. (Milan, 1994), ii, 979–1014 (998–1007).

[83] Bónis, KJE, 279.

Hungarian jurists were wary of Romanist learning.[84] The *Quadripartitum* thus referred to Cicero, explaining that the dissimilarity between polities meant that different countries needed different laws (*dissimilitudo civitatum variationem juris habeat necesse est*). It went on to explain that Hungary's climate was not the same as Rome's and its treatment of women less generous on account of the Hungarians' martial qualities. Hungary's laws and customs permitted, moreover, the retrial but not the appeal and recognized, unlike Roman Law, that attorneys might be recalled and the case restarted. It also admitted the use of violence in its procedural law, which arose again from the Hungarians' warlike character. In view of these differences of habit and disposition, the principles of Roman Law were 'greatly inconvenient'.[85] Werbőczy himself, the authors of the *Quadripartitum* averred, had succumbed to the lure of the civilians, endeavouring to force Hungarian law to the 'norm and rule' of the *ius commune*.[86] The *Tripartitum Novum*, a failed attempt from the early eighteenth century to rework Werbőczy's text, repeated these criticisms.[87]

Throughout the seventeenth and eighteenth centuries, Hungarian jurists maintained for the most part the same line, occasionally also at Werbőczy's expense. For Ferenc Fóris Otrokócsi, therefore, civilian elements were certainly present in Hungarian law and he remarked accordingly upon its vocabulary, but there were important points of difference that owed their origin to earlier Chinese influences.[88] András Huszti likewise stressed the oriental inheritance of the Hungarians, whose law was built upon 'Hunno-Gotho-Lombardo-Germanic feudal law' (*jure feudali, Hunno-Gotho-Langobardo-Germanico*). According to Huszti, it had been the Huns that had introduced the basic institutions of Hungarian law, including both the fief and the allod, the second of which owed its name to the Hungarian *eladó* ('for sale') since it might be freely sold. Werbőczy had, however, concealed these elements behind a Romanist vocabulary, using *ius possessionarium* for *feudum*, *barones* for *vasalli*, *officiales* for *valvasores*, and so on.[89] Other jurists were content to believe that the *Tripartitum* provided a faithful account of Hungarian legal practices and that such Roman Law influences as might be detected in its text were ephemeral, not detracting from its authenticity.[90]

[84] Andrew Lewis, '"What Marcellus says is against you": Roman law and Common law', in A.D.E. Lewis and D.J. Ibbetson, *The Roman Law Tradition* (Cambridge, 1994), 199–208 (199).

[85] *Quadripartitum Opus Juris Consuetudinarii Regni Hungariae* (Zagreb, 1798), pp. iii–v. A similar account may be found in Arthur Duck, *De usu et authoritate juris civilis Romanorum* (Leipzig, 1668), p. x, who explained the weakness of Roman Law in Hungary by reference to its wars. Noted in Béla P. Szabó, 'Differentiae és collatio – 17. századi munkák a római jog és a magyarországi jog(ok) összehasonlításáról', in *Igazság, ideál és valóság. Tanulmányok Kardos Sándor 65. születésnapja tiszteletére* (Debrecen, 2014), 278–89 (279).

[86] *Quadripartitum*, p. vi.

[87] *Tripartitum Novum*, OSzK, MSS, Fol. Lat., 559, praefatio (unpaginated).

[88] Franciscus Fóris Otrokócsi, *Experimentum Reductionis Juris Hungarici ad suos fontes* (Cluj, 1770), 35 (first published in 1699). For Otrokócsi's remarkable career, see Graeme Murdock, 'Responses to Habsburg Persecution of Protestants in Seventeenth-Century Hungary', *Austrian History Yearbook*, 40 (2009), 37–52 (50).

[89] Andreas Huszti, *Iurisprudentia Hungarico-Transilvanica* (Sibiu, 1742), 36–43.

[90] János Jony, *Commentatio Historico-Juridica de origine et progressu juris Hunno-Hungarici* (Levoča, 1727), 39–40.

The *Regulae Juris* were commonplaces, taken mostly from Roman or Canon Law, which were deployed throughout Western Europe to stiffen judicial decision making. The function of these pithy extracts was, as one English judgment explained, to afford, 'in deciding a case upon principle, where no direct authority can be cited from our books [...] no small evidence of the soundness of the conclusion at which we have arrived'.[91] As this English example suggests, although their use may suggest a trend towards rules of substantive law, they hardly constitute evidence that the law was shaped by Romanist methods or solutions. *Regulae* had been attached to the published collections of Hungary's statute laws from the sixteenth century onwards and they became a standard component of its collections of statute laws, the *Corpus Juris Hungariae* and its precursors, being variously added to and expanded with axioms taken from the *Tripartitum* and other Hungarian collections.

The role played by the *Regulae Juris* in Hungarian law was the subject of János Szegedi's *Manuale Jurisperitorum*, first published in 1749 for the benefit of students and attorneys. He explained that the *Regulae* were maxims or 'brocards', which were 'plainly certain and true' and which 'by the long and continuous use of the courts and of our jurists have passed into their blood and seem to have obtained authenticity'. They have thus 'obtained great authority in our courts and (where the law is lacking) incline the minds of judges', to the extent that they were cited almost daily. Szegedi urged, however, caution in their use, for they should be seen as supplementary to Hungary's laws, to be used only in its gaps, and he established in this respect a hierarchy of legal authority: 'After the written laws have been exhausted, and when statute and custom are insufficient, then trust should be placed in written instruments, in the *regulae* and general maxims, and in proverbs.'[92]

Szegedi was not, however, imposing a lawyerly scheme of his own to the problem of authority in Hungarian legal practice. A review of the arguments used in the Curia courts in the late eighteenth century was compiled, again for the benefit of students, by the *personalis* and high judge, György Galánthai Fekete.[93] We can on the basis of Fekete's study arrive at some conclusions in respect of the sources upon which judges and courts relied in arriving at their decisions. Altogether, statute laws were cited by Fekete on 212 occasions; the text of the *Tripartitum* on 208. All else was referenced to a much lesser degree. Kitonich was thus quoted on fifteen occasions; other jurists on no more than three. The *regulae juris* of the Canon Law were noted seven times and the Roman *regulae* on just six, to which we may add a stray *omnium civilistarum sensus*. A similar pattern of citation may be discerned in the principal textbook used in the middle decades of the eighteenth century, István Huszty's *Jurisprudentia Practica*, which again relied almost exclusively on the

[91] Lewis, '"What Marcellus says is against you"', 201. See also Michael Lobban, *The Common Law and English Jurisprudence 1760–1850* (Oxford, 1991), 7.

[92] János Szegedi, *Manuale Jurisperitorum Ungariae continens regulas juris patrii, pontificii et caesarei* (Győr, 1749), *praefatio* (unpaginated). Subsequent editions were published in Košice in 1751 and in Cluj in 1751 and 1763.

[93] Fekete's collection was subsequently published as *Georgii condam Fekete de Galantha Problemata Juridica*, ed. János Csaplovics (Bratislava, 1814).

*Tripartitum* and statute laws. Only in the third part of the book, dealing with the criminal law, where the *Tripartitum* and the laws gave less guidance, did the author make use of any other sources, principally Carpzow and the *Praxis Criminalis*. The Roman civil law was alluded to on only one occasion.[94] Notwithstanding, therefore, Szegedi's conviction that maxims and axioms were part of the daily debate of the courts, in practice it would seem that they were scarcely relied upon. As far as the Curia courts and the practical advice given to lawyers were concerned, the place of Roman Law in the Hungarian hierarchy of legal authority was, indeed, low.

The relative unimportance attaching to Roman Law in Hungary's legal development during the early modern period is reflected in legal education and training. Until the nineteenth century, lawyers and attorneys were not required to have a legal qualification. Before that time, their education was primarily in the arts and theology, and received at one of the several hundred grammar schools and colleges in Hungary and Transylvania.[95] In the sixteenth and seventeenth centuries, the curriculum mostly excluded the law, although some Jesuit foundations and Honterus's school in Braşov were exceptional in this regard.[96] The neglect of legal studies at the Protestant colleges was a cause of complaint among educational reformers, but it was not until the eighteenth century that colleges specifically dedicated to teaching the law were established for the benefit of Protestant students, mainly to compensate for their exclusion from other institutions of higher learning.[97] Even so, most practitioners acquired their knowledge of the law not from academic study but from pupillage. Upon leaving school, they were apprenticed to established attorneys, whom they served in the manner of clerks and *amanuenses*, being released after an agreed term to practise on their own.[98] Their training thus took place *in patvariis*, a Hungarism that meant literally 'in wrangling', and was thus exclusively in Hungarian law.[99] Doubtless, many also learned some of the more disreputable skills of the provincial lawyers, on which account they were often apostrophized as 'contorters of laws' and 'extorters of goods' (*legum contortores, bonorum extortores*), devoid of both principles and knowledge.[100] A particular complaint was lawyers' use of 'no win–no fee' agreements, which often resulted in clients being stripped of the compensation due to them.[101]

[94] Stephanus Huszty, *Jurisprudentia Practica seu Commentarius Novus in Jus Hungaricum*, 3 parts (Trnava, 1766), iii, 57 (first published in 1745).

[95] Little distinction existed at this time between academy, college, *paedagogium*, lyceum and *schola trivialis*, all of which descriptions might apply at any one time to the same institution. See József Hörk, *Az eperjesi ev. ker. collegium története*, 2 vols. (Košice, 1896–7), ii, 4.

[96] János Ravasz, László Felkai, Béla Beller and Gyula Simon, *A magyar nevelés története. A feudalizmus és kapitalizmus korában*, 3rd edition (Budapest, 1968), 21–8. Honterus's school in Braşov also included legal studies. See Szabó, 'A jogtudós Honterus', 36.

[97] MJL, iv, 440, 458.

[98] For a description of *amanuenses*, see MNL OL, O 10, *Normalia*, Bundle 1, fol. 32 (1777).

[99] The etymology and meaning were attempted by János Szegedi (*Tripartitum Juris Hungarici Tyrocinium*, 1764, 20), as a *magyarizatus, unde patvarkodom, litigo*.

[100] Endre Varga, 'A hivatásos ügyvédi osztály kialakulása', *Emlékkönyv Domanovszky Sándor* (Budapest, 1937), 624–42 (624–6, 632).

[101] János Zlinszky, *Az ügyvédség kialakulása Magyarországon és története Fejér megyében* (Székesfehérvár?, 1976?), 25.

Although we know of several universities founded in Hungary during the Middle Ages, none can be shown to have had a duration of more than a few decades.[102] It is perhaps telling that the continued existence of one such university is known only on account of the murders done by its students.[103] For higher education, Hungarians perforce went abroad, to Vienna, Cracow, Prague, Paris and Italy. During the sixteenth century, Wittenberg and, subsequently, Heidelberg and the Dutch universities became preferred destinations for Protestant students, and Padua for their Catholic counterparts.[104] Within Hungary itself, a leading role was played by the city of Trnava where the Archbishop of Esztergom took up residence in the 1540s. Trnava was host to a chapter school as well as to the ambitions of the prelates from the region of Hungary conquered by the Turks. A Jesuit teaching foundation was briefly set up there by Archbishop Miklós Oláh in 1561, but it was not until 1615 that the college was placed on a firm institutional basis, by Archbishop Péter Pázmány. Pázmány was initially reluctant to expand his foundation, but he was prevailed upon to convert it into a university, the charter for which was issued by Ferdinand II in 1635. At that time, the new university had only two faculties, of philosophy and theology, probably on account of which Pope Urban VIII initially refused it recognition. There was, however, continued pressure for the university to establish a faculty of law, to which end Catholic noblemen regularly included special bequests in their wills.[105] Eventually, in 1667, the 'long desired' faculty was established, with a complement of four teachers.[106]

The curriculum in the new faculty sought to achieve a balance between Hungarian, Canon and Roman Law. From the very first, however, the emphasis was on Hungarian law, which was taught by two of the professors, with a third and fourth teaching Roman and Canon Law respectively. Although Roman Law was taught for slightly longer on a daily basis, Hungarian law later took over its two-hour slot in the timetable.[107] During the late 1680s, the teaching of Roman Law was temporarily abandoned as part of a reorganization brought about by low enrolment. It was subsequently either combined with the teaching of natural law or, alternatively, undertaken by professors whose principal expertise lay in Hungarian law. In the second half of the eighteenth century, Roman Law was reduced to a first-year

[102] Universities were established at Pécs in 1367; Buda in 1389 (refounded in 1410); and Bratislava (the so-called 'Universitas Istropolitana') in 1467. See L.S. Domonkos, 'The State of Education in Hungary on the Eve of the Battle of Mohács (1526)', *Canadian-American Review of Hungarian Studies*, 2 (1975), 3–20.

[103] Hence our knowledge that the university at Pécs survived until 1400, for which see Astrik L. Gabriel, *The Medieval Universities of Pécs and Pozsony* (Frankfurt a/M, 1969), 29.

[104] For Transylvanian students at the Dutch universities, see now Réka Bozzay, 'Erdélyi diákok a Leideni Egyetemen a 17–18. században', in Gudor Botond, György Kurucz and Enikő Sepsi, eds., *Egyház, társadalom és művelődés Bod Péter korában* (Budapest, 2012), 58–72 (58–60).

[105] István Sinkovics, *Az Eötvös Loránd Tudományegyetem története 1635–1985* (Budapest, 1985), 20–35.

[106] Tivadar Pauler, *A budapesti Magyar Királyi Tudomány-Egyetem története* (Budapest, 1880), 481. The charter of the faculty's foundation is given in Pauler, *A budapesti Magyar Királyi Tudomány-Egyetem*, 484.

[107] Ferenc Eckhart, *A jog- és államtudományi kar története 1667–1935* (Budapest, 1936), 27, 44.

course.[108] The largest prestige attached to the teaching of Hungarian law, which numbered among its professors Ferenc Koller, Mihály Bencsik and Pál Khlósz.[109] János Szegedi, editor of the 1751 edition of the *Corpus Juris* and author of several works on Hungarian law, was, however, a professor of Canon Law at the university, but he was soon distracted by administrative duties.[110]

Law was studied over three (later two) years, mostly through lectures dictated in Latin, which were supplemented by moots and debates.[111] Hungarian law consisted almost entirely of the study of the *Tripartitum* and of Kitonich's *Directio Methodica*, which were perversely taught over a twelve- or fifteen-year cycle, with the Prologue occupying the best part of ten months.[112] The course on Hungarian law was divided between theoretical elements and practical skills, with an emphasis upon procedural law, which was learned through the study of formulary books.[113] Upon completion of the course, students could either progress to a doctorate, which required a further one or two years of study, or embark upon pupillage.[114] Pupils were placed under the supervision of approved masters, with whom they often lodged, but remained registered at the university so that they might continue to attend debates. Even so, the number of law students attending the university was never great, scarcely amounting to more than fifty. Their numbers were depleted by injuries and murders, in which respect it did not help that law students conventionally carried swords. The transfer of the university to Buda in 1777 and thence to Pest seven years later enlarged the opportunity for late-night carousing. As Francis I was later to complain, the behaviour of law students was 'not always as parents, the fatherland and the most august lord and prince desire and expect'.[115]

The small number of students attending the university meant that most lawyers continued to learn their trade by pupillage, without a formal education in the law. Moreover, graduates in law were often recruited into government service or the employment of large landowners as estate managers. The number of practising lawyers was accordingly few. In 1725, there were no lawyers at all in Székesfehérvár, at that time a city with a population of several thousand or more, and only six in the whole of Fejér County.[116] Half a century later, there were still only ten in

[108] MNL OL, O 111, Dunántúli Kerületi Tábla levéltára. *Szabályrendeletek, ügyviteli iratok 1797–98*, no. 18 (petitions for admission to the provincial bar, with course transcripts).

[109] Eckhart, *A jog- és államtudományi kar*, 11, 15–19.

[110] Alajos Degré, 'Szegedy János, az egyetem első jogtörténésze (1699–1760), in *Jogi professzorok emlékezete* (Budapest, 1935), 17–23 (18–19).

[111] Eckhart, *A jog- és államtudományi kar*, 31, 35. The *Ratio Educationis* of 1806 sought to restore the three-year curriculum, but in practice the three years were squeezed into two. See Katalin Gönczi, 'Jogászképzés a királyi akadémiákon a felvilágosodás korában és a reformkorban', *Jogtörténeti Szemle*, (2006, no. 2), 1–3 (1–2).

[112] Eckhart, *A jog- és államtudományi kar*, 21.

[113] Katalin Gönczi, *Die europäischen Fundamente der ungarischen Rechtskultur* (Frankfurt a/M, 2008), 23.

[114] For the doctorate, which was obtained by oral examination and public disputation, see Béla P. Szabó, 'Magyarországi jogi doktorok számbavétele 1680-ból', *Acta Juridica et Politica*, 73, no. 47 (2010), 701–24 (702–5).

[115] Matters of student discipline are discussed in MNL OL, O 10 *Normalia*, Bundle 1, fols. 33–4 (1777), 67 (1800).

[116] Zlinszky, *Az ügyvédség kialakulása*, 30–1.

Bihar County, two in Szeged, and eight in Buda.[117] The number of lawyers increased as a consequence of the foundation of law colleges during the first decades of the eighteenth century. The earliest consisted of departments of law that were added onto existing Protestant schools and colleges. Rival Catholic colleges were soon established, most notably at Eger and Győr.[118] To their number were added the five colleges founded by Maria Theresa in 1777 as part of the educational reform that she implemented in the wake of the secularization of the Jesuits.[119] Enterprising landlords, like György Festetics, would later establish their own academies for the legal education of a future generation of estate managers and private lawyers.[120]

The education received at the colleges was almost entirely vocational. Hungarian law predominated, with at best only one course on Roman Law, usually a study of the *Institutes*.[121] Since college graduates frequently went into government service, courses were included on public policy, finance and commerce, which meant in practice rote-learning Joseph von Sonnenfels's massive *Grundsätze der Polizey, Handlung und Finanzwissenschaft* (1765–7).[122] To make the *Grundsätze* more accessible to Hungarian students, a Latin version was published at Bratislava in 1808. For those who intended to become practising lawyers, a further year of pupillage was required, after which they were examined and sworn. The examination was oral and consisted of giving answers to practical questions posed by court officers, usually the protonotaries. The Curia firmly resisted any suggestion that the examination should involve intellectual or philosophical concerns, arguing that 'the best examination is a test of memory; legal knowledge consists more of practice than of theory'.[123] The oath, which had been a formal requirement for new lawyers since the 1690s, committed the prospective attorney not to cheat his client by collusion with his adversaries, to charge reasonable fees, and to serve both the rich and the poor.[124] After the examination and oath, lawyers who intended to practise in the Curia or provincial branches of the Royal Table were required to spend a further year in service as *jurati*, during which time they performed tasks on the court's behalf, such as conducting inquests, perambulating boundaries, copying deeds and taking depositions.[125]

[117] Figures are given in Gusztáv Wenzel, *Visszapillantás az előbbi magyar királyi curiának 1724–1769-iki működésére* (Budapest, 1875), 124–6.

[118] Gönczi, *Die europäischen Fundamente*, 24; MJL, iv, 436–50.

[119] Gönczi, 'Jogászképzés a királyi akadémiákon', 1; at Zagreb, Győr, Košice, Trnava and Oradea.

[120] György Kurucz, *Keszthely grófja. Festetics György* (Budapest, 2013), 218.

[121] Gönczi, 'Jogászképzés a királyi akadémiákon', 2.

[122] By 1798, the *Grundsätze* was already in its sixth edition. See Gönczi, *Die europäischen Fundamente*, 30.

[123] Wenzel, *Visszapillantás*, 128. See also Martyn Rady, 'Judicial Organization and Decision Making in Old Hungary', SEER, 90, no. 3, 2012, 450–81 (452).

[124] Zlinszky, *Az ügyvédség kialakulása*, 25–30.

[125] MNL OL, O 4, *Inquisitiones Juratorum*, Box 1, fols. 11–18, 83, 114, 167–8 (1722) etc. The practice of perambulation (*reambulatio*) is vividly described in R.W. Gray, 'Etching the Law on the Land: The Role of Landscape and Custom in Defining the Space of the Hungarian Village in the Eighteenth and Nineteenth Centuries', *Central Europe*, 11, no. 2 (2013), 82–101 (83–7).

Since the examination required only practical knowledge, a formal education in the law was unnecessary. Thus it was entirely possible to be admitted as a lawyer, and subsequently practise as an attorney, without having been to university or a college of law. An academic qualification in law was only made mandatory in 1804.[126] Before this time, we should reckon that the vast majority of practising lawyers had learned their trade not through higher education but exclusively *in patvariis*, as the apprentices and pupils of more experienced lawyers. It was thus calculated around 1770 that there were 800 lawyers in the kingdom, but fewer than forty were qualified to serve in the Curia courts, which suggests a significant imbalance between those with the academic qualification necessary for employment in the highest courts of the kingdom and those whose training had been by pupillage alone.[127] Plainly, however, even for those who had attended university or college, instruction had been mainly in Hungarian law and in Sonnenfels. Roman Law had formed only a little part of their studies. In this respect, their intellectual attainments were as much restricted to vocational skills as those of their country cousins who had learned their trade exclusively 'in wrangling'.

* * *

During the early modern period, Hungary remained distant from Romanizing trends, having neither a Roman Law reception in the manner of Germany nor a scholarly engagement with Romanist literature such as occurred throughout much of continental Europe. In Hungary, Romanist texts were eschewed and Roman Law was little taught, even at the university. The *Tripartitum* and Kitonich dominated Hungarian legal literature and practical knowledge took over the academic curriculum. The kingdom's insulation from Roman Law had a devastating consequence for its legal development. Roman Law communicated a system of cognitive principles into which the substance of the law might be pressed. Under the impact of Roman Law, judging was no longer a matter of finding a remedy in respect of the facts of the case but instead an act determining the law's relation to the facts. This may be called syllogistic reasoning—if A then B, and a so b—or judicial subsumption.[128] Both presuppose, however, that the law is not found, still less negotiated, but that it is consistently applied by reference to a set of fixed categories. By deliberately eschewing Romanist learning, Hungary remained locked in its legal past, not moving beyond the traditions of justice that it had inherited from the Middle Ages. Even though the *Tripartitum* and successive editions of the kingdom's statutes had fastened a part of the kingdom's law in writing, the underlying assumptions of an earlier customary regime persisted in respect of the indeterminacy and malleability of the law's substance.

[126] MJL, vi, 826.

[127] Lajos Králik, *A magyar ügyvédség. Az ügyvédi kar*, 2 vols. (Budapest, 1903), i, 196. See also Wenzel, *Visszapillantás*, 124–6.

[128] Franz Wieacker, *A History of Private Law in Europe*, trans. Tony Weir (Oxford, 1995), 141.

# 10

# Codification After the *Tripartitum*

## THE *QUADRIPARTITUM* AND THE *TRIPARTITUM*

Notwithstanding the apparent enthusiasm that greeted the *Tripartitum*'s publication, doubts soon arose in respect of the comprehensiveness of its treatment. The Hatvan diet of 1525 thus instructed that a fresh attempt be made to gather together the kingdom's laws. The call for a revision of the laws was repeated after the Habsburg succession, in 1527 and 1538. On the first of these occasions, the diet instructed Ferdinand to assemble and edit the laws of his predecessors (*universa decreta praedecessorum suorum*); on the second, to publish a new collection of the kingdom's laws and customs with the aim of amplifying the *Tripartitum*.[1] It was only, however, in 1548 that Ferdinand finally acceded to the diet's request, appointing a committee under the presidency of Bishop Pál Gregoriánczy of Zagreb to revise the laws of the kingdom and to bring these into line with justice and divine law.[2] The inspiration behind this endeavour almost certainly lay with Ferdinand, who nursed a distrust of Werbőczy on account of his support for King John Zápolya, and who thus sought to have memory of Werbőczy and of his work effaced.[3]

The work of the committee proceeded slowly, with the diet urging in 1550 that it hasten its labours.[4] By 1553, a text was ready and the diet instructed that representatives of the counties, cities, and chapters, as well as of the regions of Transylvania and Slavonia, join together with the kingdom's judges, their deputies and protonotaries to review its content, matching it against justice and actual practice, after which it should with the royal approval be confirmed by the diet.[5] No such inspection took place. Although the compilation was drafted in full, it languished, surviving only in manuscript copies. Its eventual publication, which was controversial on account of the interpolated version that was used and the identity of its publishers, had to wait until 1798.[6] Although subsequent generations of scholars had access to it in manuscript form, the text over which Bishop Gregoriánczy's committee laboured, had almost no impact upon Hungary's subsequent legal history.

[1] 1527: 3; *Monumenta Comitialia*, ii, 62, 93. [2] 1548: 21.

[3] As argued by Emericus (Imre) Kelemen, *Institutiones Juris Privati Hungarici*, 3 vols. (Pest, 1814), i, 41; noted by József Illés, *A Quadripartitum közjogi interpolátiói* (Budapest, 1931), 4.

[4] 1550: 10. [5] 1553: 15.

[6] Published as *Quadripartitum Opus Juris Consuetudinarii Regni Hungariae* (Zagreb, 1798). The Josephinist imperial counsellors Anton Novosel and József Izdenczy were behind its publication.

The text produced by the committee was known as the *Quadripartitum* on account of its arrangement in four parts. Its title indicates its indebtedness to the *Tripartitum*, the merits of which the authors of the *Quadripartitum* grudgingly acknowledged.[7] The organization of the *Quadripartitum* largely followed its predecessor, notwithstanding its arrangement into four parts, and is equally clumsy in the division of its subject matter. The first part purported to deal with the rights of persons—principally the king and noblemen—but added in the material on letters and seals that had been included in the earlier chapters of the *Tripartitum*'s second part. In discussing the oath given by the ruler at his coronation, the *Quadripartitum* included the entire text of the Golden Bull of 1222, even though this was not part of what the king swore.[8] The second part of the *Quadripartitum* corresponds closely to the first part of the *Tripartitum*, largely repeating its text. The third part of the *Quadripartitum* is the second part of the *Tripartitum* with some parts of the Prologue included in respect of the qualities of a judge. The fourth part is the jumble of the *Tripartitum*'s last part, with material transferred from the first part in respect of the estimation of buildings, appurtenances, agricultural land, cattle, and so on. The four parts were not preceded by a Prologue, but by an effusive sixteen-page dedication to the monarch.

The authors of the *Quadripartitum* admitted that they had largely kept to the scheme of the *Tripartitum*, explaining that on account of its widespread use over many years it would be unwise to depart too radically from its arrangement.[9] They promised, however, to render a more faithful account of the kingdom's laws and customs than Werbőczy had done, who—so they claimed—had left out much that was important and had been unduly influenced by Romano-canonical procedure.[10] They stressed in particular the use that they had made of the kingdom's written laws, which they had lengthily perused, ignoring those that were no longer relevant, saving always, however, the rights and special privileges of the nobility.[11] In fact, the *Quadripartitum* added little of substance to the *Tripartitum*'s text. It is longer and thus able to give more detail, most notably on the operation and membership of the kingdom's courts, including the county courts, the taking of oaths, the holding of inquests, modes of knowing, and so on. It is also more thoroughly based on statute law, relying upon a wide range of articles included in previous legislation of the diet—possibly as many as 145 articles taken in all from twenty-five separate laws of the diet, although mostly mediated through other sources.[12] Extraordinarily, however, the committee ignored the most salient legislation passed since publication of the *Tripartitum*—namely the provisions aimed at the restoration of the Catholic religion and the law of 1547 establishing the hereditary right of the house of Habsburg to the throne of Hungary.[13] It is in this respect that we should seek explanation for its failure.

[7] *Quadripartitum*, p. vi. [8] Illés, *A Quadripartitum közjogi interpolátiói*, 34–42.
[9] *Quadripartitum*, p. xv. [10] *Quadripartitum*, p. vi. [11] *Quadripartitum*, p. xiv.
[12] Alajos Degré, *A Négyeskönyv perjogi anyagi* (Budapest, 1935), 250–3.
[13] For the legislation of the diet in respect of Protestantism, see Mihály Zsilinszky, *A magyar országgyűlések vallásügyi tárgyalásai a Reformatiótól kezdve*, 4 vols. (Budapest, 1881–7), i, 14–49. The relevant laws of the diet are 1523: 48 [54] (DRMH 4, 263); 1548: 5–12; 1550: 12–20.

Upon receipt of the committee's text, Ferdinand reviewed its contents and found much that was unsatisfactory. In return for the ruler's promise that he would remain in the kingdom, the law of 1547 (Article 5) had committed the Hungarian estates always to defer to the *imperium* and *potestas* of Ferdinand's male heirs (*haeredes*), thus acknowledging the hereditary character of Hungarian kingship and its connection to the house of Habsburg.[14] The text of the *Quadripartitum*, however, blended this with the Rákos decision of 1505, altering its meaning. First, while affirming that the first born son should succeed, it added the condition that his automatic succession still rested on election. Secondly, in the event of the king having no sons, the nobility might choose whomever they wished as successor. In concluding its discussion, the *Quadripartitum* declared that the Hungarian monarchy was by long custom elective and that as a result 'no one may be constituted as the king of Hungary except by coronation and by the free election of the gentlemen of the realm.'[15]

Besides the omission of the laws on the establishment of the Catholic religion and the alteration to the law of 1547 on the succession, Ferdinand found much else to dislike.[16] In the event of a royal donation being contested because it turned out that the land involved had been unlawfully sequestrated by the ruler, the *Quadripartitum* posited that the palatine had a right to intervene and to summon the king to court. In previous cases, actions of this sort had normally been resolved between the recipient of the donation and whoever claimed prior right of possession. The *Quadripartitum* additionally assigned to the palatine the right to receive embassies in the king's absence, thus giving him a role in the making of foreign policy, and made it possible to launch actions against marauding troops through the courts rather than through their officers.[17] The full text of the Golden Bull was evidently also considered obnoxious, doubtless on account of its inclusion of the right of resistance.

Accordingly, Ferdinand instructed a revision of the text that was duly undertaken by his counsellors in Vienna. The reworking made a number of alterations. The opening chapter of the first part established the primacy of the faith and threatened heretics 'with the punishment of eternal fire in the beyond, and in this life with the enduring stain of perfidy, and the punishments that are due, according to the laws of the realm'.[18] The succession was now defined as entirely hereditary, although only through the male line. Thus, if the king had no sons, the royal office passed to collateral heirs, thereby admitting the rights of Ferdinand's brother and nephew, Emperor Charles V and Archduke Philip (of Spain), and of their male descendants. The right of election pertained only in the event of there being no royal kinsmen whatsoever.[19] Similar adjustments were made in respect of the adjudication of troops, the process for revoking donations and the rights of the palatine. The text of the Golden Bull was omitted.[20]

[14] 1547: 5. [15] Illés, *A Quadripartitum közjogi interpolátiói*, 42.
[16] János Szegedi, *Rubricae sive Synopses Titulorum*, 3 vols. (Trnava, 1734), ii, 113.
[17] Illés, *A Quadripartitum közjogi interpolátiói*, 13–15, 27–8, 46–7, 50–1.
[18] *Quadripartitum*, I. 1. [19] *Quadripartitum*, I. 18
[20] The relevant alterations are given in the appendix to Illés, *A Quadripartitum közjogi interpolátiói*, 30–49.

Ferdinand hoped that Gregoriánczy's committee would accept the alterations made in Vienna. Indeed, he left the way open for negotiation by including the passage from the *Tripartitum* which spoke of the mutual and reciprocal bond between king and nobles, as expressed through the king's creation of noblemen and the nobility's election of the monarch.[21] Doubtless, he considered it to be largely rhetorical. The committee, however, refused to compromise, declaring that what it had written comported faithfully with the kingdom's ancient laws, statutes and customs (*antiquis legibus, decretis, atque consuetudine*), and that it was not in its power to alter these. If the king wanted changes, he should pursue them through the diet.[22] Since this would have meant interminable wrangling that would have held up the more important business of raising troops and cash, Ferdinand abandoned the *Quadripartitum*. An attempt made in 1563 to resurrect the project came to nothing.[23]

The failure of the *Quadripartitum* was the triumph of the *Tripartitum*. Despite the *Tripartitum*'s flaws, the work intended to replace it had foundered. Nevertheless, Gregoriánczy's committee had started from the premise that the *Tripartitum* might be adjusted and, in their response to Ferdinand, they had acknowledged that what had been established as the customary law of the kingdom might be altered with the consent of the diet. In this respect, they confirmed the principle given in the *Tripartitum*'s Prologue that a customary law might be altered by a later statute. The problem was that no one knew at the time of the *Quadripartitum*'s composition what the content of statute law was, where it might be found, and how it might be recognized as law.

## THE *CORPUS JURIS HUNGARICI* AND ITS ANTECEDENTS

The history of the *Tripartitum* goes back to 1498 and to the commission originally given to Adam Liszkai to write up the ancient customs of the realm. The origin of Hungary's *Corpus Juris* may for its part be discerned only a few years later, in the law of 1504 that required the monarch 'to bring together in a single edition all the decrees and statutes previously dispersed in different places'.[24] A decade later, upon presentation of the *Tripartitum*, the diet once more urged that 'all the statutes be now gathered and brought together as one', a plea that they repeated in 1525 and 1527.[25] On these occasions, the diet commanded that the laws, having been collected, be submitted to it for approval before receiving the royal seal. This, however, was never done. The laws of the kingdom were instead collected and published as private compilations, first as manuscripts and then, after 1581, in printed form.

[21] *Quadripartitum*, I. 12.

[22] Illés, *A Quadripartitum közjogi interpolátiói*, 50.

[23] 1563: 30. See Mihály Párniczky and János Bátyka, *A magyar Corpus Juris (Az első kiadások forrásai)* (Budapest, 1936), 33; 1608 (*ante cor.*): 16; 1609: 69.

[24] 1504: 31 (DRMH 4, 172). The instruction is repeated verbatim in 1507: 20.

[25] 1514: 63 (DRMH 4, 206); 1525 (Hatvan): 23; 1527: 3.

The publication of the kingdom's statutes and of its customs at separate times and in separate works gives superficial credence to the 'two-track' theory of Hungarian law.[26] By this measure, Hungarian law rested on the double foundation of custom and of written statute, both of which constituted free-standing repositories of legal authority. As a little verse put it at the time:

> 'Whence the law? Do tell me please!'
> 'Well, you'll find a part in the decrees.
> And in "received use." But you must see
> That this develops incrementally.'[27]

Notwithstanding their supposed equivalence, custom and statute existed in an unequal relationship. In order to retain cogency, statute law had to assume the character of custom and to be absorbed within it. This was not just a lawyerly opinion but also the consequence of the behaviour of government and local bodies. Statutes once enacted were not inscribed on something like a parliamentary roll, but were filed away in the chancellery and many were lost over time. They were certainly not entered into the Royal Books, wherein (upon payment) noblemen might choose to have their most important deeds recorded.[28] Right through until the 1480s, we know of diets that enacted laws but for which no records survived even in the next century. Decisions of the diet might be held up in the chancellery, while the king ruminated over their content, eventually becoming forgotten. After promulgation and the despatch of manuscript copies by the chancellery to the counties, cities, chapters and leading men of the kingdom, the laws might be read out for all to hear, mostly in market places, but their texts were thereafter lodged in the chests that counted as archives. Since the recipients of these texts had to pay the chancellery for the labour of writing them out, it is probable that many institutions either chose not to receive them or else relied upon summaries.[29] Certainly, there were a few statutes that were considered of such weight that they were retained in the original version received from the chancellery as well as preserved in transcripts. The 1351 law of Louis the Great, which contained the text of the Golden Bull, thus survives in eight originals and in a further eight late fourteenth- and fifteenth-century copies.[30] Once they had been proclaimed, however, the majority of the kingdom's written laws gathered mildew. Only those that conveyed important rights or instituted major changes were recalled and acted upon in such a way as to ensure their continued observance. In this respect, the notion that the authority of statute rested upon its acceptance as custom accurately conveyed the way in which legislation to be efficacious over time needed to be so embedded in established practice as to be capable of recollection and recovery.

26 The literature is discussed in László Péter, 'The Irrepressible Authority of the *Tripartitum*', in DRMH 5, pp. xi–xxvi (pp. xxi–xxiii); Péter, 'The Primacy of *Consuetudo* in Hungarian Law', in CLCH, 101–11 (108–11).

27 Ferenc Szentpáli Nagy, *Verbötzi István törvény könyvének compendiuma* (Cluj, 1798), 51 (first published in 1701).

28 The Royal Books are described in SEER, 81, no. 3, 2003, 554–6.

29 Béla Iványi, *Mossóczy Zakariás és a magyar Corpus Juris keletkezése* (Budapest, 1926), 50–3.

30 DRH 1301–457, 126–7.

The powers accumulated by the diet and the proliferation of legislation in the second half of the fifteenth century required, however, a means whereby the content of statute might be recalled. Little point attached to the diet's deliberations if its decisions were left to human memory and to the vagaries of documentary survival. The initiative taken by the diets after 1504 in pushing for the codification of the kingdom's statutes was accompanied by private activity and by the earliest endeavours to preserve and gather information on the kingdom's statutes. In 1488–90, the text of the laws agreed at the diet of 1486, which mainly affected procedure in the courts, was printed in two editions.[31] Plainly, the publishers intended their contents to be more enduring and disseminated more widely than the manuscript copies sent out by the chancellery. At around the same time, we have evidence of ancient laws being collected and written down together in single volumes. The earliest example, probably from the late fifteenth century, includes (among much other heterogeneous material) the eleventh-century laws of SS Stephen and Ladislas, and of Coloman, and may have been intended for devotional use.[32] Hereafter, manuscript collections proliferate, becoming increasingly comprehensive and occasionally supported by indexes. Some of these were produced in the kingdom's cities—those drawn up in the northern city of Banská Štiavnica were remarkably complete, containing the bulk of fifteenth-century legislation as well as individual items from the preceding centuries.[33] Most collections were, however, the work of churchmen, notably of István Ilosvay (1500–59), auxiliary bishop of Oradea, and of the circle around Bishop Pál Gregoriánczy.[34] The first part of Ilosvay's compendium, completed in 1544, included the laws of Hungary's eleventh-century kings, the full text of the 1351 law, together with the Golden Bull, and much of the legislation passed by the diet in the fifteenth century, down to 1492.[35] A continuation by a second compiler (probably Miklós Telegdi) extended the collection to 1567.[36] Ilosvay's collection is not arranged chronologically, is interspersed with several privileges, and includes the decisions of the 1507 diet, which had never in fact received the king's approval.[37] Gregoriánczy's compendium, which was the work of several compilers, is even more diverse in its content. Besides the texts of many of the laws promulgated in the several centuries before Gregoriánczy's death in 1565, it includes verses, descriptions of coats-of-arms, short historical sketches and several humorous anecdotes.[38]

The interest of churchmen in recording the laws may be explained in several ways. Like the cities, episcopal chapters were used to preserving documents and

[31] DRMH 3, 106; see now also, János M. Bak, 'Tradition and Renewal in the Decretum Maius of King Matthias', in *Matthias Rex 1458–1490: Hungary at the Dawn of the Renaissance* (Budapest, 2013), unpaginated, online resource.

[32] J. N. Kovachich, *Notitiae Praeliminares ad Syllogen Decretorum Comitialium* (Pest, 1820), 341.

[33] Described in Kovachich, *Notitiae Praeliminares*, 337–400; for Banská Štiavnica, see 368–76.

[34] Ilosvay's career, which included discovery of the Várad Register, is summarized by Vincze Bunyitay, *A váradi püspökség története*, 4 vols. (Oradea and Debrecen, 1883–1935), ii, 55–7.

[35] *Codex Ilosvay*, OSzK, MSS, Fol. Lat. 4023, fols. 40–204.

[36] *Codex Ilosvay*, fols. 205–376.

[37] DRMH 4, p. liii.

[38] Monika Jánosi, 'Gregoriánczi Pál kéziratos törvénygyűjteménye a xvi. század középéről', *Magyar Könyvszemle*, 104 (1988), 54–64 (58–64).

their role as *loca credibilia* obliged them both to guard their records and to pay for copies of the latest statutes. More importantly, at this stage the churchmen who laboured over the kingdom's laws conceived of their activity as comporting with the humanist vocation of collecting, collating and emending historic manuscripts. They did not understand their role to be one of affirming the equivalence of the written law to custom, still less the primacy of legislation over judicial decision making, for they were working largely as historians and philologists. Like Ilosvay, therefore, they often did not include the latest laws in their collections, but instead confined their examination to laws of an older provenance, often combining these with other material of a largely antiquarian interest.

The link between collection and humanist endeavour is evident in respect of the first printed edition of Hungary's laws. Published by the collector and polymath, János Zsámboki (Sambucus), it was included along with various literary texts as an appendix to his 1581 edition of Bonfini's history of Hungary. Zsámboki's selection is indiscriminate, including privileges and charters that had no obvious legislative content. In his address to the reader, Zsámboki explained that the appendix might be of some use in the courts, to which end he also included a list of the legal terms that had arisen in his text (*Aliquot insolentium vocum in articulis*). Nevertheless, his principal concern in communicating the laws of the realm was, as he explained, to illustrate Bonfini's historical narrative.[39] Since Bonfini's account ended with the last years of the fifteenth century, Zsámboki included only such laws as had been enacted up to the 1480s. The value of his compendium to lawyers and the courts could only have been slight.[40]

Zsámboki's edition of the kingdom's laws was not only highly selective but also replete with errors and misprints. The task of compiling a new edition fell to the bishops of Nitra and Pécs, respectively Zakariás Mossóczy and Miklós Telegdi. In a rare example of episcopal cooperation, Telegdi provided Ilosvay's earlier manuscript, the money and the printing press, while Mossóczy took on the labour of editing.[41] The text that they produced was published in 1584 in Trnava under the title *Decreta, constituciones et articuli regum inclyti regni Ungariae*. It is indeed a most scholarly work that notes in the margin variant readings—*alii hic legunt, leguntur hic quoque*, and so on—demonstrating that it was not entirely derivative of Ilosvay's manuscript version.[42] Notwithstanding its critical apparatus, the Mossóczy–Telegdi edition had a practical as well as a scholarly purpose. In order to aid the reader, Mossóczy included, therefore, summaries or *rubricae* of individual

[39] Zoltán Kérészy, 'A Corpus Juris Hungarici mint irott jogi kútfő', *A Magyar Királyi Erzsébet Tudományegyetem 1934/35. tanévi irataiból*, 2 (1935), 11–45 (22). The list of terms is unpaginated and precedes immediately his collection of the laws.

[40] For Zsámboki's career, see Gábor Almási, *The Uses of Humanism: Johannes Sambucus (1531–1584), Andreas Dudith (1533–1589), and the Republic of Letters in East Central Europe* (Leiden and Boston, 2009), 145–235, and esp. 173–6.

[41] Kérészy, 'A Corpus Juris Hungarici', 24–6. Telegdi's ownership of the *Codex Ilosvay* is evident on the membrane attached to the verso of the front cover, which records that he gave it to Mossóczy in 1582. On the close relationship between Ilosvay and Telegdi, on whose estate Ilosvay had once served as a parish priest, see Bunyitay, *A váradi püspökség története*, ii, 55.

[42] Párniczky and Bátyka, *A magyar Corpus Juris*, 54–5.

articles, to which he also in places gave a numbering of his own, as well as an index. Like Zsámboki, he also intended his new edition to be of use in the courts. In the dedication to King Rudolf (Emperor Rudolf II), Mossóczy thus observed that the laws of the kingdom were so dispersed that judges often had to consult ten or more separate books in order to establish the relevant texts. He noted the frequent but vain appeals made by the diet for a comprehensive collection of the laws and lamented the failure of the *Quadripartitum* to fulfil Ferdinand's aim of bringing the laws together 'in a single and harmonious whole'. The edition aimed to be comprehensive, including as many of the laws as were known and extending up to 1583. As a further aid to his readers, Mossóczy included the texts of the oaths to be sworn by the principal royal judges and officers, attorneys and witnesses at inquests as well as a short description, taken from the *Quadripartitum*, of the procedures to be followed in courts of honour where the duel was still commonplace. The addition, however, of short biographies of Hungary's kings and lists of the historic holders of the principal ecclesiastical offices in the realm indicates that Mossóczy had not made the complete intellectual transition from humanist eclecticism to a lawyerly comprehension of the law.

The Mossóczy–Telegdi edition obtained widespread circulation, putting an end to the further creation by churchmen and others of their own manuscript collections. Whereas, therefore, almost forty of these survive for the century before 1584, only two are known to have been compiled in the succeeding period and these both date from the early 1590s.[43] A unified and apparently authoritative body of the kingdom's legislation had thus come into being, mirroring the way the *Tripartitum* had conveyed in written form the kingdom's customary law. Nevertheless, since the two texts carried a broadly analogous authority as normative texts, it made no sense to keep them separate. Both the *Tripartitum* and the published laws of the kingdom were routinely referred to in the course of litigation and together they provided the grounds most frequently given for court decisions and what was understood to be lawful conduct. Kitonich's own account of the kingdom's procedural law made thus ample and indiscriminate use of both sources of authority. As early as 1602, therefore, Péter Pázmány recommended that the *Tripartitum* be published together with laws as a single body and volume. Pázmány's own correspondence demonstrates the way in which to press home a legal point he would alternate between the texts of the laws and of the *Tripartitum*, picking out and combining whatever was relevant to his case.[44] It was not until 1628, however, that the two works were conjoined and then not in a single volume, as Pázmány had recommended, but in three. The Vienna edition of 1628, which was published at the university in Trnava by Caspar von Rath, thus had as its first volume the text of the *Tripartitum* (taken from its 1581 edition), as its second volume the Mossóczy–Telegdi text of the laws up to 1583, and as its third the kingdom's laws promulgated between 1584 and 1604. In his dedication to Ferdinand III, von

[43] Párniczky and Bátyka, *A magyar Corpus Juris*, 60.

[44] Párniczky and Bátyka, *A magyar Corpus Juris*, 61; Ferencz Hanuy, ed., *Petri Cardinalis Pazmany epistolae collectae*, 2 vols. (Budapest, 1910–11), i, 439, 616.

Rath explained that he was unable to include legislation after 1604 as this would have made the third volume too large. Since, however, this is the slimmest of the three parts, it must be suspected that Rath baulked at including the terms of the 1606 Treaty of Vienna and of the laws extending religious freedom that had been agreed by Matthias II.[45] Supplements making up for this deficiency were, however, published independently in 1653 (at Sárospatak, by George II Rákóczi) and in 1668 (at Pottendorff, in Lower Austria, at the press of Ferenc Nádasdy).[46]

Publication of the kingdom's laws in a single corpus that included the *Tripartitum* hastened the integration of the written customary law of the kingdom with its statute laws, both of which might now be seen as complementary legislation. From the last decades of the sixteenth century, therefore, the statute laws agreed by the diet often included reference in their texts both to previous statutes and to the content of the *Tripartitum*, demonstrating that the new enactment either reinforced or amplified existing provisions.[47] Where the texts of individual laws did not expressly refer to previous legislation or to the *Tripartitum*, successive editions of the laws added references of their own, either as glosses in the margin or as footnotes. In time, the separate indexes to the laws and to the *Tripartitum*, first published in 1584 and 1572 respectively, were also joined together to make a single guide or *Cynosura*, arranged alphabetically under headings. The first of these was published at the Pottendorff press in 1668. Thirty years later a revised version of the *Cynosura* was included as an appendix to a new edition of the laws, published in Trnava in 1696 by Márton Szentiványi.[48]

Szentiványi's edition carried for the first time the title of *Corpus Juris Hungarici* (CJH). Like the Vienna edition of 1628, it too was arranged in three volumes. The first gave the text of the *Tripartitum*; the second the laws of the realm up to 1583; and the third the laws published between 1588 and 1687. Szentiványi's edition was reprinted several times, with updates. It was eventually superseded in 1751 by a new two-volume edition, published by János Szegedi, which like its predecessors combined the statutes of the realm with the *Tripartitum*. Szegedi's edition was remarkable in respect of its critical apparatus, which cross-referenced in its footnotes previous legislation and the text of the *Tripartitum*, as well as drawing attention to relevant passages in civilian and other legal literature. In order to facilitate their comparative use, the articles of the laws and the chapters of the *Tripartitum*

[45] *Tripartitum Opus, Decretorum, Constitutionum et Articulorum Regum Inclyti Regni Ungariae, in tres tomos divisum*, 3 vols.

[46] *Articuli Universorum Statuum et Ordinum inclyti Regni Hungariae* (1668). See Gedeon Borsa, 'Nádasdy Ferenc pottendorfi és lorettomi nyomdái', *Magyar Könyvszemle*, 91 (1975), 201–7 (201–2). The Nádasdy press was operated by Hieronymus Verdussen III of Antwerp, whose name appears on the title page. The 1653 Sárospatak edition (publ. Georgius Renius) is entitled *Incipiunt articuli Regni Hungariae in diversis Generalibus Diaetis per Status et Ordines eiusdem Regni Hungariae conditi*.

[47] 1588: 24; 1622: 11; 1647: 16; 1647: 81; 1655: 54; 1659: 31; 1659: 116 etc. See József Illés, *Bevezetés a magyar jog történetébe. A források* (Budapest, 1910), 192.

[48] Szentiványi's *Cynosura* was published in 1699 and subsequently attached to the 1696 edition as a supplement. The Pottendorff (Verdussen) edition is entitled *Cynosura iuristarum loca Decretalia et Articulos* [...] *breviter repraesentans*. The debt which these editions owed to Ludovicus Bodo's *Farrago Communium Locorum Decretalium & Constitutionum Regni Hungariae* (*c.* 1636), which circulated in MS versions, is uncertain.

were subdivided by Szegedi into numbered sub-sections.[49] Szegedi's edition provided the basis for all subsequent editions of the CJH, including the expansive Millennium edition, the initial parts of which were published at the very end of the nineteenth century.[50] Even though most of its provisions had by this time been superseded, the *Tripartitum* still stood at the head of the Millennium edition, as the first volume in its series.

From the very first, the laws of the realm were published with supplementary material and appendixes—formulas for oaths, indexes, historical lists of bishops, counties and so on. To these the Vienna 1628 edition added as an appendix legal maxims deriving from the *Digest*.[51] Szentiványi retained these, promising to augment them with further maxims and with legal rules deriving from Canon Law.[52] In subsequent printings of the CJH, Szentiványi added new appendixes, almost it would seem as an afterthought, because he found that he had space to spare.[53] Thus, reprints of the 1696 edition included the *Praxis Criminalis* of Ferdinand III, which had never been proclaimed in Hungary, an edited version of Kitonich's *Directio Methodica*, and a further item by Kitonich, the *Centuria certarum contrietatum et dubietatum*, which was a scholastic work first published in 1619 that was intended to resolve apparent contradictions in the *Tripartitum*'s text. Szegedi's 1751 edition went still further, adding the *Articuli Juris Thavernicalis*, which were intended for use in litigation involving citizens; Maria Theresa's *Regulamentum Militare* of 1747, which laid down the composition of the imperial forces; Canon Law maxims taken from the decretals; and the so-called *Regulae Juris Patrii*, which were maxims excerpted from the *Tripartitum*, the laws and the *Cynosura*.[54] At the same time, Szegedi went through the laws (but not the *Tripartitum*), cutting out those sections that he deemed to have become irrelevant, but he pursued this task with neither vigour nor discernment.

Mossóczy, Szentiványi and Szegedi worked in a private capacity only. Maria Theresa had given the Jesuits in 1743 and, later, the university at Trnava exclusive right to publish the realm's statutes (but not the *Tripartitum*). This did not, however, convey upon the editions a public character. Their authority rested, instead, upon their use by the courts and in litigation. As for the appendixes, they themselves acquired a customary authority over time by virtue of being included in the volumes to which lawyers and the courts had the most frequent recourse. The maxims were thus occasionally advanced in litigation as self-evident truths. Likewise, courts

[49] These are given in square brackets in DRMH 4–5.

[50] *Corpus Juris Hungarici. Magyar Törvénytár 1000–1895*, ed. Dezső Márkus (Budapest, 1897 etc.). The *Tripartitum* is published as *Magyar Törvénytár. Werbőczy István Hármaskönyve*.

[51] These had been first published by Sambucus as an appendix to his 1581 Vienna edition of the *Tripartitum*. See István Csekey, *Werbőczy és a magyar alkotmányjog–A Tripartitum bibliográfiája* (Acta Juridico-Politica, 2) (Cluj, 1942), 64, no. 9.

[52] These were supposedly published in his *Curiosora et Selectiora Variarum Scientiarum Miscellanea* (Trnava, 1689), but the editions I have seen do not contain them. See Párniczky and Bátyka, *A magyar Corpus Juris*, 66.

[53] Párniczky and Bátyka, *A magyar Corpus Juris*, 67.

[54] The Canon Law maxims are taken from the Liber Quintus of Gregory IX and the Liber Sixtus of Boniface VIII. See *Corpus Iuris Canonici*, eds. E.L. Richter and E. Friedberg, 2 vols. (Leipzig, 1879–81), i, cols. 927–8, 1122–4.

treated the *Praxis Criminalis* of 1656 as a guide, even though they acknowledged that it was not strictly a part of the kingdom's law.[55] The result was suitably perverse. The written customs of the realm had acquired the character of legislation on account of the inclusion of the *Tripartitum* into the volumes of the kingdom's laws and by the cross-referencing and common indexing of their respective texts. Yet, the authority of these texts and what was understood to be law rested itself upon customary use. *Consuetudo* had become *lex*, but the content of *lex* was now defined by *consuetudo*.

## THE *EINRICHTUNGSWERK* AND THE COMMISSIO SYSTEMATICA

The Roman Law consisted of both republican and imperial texts and might be used politically in several ways. In the first, it could be deployed for what it said on the popular origins of legal authority and on the importance of custom as an expression of the people's will. The Prologue of the *Tripartitum* is one example of this trend, which would through the *mos gallicus* gather pace during the course of the sixteenth century.[56] In the second, the Roman Law might be plundered for its imperial content and as a way of advancing the prince's claim to be *legibus solutus*. The Habsburg monarchs followed the second of these routes, although in the case of Hungary their claims were more muted. Hungary's rulers might, therefore, act as if they were possessed of a complete legal authority, but until the nineteenth century they never explicitly invoked a *ius legis ferendae*. Instead, they either shied away from revealing the full extent of the powers that they claimed, for fear of offending their coronation oaths, or else they relied upon the ruler's general right of supervision (*Aufsichtungsrecht*), as acknowledged in statute law. The text of 1526: 1, which permitted the monarch to use his *auctoritas* and *potestas* to do all that was necessary for 'the defence, liberty and other needs of the realm', might thus be invoked to permit legislation by decree in matters that did not infringe established freedoms.[57]

Nor did Hungary's rulers explicitly invoke the doctrine of forfeiture (*Verwirkungstheorie*) with its Romanist assumption that all rights and liberties were in fact *leges privatae* which, since they derived from the royal grace, might be revoked by the ruler.[58] During the 1670s, in the aftermath of a conspiracy that resulted in the prosecution of several hundred Hungarian noblemen, Leopold I did not therefore propose a sequestration of noble rights in the manner done by Ferdinand II in

[55] György Galánthai Fekete, *Problemata juridica seu Quaestiones in causis*, ed. János Csaplovics (Bratislava, 1814), 230.

[56] Magnus Ryan, 'Legal Humanism and Empire', unpublished lecture, Institute of Historical Research, London (20 January 2010).

[57] János Zlinszky, *Az ügyvédség kialakulása Magyarországon és története Fejér megyében* (Székesfehérvár? 1976?), 26.

[58] The Roman Law contribution to *Verwirkungstheorie* is discussed in Hugo Toman, *Das böhmische Staatsrecht und die Entstehung der österreichischen Reichsidee von Jahre 1527 bis 1848* (Prague, 1872), 43.

Bohemia fifty years before.[59] Certainly, he abolished (temporarily, as it turned out) the freedom of the nobility in regard to taxation and exercised his rule through a gubernium that paid little heed either to noble privileges or to previous guarantees of religious liberty. The gubernium was installed in 1673, in a drunken ceremony, but collapsed four years later under the double-impact of civil war and the plague.[60] Its persecution of Protestant preachers through specially convened tribunals acquired international notoriety, even though Leopold attempted to curb the worst excesses of the courts.[61] Historians have often seen Leopold's appointment of the gubernium as foreshadowing the constitutional forfeiture practised on Hungary after 1849, but Leopold himself did not ground his actions on any such doctrine. A pamphlet by a court publicist that promoted the doctrine of forfeiture by suggesting that the Hungarians be squeezed into Czech breeches (*Der in böhmische Hosen ausgekleidete ungarische Libertiner*) was thus publicly burnt at Leopold's instruction.[62]

The largest threat to noble privilege and along with it the edifice of rights and provisions contained in the *Tripartitum* came not from the Roman Law but instead from the doctrines of natural law. Hungary's Habsburg rulers would never subscribe to the full terms of the 'double covenant' proposed by Pufendorf, for this implied that they held their power by a compact with the people, following upon the people's own agreement to found a civil society. Nor would they subscribe to the principle of confessional toleration, except in the context of encouraging immigration to the areas recently freed from the Turks. They did, however, embrace the notion that government existed for the purpose of the common welfare and that the people's good was the touchstone against which policy and institutions should be measured. In this respect, natural law theory constrained absolutist ambitions by subjecting policy to the test of benevolence, while simultaneously investing the ruler with the power to set aside conventions and privileges that might be deemed injurious to public well-being.[63]

Although their systematic connection was not elaborated before the eighteenth century, natural law theory was complementary to 'treasury science' (*Kameralwissenschaft*; cameral science).[64] Both shared a common purpose in seeking to maximize the country's wealth through good government, were opposed to entrenched privileges that were injurious to prosperity, and disparaged the traditional organization of the *Ständestaat* and the pretensions of an ultramontane ecclesiastical

[59] László Benczédi, *Rendiség, absolutizmus és centralizáció a xvii. század végi Magyarországon (1664–1685)* (Budapest, 1980), 38. See also Charles W. Ingrao, *The Habsburg Monarchy 1618–1815* (Cambridge, 1994), 69–71.

[60] Árpád Károlyi, *A magyar alkotmány fölfüggesztése 1673-ben* (Budapest, 1883), 64.

[61] John P. Spielman, *Leopold I of Austria* (London, 1977), 71.

[62] By Johann Flämitzer (Würzburg, 1688). See János J. Varga, 'Die Notwendigkeit einer neuen Einrichtung Ungarns nach die Türkenzeit', in János Kálmár and János J. Varga, eds., *Einrichtungswerk des Königreichs Hungarn (1688–1690)* (Stuttgart, 2010), 47–8. Flämitzer's opinion was hardly new. See Jean Bérenger, 'The Austrian Lands: Habsburg Absolutism under Leopold I', in John Miller, ed., *Absolutism in Seventeenth Century Europe* (Basingstoke and London, 1990), 157–74 (166).

[63] Theodor Mayer, *Verwaltungsreform in Ungarn nach der Türkenkrieg* (Leipzig and Vienna, 1911), 76.

[64] T.J. Hochstrasser, *Natural Law Theories in the Early Enlightenment* (Cambridge, 2000), 168–9.

establishment. The ideal of both was selfless government, in which the ruler acted as 'the mirror and watchman of the common people' (Becher) and 'best judge of the common good' (Pufendorf).[65] From the sixteenth century onwards, the Hungarian treasury had railed against the privileges of the nobility not only because they limited its power of taxation but also on account of the social injustices to which they gave rise. Natural law theory imbued treasury science with the moral authority, deriving from the first principle of human 'sociability', to enforce its precepts in the interests of both state and people.

From the 1670s onwards, it was a common enough pursuit to devise schemes for Hungary's reorganization. Some were born of frustration. Writing at the end of the decade, Prince Raimondo Montecuccoli, the victor over the Turks at St Gotthard (1664), reviewed the history of Hungary, concluding 'that at no point was Hungary at peace'. He blamed for this the Hungarians' lawless and malicious disposition that made them akin to wild animals and robbers. Montecuccoli's solution was rule by an iron rod, the removal of all tax exemptions to pay for an army of occupation, the enforcement of the Catholic religion, and the abolition of Hungary's government and diets. Montecuccoli had no confidence in Hungary's laws. He wrote, 'The Hungarian law book or *Tripartitum* should be straightened out, since (1) its individual provisions contradict one another. Some are unjust, others are out-of-date, and some are good but not followed; and (2) Justinian did so in his own time and so did Wladislas [II].'[66] Johann Caspar von Ampringen, who had served with Montecuccoli at St Gotthard, gave a more restrained opinion. Appointed head of the gubernium in 1673, he concluded that a thorough reorganization of Hungary's laws and institutions, including the *Tripartitum*, should be undertaken, but only after peace had been restored. In the meantime, he pressed for the existing institutions of justice to be made to function properly, and even succeeded in having the Royal Table briefly assemble.[67] In similar fashion, Leopold's director of pyrotechnics and chief of the Buda fire brigade, Gabriel Gautieri (Tüzes Gábor), inveighed against the excessive liberties of the nobility, the powers accumulated by Hungary's diets, the insufficiencies and delays inherent in the kingdom's legal and judicial organization, and the content of the *Tripartitum*, which he deemed constraining upon a royal programme of reform.[68] For his part, the head of the imperial council (Hofrat), Wenzel Lobkowitz recommended that the confusion of Hungary's laws be subject to a thorough revision as the first step in the kingdom's pacification.[69]

[65] Alfred Dufour, 'Pufendorf', in J.H. Burns, ed., *The Cambridge History of Political Thought 1450–1700* (Cambridge, 1991), 561–88 (577); Hubert C. Johnson, 'The Concept of Bureaucracy in Cameralism', *Political Science Quarterly*, 79, no. 3 (1964), 378–402 (386).

[66] Alois Veltzé, ed., *Ausgewaehlte Schriften des Raimund Fürsten Montecuccoli*, 4 vols. (Vienna and Leipzig, 1899–1900), iii, 447–58.

[67] Károlyi, *A magyar alkotmány fölfüggesztése*, 54–5.

[68] Anon. (Sándor Takáts?), 'Tüzes Gábor emlékirata Magyarország kormányzásáról', *Történelmi Tár* (1900), 219–63 (220, 227, 252, 262). See also János J. Varga, 'Die Notwendigkeit einer neuen Einrichtung Ungarns nach die Türkenzeit', in János Kálmár and János J. Varga, eds., *Einrichtungswerk des Königreichs Hungarn (1688–1690)* (Stuttgart, 2010), 9–83 (49).

[69] Károlyi, *A magyar alkotmány fölfüggesztése*, 81. A committee was duly appointed.

To these strands of discontent, treasury science and natural law offered remedies that were both coherent and cogent. They found their most complete expression in the project known as the *Einrichtungswerk* ('Work of Instauration'), which was undertaken in 1689–90 under the direction of Cardinal Leopold Kollonich, previously head of the Hungarian treasury. The purpose of the project was to make recommendations on how to organize the Hungarian territories recently liberated from the Turks, but its brief was rapidly extended to encompass the management of the kingdom as a whole, in which respect it built on previous initiatives.[70] Kollonich viewed the kingdom as a *tabula rasa* and as an experiment in the application of treasury science and natural law theory.[71] Over more than eighty sessions, the sub-committee that he headed (it reported to a Hauptdeputation under the high chamberlain, Ferdinand von Dietrichstein) assembled a catalogue of recommendations that embraced the reorganization of the kingdom's administrative, judicial, ecclesiastical, financial and military affairs (*politica, iuridica, spiritualia, cameralia seu oeconomica, et militaria*).[72] Kollonich went back to first principles, paying little heed to pre-existing rights and institutions. The *Einrichtungswerk* thus proposed a proper government for the kingdom that merged the regency council with the office of palatine and established the chancellery on a permanent footing; a programme of 'mild recatholicization' to include unions with Hungary's Orthodox churches; the encouragement of commerce and manufacturing; and proper quartering arrangements for the army to replace the prevailing methods of forage and requisition. In respect of the *neo-acquistica*, the territories freed from the Turks, the *Einrichtungswerk* recommended the cautious return of property to its previous owners combined with a programme of 'in-population' from abroad. The purpose of this immigration was not only to increase cultivation and thus the flow of income to the treasury but also 'that the kingdom, or at least a greater part of it, might become increasingly Germanicized, that the Hungarian blood, which is naturally inclined to revolution and disquiet, might be tempered with the German, and thereby brought to a constant trust and love of their natural, hereditary monarchy and nobility'.[73]

These proposals were partly welcome to an assembly of the estates (a surrogate of the diet) that gathered under the presidency of the palatine and put forward its own recommendations, principally in respect of the adoption of mercantilist policies to aid manufacturing and commerce. It disagreed, however, with a good deal else. The *Einrichtungswerk* interfered in the relationship

[70] Brian A. Hodson, 'The Development of Habsburg Policy in Hungary and the Einrichtungswerk of Cardinal Kollonich, 1683–90', *Austrian History Yearbook*, 38 (2007), 92–107 (103–6).

[71] János J. Varga, 'Berendezési tervezetek Magyarországon a török kiűzésének időszakában. Az Einrichtungswerk', *Századok*, 125 (1991), 449–88 (453–4).

[72] Varga, 'Die Notwendigkeit einer neuen Einrichtung', 24–5.

[73] William O'Reilly, 'Divide et impera: Race, Ethnicity and Administration in Early 18th-Century Habsburg Hungary', in Guðmundur Hálfdanarson and Anne Katherine Isaacs, eds., *Minorities in Europe* (Florence, 2003) (internet version), 77–103 (79). This notorious passage is put in its proper context by László Benczédi, 'Kollonich Lipót és az Einrichtungswerk', in Mihály Praznovszky and Istvánné Baginszky, eds., *Gazdaság és mentalitás Magyarországon a török kiüzetésének idején* (Salgótarján, 1987), 153–8 (155–6).

between lord and peasant, recommending an upper limit on peasant services and restoration of the peasants' right to free movement. It also advocated the taxation of noble land together with the removal of the nobility's right of exemption from tolls.[74] This was indeed a solution to impoverishment, consonant with the principles of natural law, that Kollonich had long espoused and that he would continue to promote. As he later explained, 'The numerous privileges of the nobility in respect of public burdens contradict the principles of all good government [...] In order to avoid all injustices and irregularities in the allocation of tax and other public burdens, it is necessary to establish a permanent and lasting tax that should be justly apportioned in the same way as in the other lands and provinces of His Majesty.'[75] It was not, however, an intrusion that the estates assembly welcomed.

The *Einrichtungswerk*'s recommendations in respect of the kingdom's judicial organization and the disposition of its laws were no less controversial. First, it proposed the establishment of territorial courts, in Bratislava or Buda under the palatine, in Košice under the high judge, and in Zagreb under the ban. These would exercise an appellate jurisdiction over cases arising in the cities and counties (whose jurisdictional authority would in any case be diminished). Secondly, it advised of 'the highest necessity' that the kingdom's laws be rewritten and criticized the *Tripartitum* and the published collections of the kingdom's statute laws as containing too much that was either contradictory or anachronistic, 'which bring nothing beneficial to the parties or judge in the administration of justice and the greatest irreparable harm to the kingdom and His Majesty'. The *Einrichtungswerk* singled out the protonotaries' courts, which it condemned on account of their corruption as 'plagues of justice' (*pestes Iustitiae*), the many delays brought about by petitions for retrial, the injustices done to wards and orphans, and the unnecessary severity of the courts in criminal matters.[76] As part of its proposals for reform, the *Einrichtungswerk* drew attention to a scheme undertaken by the Lower Austrian counsellor and member of Kollonich's sub-commission, Johann Georg Hoffmann.[77] Hoffmann had outlined a 'universal plan' (*idaea universalis*) for the revision of the kingdom's laws that he named the *Corpus Juris Hungarici Quintopartitum*. The *Quintopartitum* never, however, succeeded in becoming anything more than an ambitious collection of headings, over 1,200 in all, arranged in five categories that corresponded with the sub-committee's own division of administrative, ecclesiastical, judicial, military and financial matters. Its name and internal organization, nevertheless, betrayed its purpose—the comprehensive revision of the *Tripartitum* and the coordination of its content to match the aims of the *Einrichtungswerk*.[78]

[74] Mayer, *Verwaltungsreform in Ungarn*, 56–68.

[75] Varga, 'Die Notwendigkeit einer neuen Einrichtung', 68.

[76] Kálmár and Varga, *Einrichtungswerk des Königreichs Hungarn*, 100–2.

[77] Kálmár and Varga, *Einrichtungswerk des Königreichs Hungarn*, 101.

[78] The text of the *Quintopartitum* is given by Béla Baranyai, 'Hoffmann János György magyar közjogi codex-tervezete (1698–90)', in Baranyai, *A lengyel királykoronázás. Négy közlemény a magyar jog- és alkotmány-történetéhez* (Karcag, 1927), 39–84.

As far as the assembly of the estates was concerned, the problem was not the insufficiency of the kingdom's laws and institutions, but the disrepair into which they had fallen as a consequence of warfare, neglect and excessive reliance upon mandates. Moreover, as it explained to Leopold, the threat to noble privileges was scarcely just reward, given that the diet had only recently acknowledged the monarchy as hereditary and repudiated the resistance clause.[79] In Vienna, meanwhile, the head of the Bohemian chancellery, Franz Ulrich Kinsky, complained that the *Einrichtungswerk* was too modest a proposal since it did not give the king 'the authority and power to command the estates'. Caraffa, the imperial commander, insisted meanwhile that his troops stationed in Hungary continue to have rights of forage.[80] Political opposition, together with the onset of a new French war and a Turkish offensive in the Balkans, meant that Kollonich's ambitious programme of reform was never undertaken in its entirety. Some of its individual parts were, nevertheless, implemented—not least the repopulation by immigrants of the newly conquered territories, especially in the Banat of Timișoara; religious toleration in the areas of settlement; union with the Romanian and (later) Armenian Orthodox churches; and the partial reorganization of the kingdom's government.[81] In respect of the kingdom's judicial administration, the subsequent establishment of district branches of the Royal Table and the development of methods of appeal followed closely the *Einrichtungswerk*'s recommendations. A part of the programme promoted by Kollonich, as it related in particular to the kingdom's commerce, was briefly put into effect by Ferenc Rákóczi for a few years after 1705.[82]

Notwithstanding its partial adoption, the *Einrichtungswerk* stood as a metaphor for the disregard that Hungary's Habsburg rulers had for noble rights and status. It thus combined with the injustices wrought by special tribunals, the depredations done by the treasury administration, the bluster of Montecuccoli and the irregularities of the Ampringen government, to create an association between the preservation of noble liberties and the retention of the *Tripartitum*'s text. Kollonich's proposals for the reform of the law and for the law's convergence with the principles of natural justice and treasury science thus achieved the

[79] Varga, 'Die Notwendigkeit einer neuen Einrichtung', 37–8; Varga, 'Berendezési tervezetek Magyarországon', 475. See also István Soós and János J. Varga, 'A pozsonyi rendi bizottság tervezete. Az ún. "Magyar Einrichtungswerk"', *Századok*, 125 (1991), 500–16 (509).

[80] Mayer, *Verwaltungsreform in Ungarn*, 88, 92. See also, R.J.W. Evans, *Austria, Hungary and the Habsburgs. Essays on Central Europe c. 1683–1867* (Oxford, 2006), 5.

[81] The literature on the resettlement of the Banat is considerable. See now, János Kálmár, 'Das *Einrichtungswerk des Königreichs Hungarn* und die Einrichtung des Temeswarer Banats im 18. Jahrhundert', in Kálmár and Varga, *Einrichtungswerk des Königreichs Hungarn*, 459–70; Irina Marin, *Contested Frontiers in the Balkans: Ottoman, Habsburg and Communist Rivalries in Eastern Europe* (London and New York, 2012), 26–30. A highly original contribution to the study of the early-modern Banat is by William O'Reilly, 'Conceptualizing America in Early Modern Central Europe', *Pennsylvania History*, 65 (1998), 101–24. For the name of Banat, see Martyn Rady, 'Controverse istorico-istoriografice privind toponimul Banat', in Victor Neumann, ed., *Cultură și Identitate. Studii privind istoria Banatului* (Bucharest, 2009), 18–24.

[82] Gusztáv Heckenast, 'A merkantilizmus és Rákóczi gazdaságpolitikája', in Kálmán Benda, ed., *Európa és a Rákóczi-szabadságharc* (Budapest, 1980), 189–93 (189–92).

very reverse of his intentions—the further embedding of the old law as an emblem of noble freedom.[83]

* * *

During the 1690s, the principal courts of the realm that met in the Curia had begun to meet more frequently. Their recovery was, however, impeded by the outbreak of rebellion in 1703 and by continued disagreements over their composition and organization. Conflict over the kingdom's legal administration extended over several decades—throughout the reign of Joseph I and into the first dozen years of Charles III's. The Lower House of the diet was fearful that the Septemviralis court, which had emerged out of the judicial sessions of the regency council, would be reconstituted as an office or *dicasterium* that combined administrative and judicial functions and would thus be open to political interference. The recently reorganized Hungarian chancellery in Vienna provided an obvious means of meddling. Similarly, while the justice administered by the roving courts of the protonotaries was a frequent cause of complaint, their replacement by district courts suggested a new measure of intrusion into the independent activity of the counties. Protracted negotiations between king and diet had thus achieved by 1715 no more than an agreement that some of the powers of the protonotaries and treasury officers be curbed and that a new committee be appointed to examine the question of legal reform.

The new committee or Commissio Systematica appointed in 1715 was empowered with the double mandate (*mandatum bimembre*) to overhaul the kingdom's judicial organization and to improve its laws. Nevertheless, the same objections as had met previous attempts at judicial reform resurfaced, with the diet pushing strongly for the reinvigoration of the counties as a way of rendering the district courts superfluous. It did not help that the leader of the imperial side in the negotiations was Imre Esterházy, the excessively *kaisertreu* bishop of Zagreb.[84] Concessions, threats and deft management by Charles III enabled, however, the reorganization to be agreed. The Curia courts of the Septemviralis and Royal Table were extended to allow in a larger number of noble assessors; the district courts were made filial courts of the Royal Table so that the competence of the counties was not diminished; and the Curia was moved to Pest to put a distance between it and the seat of government in Bratislava. The new arrangements were incorporated in the law of 1723: 24–34, which provided the legal basis for the operation of the kingdom's courts until 1868. As we have remarked, the appeal of cases between the several layers of the courts contributed to their organizational uniformity.

The reform of the kingdom's laws proved, however, impossible. From the very first, the diet maintained that the laws were good; it was simply that they had been

[83] Varga, 'Die Notwendigkeit einer neuen Einrichtung', 66.

[84] Esterházy's position was well summed up by his remark in 1723, 'if I could, I would have the whole world subject to the overwhelming power of the most august house of Austria.' He consistently failed to understand that the reform of the courts required the consent of the diet, not least because the law of 1715 obliged this. See Bónis, *A bírósági szervezet megújítása III. Károly korában*, 82, 102–3.

neglected or misapplied. Accordingly, when Joseph I had proposed to the diet in 1709 a revision of the laws, his plea had been rejected on four occasions. As the imperial commander, Sigbert Heister, observed on this occasion, 'although those attending the diet profess themselves loyal, their conduct is from what they say more akin to rebels'.[85] Similar objections attended the work of the Commissio Systematica, where a sub-committee busied away on the reform of the law, under the direction of the Protestant lawyer, Pál Prileszky. Prileszky's methodology was to achieve a 'concentration of the laws' by glossing the *Tripartitum* with the contents of the kingdom's statute laws and with what he and the sub-committee knew of the practices of the courts. The first draft, the so-called *Observationes in Tripartitum*, was a muddle, after which Prileszky was instructed by the chancellery to reorganize its contents after Werbőczy's original scheme of persons, things and actions. The revised draft was grandly named the *Tripartitum Novum* and referred to the monarch in 1719 for approval. Charles duly passed it to the Hungarian treasury for comment, which only after much delay responded with suggestions. The sub-committee incorporated these at a session held in July 1722, by which time all interest in its work had been lost. The contents of the *Tripartitum Novum* thus made no impression on the legislation of 1723. A few of the sub-committee's recommendations were, however, picked up from a subsequent version of the *Observationes* that had been reworked by the high judge, István Koháry.[86]

The failure of the *Tripartitum Novum* was not just due to bureaucratic mismanagement, for it was, indeed, a sorry thing.[87] After a preface that borrowed extensively from the *Quadripartitum*, it rehearsed the contents of the *Tripartitum*, although in a different order, often in its arrangement borrowing from the *Quadripartitum*.[88] Bizarrely, the Prologue, which otherwise repeated Werbőczy's theoretical considerations on the law, included sections on the different customs of Transylvania and Slavonia.[89] The first part of the *Tripartitum Novum*, being the legal examination of persons, discussed the status of nobles and ignobles, townsfolk and (interestingly) *libertini* or freemen, who lived outside the seigneurial nexus.[90] The second part included much of the *Tripartitum*'s first part, but incorporated chunks of procedural law as well as a discussion of charters and privileges. The third part of the *Tripartitum Novum* was largely the second part of the *Tripartitum*. Although we will notice occasions when statute law or court practice is cited, these are consistently presented as explanatory of the *Tripartitum*'s text and as amplifying rather than modifying its content.

It is easy to disparage Prileszky's work, and to agree with the verdict that 'self-assuredness, innovation and originality were missing from it'.[91] The preface to the

[85] Bónis, *A birósági szervezet megújitása III. Károly korában*, 54.

[86] *Commissio Systematica. Observationes in Tripartitum*, OSzK, MSS, Qu. Lat. 2378, unpaginated flyleaf. See also Bónis, *A birósági szervezet megújitása III. Károly korában*, 118. The legislation mainly affected the operation of the kingdom's surviving *loca credibilia*.

[87] *Tripartitum Novum*, OSzK, MSS, Fol. Lat., 559.

[88] Bónis (*A birósági szervezet megújitása III. Károly korában*, 99) is mistaken in assuming that the compilers of the *Novum Tripartitum* did not refer back to the *Quadripartitum*.

[89] *Tripartitum Novum*, 22–3. [90] *Tripartitum Novum*, 56.

[91] Bónis, *A birósági szervezet megújitása III. Károly korában*, 99.

*Tripartitum Novum* suggests, nevertheless, the intellectual constraints under which Prileszky and the sub-committee laboured. The preface explained the purpose of the work as the integration of custom and statute law. Custom, however, always took precedence over statute law, for only such laws carried weight as had been 'received by very long practice' (*longaevo usu assueti*). As the *Tripartitum Novum* explained, Werbőczy's *Tripartitum* had been in use for more than two centuries in Hungary. It had thus acquired by virtue of its historical application an authority over time that was undisputed.[92] The *Tripartitum Novum* might accordingly rearrange its parts and comment upon its text, but its content was not to be changed. In this respect, the outcome of Prileszky's sub-committee was bound to be a conservative statement and a work of reorganization rather than of reinvention.[93]

Similar considerations constrained the work of János Szegedi, whose massive *Tripartitum juris Hungarici Tyrocinium*, first published in 1734, built on the Commissio Systematica's *Observationes*. Szegedi sought to combine the laws, current practice and elements of Canon and Roman Law with the text of the *Tripartitum*.[94] Unlike the *Tripartitum Novum* (of which Szegedi seems to have been unaware), the *Tyrocinium* adhered firmly to Werbőczy's original arrangement, not shuffling the *Tripartitum*'s individual chapters in an attempt to improve upon its organization. Nevertheless, the extensive use to which Szegedi put the *Observationes* means that we should see the *Tyrocinium* as properly the fruit of the Commissio Systematica's labour of reorganizing the law. Szegedi's method was, as with previous Hungarian attempts to modernize the *Tripartitum*, to amplify Werbőczy's text, adding details but not detracting from it. It was only in respect of the succession and right of resistance that he made any profound modification, as a consequence of the law of 1687 and of the Pragmatic Sanction.[95] Roman Law influences were slight, as for instance an explanation culled from the *Digest* in respect of the right of entry to repair river banks, or rendered obliquely, as in Szegedi's verdict that the prince was as a consequence of his coronation oath no longer *legibus solutus*.[96]

Szegedi intended the *Tyrocinium* for the use of students, on account of which it contained a gazetteer to help them locate the kingdom's courts. The cost of its volumes (between two and four, depending on the edition) must surely, however, have been prohibitive. Although published in a dozen editions between 1734 and 1764, the *Tyrocinium* did not outlive its author, who died of the plague in 1770. More successful was Szegedi's *Werbőczius Illustratus*, first published in 1740 and frequently

92 *Tripartitum Novum*, *praefatio*, unpaginated.

93 Bónis, *A bírósági szervezet megújítása III. Károly korában*, 99–100.

94 János Szegedi, *Tripartitum Juris Hungarici Tyrocinium juxta ordinem titulorum operis tripartiti, complures juris canonici, civilis et Ungarici decisiones combinans*, Trnava, 1734. The full title of the *Tyrocinium* altered with successive editions, subsequently omitting the references to civil law and judicial decisions. For our purpose, we rely on the 1751 Košice edition.

95 Szegedi, *Tripartitum Juris Hungarici Tyrocinium* (1751), 68, 83–8 (I. 3; I. 9). The Pragmatic Sanction made the royal succession cognatic.

96 Szegedi, *Tripartitum Juris Hungarici Tyrocinium* (1751), 184 (I. 87), 264–5 (II. 5); *Digest*, 43. 15.

reprinted over the next eighty years.[97] The *Werbőczius Illustratus* was, however, little more than a re-edition of the *Tripartitum*. The *Tripartitum*'s text was preserved intact, although Szegedi introduced the scheme of numbering the sub-sections of chapters that he would later use in his 1751 edition of the CJH. Commentary on the *Tripartitum*'s text was confined to footnotes that mainly cross-referenced to Kitonich's *Directio Methodica*, the *Tyrocinium* and the *Observationes*. The notes—there are roughly two per page—were, for the most part, of slender content, being mainly intended to explain points or terms of law. Only in a few places did they materially add to the substance of the *Tripartitum*.

In the opening pages of the *Tripartitum Novum*, the unification of the kingdom's laws was presented by Prileszky and his sub-committee as a historic endeavour that reached back through the *Quadripartitum* to Wladislas II's original commission.[98] We can, in similar fashion, draw a line of descent from the Commissio Systematica, through the *Observationes*, to Szegedi's *Tyrocinium* and *Werbőczius Illustratus*. The Commissio Systematica had been instructed as one of its tasks to rewrite the kingdom's laws, an endeavour that had been previously urged in the *Einrichtungswerk* and by many others. In the event, the Commissio Systematica failed. Neither the *Observationes* nor the *Tripartitum Novum* had any significant impact on the kingdom's legislation. The slender outcome of the Commissio Systematica's work of rewriting the law thus left the *Tripartitum* intact. In this respect, the Commissio Systematica's most enduring legacy was Szegedi's *Werbőczius Illustratus*—the republication for the benefit of generations to come of the *Tripartitum*'s text, whole and intact, with only light annotation at the feet of its pages.

## PUBLIC LAW, THE CJH AND THE HISTORIANS

Despite the republication in successive editions both of the realm's statutes and of the *Tripartitum*, little effort was made to improve their texts. The laws remained largely as they had been received from Ilosvay and published by Mossóczy. Mossóczy's edition was, however, defective, for although noting variant readings he had made no attempt to reconstruct the original texts of the laws. Successive editions had added in printing errors, corrections and 'improvements' not only to the laws but also to the *Tripartitum*'s text. Even though statutes promulgated after 1600 were usually distributed in printed form, with the royal seal and signature, the CJH still managed to garble these, even in editions published in the nineteenth century that communicated laws that were just a few years old![99] The extent of deviation from the originals is considerable. For instance, the version of the law of 1492 given in the 1779 edition of the CJH (which was an updated reprint of Szegedi's 1751

97 Anon., *Werbőczius Illustratus* (Trnava, 1740). For Szegedi's authorship, see István Csekey, *A Tripartitum bibliográfiája*, Acta Juridico-Politica, 2 (Cluj, 1942), 173.

98 *Tripartitum Novum*, *praefatio*, unpaginated.

99 Párniczky and Bátyka, *A magyar Corpus Juris*, 37; J.N. Kovachich, *Lectiones Variantes decretorum comitialium* (Pest, 1816), 452–4.

edition) contained 600 errors; the text of the *Tripartitum*, as published in the same collection, had about 2,000, including even the length of the bar that supposedly determined the kingdom's scheme of measurement.[100] It was later estimated that the entire body of the CJH contained over 13,000 errors.[101] Certainly, the great majority of these were inconsequential, but a few affected the meaning of the relevant legislation—*numerum* to *munerum*, *consilium* to *regnum*, *castretur* to *castigetur*, *filiae et sorores* to *sorores* alone, and so on.[102] Likewise, successive editions of the laws had included material that could hardly be considered legislation, as for instance the 'cameral contract' of 1342 regulating the farm of the kingdom's mints, or that constituted 'failed legislation', like the law of 1507, or that was of dubious provenance, most obviously a supposed law of Andrew I. At the same time, the compilations left out many of the laws that had been proclaimed, for successive editors were unaware that their texts had survived. The entire corpus of thirteenth-century legislation was overlooked, with the sole exception of the 1222 Golden Bull. The statutes of 1385, 1404 (6 April), 1421, 1427 (both statutes of that year), 1421, 1439, 1440, 1443, 1444 and 1458 (8 June) were likewise omitted.

Ilosvay, Mossóczy, Szentiványi and Szegedi were all priests. The connection between churchmen and the business of collecting and editing historical texts remained strong throughout the eighteenth century. It is demonstrated in the successive achievements of the Jesuits Gábor Hevenesi (1656–1715), István Kaprinai (1714–86) and György Pray (1723–1801), the last of whom discovered the earliest text in the Hungarian language, and Bishop Ignác Batthyány of Transylvania (1741–98), founder of the Batthyaneum Library in Alba Iulia and editor of the three-volume *Leges Ecclesiasticae Regni Hungariae*.[103] Rival collections of sources were gathered by Protestant luminaries. The Protestant 'source-collecting school' went beyond composing an alternative narrative of Hungarian ecclesiastical history, being also involved in the editing of some of Hungary's earliest chronicles and in the publication of topographical gazetteers and *Landeskunde*. Preeminent among these were the encyclopaedist, David Czvittinger (*c*. 1680–1743), Mátyás Bél (1684–1749), author of the five-volume *Notitia Hungariae Novae Historica-Geographica*, and Bél's Austrian student, Johann Georg Schwandtner (1716–91), whose *Scriptores rerum Hungaricarum* published for the first time the celebrated *Gesta* of the Hungarian Anonymus.[104] In the course of his research, Czvittinger in particular became aware of the deficiencies of the CJH and of its many omissions.[105]

The principal spur to a critical evaluation of the kingdom's published (and unpublished) legislation came out of the historical study of Hungary's public law. Hungarian public law, in the sense of its constitutional arrangements, is frequently

[100] Trip., I. 133 [47] (DRMH 5, 220); Kovachich, *Lectiones Variantes*, 113–38, 461–517.

[101] Éva V. Windisch, *Kovachich Márton György, a forráskutató* (Budapest, 1998), 184.

[102] Kovachich, *Lectiones Variantes*, 124, 200, 209, 213.

[103] 1785–1827, Alba Iulia and Cluj.

[104] Steven Bela Vardy, *Modern Hungarian Historiography* (Boulder, Guildford and New York, 1976), 24–31.

[105] Adam Francis Kollar, *Originibus et usu perpetuo potestatis legislatoriae circa sacra Apostolicorum* (Vienna, 1764), 116.

portrayed as customary and as being regulated by largely unwritten norms.[106] There is some truth in this, for a part of the kingdom's public law derived from historical practice and observation—as, for instance, the procedure of *diaetalis tractatus* and of bargaining between monarch and diet; the convention that some sort of royal election should be held or, in its place, a negotiation between ruler and estates over the terms of the inaugural diploma; the participation of Croatian delegates at the diet, and so on.[107] These constitutional arrangements were not sanctioned in written law but were rooted in repetitive acts that served to perpetuate their recollection and use. A good part of the kingdom's public law was, however, so lacking in normative substance as to defy the description of custom. Its content was for the most part fleeting and arbitrary, depending upon the relative political balance of monarch and estates. Even matters that might be thought to have acquired a customary character were liable to sudden erosion, often by way of a deliberate act of forgetfulness, or else radically expanded beyond the ambit of their previous application. The right, therefore, of the ruler to make law through decree, by his or her own volition (*proprio motu*), was long contested, and it was never certain whether this right might only be deployed to fill in gaps in the existing law or whether it amounted to a complete legislative competence. The so-called *Revisionsklausel*, included from 1687 in either the royal oath or the inaugural diploma (or indeed both), was also capable of several interpretations. The *Revisionsklausel* compelled the monarch to uphold the nobility's rights 'as the king and the assembled estates shall agree on the interpretation and application thereof' (*prout super eorum intellectu, et usu, regio ac communi statuum consensu diaetaliter conventum fuerit*) and so might be used either to oblige the monarch to maintain the nobility's privileges and rights or to permit him to bypass them.[108] Similarly, the monarch's power to appoint prelates of the church could, by an act of the royal will, be extended to include other ecclesiastical dignitaries, even parish priests, or be applied in such a way as to diminish the rights of patronage previously practised by corporations.[109] The right of the diet, considered customary by the late fifteenth century, to vote taxation might still be challenged as an *abusus* and, at the diet of 1765 as well as subsequently, a contrary royal right proposed in this regard.[110]

The kingdom's public law rested, thus, less upon convention as upon contestation, being in this respect 'normatively non-normative'. In the struggle over the content of the kingdom's public law, monarch and estates sought to buttress their respective positions by appealing to history, hunting out precedents and pointing

[106] On the customary content of public law in Hungary, see László Péter, 'Die Verfassungsentwicklung in Ungarn', in Helmut Rumpler and Peter Urbanitsch, eds., *Die Habsburger Monarchie*, vol. 8 (*Verfassung und Parlamentarismus*), 2 parts (Vienna, 2000), i, 239–540 (242–5); István M. Szijártó, *A diéta. A magyar rendek és az országgyűlés 1708–1792* (Budapest, 2005), 40–3.

[107] For the *diaetalis tractatus*, see László Péter, 'The Hungarian *Diætalis Tractatus* and the Imperial Constitutional Systems: A Comparison', *Central Europe*, 6, no. 1 (2008), 47–64 (58–63).

[108] 1687: 1. See László Péter, 'The Primacy of Consuetudo in Hungarian Law', in CLCE, 101–11 (104).

[109] Andor Csizmadia, *Feudális jogintézmények továbbélése a Horthy korszakában* (Budapest, 1961), 6–9.

[110] Szijártó, *A diéta*, 248–50.

to earlier trends that had, so it was alleged, been obliterated by the passage of time. The rights of the church and diet were among the first to be investigated by a new generation of historians, who were motivated to search out and reread the manuscripts of the past for avowedly political purposes. The debate over the kingdom's public law thus led directly to the critical evaluation of the legal and other sources collected over the course of the preceding centuries. The earliest activity in this respect lay with the circle around Cardinal Archbishop Kollonich, which during the course of the 1680s investigated the texts of previous statutes and treaties with the aim of proving the hereditary nature of Hungarian kingship.[111] It was also evident in the next century, albeit at a humbler level, in the actions of the royal officials who combed through Hungary's oldest charters to prove the crown's right to treasure trove.[112] The examination of the kingdom's historic public law is, however, most closely associated with the imperial librarian, Ádám Kollár (1718–83), who with the encouragement of Maria Theresa and the Staatsrat brought his learning to bear on the issue of the monarch's right to raise taxation without the consent of the diet and to control all church preferments.[113] Certainly, Kollár overplayed his hand, variously arguing that St Stephen had been possessed of an apostolic authority that owed nothing to papal gift, that the Golden Bull was an invention of Bonfini, and that the diets had usurped an authority that had formerly belonged to the monarch alone. He also highlighted the *Tripartitum*'s failure to acquire the royal seal, on the basis of which he denied its legal authority, as well as the many gaps in its text, particularly as they related to the kingdom's public law.[114] Nevertheless, in the course of his research Kollár established the defective nature of the CJH, not least its many omissions and misprints, and he called as a matter of urgency for a new edition, to be completed with 'greater devotion, knowledge and care'.[115] Kollár's opinions outraged the diet and were regarded as a step too far by the queen-empress, who put him instead to researching Hungary's historic claims to southern Poland and to the reform of public education.[116]

The most important assault on the CJH came, however, from the other side of the political spectrum. In the wake of Joseph's attack on Hungary's laws, the librarian and archivist, Márton György (Martinus Georgius) Kovachich (1744–1821), began to collect evidence in particular of the work of the kingdom's diets. It was Kovachich's purpose to demonstrate that Hungary's diets had a continuous

[111] Gustav Turba, *Die Grundlagen der Pragmatischen Sanktion. 1. Ungarn* (Leipzig and Vienna, 1911), 21.

[112] MJL, iv, 793; Antal Mózes Cziráky, *Conspectus Juris Publici Regni Hungariae*, 2 vols. (Vienna, 1851), i, 175.

[113] Andor Csizmadia, 'Az absolutizmus magyarországi jogtörténetirói. Kollár, Benczúr, Krčelić', in Kálmán Kovács, ed., *A magyar politikai es jogi gondolkodás történetéből. XVIII.–XIX. század* (Budapest, 1982), 21–38 (25).

[114] Adamus Franciscus Kollar (Ádám František Kollár), *Originibus et usu perpetuo potestatis legislatoriae circa sacra apostolicorum regum* (Vienna, 1764), 117. See also Csizmadia, 'Az absolutizmus magyarországi jogtörténetirói', 28.

[115] Cited in Andor Csizmadia, *Adam Franz Kollár und die ungarische rechtshistorische Forschung* (Vienna, 1982), 23.

[116] Csizmadia, *Adam Franz Kollár*, 7–11, 17–18, 22–3, 28, 39–41; Csizmadia, 'Az absolutizmus magyarországi jogtörténetirói', 25–30; Kollar, *Originibus et usu perpetuo*, 116. See also Andor Csizmadia, 'Previous Editions of the Laws of Hungary', in DRMH 1[2], pp. xvii–xxxiii.

existence that could be tracked back to the conquest period, and that they and not the ruler were the kingdom's true legislators.[117] In this way, Kovachich took head on the claims previously advanced by Kollár and variously maintained by a subsequent generation of Josephinist historians and monarchical enthusiasts. Kovachich's research was solidly archival. Although denied full access to the royal collection, he toured the countryside, copying and gathering manuscripts from no less than seventy-six collections as well as maintaining a busy correspondence with scholars and antiquarians who provided him with transcripts and details of their own discoveries. The materials that he gathered amount today to no less than 300 boxes.[118]

Kovachich's prodigious energy was dissipated in many fruitless projects and ventures. His principal contribution was the two collections, the *Vestigia comitiorum apud Hungaros ab exordio regni eorum* (Buda, 1790) and the three-volume *Supplementum ad Vestigia comitiorum* (Pest, 1798–1801). Kovachich acknowledged the way that debate around the kingdom's public law had invigorated historical enquiry, explaining that the purpose of his volumes was to reveal 'the history of legislation, to illumine public law and the origin of the laws and what relates to the understanding of the state's constitution'.[119] While preparing the *Vestigia* and *Supplementum*, Kovachich came across twelve hitherto unpublished (or largely unpublished) statutes promulgated at the kingdom's diets, reference to a further sixteen diets where statutes were thought to have been issued, and another forty items the provenance and legal character of which were uncertain. Subsequent research yielded a dozen more unpublished statutes.[120] In comparing the published versions of the laws, as given in the CJH, with the originals that he had discovered, Kovachich became alert to their defective nature. The full extent of their corruption was not, however, communicated until 1816, with the publication in Pest of the *Lectiones Variantes decretorum comitialium* by Kovachich's son, János Miklós (Johannes Nicolaus).

On account of the discoveries that he had made, it was only after difficulty and delay that Kovachich's works were finally approved by the censors. One problem that they raised was to prove insurmountable—if the laws as published in the CJH were incomplete and textually corrupt, did this not put in jeopardy the kingdom's legal foundations by introducing new readings?[121] Unlike the Vienna censor, Johann Christian von Engel, who was himself a historian of merit, Kovachich did not comprehend the legal minefield into which he had entered, claiming to be only a disinterested historian. Accordingly, he pressed on with plans to publish a completely new collection of the kingdom's statutes, to be entitled the *Codex decretorum comitialium*, which he intended should supersede the CJH. His repeated appeals to the chancellery, diet and palatine for permission and funding were denied.[122]

[117] Windisch, *Kovachich Márton György*, 27.
[118] Windisch, *Kovachich Márton György*, 15, 129.
[119] Windisch, *Kovachich Márton György*, 117.
[120] Csizmadia, 'Previous Editions of the Laws of Hungary', p. xxx.
[121] Windisch, *Kovachich Márton György*, 119–20.
[122] Windisch, *Kovachich Márton György*, 186–7.

Criticism of Kovachich's project largely took the form originally proposed by Engel. First, those laws that had been left out of the CJH did not belong there. Either they had been omitted from previous editions because they were deemed to have lapsed, or else they had subsequently fallen into desuetude as a consequence of their omission. There was thus no point in resurrecting them. Secondly, the errors that had found their way into the text of the CJH had been sanctified by time and so rendered 'true and holy'.[123] The diet, therefore, while acknowledging the CJH's errors, accordingly determined that since the authority of its contents had never previously been called into question, it was necessary to recognize their continued efficacy.[124] The body of the kingdom's statutes was thus a closed book or *clausum*, which might not be altered or emended, and which through its communication over time of a single text guaranteed the consistency of the law's application.[125] As successive jurists affirmed, even if they lacked the quality of historical authenticity, the defective texts of the kingdom's law retained legal authority as a consequence of their historic use, while the statutes that Kovachich had uncovered were possessed of none, for their contents had never received the sanction of observation and practice.[126] To that extent, the content of a legislative act retained only such authority as custom lent it. In seeking to unmask the history of the kingdom's public law, Kovachich's work thus inadvertently confirmed through the manner of its reception the primacy of Hungary's customary tradition.

* * *

Notwithstanding successive attempts to revise or replace its text, the *Tripartitum* endured, outliving the *Quadripartitum*, the *Quintopartitum*, the *Einrichtungswerk* and the labours of the Commissio Systematica. Its authority rested upon its customary use in the courts and in its circulation, both as part of the CJH and in its single editions. The *Tripartitum*'s continued salience in the legal life of the kingdom may be demonstrated by the work of many nameless scholars, who penned manuscripts that adumbrated its contents, sought to extract its essence or to reconcile its provisions with cases of which they knew, or endeavoured to bend its rules to fit in with theological precepts.[127] There can surely be no other secular work in Hungarian history that has been so pondered over. For its part, the CJH likewise survived attempts to re-found the laws of the kingdom by rendering them more coherent or reforming them entirely to comport with natural law principles. The strength of the CJH rested, like the *Tripartitum*, on the customary authority that

[123] Windisch, *Kovachich Márton György*, 190.

[124] *Diarium Comitiorum Regni Hungariae. Magyarország gyűlésének jegyző-könyve* (Pest, 1807), 555 (31 October 1807). The diet, however, thanked Kovachich for his labours.

[125] Kelemen, *Historia Iuris Hungarici privati*, i, 348.

[126] Párniczky and Bátyka, *A magyar Corpus Juris*, 92–3. See also Csizmadia, 'Previous Editions of the Laws of Hungary', p. xxxi.

[127] See for instance (among much else), BAR-CJ, MSS, U480, *Decretum Tripartitum Hungarico Idiomate per Quaestiones et Responsiones*; U523/A, *Regulae Expeditionum Juridicarum*; U523/B, *Directio Processualis*; U523/D, *Quaedam notabilia*; U523/F, *Omnia ad Majorem Dei Gloriam*; U849, *Compendiosa deductio iuris Stephani Verböczy*.

it enjoyed. On this account, its rendering of the kingdom's statute laws, although recognized by historians as defective, retained the authority of use. As in the Middle Ages, therefore, the law of the kingdom continued to derive from the interplay of legal text and actual observance, thus confirming its character as customary law. The manner in which the courts handled this material and adapted it to the cases before them is the subject of the next chapter.

# 11

# Courts and the Law in the Long Eighteenth Century

## CUSTOMARY LAW AND THE LOWER COURTS

Hungary's eighteenth century may be either long or short, extending from the Peace of Satu Mare in 1711, which marked the end of the Rákóczi Revolt, to either the reign of Joseph II in the 1780s or to the collapse of the old regime in 1848.[1] In this chapter, we will draw upon illustrations from the longer century to elucidate the activity of the courts, although in the next we will backtrack a little to examine responses to the Josephinist experiment. In respect of the kingdom's courts, however, the long and the short centuries are not so different. For most of their course, a part of the law was still considered to derive from the *Tripartitum* and the CJH. These did not, however, provide comprehensive solutions to the cases that came before the courts, nor was their content always appropriate in individual circumstances. In the gaps and in cases where the written law was deemed unsuitable, popular observance continued to inform decisions, in which respect the law of the courts was never exclusively lawyerly. This is most apparent in respect of the kingdom's lower courts and in the manner of their judging. Here, the Bartolist conception of custom, as emanating out of the people's will and tacit consent, found its fullest expression, being understood as emerging from the community.

The lower courts of the kingdom, in villages, counties, market towns and in seigneurial jurisdictions, had much to guide them. Although intended for a noble audience, the *Tripartitum* carried authority throughout the kingdom, and much of peasant custom converged upon it, in respect both of the substantive law and of procedure. Regarding criminal offences, the Austrian *Praxis Criminalis* was widely followed, although subject to much modification at a local level on account of the savagery of its penalties.[2] Much, however, remained uncertain, such as acts of vengeance, drunken revelry (the behaviour of Orthodox Romanians on Sundays was

[1] On some of the problems of periodization in Hungarian historiography, see László Péter, 'A Debate on the History of Hungary between 1790 and 1848', SEER, 50, no. 3 (1972), 442–7.

[2] Gábor Béli, 'Strafrechtspraxis und Strafrechtswissenschaft in Ungarn im 18. Jahrhundert', in Barna Mezey, ed., *Strafrechtsgeschichte an der Grenze des nächsten Jahrtausendes* (Budapest, 2003), 110–21 (113–14).

a recurrent complaint), and many of the disputes arising from property ownership, especially of vineyards. Although certain conventions might exist, there were no means of determining whether these were of general application, still less whether they constituted legal norms. There were thus no general principles guiding pre-emption in respect of land sales, nor any fixed rules regarding the sequestration of farmland that had been neglected. Each case had, instead, to be adjudicated according to its merits. On top of this, new circumstances might arise which required a legal response, but where the customary law was silent, or existing customary arrangements found to lead to unfair outcomes.

Under these circumstances, where custom was unsure or its applicability in concrete cases uncertain, it made sense to refer to the community out of whose habits and practices the customary law was held to derive in the first place. Accordingly, a part of the customary law as it developed in Hungary had the character of a law that was collectively found, and which developed in individual communities by way of common consent and popular approbation. We should not, of course, imagine that the judgments and decisions given out in this way were arrived at democratically. It might thus be, for instance, that the magistrates were all related to each other as well as to individual litigants, thus compromising the integrity of the court's proceedings.[3] Nevertheless, the manner in which judgments were reached and the law determined reflected the notion that the law might be established communally and defined according to the collective will.

At the lowest level, the village court, judgment was made by the headman and between four and twelve sworn village elders. These were usually elected by the village, often with the approval of the local lord.[4] For the most part, village courts adjudicated minor disputes up to the value of just a few florins and petty misdemeanours, but some had a much larger authority, including the right to judge capital crimes.[5] When tricky points of law needed resolution or a serious offence was involved, then the village might participate in the court's discussions. In Calvinist communities where the presbytery functioned as the local court, the whole congregation might be involved.[6] In market towns and smaller urban centres, analogous arrangements prevailed with an outer council or senate of up to 100 townsmen

[3] As at Dumbraveni in Târnava (Küküllő) County. See SJAN-CJ, Fond 363, Fond Familial Josika de Vlaha, no. 28, *Procese-verbale* (1782), item 5.

[4] Vilmos Sápi, 'Községi biráskodásunk a feudalizmus utolsó évszázadaiban', *Jogtudományi Közlöny*, NS, 21 (1966), 466–72 (467–8). On the subordinate relationship of village headmen to their lords, see Péter Illik, 'A falubirói funkciók a Batthyány-uradalmakban a 17. században', *Agrártörténeti Szemle*, 50, nos. 1–4 (2008), 153–69. Illik probably overstates his case. A useful corrective is Livia Magina, *Instituția judelui sătesc în principatul Transilvaniei (sec. xvi–xviii)*, PhD thesis (Babeş-Bolyai University, Cluj-Napoca, 2013), 76–7, who sees the village headman functioning in the dual role of agent of the lord and of communal representative.

[5] Ferenc Eckhart, *A földesúri büntetőbiráskodás a xvi–xvii. században* (Budapest, 1954), 10. Sentence of death required, however, the landowner's approval and, in most cases after 1781, the consent of the ruler. See Lajos Hajdú, *Bűntett és büntetés Magyarországon a xviii. század utolsó harmadán* (Budapest, 1985), 127–8.

[6] István Kállay, *Úriszéki biráskodás a xviii–xix. században* (Budapest, 1985), 75; Katalin Jávor, 'Egy 19. századi presbiteri jegyzőkönyv tanulságai', in Gyula Ortutay, ed., *Népi kultúra–Népi társadalom* (Budapest, 1971), 71–103 (73).

joining in the adjudication of weightier cases.[7] Vineyard courts, which exercised an authority over conduct in the terraces as well as in property disputes, also relied upon extensive popular participation; woodland courts less so, mainly because their jurisdiction was limited to a narrow range of easily proven offences.[8] Decisions in respect of the law and of its application to individual cases that were arrived at locally might thus be made on behalf of 'the whole community', 'from our common decision', and according to 'the law of our fathers'.[9]

The manor courts belonging to the landowning nobility likewise sought through their composition to capture communal apprehensions of the law's content. Rather than being instruments of the landlord's discretionary power, the courts in Hungary's individual lordships drew upon a wide membership. The lord himself seldom attended, although he appointed the court's presiding officer.[10] In smaller lordships, where the burden of holding courts was too onerous, landowners often also referred cases directly to the county, thus giving over their jurisdictional responsibilities.[11] This was, indeed, normal in Transylvania, where manors often amounted to just a handful of tenements and seigneurial jurisdiction was accordingly circumscribed.[12] Participation at manor courts varied according to availability, but regularly included village elders, freemen (*libertini*, often postal clerks or waggoners), estate bailiffs, citizens of nearby towns, tax collectors, the local preacher and headmaster as well as representatives of the county administration.[13] The number of those attending manor courts in a judicial capacity regularly numbered between sixteen and twenty, thereby diminishing both the landlord's influence and, indeed, the weight of the noble estate more generally in matters affecting the lives of ordinary Hungarians. Certainly, the numbers attending manor courts in a judicial capacity went into decline towards the end of the eighteenth century. As seigneurial jurisdiction became absorbed within the burgeoning county administration,

[7] Antal Miskei, *Ráckeve története a kezdetektől 1848-ig* (Ráckeve, 2003), 307; László Novák, *Nagykőrös története és néprajza a xix. század közepéig* (Nagykőrös, 1994), 333; József Nagy, *Eger története* (Budapest, 1978), 208; István Szűcs, *Debreczen története* (Debrecen, 1870–2), 510–12.

[8] Most woodland offences were dealt with on the spot, according to a fixed schedule of fines. See thus MNL OL, P 275, Festetics cs. keszthelyi levéltár, Birtokgazdálkodási iratok, Bundle 160, 'Strafprotokoll'. More serious cases of damage might be referred to the village assembly. See *Corp. Stat.*, i, 406–7; Károly Tagányi, *Magyar erdészeti oklevéltár*, 3 vols. (Budapest, 1896), i, 723. For vineyard courts and assemblies, see András Lichtneckert, *A balatonfüredi szőlőhegy és szőlőhegyi önkormányzat története* (Balatonfüred, 2008), 197–8; Melinda Égető, *Hegytörvények forrásközléseinek gyűjteménye (1470–1846)* (Budapest, 2002), 131.

[9] Etele Thury, 'Az Óvárhoz tartozó városok és falvakban levő birák és községek rendtartása 1635-ből', *Történelmi Tár* (1905), 572–89 (572); Lajos Kemény, 'A forrói jobbágyok rendtartása 1601. előtt', *Magyar Gazdaságtörténelmi Szemle*, 8 (1901), 415–16; Tagányi, *Magyar erdészeti oklevéltár*, ii, 61–3. See also István Imreh, *A rendtartó székely falu* (Bucharest, 1973), 93, 102, 107.

[10] For the continued attendance of landlords at manor courts, see PML, IV–87a, Uriszéki iratok, Fóti uradalom, Box 1, *Jegyzőkönyv*, 1835; MNL OL, P 88, Dessewffy család, *Familiaria*, Bundle 5, fasc. 79, fols. 1–8. In the second example, dating from 1820, the court was chaired by the lord.

[11] István Kállay, *A magyarországi nagybirtok kormányzata 1711–1848* (Budapest, 1980), 232.

[12] Veronka Dáné, *'Az Őnagysága széki igy deliberála.' Torda vármegye fejedelemségkori birósági gyakorlata* (Debrecen and Cluj, 2006), 39–42.

[13] Lajos Horváth, 'Közsegi közigazgatás Pest megyében a xvii–xviii. században', in Tibor Egey, ed., *Fejezetek Pest megye történetéből. Tanulmányok* (Budapest, 1990), 137–97 (154); Eckhart, *A földesúri büntetőbiráskodás*, 26–30. For manor courts in Transylvania, see Dáné, *'Az Őnagysága széki igy deliberála'*, 71.

membership of manor courts was increasingly confined to the corps of professional magistrates and judges who dispensed justice in the counties and ridings.[14] Since after 1790, it was possible to appeal cases from the manor to the county courts, the merger of their membership made obvious sense. Nevertheless, it was only on the eve of emancipation that the first comprehensive accounts of the laws and procedures to be followed in manor courts were published, and then only as private manuals of instruction.[15]

Far from being instruments of noble power, the courts of the counties were also diverse in their composition. Certainly, the *sedes iudiciaria* or *sedria*, the principal organ of county justice, together with its subordinate magistrates' courts in the ridings, was staffed exclusively by noble judges and assessors, who were elected by the noble community.[16] These courts were more lawyerly than the manor and village courts, for the principal officer, the *alispán* (deputy lord of the county; the high lord or *főispán*, a royal appointee, seldom bothered himself with routine county business), as well as the several 'judges of the table' (*táblabirák*) had usually received some formal education in the law. Indeed, service as an alispán was by the early nineteenth century regarded as part of the career path that might take an aspiring lawyer to the office of judge of the Curia.[17] Parties involved in litigation were often attended by their attorneys. As a consequence of the more lawyerly composition of its courts, the law followed in the counties stood increasingly close to the law at work in the Curia and royal courts.

Normally, the county *sedria* consisted of up to a dozen or so judges, even on such occasions as when it went into emergency session because the gaol was full.[18] It was difficult, however, to extend this number because the county courts were so busy as to make unreasonable demands on the time of all but a small number of salaried officers. Indeed, by the nineteenth century, many county courts were in more or less permanent session.[19] Much of the routine business of adjudication was therefore performed in the court of the deputy lord or in the ridings courts with just several magistrates in attendance.[20] Nevertheless, where points of law needed discussion, the matter might be referred to the county assembly for direction. Regulations and guidance might in this event be duly composed or the law be found sufficiently clear as not to need elaboration.[21] The county assembly of Pest, at which barons, magnates and prelates grandly gathered as well as ordinary noblemen, thus reserved 'hard matters' to its jurisdiction, poring over the details of the lordly ownership of individual peasant plots and discussing

[14] Imre Palugyay, *Megye-Hivatalok* (Pest, 1844), 143–4, 152; Eckhart, *A földesúri büntetőbíráskodás*, 30.

[15] See thus Carolus Pfahler, *Jus Georgicum Regni Hungariae* (Keszthely, 1820), discussed in György Kurucz, *Keszthely grófja. Festetics György* (Budapest, 2013), 218–19.

[16] The relative weight of the főispán and the county community in selecting county officers differed from place to place, and over time.

[17] Endre Varga, *A királyi curia 1780–1850* (Budapest, 1974), 164–5.

[18] *Corp. Stat.*, iv/1, 447.

[19] Iván Meznerics, *A megyei büntető igazságszolgáltatás a 16–19. században* (Budapest, 1933), 22.

[20] György Bónis, Alajos Degré and Endre Varga, *A magyar bírósági szervezet es perjog története* (Zalaegerszeg, 1996), 100–1.

[21] SJAN-CJ, Fond 4, Comitatul Alba de Sus, no. 1, *Protocollum Marchalium Congregationum 1790–1802*, fol. 48*v*.

whether divisions of noble property should be performed with the assistance of geometers.[22] County assemblies also acted as the forums wherein plaints were laid and debated in advance of their removal to the sedria or of their transmission to a higher court, on account of which the assemblies might instruct a preliminary investigation to be undertaken. Court sessions normally followed hard upon the county assemblies, to the extent that the distinction between the two is often blurred in the institutional record.

By the second half of the eighteenth century, county assemblies were usually held monthly, often at different venues, and they had a notably varied membership. All noblemen were expected to attend sessions of the assembly, although it was a frequent complaint of county officers that too few actually did. Besides noblemen, there were often in attendance village headmen, wealthy peasants, members of the local garrison, representatives of nearby towns, delegates of villages of petty nobles, distinguished visitors (like, for instance, the head of the University's Law Faculty) as well as the 'many others', whom the county notaries thought too minor to be recorded by name.[23] Although county notaries in Hungary seldom gave precise figures for attendance, their Transylvanian counterparts often did, since it was important to show that assemblies were confessionally balanced in their composition. Records for Cluj and Upper Alba counties indicate that about 100 noblemen were generally present, although the number varied considerably, from 70 up to 120.[24] In anticipation of the diet held at Cluj in 1792, almost 250 noblemen were recorded at a single meeting in Upper Alba County. On this occasion, whole families turned up rather than just a single representative.[25] Assemblies of the Transylvanian counties were generally attended only by noblemen, for they were usually poorer than their fellows in Hungary and thus more concerned to demonstrate the exclusivity of status. Because, however, the competence of most manor courts was less complete in Transylvania, a good deal of the business that would otherwise have gone before these ended up before the courts of the county, either the sedria or its subordinate forums (the *filiális* and *parciális* courts).[26] The periodic denunciation, investigation and rounding up of offenders was accomplished

[22] RL, C/67, Sárközy család levéltára, Bundle 1, no. 5; Sárközy család levéltára, Bundle 2, no. 48.

[23] Alajos Degré, 'Megyei közgyűlések a xvi–xvii. századi török háborúk korában', in György Bónis and Degré, ed., *Tanulmányok a magyar helyi önkormányzat múltjából* (Budapest, 1971), 35–52; András Borosy, ed., *Pest-Pilis-Solt vármegye közgyűlési jegyzőkönyveinek regesztái 1712–1740*, 7 vols. (Budapest, 1989–96), vii, 96, 174, 232. Peasants might, however, be refused a voice in the assembly's deliberations. See Éva H. Balázs, Lilla Krász and György Kurucz, *Hétköznapi élet a Habsburgok korában 1740–1815* (Budapest, 2007), 94. For the head of the Law Faculty, see OSzK, MSS, *Krassóvármegyei jegyzőkönyv 1779–82*, Fol. Lat. 3901, fol. 1.

[24] SJAN-CJ, Fond 3, Prefectura județului Cluj, no. 16, *Protocollum Marchalis Congregationis 1808–13*, fols. 13*v*–15 (1808), 88*v*–90 (1812); Fond 4 Comitatul Alba de Sus, no. 1, *Protocollum Marchalium Congregationum 1790–1802*, fols. 139 (1794), 157*v*–58 (1795), 215, 220 (1800).

[25] SJAN-CJ, Fond 4, Comitatul Alba de Sus, no. 1, *Protocollum Marchalium Congregationum 1790–1802*, fols. 66–72 (1790).

[26] SJAN-CJ, Fond 3, Prefectura județului Cluj, no. 16, *Protocollum Marchalis Congregationis 1808–13*, fols. 8, 51*v*; Fond 4, Comitatul Alba de Sus, no. 128, *Protocollum Partialis et Filiale Inclyti Comitatus Albensis Superioris*, fol. 6 (1757); Fond 4, Comitatul Alba de Sus, no. 1, *Protocollum Marchalium Congregationum 1790–1802*, fol. 150*v*, 167*v*.

by 'roving courts' (*cirkálás*), which also drew on a mixed membership of county officers, village headmen and peasant assessors.[27]

In the manner in which they conducted their business, Hungary's village, town, manor and county courts sought to give voice to a communal understanding of the law, enlisting either the community or what might loosely be considered its representatives as participants in the legal process. Judicial decisions were thus arrived at collectively, by consensus and agreement. At times, it is certainly possible to determine the factors that led to a judicial outcome, where the influence of a local lord in forcing through a solution satisfactory to himself is visible, or the efforts of a particularly energetic pastor.[28] On other occasions, we may note the way that imagination of a plague of cannibals gripped a county community, with fatal consequences for the local Roma population.[29] Most cases, however, show less dramatic events and less obvious suasions, where what was thought to be good and reasonable was used to achieve a solution that was acceptable to members of the court, but of which the surviving record gives only the decision, not the manner by which it was reached.

A part of the work of the lower courts that we have described involved matters of property. In this respect, the law was highly proceduralized, to a large extent borrowing the stages of the action and the modes of proof from processes followed in the higher courts.[30] Accordingly, the law was relatively easily determined and often a matter of simply following established rules. In many cases, the justice of the plaint was evident and the court's role simply one of enforcement. A particular difficulty was that peasants often concluded contracts that were too simply composed to cope with unforeseen circumstances and that adjudication was accordingly needed to unravel the commitments they had entered into, particularly if a debt had been sold on.[31] Even so, the more formal bills of exchange in which noblemen securitized their debts could be equally amateurish.[32] Under these circumstances, it was expedient for the court to adopt a midway position between rival claims—likewise in such contentious matters as rights to woodland and to tavern keeping, where the laws of property directly confronted popular notions of 'moral ownership'.[33] In more complicated commercial disputes, local practice tended to borrow from the norms followed in the towns; likewise, intestacy adhered in

[27] Dáné, *'Az őnagysága széki igy deliberála'*, 73–4.

[28] Eckhart, *A földesúri büntetőbiráskodás*, 20; Kálmán Révész, 'A presbyterium legelső nyomai hazai református egyházunkban', *Protestáns Szemle*, 4 (1892), 419–46 (431).

[29] Hajdú, *Bűntett és büntetés*, 10, 122; Lajos Hajdú, *Az első (1795-ös) magyar büntetőkódex-tervezet* (Budapest, 1971), 52–3.

[30] Kállay, *Úriszéki biráskodás*, 141–59, 327–445; Kállay, *A magyarországi nagybirtok kormányzata*, 239.

[31] For typical peasant contracts, see MNL OL, P 86, *Dessewffy család*, Bundle 50, fols. 98ff. For peasant debts being contracted through bills of exchange, see István Kállay, 'Világos adóssági per és csődeljárás az úriszékben', *Jogtörténeti Tanulmányok*, 5 (1983), 129–41 (133).

[32] See thus RL, C/71, Sigray család levéltára, 1. 2, containing a *carta bianca* from 1749 that the issuers had signed but omitted to seal, notwithstanding the protocol written on the instrument.

[33] *Corp. Stat.*, i, 376; Tagányi, *Magyar erdészeti oklevéltár*, i, 479, 603. See also R.W.B. Gray, *Land Reform and the Hungarian Peasantry c. 1700–1848*, unpublished PhD thesis (University College London, 2009), 70.

respect of legal succession to conventions that were widespread. Very many private actions might therefore come before a local court—the magistracy of the market town of Ráckeve was dealing with several hundred a year by the 1830s.[34] Most, however, were capable of speedy and satisfactory resolution. The more complicated cases involving the property rights of noblemen (who usually had extensive written evidence at hand to support or rebut a claim) were too much for the lower courts. Although some of the opening stages of an action might be done at the county assembly, or through an inquest performed at the county's instruction, they otherwise went straight to the Curia for adjudication. Generally, only a handful a year were heard by the county sedria.[35]

Criminal cases were, likewise, driven by procedural norms that had their origins in practices more generally observed. By the eighteenth century, most cases were handled by a prosecutor (*fiscalis*, *magistratus*, *ordinarius*), who had usually received some legal education, gathering the evidence of witnesses and taking a statement of the accused.[36] The questions put to the accused and recorded in the *Deutrum* followed a set pattern and were written up verbatim by the prosecutor at the time of interrogation. It was common for the culprit to admit his guilt almost at once, for most crimes were 'manifest', and indeed it was in his interest to do so, for otherwise he might be put under torture to confess. (It was widely held that capital punishment first required a confession.)[37] Even after the abolition of torture in 1776, a suspect might still expect some 'softening up' by the constable (*hajdú*) and, should he remain recalcitrant, a period in custody.[38] If the evidence was not conclusive, the suspect might still be taken to court on the grounds of 'likelihood', although his penalty was reduced should he then be found guilty. Since previous convictions were known to the court (they were given on the *Deutrum*), 'likelihood' retained a powerful place in the criminal law in Hungary, as indeed elsewhere.[39]

The difficulty for courts lay in knowing what constituted a crime and what penalty it merited. The varieties of crime included in the standard manuals of criminal law were unhelpful on account of their 'catch-all' nature, for which they invariably demanded the supreme penalty. Sodomy notoriously encompassed a range of offences, from bestiality to masturbation, and required upon conviction the death penalty, including for any animal involved.[40] Accordingly, communities tended to dispense with substantive definitions and to convict instead according to such vague categories as *vita scandalosa* or *rosszaság* (literally, 'badness') and

[34] PML, V–180 A (a), *Ráckeve tanácsi iratai*, vol. 8, 1833, 1834 (unpaginated).

[35] András Borosy, Katalin Kisfaludy and Attila Szabó, eds., *Pest-Pilis-Solt vármegye közgyűlési iratainak regesztái. Igazságszolgáltatási iratok*, 3 vols. (Budapest, 1998–2000), iii, *passim*.

[36] Prosecutors and their offices had become largely professionalized by the beginning of the nineteenth century. See András Molnár, 'Zala megye közigazgatása 1790–1848', in Molnár, ed., *Zala megye archontológiája 1138–2000* (Zalaegerszeg, 2000), 61–79 (77).

[37] Hajdú, *Büntett és büntetés*, 83.

[38] SJAN-CJ, Fond 363, Fond Familial Josika de Vlaha, no. 28, *Procese-verbale* (1782), item 8.

[39] Matthias Vuchetich, *Institutiones Iuris Criminalis Hungarici* (Buda, 1819), 78–9.

[40] Vuchetich, *Institutiones Iuris Criminalis*, 314; Gabriel Gochetz, *Systema Praxis Criminalis inclyti regni Hungariae* (Buda, 1746), 57; Mathias Bodó, *Jurisprudentia Criminalis secundum praxim et constitutiones Hungaricas* (Bratislava, 1751), 257.

promiscuity or *paráznaság*.[41] In these cases, the content of the law was principally what opinion at the time deemed it to be.[42] So, for instance, as late as the 1830s, a young man in Pest County was brought before the manor court of the Grassalkovich family at Gödöllő on grounds of bad behaviour. He had been heard swearing, had been rude to his parents and had not attended church. His neighbours and the parish priest affirmed the young man's delinquent conduct to the village elders.[43] They gathered a dossier that they sent on to the court after which the young man was gaoled. In similar fashion, the County Court of Ugoča determined in 1809, in respect of one nobleman, that 'there was no hope of his moral improvement' and that for his scandalous life of fornication, profanity and drunkenness he should forfeit his tongue.[44] Elsewhere, courts made the presumption that certain types of activity were criminal, having regard only for what they considered the right and proper manner of doing things. A young woman, who had dressed up as a man in order to gain employment as a labourer, thus received a beating from the county court of Heves, and the instruction that she be henceforth appropriately clothed.[45] An elderly man, returning from the tavern, was so drunk that he did not notice that his equally inebriated companion had collapsed in the snow and so had frozen to death. He received a month in gaol and a beating for his neglect.[46] In both cases, the act of which the accused was charged fell into no recognizable category of offence but was deemed nonetheless an infraction that merited chastisement. By the same token, offences that had long fallen into desuetude might suddenly be recalled, as in the case of twenty peasants in Trenčín County, convicted in 1782 of the antique crime of incitement to apostasy (notwithstanding the Edict of Toleration published only the previous year).[47]

The severe penalties demanded in the manuals of criminal law were rarely exacted in their full measure. Just as the content of the law was to an extent communally derived, so punishments tended to be influenced by what the community knew of the culprit and of his circumstances.[48] In respect of the young man from Pest County, the village elders soon regretted their role in bringing him to court. His imprisonment had left his wife and children destitute and thus a drain on the public purse, and so the elders petitioned for his release.[49] Compassion and a reluctance to overburden the community will explain why many courts were anxious to establish mitigating circumstances—the youth of the offender, his intoxication,

[41] See also, Gábor Béli, *Magyar jogtörténet. A tradicionális jog*, 2nd edition (Budapest and Pécs, 2009), 293.

[42] Sápi, 'Községi biráskodásunk', 470.

[43] PML, IV–87b, Úriszéki iratok, Gödöllői Grassalkovich uradalom, Box 1, *Fenyitő iratok*, 1838, no. 46.

[44] MNL OL, O 9, *Protocolla Tabulae Regiae. Causae Criminales*, 1809, 16–17. The Royal Table mitigated the punishment.

[45] Hajdú, *Bűntett és büntetés*, 115.

[46] Hajdú, *Bűntett és büntetés*, 189.

[47] Hajdú, *Bűntett és büntetés*, 40.

[48] Sápi, 'Községi biráskodásunk', 472.

[49] PML, IV–87b, Úriszéki iratok, Gödöllői Grassalkovich uradalom, Box 1, *Fenyitő iratok*, 1838, no. 46. See also Úriszéki iratok, Gödöllői Grassalkovich uradalom, Box 1, file labelled 'Hrubos Pál', 1837; Úriszéki iratok, Gödöllői Grassalkovich uradalom, Box 1, *Fenyitő iratok*, 1838, nos. 29, 46.

mental illness, somnambulism and so on.[50] A concern for expense also meant that penalties other than imprisonment were preferred—acts of public disgrace or of stigmatization (the pillory or shaving off the moustache), fines, beatings, barge-hauling, road repair, and so on. Extravagant penalties (such as suspension by the hair), even though justified by reference to local custom, might, however, result in the judges themselves being arraigned.[51] Likewise, the harsh punishments exacted by some manor courts, such as the amputation of the hand for wounding, might be blocked on appeal, as this would condemn the culprit to a life of economic inactivity.[52] It was only where the culprit was a habitual offender or had greatly antagonized the community by their behaviour over a long period that the death penalty was imposed—thus on account of persistently lewd conduct or, in one case from the 1780s, 'because he has spent his entire life drinking, squabbling and quarrelling'.[53] Remarkably, therefore, the annual number of recorded executions in Hungary in the 1770s was about sixty (although we should allow for some under-reporting).[54]

Hungary's lower courts thus tended to render a justice that was collectively derived. Where the law was unsure or its outcomes deemed unfair, communal norms were invoked or recourse had to opinions more widely held, particularly in respect of crimes and their punishment. The composition of the courts reflected the need to ground judgments on some measure of popular approbation. As it was, the lower courts of the kingdom were already crowded. Nevertheless, where difficulties arose in determining justice or the law, the court's membership was broadened, to the extent of enlarging it to include the whole community. Even in respect of the courts of the county, where justice was increasingly professionalized, decisions might still be referred to assemblies of noblemen and others, and their collective understanding of the law determine its substance and application.

## THE COURTS OF THE CURIA

The court of the Royal Table, under the presidency of the *personalis* judge, was the principal court of the privileged orders. Its membership drew on representatives of both the common and upper nobility as well as of the clerical estate. The greatest prestige attached to the court's several prelates and barons who sat closest to the *personalis* and spoke last in deliberations. These, respectively canons of the church

[50] Vuchetich, *Institutiones Iuris Criminalis*, 142–4, 152–3. The issue of drunkenness as a mitigating factor was controversial. See Pál Szlemenics, *Elementa Juris Criminalis Hungariae* (Bratislava, 1827), 84.

[51] Kállay, *A magyarországi nagybirtok kormányzata*, 253.

[52] SJAN-CJ, Fond 363, Fond Familial Josika de Vlaha, no. 28, *Procese-verbale* (1782), item 11. The judgment against a Transylvanian Romanian peasant on the Kemény lordship was appealed by Dăbâca County and referred to the Gubernium.

[53] Hajdú, *Bűntett és büntetés*, 203, in respect of an 'enhanced' sentence of death. See also, István Balogh, ed., *Katonai tábortól a mezővárosig (Böszörmény, Hadház, Nánás és Szoboszló magisztrátusi jegyzőkönyvei 1711-ig)* (Debrecen, 1999), 59.

[54] Hajdú, *Bűntett és büntetés*, 117.

and members of the higher nobility (but not necessarily barons in the sense of holders of high royal office or hereditary aristocrats), had not usually received any formal education in the law. What they knew derived from practical experience and past judicial service. Since their authority rested on their rank, it was important to address them properly, using their correct titles.[55] The court's other members comprised *jurisperiti*, who had either worked previously in the county administration or had studied law at college or university, supplemented by pupillage and service as a court *juratus*. Of these the most important in terms of their function were the referring judges (*assessores referentes*) who prepared the cases for discussion, and the protonotaries and vicegerents of the palatine and high judge, to whose superior knowledge of the law the court usually deferred. These were mostly recruited from the ranks of the common nobility. The court was also attended by the royal *director causarum* who was there to represent the interests of the crown, but who might also lead the proceedings in criminal cases.[56] Each of these might participate in discussions and cast a vote, with the exception of the director, who might not act in judgment where the monarch could directly profit from the outcome, and the two prelates who customarily absented themselves from criminal matters. There were thus altogether around twenty judges normally in attendance at sessions of the Royal Table. The jurisdiction of the Royal Table extended to most actions involving noble property rights, which proceeded there as a court of the first instance, and for appeals in criminal cases involving nobles that had been sent up from the counties. By the early 1790s, the Royal Table might also hear appeals initiated by peasants in respect of both criminal and civil actions.[57]

The Septemviralis court (or Table of the Seven) operated as the appeal court for the Royal Table. Its president was in theory the palatine, but he was usually too busy to attend and the river crossing from the palace in Buda to the Curia building in Pest was in any case dangerous for part of the year. His place was usually taken by the high judge. Only in the second half of the eighteenth century were high judges appointed who had any legal expertise, their predecessors having been for the most part superannuated soldiers. The Septemviralis court had in the seventeenth century consisted, as its name suggests, of seven judges—the palatine, three prelates and three barons. Over the course of the late seventeenth and eighteenth centuries, its membership was expanded to include up to five prelates, eight high-ranking nobles and as many as fourteen other judges. There was, however, considerable overlap between the two courts of the Curia. In particular, the referring judge or protonotary who had originally prepared the case for discussion at the Royal Table was also responsible for presenting it anew to the Septemviralis in the event of its appeal. As a consequence, the Septemviralis court usually allowed itself to be led by the decision first given and its discussions were evidently perfunctory.

[55] OSzK, MSS, Fol. Lat. 4338, fols. 14–15.

[56] László Nánási, 'Ügyészek a rendi Magyarországon', *Jogtörténeti Szemle*, (2009, no. 3), 34–8 (35–6).

[57] For the organization and development of the Curia courts, see Endre Varga, *A királyi curia 1780–1850* (Budapest, 1974); Bónis, Degré, Varga, *A magyar bírósági szervezet*, 111–14.

It was not unusual for the Septemviralis court to get through scores of appeals in a day, particularly at the start of the judicial terms when a backlog of cases had built up.[58] Both courts also shared a specialist assessor knowledgeable in mining law. In the 1840s, a separate court of the Curia—the Exchange Court or Váltófőtörvényszék—was established for litigation involving bills of exchange (*Váltó*, *Wechsel*), but with a remit that extended to adjudication of the securities on commercial loans and to proceedings for bankruptcy. The court consisted of experts in commercial law and dealt with cases appealed from either lower level bill-of-exchange courts (of which there were eight) or from town and county courts.[59] Cases that came before the Curia's Exchange Court might, however, be appealed to either the Royal Table or the Septemviralis court, depending upon which was the less busy at the time.[60]

Following the reforms of the early 1720s, branches of the Royal Table were established in the provinces, at Trnava, Kőszeg, Prešov, Oradea (thence to Debrecen in 1725) and, in Croatia–Slavonia, at Zagreb. These new courts replaced the roving protonotaries, who in concert with local assessors had previously dispensed an itinerant justice. Whereas, however, the protonotaries had not possessed a full authority but required the Royal Table to approve their decisions, the new district courts had the right to issue judgments and they did not need to refer their decisions.[61] The jurisdiction of the district courts was, however, restricted to civil disputes between nobles, mostly involving actions for debt, suits over properties that lay in more than one county, and cases involving widows, orphans and wards, and their decisions might be appealed to the Royal Table. The number of judges present at any one session seldom exceeded six.[62] Even though individual actions, as for instance over a contested will, could consume a whole day, by the end of the eighteenth century individual district courts were processing 500 cases a year.[63] The authority of the district courts was briefly expanded in the late 1780s when, as a consequence of Joseph II's reforms, they began to function as appeal courts for the short-lived *judicia subalterna* that now operated at the lowest level of the new structure of royal courts, having taken over much of the work of the county and manor courts. With the abandonment in 1790 of Joseph's experiment, the district courts returned to their former role, as subordinate branches of the Royal Table, with a circumscribed authority.[64]

58 *Sententiae in Excelsa Curia Regia*, Pest, 22 August 1822; *Sententiae in Excelsa Curia Regia*, 10 January 1825; *Sententiae in Excelsa Curia Regia*, 12 November 1827.

59 For cases being moved directly from the towns and counties, see MNL OL, O 52, Váltótörvényszék, vol. 4, 16–21 (seven examples) and *passim*. Most of the records of the Váltófőtörvényszék were destroyed by enemy action in 1956.

60 Varga, *A királyi curia*, 203.

61 Protonotaries did not, however, require a mandate to hear an action. See MNL OL, O 3, *Mandata Judiciaria*, 1654, fols. 350–84. Cf. János Marschalkó, in MJL, ii, 106.

62 MJL, iv, 692–3.

63 MNL OL, O 116, Dunantúli Kerületi Tábla levéltára, *Tanácsülési jegyzőkönyvek*, 13 (1797), 20; MNL OL, O 116, Dunantúli Kerületi Tábla levéltára, *Tanácsülési jegyzőkönyvek*, 14 (1798), 78.

64 István Stipta, *A magyar bírósági rendszer története*, 2nd edition (Debrecen, 1998), 70; Éva H. Balázs, *Hungary and the Habsburgs 1765–1800: An Experiment in Enlightened Despotism* (Budapest, 1997), 232–3.

The judges of the Curia courts were formally appointed by the ruler. This was inevitable to the extent that the Curia courts were royal courts and, perhaps more importantly, that the treasury needed a letter from the chancellery in order to start paying a judge's salary. The presidents of the Royal Table and Septemviralis court, respectively the *personalis* and (de facto) the high judge on behalf of the palatine, were invariably distinguished by the long service to the ruler that they had exhibited, having usually spent extended periods in Vienna, frequently working in the Hungarian Chancellery there. High judges were by the time of their preferment often in their sixties; the *personalis* judges a decade or so younger. The ruler took an active interest in appointment to both offices, not least because the *personalis* was also president of the Lower House of the diet. In respect of the other judges of the Curia, the ruler was less concerned, even though the protonotaries acted as clerks to the diet and were responsible for drawing up and editing the replies and resolutions of the Lower House.[65] The monarch was usually content to allow individual judges to appoint the protonotaries and their own vicegerents and for the court as a whole to select the other judges in attendance. Indeed, when Francis I (Emperor Francis II) sought in 1818 to block the appointment of a protonotary on the grounds that he was a Protestant, a great fuss arose. The *personalis* first questioned and then refused to implement the instruction, and it was only at the third time of asking that he gracelessly submitted.[66]

Except for the barons and prelates of the Curia, most of the judges were trained lawyers who had begun their careers in the counties or the royal service. Judicial office in the Curia proved an invaluable launching position for further advancement. József Ürményi (1741–1825), having studied law at Vienna and Trnava, worked to begin with as a lawyer in the royal service and then as a protonotary of the Royal Table. Thereafter, he was promoted to the chancellery, pushing through the enlightened reforms of education and of administration undertaken by Maria Theresa and Joseph II. He was subsequently appointed *personalis* (1789–95) and, after a period of disgrace, high judge (1806–25), an office that he held until well into his eighties.[67] Ürményi's contemporary, László Melczer (1755–1827), who came from a middling noble family in Šariš County, began employment in the county administration before moving in his twenties to the office of protonotary. Thereafter, he was appointed a deputy lord (alispán) of a county, returning in the 1790s to membership of the Curia, as one of the judges in the Septemviralis court.[68] His son, István (1810–96), having acquired a degree in law, also started in county service, subsequently joining the office of the *director causarum* before becoming a judge on the Royal Table in 1842 and, eventually, *personalis* judge in

[65] István M. Szijárto, 'The Diet: The Estates and the Parliament in Hungary, 1708–1792', in Gerhard Ammerer et al., eds, *Bündnispartner und Konkurrenten der Landesfürsten? Die Stände in der Habsburgermonarchie* (Vienna and Munich, 2007), 151–71 (161).

[66] Varga, *A királyi curia*, 162–3.

[67] Sándor Pruzsinszky, *Ürményi József* (Budapest, 1990).

[68] István Bakács, Gaborné Pap and Lajosné Pataky, *Kisebb családi és személyi fondok (MOL P szekció)*, 4 vols. (Budapest, 1968–76), iv, 71.

1861.[69] The careers of the two Melczers, as indeed the biographies of other leading judges of the Curia, demonstrate that there was no obvious contradiction between judicial office in the counties, traditionally viewed as hotbeds of noble resistance to the ruler, and a high position in the royal courts.

Just as the ruler generally acquiesced to the Curia courts in the matter of judicial appointments, so he or she generally refrained from interference in the conduct of cases. Certainly, there are plenty of bundles of surviving royal rescripts, mandates and *normalia* that bear witness to the ruler's concern with the activity of the courts. Most of their contents, however, are far removed from the so-called *benigna rescripta* of historical legend, the supposed instruments by which the ruler manipulated the outcome of cases for political purposes.[70] Most, in fact, deal with routine business—questions relating to legal education, salaries and pensions, the cost of wood for the Curia's stoves, the theft of money by a local attorney and so on. We will certainly notice occasions where the ruler, working through the chancellery, urged the Curia courts to hasten their deliberations, lifted a case to the Septemviralis court to close off the opportunity for it to be delayed still further by appeal, or moved to the Curia a case from a county court because a fair trial could not be guaranteed there. Very occasionally, we may spot a judgment being quashed or a case removed entirely from the Curia and sent by royal order to the chancellery for adjudication. In nearly all these cases, however, legal grounds for the interference were given.[71] Equally, though, the chancellery frequently addressed the Curia for advice in matters where the law was unclear or in order to gather its opinion on new legislation.[72] Certainly, in the 1790s and, again, in the 1830s the Curia was coerced by the ruler and chancellery to adjudicate cases which had a strong political content, and it was pressed to adopt procedures that were manifestly unjust to the defendants (most notably, restricting legal counsel and limiting the defendants' right of reply). Even so, as in the 'Jacobin' trials of 1794–5, the Curia judges showed a strong independence, prolonging the proceedings so that the evidence might be fully tested, permitting the defendants opportunities to reply normally, notwithstanding the chancellery's instructions, and throwing out cases where the

[69] *Magyar életrajzi lexikon*, 2 vols. (Budapest, 1967–9), ii, 186.

[70] Béni Grosschmid, *Magánjogi előadások. Jogszabálytan* (Budapest, 1905), 127; Henrik Marczali, *Hungary in the Eighteenth Century* (Cambridge, 1910), 331–2. See also, László Péter, 'The Autocratic Principle of the Law and Civil Rights in Nineteenth-Century Hungary', in Péter, *Hungary's Long Nineteenth Century: Constitutional and Democratic Traditions in a European Perspective* (Leiden and Boston, 2012), 281–304 (283), first publ. in *CEU History Department Yearbook, 1997–98* (Budapest, 1999) 11–34.

[71] MNL OL, O 11, *Rescripta Regia (Ad Septemviralem)*, Bundle 1, fols. 29, 91, 109; *Rescripta Regia*, Bundle 2, fols. 104–14, 159, 237, 283, 285, 512, 518; MNL OL, O 10, *Normalia*, Bundle 2, fols. 6, 20; *Normalia*, Bundle 3, fols. 13ff, 41ff contains extensive material on the Curia's stoves and the entitlements of the judges to tinder. The chancellery also gave instructions to the district courts. See MNL OL, O 111, Dunántúli Kerületi Tábla levéltára, *Szabályrendeletek, ügyviteli iratok*, 1797–8, nos. 114, 253.

[72] MNL OL, O 11, *Rescripta Regia (Ad Septemviralem)*, Bundle 1, fols. 83, 241, 327; *Rescripta Regia (Ad Septemviralem)*, Bundle 2, fols. 169, 490 (to determine on which day the feast of St Gerard should be held); MNL OL, O 10, *Normalia*, Bundle 3, fol. 111.

evidence was thin. Of the 49 alleged Jacobins against whom the royal *director causarum* brought charges, the Royal Table convicted only fourteen.[73] The stubbornness of the Curia is one reason why at the end of the trials King Francis sacked both Ürményi and Károly Zichy as *personalis* and high judge respectively.[74]

The trials of the 1790s were unusual because this was the first time that the Curia actually saw and interrogated criminal defendants, previous cases of sedition and lèse-majesté having been tried by special courts.[75] Criminal cases only otherwise came before the Curia by route of appeal and the judges confined themselves to an examination of the paperwork. Large numbers of civil cases proceeded, however, before the Royal Table as a court of the first instance and their adjudication continued to follow the conventions of Romano-canonical procedure. The trial proceeded episodically and its leisurely pace gave opportunities for the parties to settle out of court or, even, with the judges' assistance, in court.[76] The first act was the laying of the plaint, followed by the summons, the gathering of evidence and the exchange of paperwork. The second was when the matter came to court and was opened (*Levata*), in a public act that often took place in the church next to the Curia building.[77] Thereafter, the court went into closed session. Initially, the lawyers representing the parties fought over the *exceptiones*, with counsel for the respondent seeking to have the case thrown out or delayed on grounds of procedural or other error. The main part of the trial continued as before to comprise the period of *allegationes*, wherein the various claims of the plaintiff or *actor* were expounded with the respondent's lawyer replying in turn. Usually, only four exchanges were permitted, but on occasions this number might be considerably exceeded.[78] Individual points of law might be settled with interim adjudications or the case postponed for further evidence or documentary proof to be gathered. Only rarely was evidence taken directly from the parties or from witnesses. As in the medieval period, proceedings might be confused by the appearance of third parties in the action, by the need to summon warrantors, and by the bundling together of plaints, each of which required a separate adjudication. A review of Curia procedures undertaken in the early 1790s thus disclosed fifteen separate stages in an action following on from the *Levata*.[79]

[73] Kálmán Benda, ed., *A magyar jakobinusok. Iratok, Levelek, Naplók* (Budapest, 1957), 206, 311–15; Vilmos Fraknói, *Martinovics és társainak összeesküvése* (Budapest, 1884), 346–64; Kálmán Benda, *A magyar jakobinusok elleni felségsértési és hűtlenségi per iratai 1794–95* (*A Magyar Jakobinusok*, 2) (Budapest, 1952), 378–410.

[74] Both were dismissed simultaneously at the end of July 1795. Ürményi's enemies had, however, been long plotting his downfall.

[75] Varga, *A királyi curia*, 96–9.

[76] Varga, *A királyi curia*, 232.

[77] In the Church of the Franciscans, *in solito celebrandarum sessionum loco*. See MNL OL, O 9, *Protocolla Tabulae Regiae*, 59, 1817, 210. Sessions of the Septemviralis court were also customarily opened there. See MNL OL, O 8, *Protocolla Tabulae Septemviralis*, 10, 1800, 1.

[78] MNL OL, O 18, *Processus Tabulares*, Bundle 4, no. 14. Repeated attempts by the ruler to reduce the number of exchanges to three failed, which is a comment in itself on the inability of the crown to influence court practice, notwithstanding its claim to an *Aufsichtsrecht*. See Ignác Kassics, *Enchiridion seu Extractus Benignarum Normalium Ordinationum Regiarum*, 3 vols. (Pest, 1825), i, 101.

[79] MNL OL, N 105, Deputatio Regnicolaris in Juridicis, Lad. MMM, fasc. 5, *Ordo Processualis in xxviii sectiones digestus*, given in fols. 281 ff. The twenty-eight parts of the *Ordo* include preliminary and appeal procedures.

Upon the conclusion of debate between the lawyers and the submission of all paperwork ordered during the course of the trial, the judges deliberated privately upon their decision, which was then formally announced and publicly delivered. On occasions, the judges would address the *jurati* in attendance, explaining points of law and other such matters as might benefit their legal education. Providing some grounds could be found, requests for appeal or for a retrial were seldom denied by the Royal Table. Given the prolonged procedures of the Curia courts, it is unsurprising that by the 1820s the Royal Table had a backlog of more than 4,000 cases.[80] It should, however, be noted that cases once begun might yet be suspended immediately or even halfway through by the plaintiff, but still kept on the record as *Levata,* thus imposing a constraint on the respondent in regard to the issue under dispute. In cases involving land, this had the consequence of preventing the other party from disposing of his property until such a time as the case was terminated, which might of course never happen. In 1817, the Curia removed from the active record some categories of action that belonged to this type, consigning them to the archives. Their surviving content runs to no less than 140 bundles of documents.[81]

Although the period of the *exceptiones* and *allegationes* took place in closed session, the lawyers of the parties and the litigants were in attendance and minutes were kept by a notary (*protocollista*) attached to the court. In preparing the case for adjudication, excerpts were taken from the record by the referring judge or by a protonotary appointed to this task, who coupled them to notes of the various documents adduced in the course of the proceedings. In any one case, there might be several hundred separate supporting items—maps of properties, genealogies (sometimes going back to the thirteenth century), transcripts of deeds and so on. The dossier that the referring judge or protonotary compiled and which he explained to the court, provided the material upon which the Curia judges reached their decision.[82] The decision of the court constituted a matter of public record and was accordingly entered into the court protocol together with the text of the plaint and a list of judges in attendance. Indeed, during the 1790s, and for reasons that are uncertain, the Curia sometimes caused the dossier to be extracted and printed, but this initiative was soon abandoned.[83] Decisions were frequently collected by the lawyers in attendance in the expectation that their study might over time disclose the manner of judicial thinking in the Curia.[84]

Whereas the laying of the plaint and the judgment were given publicly, the discussions leading up both to the interlocutory adjudications and to the final decision were reached privately and were not a matter of public record. Nor did the

[80] Varga, *A királyi curia*, 110, 117.

[81] Endre Varga and Miklós Veres, *Bírósági levéltárak 1526–1869* (Budapest, 1989), 94–6.

[82] The class is described in Varga and Veres, *Bírósági levéltárak*, 133–7.

[83] The printed dossiers are bound in a single volume with the title *Extractus Causarum in Tabula Regia*, now held in the British Library (Printed Books S. 195/2). I am not aware that any of this material has survived in Hungary.

[84] OSzK, MSS, *Norma Processualis*, Quart. Lat. 2485, *passim*; OSzK, MSS, *Notationes circa Processum Iudiciorum*, Fol. Lat. 1869, fols. 121–53; BAR-CJ, U523/A, *Regulae Expeditionum Juridicarum*.

judgment, as entered into the protocol, disclose the grounds for the court's decision. Although on occasions the judgment might recall one of a number of legal authorities and identify those parts of the case upon which the court's decision turned, for the most part the decision of the judges was a bald *Deliberatum est, quod* [...]. Their judgment was, moreover, almost always given collectively, as a unanimous decision.[85] Even with actions of apparently signal importance, where we might otherwise have expected the grounds to have been announced, the judgment was still unmotivated.[86]

There was nothing unusual or sinister about the Curia's silence. Historically, most civil law courts have not disclosed their grounds; nor, still today, do Common Law juries. Indeed, inscrutability made good sense, limiting the opportunity for a judgment to be voided on a technicality or the basis of a decision ridiculed. For litigants and their lawyers, however, it was frustrating, for it made the judicial process unpredictable. Additionally, by hiding their reasoning and by maintaining the fiction of judicial unanimity, the Curia courts gave no hint to the losing party as to the wisdom of an appeal or retrial (which doubtless explains why so many unsuccessful litigants pressed on with these, disregarding time and money). Since lawyers and their clients had little indication as to what might be reliably thought to move the judges' thinking, they commonly presented as many arguments as possible, hoping that at least one would be found compelling. The impenetrability of judicial thinking may explain why one Hungarian Jacobin deemed it worthwhile at his trial to advance Ferguson and Blackstone as potentially persuasive authorities![87] Although the reluctance of judges to disclose 'their principal grounds and reasons' remained a complaint of both the ruler and the diet, court decisions continued to remain unmotivated.[88]

Although unmotivated, courts in recording their decisions often referred to the *Tripartitum* and the CJH as providing the grounds for their judgment. To these, they would sometimes add the brocards given in the appendices of the CJH, supplemented in the later eighteenth century by epigrams deriving from Natural Law, as contained in Karl Anton Martini's *De lege naturali positiones* (1767; German edition, 1797).[89] Since, however, these sources of authority seldom yielded straightforward solutions in law, particularly in respect of the commercial law and contracts, it was usual for the judges to work by analogy and thus to fill in the gaps

[85] Unlike the Provincial Tables, where majority decisions were recorded. See MNL OL, O 116 Dunántúli Kerületi Tábla levéltára, *Tanácsülési jegyzőkönyvek*, vol. 13 (1797), 26; Dunántúli Kerületi Tábla levéltára, *Tanácsülési jegyzőkönyvek*, vol. 14 (1798), 24, 46, 66. I have, however, found one case where the Court of the Septemviralis's determination proceeded by a *pluralitate votorum*. See MNL OL, O 8, *Protocolla Tabulae Septemviralis*, 1 (1791), 28.

[86] MNL OL, O 39, *Decisiones Curiales*, vol. 38, Part 2 (1773), 908–10, 932.

[87] Benda, *A magyar jakobinusok elleni felségsértési és hűtlenségi per iratai*, 388–9. Robert Ferguson (a supporter of Monmouth) may have been known on account of his advocacy of persecuted Hungarian Protestants. See Graeme Murdock, 'Responses to Habsburg Persecution of Protestants in Seventeenth-Century Hungary', *Austrian History Yearbook*, 40 (2009), 37–52 (46–7).

[88] Grosschmid, *Magánjogi előadások*, 718–19; Varga, *A királyi curia*, 231–2.

[89] Gusztáv Wenzel, *Visszapillantás az előbbi magyar királyi curiának 1724–1769-iki működésére* (Budapest, 1875), 28; see also Imre Szabó, *A burzsoá állam- és jogbölcselet Magyarországon*, 2nd edition (Budapest, 1980), 43–4.

in the law by a process of deductive reasoning. So for instance in the matter of whether a commercial contract should be notarized, the Curia decided that it was better (*melius*) to have this done, in the same way as it was better for a nobleman to have a coat of arms.[90] In respect of whether a debt owed on a bill of exchange could be pursued at law even if the bill had been returned to the borrower by the lender, the Curia affirmed that it might; in much the same way as a donation of land could in some circumstances be revoked, so the debt itself might still be recalled without judicial penalty even though the note had been returned.[91] As to whether inherited land could be put up as collateral on a loan, the Curia was adamant that it might not, for it presumed the possibility of the estate's alienation which was forbidden in the *Tripartitum*.[92]

These decisions did not, however, constitute a body of case law that substituted for the deficiencies of the published law. In case law, individual judgments contribute to a rule that is worked out progressively by successive judicial declarations. The courts of the Curia, by contrast, understood their role as being to bring out a rule that was latent within the existing sources of authority. In the mind of the Curia's judges, the law was not incrementally developed, added to and refined, but a text, the gaps in which might be filled in with their decisions by a process of deductive reasoning. A subsequent generation of legal scholars would criticize Hungary's judiciary for not developing a method of case law analogous to the English Common Law tradition, and thus for leaving the law unrefined and incapable of rendering sophisticated judgments.[93] The starting points of the two systems were, however, quite different. The one sought to develop and shape a rule by successive judgments, and to establish its immanence; the other aimed to tease out a rule by working from a text that was held to be authoritative, but often adjusting its meaning in the interest of finding a solution to the case before the court.

Until the end of the eighteenth century, judicial decisions were not recorded systematically. In some cases, decisions were extracted and retained in bundles both for future reference and for the benefit of students. Leading cases might also be retained in separate files, although these were often compiled with a view as much to the importance of the litigants as of the decision handed down by the court.[94] Although the surviving records seem haphazardly arranged, it was clearly possible for courts to locate at least some previous decisions relevant to the specific

[90] György Galánthai Fekete, *Problemata juridica seu Quaestiones in causis*, ed. János Csaplovics (Bratislava, 1814), 27–8. Fekete was High Judge between 1773 and 1783.

[91] Fekete, *Problemata juridica*, 21.

[92] Fekete, *Problemata juridica*, 72; Mária Homoki-Nagy, 'Az Osztrák Polgári Törvénykönyv hatása a magyar magánjogra', in Péter Antalóczy et al., eds., *Kormányzás és kodifikáció* (Budapest, 2006), 227–47 (238–9).

[93] Gusztáv Schwarz, *Magánjogunk felépitése* (Budapest, 1893), 18–23; Bernát Besnyő, *Szászy-Schwarz Gusztáv emlékezete* (Budapest, 1933), 31–2; Ernő Wittmann, *Tanulmányok az angol magánjog köréből*, (Budapest, 1907), 5–14, 44–5, discussed in Martyn Rady, 'England and Hungarian Jurisprudence: Questions of Public and Private Law', in László Peter and Rady, eds., *British-Hungarian Relations since 1848* (London, 2004), 315–27 (323–5).

[94] Varga and Veres, *Birósági levéltárak*, 55–7; MNL OL, B 53, *Index Manualis in juridicis* (1752–1827).

cases before them, including decisions more than half a century old.[95] During the 1760s, Maria Theresa pressed the Curia to publish the motivations of its decisions as part of a more general programme designed to speed up and illuminate its procedures.[96] A committee of the Curia accordingly brought together more than a thousand plaints and decisions, culled from the court protocols of both the Royal Table and the Septemviralis court. After several decades of neglect, these were published in 1800 under the title *Planum Tabulare sive Decisiones Curiales* (Bratislava).[97] The printed collection was augmented by a companion volume, *Nucleus Plani Tabularis* (ed. János Csaplovics, Bratislava, 1811) which extracted and summarized the decisions, arranging them under headings. Even so, the contents of the *Planum Tabulare* remained a muddle, a *casuistica* of randomly selected cases that for the most part simply combined the plaint with the judgment, leaving obscure the intermediate stages of judicial reasoning.[98] Nevertheless, a further volume of Curia decisions was published in 1823–4 and, after 1822, the Curia itself began selectively to print its own decisions, more or less for each day it was in session.[99] The highly abbreviated form in which the Curia recorded its decisions, again (of course) without the motivation but often also without the plaint, doubtless rendered this as insufficient a resource for lawyers at the time as it is for historians now.

Let us take by way of illustration one example of a published court decision, which is the record of a case that proceeded before the Royal Table in 1823, in the matter of János Kovács, natural father and guardian of Erzsébet Urbanovszky, against the respondent, Pál Miklóssy (and that is all we are told of the parties and the plaint!):

> The blood relationship with the deponent, Emerentia Urbanovszky, not being called into question, in respect of the joint ownership relating to the contested property listed under D., since the respondent did not furnish legal notice before the completion of sale on the property, we find for the plaintiff, and adjudge the contested property to him, and oblige the respondent to disclose as appropriate.

In this instance, it is difficult even to guess what the case is about, let alone the principle governing the judgment. It may, indeed, be a very important decision, granting the mother of a nobleman's illegitimate daughter certain rights in respect of property over which he himself had a claim through inheritance. Or it may simply reaffirm the right of a relative to be notified of a property sale. We cannot tell. Even at this late stage in its institutional history, the Curia still failed to distinguish between court record and report.[100]

[95] MNL OL, O 30, *Büntető perkivonatok fogalmazványai*, Bundle 3, fols. 1, 187–8, 457, 540; MNL OL, O 39, *Decisiones Curiales*, vol. 13, 642; Fekete, *Problemata juridica*, 154.

[96] MNL OL, O 11, *Rescripta Regia (ad Septemviralem)*, Bundle 1, fol. 166.

[97] The *Planum Tabulare* was reprinted in 1817 and a Hungarian translation by István Czövek published in 1825. See Endre Nagy and Lajos Rácz, *Magyar alkotmány- és közigazgatástörténet*, ed. Gábor Máthé (Budapest, 2007), 428.

[98] The criticism is Ferenc Deák's. See Mária Homoki-Nagy, *Az 1795. évi magánjogi tervezetek* (Szeged, 2004), 12.

[99] Stephanus Molnár de Péterfalva, *Sententiae Excelsae Curiae Regiae*, 2 parts (Pest, 1823–4); *Sententiae in Excelsa Curia Regia* (Pest, 1822 etc.).

[100] *Sententiae in Excelsa Curia Regia*, 20 November 1823.

We will occasionally notice instances when lawyers invoked previous decisions of the courts on the basis that like cases should be judged alike. Nevertheless, contemporaries remained uncertain whether previous decisions were as persuasive as statute law, thus 'substituting for it until the Diet decides matters',[101] whether they needed repetition to make them binding, or whether they individually constituted a 'yardstick'.[102] In this respect, it is instructive that the 1869 Law IV, 'On the Exercise of Judicial Power', left out the decisions of courts as one of the sources of authority to which judges should defer.[103] Nevertheless, the decisions made by the courts of the Curia yielded over time a body of rules that constituted judicial practice, a *praxis* and *usus* that disclosed a specific manner of approaching legal problems. Inevitably, given the deductive methods of reasoning that the judges employed, moving from the text of a statute or a paragraph in the *Tripartitum* to the facts of the case before them, the mood of the Curia and thus the constructions of its judges tended to be conservative. Reasoning by analogy in cases where the law was uncertain meant, in particular, that the judges conceded to almost all categories of noble land holding the same security of possession as inherited property, thus contributing to the immobility of the land market and to the prolongation of cases.[104] Because, however, there was little by way of commercial law on which the judges could build—the first statutes regulating business and finance were only passed by the Diet in 1840—the Curia was incapable of developing detailed rules of commercial contract and liability even by analogy.[105] Likewise, on account of the underdevelopment of the legal idea of the corporation in Hungary, it failed to elaborate anything approaching a modern company law.[106]

The judges were, however, only too well aware of the constraints under which they worked. In the 1760s, under pressure from the Chancellery to revise the laws, the judges of the Royal Table explained how the procedural law in particular might be improved in order to speed up the administration of justice, by eliminating some of the devices used by litigants to force retrials. For his part, the *personalis*

[101] Matthias Vuchetich, *Institutiones Iuris Criminalis*, 23.

[102] Ignácz Frank, *A közigazság törvénye Magyarhonban* (Buda, 1845–6), 89; Wenzel, *Visszapillantás*, 27; János Suhayda, *A magyar polgári anyagi magánjog rendszere* (Pest, 1862), 37; Imre Zlinszky, *A magyar magánjog mai érvényében különös tekintettel a gyakorlat igényeire*, 4th edition, ed. Sándor Dárday (Budapest, 1891), 36–7; Ferencz Raffay, *A magyar magánjog kézikönyve* (Prešov, 1904), 18; Alajos Degré, 'A Planum Tabulare keletkezésével kapcsolatos kérdések', in *Emlékkönyv Kolosváry Bálint* (Budapest, 1939), 101–9 (107–8).

[103] Judges were held to proceed and pass judgment on the basis only of 'the laws, decrees that have been proclaimed and that rest on the law, and on custom having the force of law.' See Gábor Máthé, *A magyar burzsoá igazságszolgáltatási szervezet kialakulása 1867–1875* (Budapest, 1982), 43.

[104] As noted by the protonotary of the Palatine, Antal Brunsvik, in the 1750s. See Dénes Jánossy, 'Reformtörekvések a polgári peres eljárás terén a xviii. században', *Századok*, 77 (1943), 41–77 (52–4).

[105] Mária Homoki-Nagy, 'Az Osztrák Polgári Törvénykönyv hatása', 242–3; Mária Homoki-Nagy, 'Bérleti szerződés a 19. század birói gyakorlatában', *Acta Juridica et Politica*, 69 (2007), 263–83; János Zlinszky, 'Kodifikation und Gesetzgebung des allgemeinen Privatrechts in Ungarn', in Helmut Coing, ed., *Handbuch der Quellen und Literatur der neueren europäischen Privatrechtsgeschichte*, 3 vols. in 8 parts (Munich, 1973–88), iii/2, 2141–213, 2819–38 (2824–6); Károly Szladits, in MJL, ii, 352. Problems of liability in respect of failure to transport were a particular problem. See MNL OL, O 98, *Acta Tavernici Antonii Cziráky*, Bundle 1, no. 105; *Acta Tavernici Antonii Cziráky*, Bundle 2, no. 210.

[106] Wenzel, *Visszapillantás*, 40.

judge, Ferenc Koller, argued that reform of the *praescriptio* or period of limitation might prevent rights to hereditary property being contested despite centuries of ownership in one family. Both solutions would, however, have had the consequence of overturning a good part of the procedural law contained in the *Tripartitum*, for which reason the reforms proposed required the statutory weight of the diet. This was not, however, forthcoming.[107] Likewise, the Curia considered itself bound to maintain the historical equation of landownership with the status of nobility, thus cracking down on the many forms of intermediate possession that had arisen, particularly in the territories populated after the 1680s, and obliging non-nobles to sell up properties that lay outside the seigneurial nexus.[108]

Notwithstanding its conservatism in matters of landownership, where the Curia could act progressively and carve out its own legal space it did so. In respect of the criminal law, it adopted its own rules that worked towards the mitigation of penalties, hence its frequent recourse to the formula, 'The crimes in the charge having been committed without any violence etc.'[109] Similarly, the Curia recognized such devices as the bill of exchange and (at least obliquely) the mortgage loan or *hypotheca* that reversed the standard arrangements of the pledge, even though commentators were convinced that the mortgage loan was legally impossible.[110] Even in the absence of statutory authority from the diet, the Curia began to apply the period of limitation in a more generous sense to property rights, thus putting an end to some of the vexatious and opportunistic litigation that so blighted noble property holding.[111] It was also ready on occasions to admit that local customary arrangements carried legal force, even though they were unacknowledged in statute law. In one extreme case proceeding before the Royal Table in the 1770s, the court found that the previous conduct of the parties, in this case the repayment of a pledge on land with a commercial bill of exchange, constituted a practice between them that overrode more widely followed conventions.[112]

As the last example suggests, the Curia's own body of practice was not fashioned in isolation. The passage of disputes from the counties and district courts and the manner of the Curia's own recruitment meant that it was alert to observances that were followed more widely within the kingdom as a whole. Developing customary arrangements were accordingly accommodated, eventually becoming included within the Curia's own understanding of the law. In this respect, there was no gulf, still less contradiction, between customary arrangements that had their origin in popular conventions and the lawyerly practice of the kingdom's higher courts.

[107] Jánossy, 'Reformtörekvések a polgári peres eljárás terén', 57–61.

[108] Wenzel, *Visszapillantás*, 14–27; SJAN-CJ, Prefectura judetului Cluj, Fond 3, no. 126, *Protocollum inclyti comitatus Colosiensis Generale*, 368–76.

[109] *A vádbeli büntettek minden erőszak nélkül követtetvén el etc.*: *Sententiae in Excelsa Curia Regia*, *passim* from 1838. The records of the Curia slowly shifted from Latin to Hungarian after 1835.

[110] Emericus Kelemen, *Historia Juris Hungarici Privati*, 2nd edition, 4 vols. (Buda, 1818), iii, 541–2.

[111] Wenzel, *Visszapillantás*, 70–1.

[112] MNL OL, O 39, *Decisiones Curiales*, vol. 39, Part 2 (1774), 7. Conceivably, the court's decision rested on the underlying principle that *contractus contrahentibus ponit legem*.

Such is, indeed, what might be expected, for the assumptions of lay people will often be recognized in time by the courts and thus be incorporated into law.[113] The interaction of popular and judicial practice, and in particular the way that customary arrangements that had developed locally fed into the workings of the Curia may be illustrated by the history of the Hungarian law of bankruptcy.

## BANKRUPTCY AND SEQUESTRATION

There was no permanent law of bankruptcy in Hungary before 1840.[114] Except for a brief period during Joseph II's reign, which we will discuss below, the most that existed was the opportunity, given in 1723: 107, to register or 'intabulate' debts with the county or local town magistracy. In the event of the debtor being unable to repay his obligations, priority was given to those whose loans had been so recorded, as was 'the norm observed in other kingdoms and provinces'.[115] The usual procedure followed in the kingdom's closest neighbour, Lower Austria, was, however, to delay procedures for bankruptcy until the debtor's death, since it was only at this point that his inability ever to meet his obligations was evident.[116] An analogous arrangement applied in Hungary's cities, where as a matter of routine the property of merchants was upon their death put in interim trusteeship, pending an investigation by the city magistracy into their commercial liabilities.[117] Where a debtor took on loans that he was plainly unable to repay, proceedings might be taken against him for fraud. In this case, his assets fell to whoever managed to sue first for recovery of the debt.

Peasants frequently took on debts, either to help them through lean years or for reasons of investment. Loans made to peasants were frequently intabulated at the manor court and it was thus this court that was called upon to act in cases where it was found that individual peasants were incapable of repayment on account of their 'manifest debt' (*debitum liquidum*).[118] According to the text of the *Tripartitum*, peasants who had been fined, taken on debts or been ordered to make compensation for damages, but who were unable to pay, might be handed over to their creditors and made to work off the money they owed.[119] Manor courts often resorted to this remedy, but it was found unsatisfactory, possibly because many loans were owed not to individuals but to charitable foundations (most usually the village orphans' fund).[120] Increasingly, therefore, they applied rules of bankruptcy to debtors, even

[113] J.H. Baker, *The Law's Two Bodies* (Oxford, 2001), 60.

[114] MJL, ii, 799–800.

[115] Szabolcs Somorjai, 'Pest–Pilis–Solt vármegye adósai és hitelezői a 18. század második és a 19. század első felében', *Aetas*, 25, (2010, no. 2), 5–18 (5–6).

[116] Joannes Baptista Suttinger, *Consuetudines Austriacae* (Nuremberg, 1718), 979–81.

[117] György Bónis, *Buda és Pest bírósági gyakorlata a török kiűzése után 1686–1708* (Budapest, 1962), 120–1.

[118] The opposite of 'manifest debt', which was concealed debt, constituted fraud.

[119] Trip., III. 28 (DRMH 5, 415).

[120] Zoltán Kaposi, 'Hitelintézmények Magyarországon a xix. és xx. században', *Aetas*, (1992, no. 4), 34–43 (34).

during their own lifetimes.[121] In such cases, creditors applied to the court for the peasant's property to be put in trusteeship, in respect of which a curator was appointed to make an inventory of his assets. If it was shown that the peasant's liabilities exceeded his assets, then the court compiled a list of creditors and the amounts owed, preliminary to a distribution of the bankrupt's property. The courts were exacting, sometimes leaving the debtor with no more than his or her clothing.[122] The assets were distributed according to a rank ordering that gave precedence to money owed to the court, lord and church, and by way of communal dues. Next in the list were family members and intabulated creditors, and at the bottom loans that had not been formally recorded. The aim of the distribution was to satisfy creditors higher up on the list, with the consequence that non-preferential creditors often received nothing. The creditors might, however, resolve among themselves on a different method of distribution, agree to take personal possession of the debtor's property or to put it up for auction. As an alternative to formal bankruptcy, a debtor might subscribe to what might loosely be called a 'debt management scheme', whereby his debt was securitized in the manner of a bill of exchange, with an accompanying schedule of repayments. The securitized debt was then sold on, with the proceeds of the bond's sale distributed among the creditors.[123]

During the course of the eighteenth century, the Curia developed its own procedures in respect of bankruptcy that borrowed from the methods of the manor courts. These constituted a body of practice which the Curia employed with increasing refinement. It thus adopted the principle of the curatorship of the debtor's assets and worked out its own scheme of rank ordering that took into account obligations due to daughters, in respect of the quarter, and the rights of wives to the dower and over revertible property that they had brought into the marriage. These were given priority over other liabilities, unless the women had contracted the debt or a portion of it as joint-signatories.[124] In respect, however, of inherited land, the Curia was perforce obliged to adopt a midway position. Notwithstanding the difficulties that István Széchenyi experienced in trying to raise a loan on the security of his estates, it was entirely possible for nobles to borrow money, using their estates as collateral. (Széchenyi was refused credit by the Eskeles bank because he was rightly recognized as a spendthrift.) By the beginning of the nineteenth century, a few noblemen were even converting their estates into companies and selling the share capital.[125] The difficulty was that inherited land might not be seized by creditors, since as *aviticitas* it did not belong exclusively to the debtor. Accordingly, the Curia placed either all or some of the inherited property of a noble debtor under trusteeship, using an order of sequestration, after which the creditors took the profits, with the estate still remaining in the debtor's legal

[121] István Kállay, 'Világos adóssági per és csődeljárás az úriszékeken', *Jogtörténeti Tanulmányok*, 5 (1983), 129–41 (129).

[122] Kállay, 'Világos adóssági per', 137.

[123] Kállay, 'Világos adóssági per', 133.

[124] Wenzel, *Visszapillantás*, 87–8.

[125] B.G. Iványi, 'From feudalism to capitalism: the economic background to Széchenyi's reform in Hungary', *Journal of Central European Affairs*, 20 (1960), 270–88 (282–3).

possession. It was not always possible, however, to have the counties enforce orders of sequestration and of trusteeship.[126]

The first Hungarian law of bankruptcy was decreed by Joseph II in 1786 and published as the *Ordo Judiciarius pro omnibus tribunalibus et foris judiciis regni Hungariae.*[127] Notwithstanding its title, the *Ordo Judiciarius* is predominantly concerned with debt, the rank ordering of creditors, and the management of noble estates that were subject to judicial sequestration. Although the *Ordo Judiciarius* did not survive Joseph's reign, many of its provisions were incorporated into Article 22 of the law of 1840 that regulated bankruptcy. Until this time, the method of proceeding in cases of manifest debt depended upon rules applied by the Curia that derived themselves from the methods followed at a local level, predominantly in the manor courts. In this respect, Curia practice and practices observed more generally within kingdom converged, with conventions that had been adopted locally being assumed by the Curia and given through its adjudication an increasingly normative weight.

* * *

Custom was not, therefore, immobile. Lower courts continued right through to the nineteenth century to apply the customary regime of the law with considerable latitude, often administering the law with regard for communally derived notions of the law's proper application and adjusting penalties accordingly. The higher courts demonstrated a similar flexibility, bending the law's content to accommodate practice, particularly in respect of the kingdom's developing commercial law. In this respect, it helped that the courts were not bound by precedent or case law, but relatively free to discover a solution of their own to meet both changing circumstances and the case before them. The two spheres of the law—the communal law practised in villages and manor courts and the more lawyerly law of the Curia—did not, however, operate in isolation. As in the Middle Ages, the flow of persons and cases between the different layers of the courts contributed to the convergence of practice, which was enhanced by the development of the appeal and by the new hierarchy of courts established in the 1720s. Indeed, in respect of bankruptcy law we may note how practices and procedures that were developed in the villages and manor courts came in time to influence and be adopted by the courts of the Curia. The customary law of Hungary may have been uncertain in its application and an amalgam of elements deriving from the *Tripartitum*, statute law, *regulae* and brocards. Confirmed, adjusted and expanded by the practice of courts, it nevertheless retained a reputation and adaptability that lent it continued efficacy.

[126] Iványi, 'From feudalism to capitalism', 283; Béla Iványi-Grünwald, 'Gróf Széchenyi István Hitel cimű munkája. Történeti Bevezetés', in *Gróf Széchenyi István összes munkái*, 15 vols. (Budapest, 1930–9), ii, 1–264 (61–71).

[127] *Ordo Judiciarius pro omnibus tribunalibus et foris judiciis regni Hungariae* (Bratislava, 1786). An excerpted version with a Hungarian translation was published as *Novus Ordo Judiciarius–Újj törvényes rend tartás* (1786, no place given).

# 12

# Custom and Law in the Modern Period

## THE LIMITS OF REFORM

The customary law and its institutions were torn up by Joseph II in the 1780s. In the decade of his rule, Joseph pushed through an experiment in enlightened absolutism that turned the established legal order on its head. Joseph's measures aimed (among much else) at the emancipation of the peasantry through the monetization of seigneurial obligations, the taxation of noble land, the introduction of new civil and penal codes that eliminated both *aviticitas* and the privileges of the nobility, and the separation of justice from administration through the reorganization of the kingdom's lower courts. Joseph's reforms were all introduced by decree or patent, without any involvement of the estates. His assault on the privileges of the Hungarian nobility was combined with a propaganda offensive that both disparaged the *Tripartitum* and demonstrated that Hungary's historic arrangements of public law had been perverted by noble self-interest.[1] It brought the kingdom to the verge of rebellion and of a new Prussian invasion. In anticipation of an imminent change of regime, one Hungarian conspirator (Remigius Franyó) sent Frederick William II of Prussia a copy of the *Tripartitum* for his edification.[2]

On his deathbed, Joseph II retracted most of his legislation for Hungary. In order to pacify the kingdom, Joseph's successor, Leopold II, hastily summoned a diet, the first in thirty-five years. Leopold hoped to convince the diet to agree to a broad measure of reform.[3] Most deputies to the diet that met in 1790 aimed only, however, at a *restitutio in integrum*, but there were some who argued that Joseph's rule had broken the contract between the political nation and the house of Habsburg and had thus severed the thread of succession (*filum successionis*). They accordingly

[1] See thus (László Kövesdy), *Examen Verböczyanum, quod hactenus sub titulo Regni Anti-Verböczyani, per amicos tres, Tripartitum inter se dividentes* (Pest, 1785); also (József Izdenczy), *Etwas über Werbőcz.* The *Etwas* was published in 1795 in *Statistische Aufklärungen über wichtige Theile und Gegenstände der österreichischen Monarchie*, i, ed. G. Grellmann (Göttingen, 1795), 459–68, but as a reprint of an earlier, undated, pamphlet. Izdenczy's many publications in support of Joseph's reforms are listed in Ferenc Strada, 'Izdenczy József. Az államtanács első magyar tagja', *A Gróf Klebelsberg Kunó Magyar Történetkutató Intézet Évkönyve*, 10 (1940), 54–149 (69). Strada and others continue to ascribe the *Irrthümer in den Begriffen der meisten Ungarn* (1790) to Izdenczy, even though it was recognized in the 1920s as the work of Franz Matthäus Grossinger. See Derek Beales, 'The False Joseph', *Historical Journal*, 18, no. 3 (1975), 467–95 (489–90).

[2] Robert Gragger, *Preussen, Weimar und die ungarische Königskrone* (Berlin and Leipzig, 1923), 9.

[3] On the reform movements during Leopold II's reign, see Gábor Pajkossy, 'West European models and national traditions: reform projects in late eighteenth-century Hungary', *Transactions of the Seventh International Conference on the Enlightenment*, i (Oxford, 1989), 349–52 (349–50).

advocated the restoration of an elective monarchy, the reinstatement of the right of resistance, and the prosecution of Joseph's Hungarian advisors on the (dubious) grounds of *crimen laesae nationis*.[4] In order to recapture the middle ground, Leopold enlisted firebrands from within the nobility to urge a radical programme that aimed at the empowerment of the 'fourth estate' and the taxation of the nobility. Some of these would later go on to embrace the cause of revolution, ending their lives on the executioner's block.[5]

Consensus could, however, be reached on a scheme that aimed to render impossible any repetition of Joseph's rule. Joseph's reforms had all been introduced by patent. There was nothing unusual about the use of mandates of this type, which were deemed to flow from the supervisory role that the monarch discharged. Previous statutes had sought to hem in the use of royal mandates, confirming that they might not be used against the rights and laws of the kingdom.[6] Most mandates and patents were, indeed, purely administrative instruments, of only temporary significance, dealing with routine business—prognostication in markets, the excessive use of post horns, the hooding of pipes for smoking tobacco, and so on.[7] In this respect, they were as unexceptionable as the vast bulk of *normalia* addressed to the courts. Some, such as Maria Theresa's patents that had forbidden torture, eliminated the crime of witchcraft or regulated peasant obligations, comported less happily with the laws and practices of the kingdom—and in the case of the last of these, published in 1767, might be considered a direct assault upon the established rights of the nobility. Joseph's patents belonged unequivocally, however, in the category of mandates that were *illegitima* insofar as they were self-evidently *contra jura et leges regni*, *contra Decreta regni*, and not in conformity with the kingdom's customary law. In order to prevent any further abuse of patents, the diet as a first step obliged Leopold to confirm that he would not use these instruments, unless they were in line with the kingdom's laws—*nonnisi in sensu legum*. Leopold agreed to this.[8]

The problem was that the laws to which the diet appealed were by no means established. Their content was uncertain and their applicability not obvious. Hungarians had, however, recently learned from Montesquieu that the bundle of customs and conventions that governed the rights of the nobility amounted to a constitution. (The 1792 Transylvanian diet subsequently opened in Cluj with a trio sung by personifications of the three powers.)[9] Many noblemen accordingly demanded a comprehensive written settlement, in the manner of a constitution,

[4] Gyula Mérei and Károly Vörös, eds., *Magyarország története tiz kötetben, 1790–1848*, 2 vols. (Budapest, 1980), i, 88; Lajos Hajdú, *Az első (1795-ös) magyar büntetőkódex-tervezet* (Budapest, 1971), 60. See also, Adam Wandruszka, *Leopold II*, 2 vols. (Vienna and Munich), ii, 275–314.

[5] Ernst Wangermann, *From Joseph II to the Jacobin Trials* (Oxford, 1959), 86–8.

[6] 1543: 31; 1563: 80; 1608: 6; 1625: 5. Discussed in BAR-CJ, MSS, U523/F, *Omnia ad Majorem Dei Gloriam*, 701. Despite its current location, this mid-seventeenth century work was intended for a Hungarian audience.

[7] Epitomes of royal decrees are given in Ignác Kassics, *Enchiridion seu Extractus Benignarum Ordinationum Regiarum*, 3 vols. (Pest, 1825).

[8] Wandruszka, *Leopold II*, ii, 332.

[9] László Péter, 'Montesquieu's Paradox on Freedom and Hungary's Constitutions 1790–1990', in Péter, *Hungary's Long Nineteenth Century: Constitutional and Democratic Traditions in a European*

which would fill in the legal gaps wherein royal patents might otherwise intrude, thus guaranteeing their liberties against any future erosion.[10] Leopold was supportive of their request, for he hoped through a revision of the laws to effect the modernization of Hungary's institutions.[11] Because, however, Joseph's reforms had been so comprehensive, involving most aspects of the kingdom's life, the idea of a constitutional settlement was rapidly eclipsed by the more ambitious plan of defining the legal scope and character of every institution in the country. The diet accordingly appointed no less than nine committees of the estates or, as they were known, Deputationes Regnicolares to work out a thorough legislative settlement. This was to include not only the elaboration of codes of criminal, civil, commercial and procedural law, but also public administration, taxation, peasant obligations, the national economy, mining, ecclesiastical matters, education and culture, and the miscellaneous complaints of the diet.[12] The plan, as originally envisaged, was for the committees to work together to produce a body of draft legislation that would be put to a future diet for approval, as 'a single uniform scheme [...] all parts of which should make up an orderly and coherent whole'.[13]

The committees had completed their work by 1795. By this time, however, the repression attending the Jacobin trials had rendered all talk of reform not only otiose but also politically dangerous. Their draft legislation was accordingly consigned to the archives. Although they were occasionally dusted down, it was not until 1827 that the diet instructed their investigation and revision. A further round of consultation took place and amended versions of the drafts, with minority reports added in, were duly published. On this occasion, the stumbling block was the conviction that the drafts needed to be made into law simultaneously, as an organic whole, but no consensus could be obtained on what the corpus, in its entirety, should contain. Once again, therefore, the work of the Deputationes was consigned *ad acta*.[14]

Although its scope was immense, the draft legislation drawn up by the committees was generally cautious. Certainly, the Deputatio entrusted with economic affairs came up with an ambitious scheme of free trade, predicated on the removal of the customs barrier between Hungary and the rest of the Monarchy.[15] Its ecclesiastical counterpart drove a noticeably Josephinist agenda that fell short of restoring church property, and the cultural committee made some thoughtful recommendations for the establishment of commercial and agricultural colleges.[16] Likewise, the

*Perspective. Collected Studies* (Leiden and Boston, 2012), 152–82 (157). First published in *History of Political Thought*, 16 (1995), 77–104.

[10] Elemér Mályusz, *Sándor Lipót főherceg nádor iratai 1790–1795* (Budapest, 1926), 13–14.

[11] Wandruszka, *Leopold II*, ii, 275.

[12] The remit of the nine committees is given in 1790–91: 67.

[13] Mályusz, *Sándor Lipót főherceg*, 120.

[14] George Barany, *Stephen Széchenyi and the Awakening of Hungarian Nationalism, 1791–1841* (Princeton, NJ, 1968), 200, 282–5.

[15] Éva Hoós, *At the Crossroads of Ancient and Modern: Reform Projects in Hungary at the End of the 18th Century* (Budapest, 1996), 4–5; Katalin Gönczi, *Die europäischen Fundamente der ungarischen Rechtskultur* (Frankfurt a/M, 2008), 147–8.

[16] Éva H. Balázs, *Hungary and the Habsburgs 1765–1800: An Experiment in Enlightened Absolutism* (Budapest, 1997), 314–15.

Deputatio Juridica entrusted with the renewal of the CJH produced some impressive work in respect of the commercial law. Its *Codex Cambio-Mercantilis* was not the first attempt to institute a comprehensive commercial code, for Joseph had previously urged the Curia to devise legislation in this regard and had sent for the judges' instruction a code that he had commissioned to regulate bills of exchange.[17] Nevertheless, the *Codex* was thorough and wide-ranging, including draft legislation on bills of exchange, bankruptcy, partnerships and companies, including limited liability and joint-stock.[18] Its text was, for the most part, derivative of foreign laws, on account of which it forbade the use of 'dry bills' (*trockene Wechsel*; *cambiales siccae*), where the drawer and payer were identical, on the grounds that these instruments were potentially usurious. In fact, as a type of promissory note, dry bills were a vital ingredient of capitalist transformation.[19]

In most areas of the law, the Deputatio Juridica adopted a conservative position. Its draft on the criminal law eliminated the distinction between 'private wrongs', which included many types of violence, and the large number of acts that had been brought under the heading of *nota infidelitatis*, thus constituting *publica delicta*.[20] The substantive part of the text divided offences into the categories of crimes against public security, the person, property and morals.[21] Nevertheless, the code admitted that there was a range of lesser offences that it had not had time to consider, such as gambling, breaking quarantine restrictions, diverting watercourses and so on. The prosecution of these crimes was left to judicial discretion, thus vitiating the code's claim to be both comprehensive and motivated by the principle of *nulla poena sine lege*.[22] This deficiency subsequently passed into the Hungarian criminal law, when it was eventually codified in 1878–9.[23]

In its treatment of the procedural and civil law, the Deputatio Juridica embraced the opinion that the existing laws were good and only needed to be better arranged. Advice received from the counties and from other agencies of government confirmed the view that the law's application, rather than the law itself, was at fault, mainly on account of judicial negligence and the wrangling of lawyers.[24] The Deputatio Juridica's recommendations on procedure thus amounted to little more than a rewriting of Kitonich and to detailing the stages of an action.[25] When it

17 MNL OL, O 11, *Rescripta Regia*, Bundle 1, fol. 327 (1781). See also MJL, iv, 649, which suggests an even earlier plan for a commercial code, originating in 1779.

18 János Zlinszky, 'Hungarian Private Law in the 19th and 20th Centuries up to World War II', in András Gergely and Gábor Máthé, eds., *The Hungarian State: Thousand Years in Europe* (Budapest, 2000), 305–34 (312).

19 Larry Neal, *The Rise of Financial Capitalism: International Capital Markets in the Age of Reason* (Cambridge, 1990), 7–8. The *Codex Cambio-Mercantilis* is printed in an amended version as the fifth, repaginated part of *Opinio Excelsae Regnicolaris Deputationis ad Deputationem Juridicam Relata* (Pest, 1831).

20 Hajdú, *Az első (1795-ös)*, 224, 297.

21 The text is given in Hajdú, *Az első (1795-ös)*, 389 et seq.

22 Hajdú, *Az első (1795-ös)*, 37. Given in Part 4, para. 54 of the code.

23 See thus Law XL of 1870, para. 12. Discussed in Béni Grosschmid, *Magánjogi előadások. Jogszabálytan* (Budapest, 1905), 151–2.

24 See thus MNL OL, N 105, *Deputatio in Juridicis*, Lad. MMM, Bundle 5.

25 *Ordo processualis in xxviii sections digestus*, in MNL OL, N 105, *Deputatio in Juridicis*, Lad. MMM, Bundle 5, fols. 281 et seq.

came to the civil law, the Deputatio confined its activity to a reorganization of the *Tripartitum*, adding in material gathered from the CJH. In a few places, as for instance the law of treasure trove, the Deputatio Juridica was inventive.[26] Nevertheless, it failed to elucidate several tricky areas of law, such as what to do with the goods of a priest who had died intestate or whether prefected daughters might freely dispose of their inheritance as *acquisita*.[27] Its brief foray into bankruptcy failed to acknowledge procedures as actually followed and contradicted the *Codex Cambio-Mercantilis*.[28] It retained the distinction between *delictum privatum* and *delictum publicum*, even though this had been removed in the draft criminal code.[29]

It would be a mistake, however, to conceive of the work of the Deputatio Juridica as a further instance of a failed blueprint. First, the content of the drafts provided elements that might be deployed to support a programme of reform. Once the notion of organic, comprehensive change had been abandoned, individual parts of the Deputatio Juridica's work might accordingly be converted piecemeal into legislation. This decoupling of the parts from the whole was embraced by the diets of 1832–6 and 1839–40 and resulted in the adoption of single legislative items that introduced chunks of the *Codex Cambio-Mercantilis* into law. In 1840, Hungary thus obtained its first statutes regulating bills of exchange, commercial transactions, factories, companies, transportation, and bankruptcy (although not limited liability).[30] Four years later, the law on property holding was changed to permit non-nobles the right of landownership.[31] Secondly, the work of drafting, both in the 1790s and in the late 1820s, had been undertaken by committees of the diet, at the diet's own commission. It thus put the diet at the forefront of the legislative process, charging its representatives with the business of initiating legislation, rather than of responding to the royal propositions by advancing counter-proposals and grievances (*gravamina*). From this point onwards, legislation by statute would become the instrument of choice for reformers and the means of Hungary's modernization. In these respects, Kossuth's praise for the work of the committees as laying down the foundations for the reform movement before 1848 was not rhetorical.[32]

The achievements of the reform diets of the 1830s and 1840s should not, however, be over-estimated. In respect of the criminal law, the trials of Lovassy, Kossuth and Wesselényi in the late 1830s, on grounds of lèse-majesté, indicated the procedural deficit under which the criminal law worked.[33] Deák's plan presented in 1843 for a criminal code proved, however, stillborn, mainly on account of its abolition

[26] Mária Homoki-Nagy, *Az 1795. évi magánjogi tervezetek* (Szeged, 2004), 113–14.
[27] Homoki-Nagy, *Az 1795. évi*, 41–2, 90.
[28] Homoki-Nagy, *Az 1795. évi*, 204.
[29] Homoki-Nagy, *Az 1795. évi*, 210–13. Homoki-Nagy sees this inclusion as contributing to the law on damages.
[30] 1840: 16–22. Limited liability was only fully admitted in law in 1930.
[31] 1844: 4.
[32] Lajos Kossuth, *Felelet Gróf Széchenyi Istvánnak* (Pest, 1841), 13.
[33] Gönczi, *Die europäischen Fundamente*, 241.

of the death penalty and the concomitant expense of imprisonment.[34] Likewise, the redemption of services proceeded slowly. This was not only because peasants saw no reason to commute future dues into costly lump-sum payments, but also because the reform of seigneurial relations aroused a visceral response among supporters of the old order.[35] As one of their spokesmen at the diet put it in the 1830s, 'What is my freedom worth if all the people are free?'[36] The same objections frustrated the introduction of a new civil code, which might have laid the foundations of the modern 'civil society', to which reformers inclined, since its discussion necessarily called into question the privileges of the nobility. Even though Széchenyi had shown how *aviticitas* impoverished noblemen by denying them complete ownership of their estates and thus the collateral upon which to obtain credit, the association of *aviticitas* with noble status rendered its abolition politically impossible.[37]

We may, nevertheless, discern a rhetorical shift. The *Tripartitum* and Hungary's ancient law had long been considered emblematic of noble liberty and the country's main bulwark against Habsburg centralization and misrule. Increasingly, however, the *Tripartitum* was widely perceived, from no later than the 1830s, as locking the kingdom in immobility and preventing even the sort of measured change to which conservative reformers aspired. In the counties and in preliminary meetings of the diet (where a good part of legislative business was first hammered out), nobles and deputies inveighed against the dead hand of tradition, while in the burgeoning Hungarian literature and letters of the period, the antique nobleman, a Don Quixote with *Tripartitum* in hand, was rendered an object of ridicule or disgust.[38] István Széchenyi's celebrated ambition to consign nine-tenths of the *Tripartitum* and *Corpus Juris* to the flames may well have been a legal pun on the ninth and the tithe, but it articulated a mood that was prepared to sacrifice the old rural order for economic improvement, and privilege for the 'ennoblement of the nation'.[39] In this respect, it is telling that the diet of 1839–40 was ready to dispense with its adherence to the existing law even to the extent of actively seeking out foreign legislative models that could be adapted to meet Hungarian conditions.[40]

[34] Gönczi, *Die europäischen Fundamente*, 169; György Ráth, *Az országbirói értekezlet a törvénykezés tárgyában*, 2 vols. (Pest, 1861), i, 60, 192.

[35] Only two per cent of villages had reached redemption agreements with their lords by 1848.

[36] István Barta, Gábor Pajkossy and István Sinkovics, eds., *Kossuth Lajos összes munkái*, 15 vols. (Budapest, 1948–89), iii, 719 (Károly Lamotte).

[37] Ferenc Mádl, 'Kodifikation des ungarischen Privat- und Handelsrecht im Zeitalter des Dualismus', in Andor Csizmadia and Kálmán Kovacs, eds., *Die Entwicklung des Zivilrechts in Mitteleuropa* (Budapest, 1970), 87–119 (96–8).

[38] Lóránt Czigány, *The Oxford History of Hungarian Literature* (Oxford, 1984), 160–78. For this description of a Hungarian nobleman, see Gyula Mérei and Károly Vörös, eds., *Magyarország története tiz kötetben, 1790–1848*, 2 vols. (Budapest, 1980), i, 106. For the changing nature of political discourse in the 1830s, see József Takáts, *Modern magyar politikai eszmetörténet* (Budapest, 2007), 14–21.

[39] Tamás Vécsey, *Széchenyi és a magyar magánjog* (Budapest, 1895), 2–3; Katalin Gönczi, 'Werbőczy's Reception in Hungarian Legal Culture', in CLCE, 87–99 (93); Gönczi, *Die europäischen Fundamente*, 155.

[40] Gönczi, *Die europäischen Fundamente*, 165–6.

Reform, however, foundered on the sheer scale of what was required. The good noblemen of Satu Mare County may thus in 1841 have urged a thorough-going reform of institutions, including the abolition of *aviticitas* and of seigneurial obligations, but what they proposed involved nothing less than the destruction of the three pillars upon which the social order was considered to stand—the system of land donation and noble privilege, the rights of the noble kindred, and the historic relationship of the tenant peasantry to their lords.[41] The hope, therefore, remained that the existing law and legal institutions might be modernized in such a way as to provide the foundation of a renovated society rather than cast aside entirely. In this spirit, the diet commissioned in 1840 the newly founded Academy to translate the CJH into Hungarian, a work which was overseen from a literary point-of-view by the poet, Mihály Vörösmarty. The first fruit of this labour was a new translation of the *Tripartitum*, published in 1844.[42] A dictionary of Werbőczy's legal vocabulary was published in the same year, with the original Latin terms translated into their supposedly Hungarian equivalents.[43] Meanwhile, conservative lawyers, such as Ignác Frank, busied away at adjustments to Hungarian legal institutions, such as the application of the *praescriptio* to inherited noble property, which might put rights in land upon a surer footing, without the need to abolish *aviticitas*.[44] In similar vein, András Michnay and Pál Lichner published in 1845 an edition of the fifteenth-century Buda *Stadtrecht*, with the aim of grounding future commercial legislation on historical foundations, 'since all laws rest upon older laws and customs'.[45] The collapse of Habsburg rule in the spring of 1848 put paid, however, to all these attempts and ushered in a period of rapid and radical change.

## NEO-ABSOLUTISM AND THE HIGH JUDGE CONFERENCE

Between 1848 and 1859, Hungary underwent a succession of constitutional and legal revolutions. The April Laws of 1848 converted Hungary's 'real union' with the rest of the Monarchy into a personal union between kingdom and king, and Hungary acquired for the first time a recognizably parliamentary form of government. (For this reason, we will now speak of Hungary's parliament rather than of

[41] Mária Homoki-Nagy, 'A magyar magánjog kodifikációja a 19. században', *Jogtörténeti Szemle*, (2004, no. 1), 4–8 (5).

[42] *Verbőczi István Hármaskönyve* (Pest, 1844). The translation of the statutes was only published much later beginning in 1899, with the first volume giving the laws up to 1526. The initial five volumes of the so-called Millennium collection, taking the laws up to 1835, were published over the next two years by Franklin (Budapest).

[43] Gönczi, 'Werbőczy's Reception', 95; József Ponori Thewrewk, *Werbőczy István deák műszavai régi magyaritásokkal* (Bratislava, 1844).

[44] Ignácz Frank, *Ősiség és elévülés* (Buda, 1848), 17. In fact, Frank's suggestion had been partly anticipated by the Deputatio Juridica in 1795. See Homoki-Nagy, *Az 1795. évi*, 177.

[45] Andreas Michnay and Paul Lichner, *Ofner Stadtrecht von MCCXLIV–MCCCCXXI* (Bratislava, 1845), p. v. Discussed in Gönczi, *Die europäischen Fundamente*, 259–60; János Zlinszky, 'Die historische Rechtsschule und die Gestaltung des ungarischen Privatrechts im 19. Jahrhundert', *Acta Juridica et Politica*, 33, no. 30 (1985), 433–45 (437).

its diet.) The old system of *tractatus* and of exchanging propositions and counter-propositions was henceforth replaced by the laying of individual bills for the royal signature. Executive authority was, moreover, to be vested in a ministry that was responsible to the new parliament as well as to the monarch, and decrees of the ruler henceforward required ministerial counter-signature. Transylvania's separate status within the Hungarian crown lands was abolished. Besides their constitutional provisions, the April Laws implicitly put an end to the status of the nobility, unravelled the seigneurial nexus, creating thereby a free peasantry, and abolished the traditional system of noble landholding that rested on the principle of *aviticitas*.[46] The details whereby these measures were to be implemented were not enunciated at the time, being left over for future discussion. The intended legislation was not, however, forthcoming. On account of Ferdinand V's disregard for the April Laws and the machinations of his generals, war instead broke out between Hungary and the monarch. In December 1848, Ferdinand was dethroned in a coup and replaced as king and emperor by his talentless nephew, Franz Joseph.

Following Hungary's defeat in 1849, its constitutional relations with both the other lands of the Monarchy and the ruler were dramatically reversed. Relying on the doctrine of forfeiture, Franz Joseph declared Hungary to have lost the right to its own laws on account of its rebellion and thus to be subject to the royal will. Accordingly, Hungary was deprived both of its parliament and of its local organs of self-government. Following Franz Joseph's decision to forego any semblance of constitutional rule as Emperor and to extend the practice of 'neo-absolutism' throughout the Monarchy, Hungary was governed in the manner of his other lands and kingdoms and administered centrally from Vienna. Hungary's absorption into the Austrian *Gesamtstaat* was, however, accompanied by measures that carried forward the legal revolution begun in 1848. Although centralizing and despotic in the practice of its government, the neo-absolutist regime was radical in its social and economic policies. In 1852, new principles of landownership were enunciated that laid down how, following upon the abolition of *aviticitas*, properties were in future to be transferred, inherited and given in pledge, adumbrating transitional arrangements. The next year, the Urbarial Patent adumbrated the terms under which land was to be assigned to the peasantry and former landlords to be compensated. In 1855, the institution of the land registry was established and regional offices set up to record all property holdings as well as the mortgages and liens attaching to individual portions. The early 1850s also saw the introduction of the Austrian Civil Code as well as the imposition of a new criminal law.[47] The highest court for Hungary, the Supreme Court and Court of Cassation, now sat in Vienna, administering Austrian law, although to overcome the barriers of language its Hungarian

[46] The status of nobility was not abolished by the April Laws, although legal equality (*jogegyenlőség*) is alluded to in the provision joining Transylvania to Hungary (1848: 7. 5).

[47] On the impact of the Austrian Civil Code on aspects of Hungarian private law, see Mária Homoki-Nagy, 'Az Osztrák Polgári Törvénykönyv hatása a magyar magánjogra', in Péter Antalóczy et al., eds., *Kormányzás és kodifikáció. Tanulmányok az újkori Európa jogfejlődéséről* (Budapest, 2006), 227–47.

business was overseen by a dedicated Hungarian section.[48] These measures were carried forward by over 100 supplementary patents and by a centralized bureaucracy that was governed by ministries in Vienna. Their implementation in Hungary was accompanied by a 'state of siege' lasting until 1854 that brought crimes of obstruction or dissent before military tribunals, and by a press law imposed in 1852 that put in place savage penalties for criticism of the *Gesamtstaat* and of its sovereign.[49]

The 1850s witnessed some spectacular illustrations of Hungary's modernization—new institutions of education, post and telegraph offices, a modest railway boom, credit banks for industry and agriculture, the standardization of weights, measures and clock-time, *Trafik* shops for the sale of tobacco, and so on.[50] In this respect, neo-absolutism achieved more of lasting consequence than Joseph II's reforms, many of which had not been implemented in Hungary at the time of their withdrawal. Nevertheless, direct rule achieved rather less than both contemporaries and later historians have often averred. On the ground, much of the work of daily administration had to be performed by low-paid Austrian bureaucrats, who struggled to comprehend both the artless country folk over whom they were appointed and the welter of regulations coming out of Vienna.[51] The distribution of land to the peasantry proceeded slowly, partly because peasants held back from coming into final accord with their lords in the hope of negotiating a better deal.[52] In similar fashion, most disputes involving land held under *aviticitas* were postponed (many had been rumbling for decades and so further delay was little hardship).[53] The application of Austrian law did, however, facilitate the breakup of communally held property when no agreement on division could be reached by the *compossessores* (a not uncommon situation).[54] Even so, there were the usual stories of wards being cheated out of their inheritance.[55] For its part, the registration of land, although generally regarded by property holders as a beneficial development since it gave added security to ownership, proceeded slowly. By 1861, under a half of the kingdom's properties had been registered and, even then, many entries were believed to be either fictional or fraudulent.[56] The difficulty of reconciling entry in the land register with the *praescriptio* and property held in mortgage

[48] Oszkár Sashegyi, 'A neoabszolutizmus rendszere 1849–1867', in Ferenc Pölöskei and György Ránki, eds., *A magyarországi polgári államrendszerek* (Budapest, 1981), 81–139 (102).

[49] MNL OL, Ö 142, Justizministerium. Akten-Ungern, Bundle 1, file marked '800-as'. I know the decree on the press only in MS form; there is doubtless a printed version somewhere. For distributing materials dangerous to common security the penalty was a week to six months in gaol; for advocating resistance to the 'united Austrian empire' up to twenty years of hard labour.

[50] Ágnes Deák, *From Habsburg Neo-Absolutism to the Compromise 1849–1867* (Boulder and Highland Lakes, NJ, 2008), 125–42.

[51] See thus, Anon. (Josef Wizdalek), *Acht Jahre Amtsleben in Ungarn von einem k.k. Stuhlrichter in Disponsibilität* (Leipzig, 1861), 6–24.

[52] Károly Kecskeméti, *Tök község parasztsága az Urbáriumtól az úrbéri per végéig 1770–1879* (Tök, 2009), 68. See also Endre Kovács and László Katus, eds., *Magyarország története tiz kötetben, 1848–90*, 2 vols. (Budapest, 1979), i, 673.

[53] János Balogh, *A magyar magánjog visszaállitásának kérdései* (Pest, 1861), 11.

[54] Homoki-Nagy, 'Az Osztrák Polgári Törvénykönyv', 238–9.

[55] Balogh, *A magyar magánjog visszaállitásának kérdése*, 12.

[56] Balogh, *A magyar magánjog visszaállitásának kérdése*, 13; Ráth, *Az országbirói értekezlet*, ii, 189.

created additional uncertainties.[57] The confusion of laws, and the uncertainty of the courts as to which law to follow, was likened to conditions in the American Wild West.[58]

* * *

The crisis provoked by Franz Joseph's military humiliation in Italy in 1859 obliged the ruler to don the mask of constitutionalism. In the October Diploma of 1860, Franz Joseph promised to restore the institutions that he had abolished only a decade before and to make law by ostensibly parliamentary means rather than by decree. A Hungarian parliament duly assembled in April the next year. Since it had not been convoked according to the terms of the April Laws, it spent most of its brief life debating its own existence and how best to translate *indignatio* into Hungarian.[59] Dismayed at its obduracy, Franz Joseph eventually closed the parliament down in August.

The convocation of the parliament was accompanied by a meeting held in close parallel to debate the restoration of the kingdom's laws. The legislation of the previous decade had been introduced by decree, without counter-signature, and was thus by the terms of the April Laws invalid.[60] Its content in respect both of substantive and of procedural law was, however, so far reaching that it could not be simply declared void in the manner of Joseph II's decrees. It was, nevertheless, not at all obvious which of the innovations introduced under neo-absolutism were worth keeping and what sort of mechanism was needed to give these a basis in law. The meeting, which included some sixty former judges and lawyers, was convoked under the presidency of the former chancellor, György Apponyi, who had been appointed to the restored office of High Judge in January 1861.[61] To begin with, Apponyi seems only to have envisaged the High Judge Conference (Országbirói Értekezlet) reaching agreement on some temporary arrangements that would then be authorized by a royal patent.[62] Apponyi did not understand that the legality of these arrangements had to rest on

[57] Imre Zlinszky, *A telekkönyv intézmény befolyása a tulajdonjog szerzésére* (Budapest, 1876), 24, 44. Because the right in land rested on the entry in the register, and not on formal possession, the *praescriptio* applied from the time of the written entry. There was no requirement to adjust the entry in the event of a mortgage being contracted upon the right. For further inadequacies, approvingly explained by reference to a Cheshire Cat, see Charles Szladits, 'A Comparison of Hungarian Customary Law with English Case Law', *Journal of Comparative Legislation and International Law*, 3rd series, 19, no. 4 (1937), 165–78 (171–2).

[58] Endre Nizsalovszky, 'Deák Ferenc és a magyar polgári magánjog kialakulása', *Tanulmányok Deák Ferencről* (*Zalai Gyűjtemény*, 5) (Zalaegerszeg, 1976), 61–84 (74). The American analogy became increasingly powerful in Hungarian discourse. See Gwen Jones, *Chicago of the Balkans: Budapest in Hungarian Literature 1900–1939* (Oxford, 2013), 1–4.

[59] *Az 1861-ik évi magyar országgyűlés*, 3 vols. (Pest, 1861), ii, 102–3. The exchanges between monarch and parliament are conveniently given in *The Addresses of the Hungarian Diet of 1861, translated and presented to Members of Both Houses of the British Parliament by J. Horne Payne, MA* (London, 1862).

[60] The October Diploma had also limited the monarch's right to issue patents.

[61] Apponyi was very much a last resort. Franz Joseph had previously approached Deák and János Cziráky. See György Szabad, *Forradalom és kiegyezés válaszútján (1860–61)* (Budapest, 1967), 319.

[62] MNL OL, O 125 Országbirói Hivatal, Bundle 1, fols. 30–2.

something other than this type of royal instrument, the constitutional invalidity of which had brought the Conference into being in the first place. A flood of petitions from the counties as well as a congress of lawyers meeting in an unofficial capacity thus reminded Apponyi that 'the making, abolition and determination of the law can only take place with the agreement of a legally convened parliament' and that Hungary already had its own laws in the form of those enacted in April 1848.[63]

Notwithstanding doubts about the Conference's competence and deliberate attempts to sabotage its proceedings, a consensus of sorts prevailed.[64] A *restitutio in integrum* of Hungary's laws was not possible. Social and economic developments since 1848 had moved too fast and too far to permit this beguiling expedient. But the legislation introduced under neo-absolutism was not welcome either. Certainly, no one opposed land registration which, despite its faults and the tardiness of its introduction, was generally acknowledged to be a good thing and, indeed, 'a daily necessity'.[65] The Austrian Civil Code, however, was deemed overly cumbersome and to permit too many ways by which cases might be prolonged. The Austrian Criminal Code had, for its part, many uncertain clauses, particularly in respect of political crimes.[66] The solution that gradually emerged was to review all aspects of the law, balancing the demands of the new age and the spirit of the April Laws with the traditions of Hungarian law, although not to the extent of 'restoring its medieval institutions'.[67]

A compromise between national traditions and current needs suited members of Hungary's nascent historical law school, whose exponents gave intellectual grist to the Conference's discussions. Paradoxically, the ideas of the historical law school had been fostered during neo-absolutism by the work of the education minister, Leo Thun-Hohenstein, who had introduced to the university curriculum approaches to legal enquiry borrowed from the German lands.[68] For Hungary's historical law school, the study of legal institutions disclosed the spirit of the people and their cultivation promoted the organic growth of the nation. As Tivadar Pauler explained, 'The law develops out of the life of the nation in the manner of a plant, whose roots rest in the conviction of the people and evolve through customary practices.'[69] In its rejection of codification and its distrust of legislative solutions that hindered the development of the national will, the historical law school came near to the *Tripartitum*'s earlier account of the relationship of statutory law to customary law.[70] Nevertheless, it qualified the derogatory power of statute over custom, affirming instead that the law which emerged voluntarily

63 MNL OL, O 125 Országbirói Hivatal, Bundle 1, fols. 118, 121–4, 148, 152.

64 For Hungarian attempts at sabotage, see Szabad, *Forradalom és kiegyezés*, 321.

65 Ráth, *Az országbirói értekezlet*, i, 54.

66 Ráth, *Az országbirói értekezlet*, i, 19, 187.

67 Ráth, *Az országbirói értekezlet*, i, 56.

68 Andor Csizmadia, ed., *Magyar állam- és jogtörténet* (Budapest, 1978), 17.

69 Katalin Gönczi, *Die europäischen Fundamente der ungarischen Rechtskultur* (Frankfurt a/M, 2008), 260.

70 Noted by Gönczi, *Die europäischen Fundamente*, 263.

from the moral unity of society, constituted the true expression of the nation's historic nature and purpose.[71]

The problem now became to identify the traditional law of the nation. Rapidly, both in the committees that looked into individual branches of the law and in the plenary sessions, the search for the historic springs of Hungarian law became conflated with ideas of the 'national genius' and the 'inheritance of a thousand years'.[72] As with all attempts to ground national identity on objective modes of conduct, establishing the marks of exceptionalism proved hard. Was it that Hungarian law exempted women from the birch?[73] That it obliged those who had lost a suit to vacate a contested estate and appeal for recovery while *extra dominium*?[74] (Hungarian law actually provided a myriad of ways by which to circumvent this obligation.) That it was chivalrous (*lovagias*) in its treatment of widows?[75] That the disposition of property in the absence of direct heirs followed the principle of *paterna paternis, materna maternis*? (A commonplace civilian expression.)[76] That Hungarian law prevented foreigners, such as Austrian officers, laying hands on ancestral land? As it turned out, in respect of relations of private law, this last consideration, voiced by Deák, proved particularly compelling.[77]

The Austrian Civil Code had, with certain safeguards for heirs, permitted the free ownership and disposition of property, as well as the widow's right to inherit a part of the landed estate of her dead husband (and so, by extension, allow any second husband to obtain possession of that part, should she predecease him). *Aviticitas*, by contrast, vested property in the extended family and incorporated strict rules of inheritance that kept the estate within the kindred. Increasingly, as the pressure mounted to define the national genius as manifested in Hungary's legal institutions, *aviticitas* became viewed as the most enduring legacy of Hungary's millennial history—'the inheritance of our ancestors', 'the pillar of the nation' and so on.[78] Only a short time before, *aviticitas* had been jettisoned as an impediment to the nation's improvement and its abolition feted by many as one of the triumphs of the April Laws. Some deft legal footwork was accordingly required and this became one of the major achievements of the High Judge Conference.

The solution adopted was to confirm the abolition of the following: first, the distinction between noble and non-noble land (although a rear-guard sought to restore it);[79] secondly, the principle that all land had its origin in the ruler's gift and so might eventually return to him; and, thirdly, all preferential arrangements laid

[71] We paraphrase here Károly Szász (1798–1853). See Géza Kiss and Sándor Turnowsky, eds., *Szász Károly* (Bucharest, 1955), 106–8, 113.

[72] Ráth, *Az országbirói értekezlet*, ii, 219–20.

[73] Ráth, *Az országbirói értekezlet*, i, 250.

[74] Ráth, *Az országbirói értekezlet*, i, 37.

[75] Ráth, *Az országbirói értekezlet*, ii, 248.

[76] Ráth, *Az országbirói értekezlet*, ii, 220.

[77] Endre Nizsalovszky, 'Deák Ferenc és a magyar polgári magánjog', 77; Ráth, *Az országbirói értekezlet*, ii, 221.

[78] Mádl, 'Kodifikation des ungarischen Privat- und Handelsrecht', 102–3.

[79] Ráth, *Az országbirói értekezlet*, ii, 217.

in respect of the property rights of daughters and spinsters. In other respects, however, the decision of the Conference was to retain the principle of 'familiness' (*családiság*) that underscored the 'legal and blood community' of *aviticitas* while making nods in the direction of the *Tripartitum* and of Hungary's historic arrangements of landholding.[80] Thus, the alienation of land was permitted, but not if it was to be squandered; at that point a closure (*zárlat*) on further sales might be imposed. In wills, at least a half of the estate was bound to go to direct heirs; in the absence of these the half went to parents and then to collateral branches of the kindred.[81] Tellingly, this reserved part of the estate was not referred to as the 'obligatory portion' (*köteles rész*) but as the 'divisional portion' (*osztályrész*), thus harking back the vocabulary of *aviticitas*.[82] Most remarkably, in its treatment of the rights of widows, the Conference revived the distinction between 'ancestral' and 'acquired' goods, which both the April Laws and the Austrian Civil Code had removed.[83] A widow might thus inherit the acquired goods of her late husband, but not the ancestral property unless there were no direct or collateral heirs. In this way, Austrian officers might be prevented from laying hands on Hungarian land even at the price of a less than chivalrous regard for the welfare of Hungarian widows.[84]

In respect of other branches of law, the Conference maintained a largely conservative stance. Older commercial laws were revived, although in respect of mining activity the terms of the 1854 Mining Patent (which had controversially introduced some elementary safety regulations) were carried over intact.[85] Land registration and the 1855 Patent on its adoption were preserved. In its treatment of the criminal law, however, the Conference eschewed any substantive considerations, confining its work to an elaboration of procedure, and Deák failed in his attempt to reintroduce the draft he had presented to the diet in 1843.[86] Nevertheless, the Conference skilfully retained the exemption from birching for nobles and their families, extending their privilege to members of the professions (*Honoratioren*) and Jews.[87] The retention of corporal punishment for the labouring classes provoked outrage among liberals at home and foreign correspondents.[88] As it turned out, corporal punishment was later withdrawn as a penalty in Law LII of 1871, but restored in Law XXVI of 1920 for lesser infractions, although the courts refused to impose it.[89]

[80] Ráth, *Az országbirói értekezlet*, ii, 248.

[81] *Ideiglenes Törvénykezési Szabályok* (1861), I, paras 4, 7. The principle is retained in Hungarian civil law. See Act V of 2013, 7.75–82.

[82] The term *köteles rész* had originally been used during the Conference.

[83] Mór Katona, *A mai érvényű magyar magánjog vezérfonala* (Bratislava, 1899), 30.

[84] *Ideiglenes Törvénykezési Szabályok* (1861), I, para. 14. The 2013 Civil Code adopts the same precautions in respect of matrimonial property rights. See Act V of 2013, Section 4. 38.

[85] *Az 1861-ik évi magyar országgyűlés*, 3 vols. (Pest, 1861), ii, 66–7.

[86] Ráth, *Az országbirói értekezlet*, i, 60, 190–2. Deák's critics mainly feared the expense of establishing prisons with individual cells.

[87] Ráth, *Az országbirói értekezlet*, ii, 305–9; *Ideiglenes Törvénykezési Szabályok* (1861), II, para. 5.

[88] Szabad, *Forradalom és kiegyezés*, 353–4.

[89] Salamon Beck, 'Peschka Vilmos. Jogforrás és jogalkotás', *Állam- és Jogtudomány*, 9, no. 3 (1966), 480–7 (484). The attempt by Hungary's first female MP, Margit Slachta, to extend corporal punishment to women on humanitarian grounds (!) was defeated in the Lower House.

The deliberations of the High Judge Conference were completed at the beginning of March and the draft it had composed was reworked by a committee of the re-established Septemviralis Court, to be shortly thereafter published as the 'Provisional Judicial Regulations' (ITSz: *Ideiglenes Törvénykezési Szabályok*).[90] The ITSz was celebrated at the time as achieving a settlement between older Hungarian foundations and new legal outlooks, forms and landed relations, and as bringing the Hungarian law of property and persons into accord with the spirit of the age. Later writers would indeed compare it to the *Corpus Juris*.[91] In fact, for all the cleverness of some of its parts, the ITSz was regarded by the imperial counsellors in Vienna as a shambles, full of contradictions and inconsistencies.[92] They were right. Great gaps existed in the inheritance law that the Conference had crafted, as for instance in regard to the allocation of estate within the 'divisional portion'. Likewise, by confirming the institution of the land registry and referring back to the Austrian Civil Code as explanatory of this, the ITSz provided a gateway through which further provisions of the Code might be deemed applicable to Hungary.[93] On 22 March, Apponyi excused the ITSz as a 'lesser evil' to the current legal confusion, but Franz Joseph was unconvinced. It was only Apponyi's threat of resignation that brought the king round.[94]

The imperial counsellors—principally the Archduke Rainer and the interior minister, Anton von Schmerling—had, however, identified a further and obvious problem with the ITSz. How was it to be enacted? Incredibly, despite all the criticism voiced by the Conference at its opening session and amplified in the petitions of the counties, Apponyi still thought it possible to publish the ITSz in the form of a royal patent. How could the king actually do this, the counsellors asked, given the constitutional irregularity of a patent?[95] It was, indeed, at their insistence that the ITSz was laid before the Lower House of the Hungarian parliament where, in June, it was cursorily debated and approved by 152 votes to 70. (It passed through the Upper House unanimously.)[96] Yet, of course, this was not a properly convened parliament, on account of which it considered itself incapable of making legislation but only of advancing recommendations. Notwithstanding parliament's approval and the grudging consent of the ruler, therefore, the ITSz still lacked a basis in law. In a stroke that might be considered masterful were it not that its implications were clearly lost on him, Apponyi sent on 23 July the text of the ITSz

[90] Albert Berzeviczy, *Az absolutizmus kora Magyarországon 1849–1865*, 3 vols. (Budapest, 1922–32), iii, 187–8.

[91] Berzeviczy, *Az absolutizmus kora*, iii, 189; Gusztáv Beksics, *Ferencz József és kora* (Budapest, 1898), 593.

[92] *Idősb Szögyénÿ-Marich László országbiró emlékiratai*, eds. by his sons, 3 vols. (Budapest, 1903–18), iii, 88.

[93] Gusztáv (Szászy-) Schwarz, *Magánjogi felépitése* (Budapest, 1893), 10–11.

[94] *Idősb Szögyénÿ-Marich László*, iii, 88–90. Franz Joseph needed a High Judge in office to give one of the addresses at the opening of the parliament, scheduled for April.

[95] *Idősb Szögyénÿ-Marich László*, iii, 88.

[96] Speeches opposing the ITSZ are not given in *Az 1861-ik évi magyar országgyűlés*, but published separately in Balogh, *A magyar magánjog visszaállitásának kérdése*, which also gives detail of the vote in the Lower House. For the vote in the Upper House, see MNL OL, O 125, Országbirói Hivatal, Bundle 1, fol. 342.

to the lower courts on behalf of the Curia. Recommending that it be henceforth regarded as a guide (*zsinórmértékül*), he advertised that its provisions 'be considered by litigants and judges alike as temporary instruments of assistance and direction'.[97] Even so, while some litigants and judges considered that the ITSz should be 'used from this day on as legally valid', there was considerable disquiet over the manner of its introduction, which smacked of an octroy.[98]

The ITSz was regarded to begin with as a purely provisional measure that would be replaced in short time by fuller legislation and a civil code, authorized by a properly constituted parliament. Although, following the establishment in 1867 of a lawful parliament, legislation was passed that superseded portions of the ITSz, much of its text remained in force until the implementation of the Communist Civil Code in 1960. Once it had been issued, however, no difficulty arose in respect of finding authority for the ITSz. The parallel between Werbőczy's decision to send out the *Tripartitum* to the counties, even though it lacked the royal seal, and Apponyi's own decision to publish the ITSz, even though it had no legislative authority, were obvious and compelling.[99] The validity of the ITSz was thus deemed customary and it might accordingly be listed among those instruments and practices the weight of which rested upon custom. Law IV of 1869 on 'The Exercise of Judicial Power', therefore noted in its fourth paragraph that 'The judge shall proceed and pass judgment on the basis of the laws, decrees that rest on the law, and custom having the force of law.' Insofar as the ITSz was neither a law nor a decree, it had already been apprehended within the broad category of 'custom having the force of law'.

As Béni Grosschmid later observed, the contents of the ITSz were not customary but were instead a medley of norms taken mainly from Austrian law, fleshed out with some of Hungary's legal traditions.[100] In fact, Grosschmid observed, the High Judge Conference might as well have adopted the Austrian Civil Code, except that it was important for the nation to believe that it lived by its own law. For Grosschmid, the importance of the ITSz as a customary instrument rested not with its content but in the manner of its introduction, which presupposed the right of the courts to determine the content of custom on the basis of what they chose to observe.[101] In order to retain custom's roots in popular observance, the first commentator on the ITSz hesitantly invoked a *tacitus consensus populi*, by which court practice became embedded over time in the people's habits, but even he was unconvinced.[102] Grosschmid's conclusion was thus inescapable—that the manner

97 MNL OL, O 125, Országbirói Hivatal, Bundle 1, fol. 344.

98 MNL OL, O 125, Országbirói Hivatal, Bundle 1, fols. 378, 400 et seq.

99 Imre Zlinszky, *A magyar magánjog mai érvényében*, 4th edition, ed. Sándor Dárday (Budapest, 1891), 40.

100 His comment was not hyperbole, but a criticism also voiced in the 1861 parliament. See *Az 1861-ik évi magyar országgyűlés*, iii, 136–7; also, János Zlinszky, in *Handbuch der Quellen und Literatur der neueren europäischen Privatrechtsgeschichte*, ed. Helmut Coing, 3 vols. in 8 parts (Munich, 1973–88), iii/2, 2153.

101 Grosschmid, *Magánjogi előadások*, 868–9.

102 János Suhayda, *A magyar polgári anyagi magánjog rendszere az Országbirói Értekezlet által megállapitott ITSz-hoz alkalmazva* (Pest, 1862), 34.

of the ITSz's introduction had judicialized custom to the extent that customary law and the law of the courts were now synonymous. Or, as it was later perversely explained, custom was the practice of the courts, which originated in what the courts practised.[103]

## COURTS AND THE LEGISLATIVE DEFICIT

The ITSz had restored the organization of the kingdom's courts as it had been before 1848 with only a few modifications. The principal adjustments lay in regard to the administration of the land registers and land use, which resulted in tens of thousands of suits coming before the courts every year.[104] The ITSz had also allowed the principal instrument of local justice, the county court, to operate as autonomously as possible, even to the extent that 'the maximum number of members of the court shall not be laid down, but be requisite with the administration of justice, for the court to decide.' Although membership of the county courts had become less numerous in the first decades of the nineteenth century, their tables often still included more than a dozen judges, county officials and assessors. The courts of the Curia, which the ITSz restored, continued to be packed with barons, prelates, assessors and others.[105] The ITSz did, however, confirm the reduction in the size of village and other local courts, where procedures were only oral, to just three officers.[106] Seigneurial courts were not, however, reinstated. Most of their work was taken over by courts in the ridings or járásbiróságok (there were 360 of these by 1871), the competences of which had been expanded during the period of neo-absolutism.

Following the Settlement or Compromise of 1867, by which Franz Joseph gave Hungary home rule, laws were introduced by the Hungarian parliament for the modernization of the kingdom's judicial administration. These aimed in the first instance at creating a career judiciary, appointment to which was by special examination. The function of the judges as civil servants was qualified by measures intended to ensure their impartiality, but since judicial appointments rested on ministerial approval, the judges were a generally compliant lot.[107] Judges were, moreover, paid badly in comparison to practising lawyers, on account of which their reputation suffered. Their background and education were also generally poorer, and their previous experience usually lay in clerking and not in litigation.[108] At the same time,

[103] Gyula Paraszkay (ifj), *A biról gyakorlat mint jogforrás* (Miskolc, 1929), 17, offprint of *Miskolci Jogászélet* (1929, no. 6).

[104] Some later figures for disputes over land registration are given in Lajos Králik, *A magyar ügyvédség. Az ügyvédi kar*, 2 vols. (Budapest, 1903), i, 265–8. Králik surely confuses the act of registration, which was notarial, with an action over registration, although both proceeded in the first instance before the same forum.

[105] György Bónis, Alajos Degré and Endre Varga, *A magyar bírósági szervezet és perjog története* (Zalaegerszeg, 1996), 215.

[106] Originally laid down in 1836: 20, but in a different context. This provision was routinely ignored.

[107] Bónis, Degré and Varga, *A magyar bírósági szervezet*, 216.

[108] Králik, *A magyar ügyvédség*, i, 245–8, 255. The requisite education and professional experience of judges was described in Law IV of 1869 (para. 7).

however, the role of the judge was enlarged by the removal of assessors and other officers from the courts. The Royal Curia court (which superseded the Septemviralis court) generally operated with between five and seven judges in attendance; the two (later eleven) courts of the Royal Table had five (later three) judges; and the city and county courts had three. Courts in the ridings were headed by single judges.[109]

Behind the changed status of the judiciary and the slimming down of court membership lay the assumption that jurisprudence was a mechanical act that simply required the facts before the court to be fitted to the relevant piece of legislation. As is typical in continental jurisdictions, judges were considered no more than, as Montesquieu had put it, 'the mouth that pronounces the words of the law, inanimate beings who can moderate neither its force nor its rigour'.[110] It was only where the quality of the facts was in dispute, most notably in respect of whether an article in the press was defamatory or seditious, that a wider constituency of opinion, in the form of a lay jury, was considered necessary.[111] The principle of judicial subsumption, which guides many continental jurisdictions, requires, however, that the law be both known and scrutable. In Hungary, however, this was not the case. Law IV (para. 19) of 1869 had, as we have seen, required that judges adjudicate by reference to statute, lawful decrees and custom having the force of law. It was moreover now specified that the lawful text of any statute was the one proclaimed in parliament and deposited in the National Archive, and thus not by implication any customized version.[112] Nevertheless, there was no obvious way of measuring the legality of a decree or custom by reference to its relationship to statute or to the force of law, for large areas of the law continued, as before, to remain without any regulation or guidance in statute.

* * *

Hungary's parliaments were never less than busy. Between 1870 and 1890, a thousand bills became law, a number that would more than double by 1930.[113] Some of these were intended to lay the liberal foundations of a modern civil society—regulating the rights of members of national minorities (before 1918, less than half of Hungarians were native Hungarian-speakers), establishing religious toleration, renewing the kingdom's commercial legislation, establishing a new criminal code, and so on. Nevertheless, statutory legislation tended to be piecemeal rather than comprehensive. Large parts of the law, particularly those affecting legal equality and the remaining encumbrances on peasant tenures were dealt with in a

[109] István Stipta, *A magyar bírósági rendszer története*, 2nd edition (Debrecen, 1998), 126–33.

[110] Montesquieu, *The Spirit of the Laws*, eds. Anne M. Choler et al. (Cambridge, 1989), 163 (11. 6).

[111] Jury trials were established in 1867 for press trials and extended in 1897 to include the most serious criminal and political offences. They were suspended in 1914 and not reinstated. See Tamás Antal, 'The Codification of Jury Procedure in Hungary', *Journal of Legal History*, 30, no. 3 (2009), 279–97; also Rieko Ueda, 'The Hungarian Jury System under a Dual Monarchy System', *Slavic Studies*, 47 (2000), 218–300 (in Japanese, with English-language summary).

[112] Law III of 1868.

[113] Zoltán Magyary, *The Rationalisation of Hungarian Public Administration* (Budapest, 1932), 11.

fragmentary fashion.[114] Still, at the beginning of the twentieth century, there were categories of woodland where rights of peasant usufruct had not been legally resolved.[115] The overwhelming share of legislation passing through parliament was given over to measures of only fleeting significance, being mainly nuts-and-bolts administrative and budgetary provisions. Possibly as much as eighty per cent of parliamentary legislation fell into this category.[116]

Legislation was not only partial, but it was also often derivative. It was much easier to borrow foreign legislative acts than to draft bills from scratch. The problem was that the importation of models from abroad introduced a vocabulary and distinctions in law that were not applicable to Hungary. In copying the German *Strafgesetzbuch* of 1871, the criminal code of 1878–9, devised by Károly Csemegi, introduced a threefold classification of crimes, dividing these between *bűntett*, *vétség* and *kihágás* (corresponding to the German *Tat*, *Verbrechen* and *Vergehen*), that had no basis in Hungarian practice.[117] The commercial legislation of the late 1870s was similarly taken from German law and smuggled in provisions of consumer protection without establishing a context for their implementation.[118] A further round of borrowing during the 1880s saw the establishment of a financial-administrative court for the resolution of disputes over taxation, fines and exemptions. Its competence was extended to other branches of the administration in 1896 and included most cases for legal redress against excesses or derelictions of duty by organs of state and local government. The inspiration for this development came primarily from the examples of the Austrian Reichsgericht (1869) and Verwaltungsgerichtshof (1875). Even at the time, however, the introduction of administrative courts was considered contrary to established Hungarian practice. Hitherto actions against officials had fallen within the purview of the ordinary courts.[119]

The establishment of administrative courts created an artificial distinction between public and private law that opened up new problems of jurisdiction and of the appropriate forum for adjudication. This is precisely what we might expect, given that the 'continental distinction' was as foreign to Hungary then as it is to England today.[120] Rather than tackle the problems of competence head on, however, successive governments chose not to legislate at all. Whole areas of activity were thus not covered by legislative provision, particularly in respect of the rights

[114] László Péter, 'The Aristocracy, the Gentry and their Parliamentary Tradition in Nineteenth-Century Hungary', in Péter, *Hungary's Long Nineteenth Century: Constitutional and Democratic Traditions in a European Perspective. Collected Studies* (Leiden and Boston, 2012), 305–42 (311–13). First published in SEER, 70 (1992), 77–110.

[115] Ferencz Szilárd, 'Az úrbéres erdők ügye', *Erdészeti Lapok*, 49, no. 21 (1 November 1910), 809–20.

[116] Magyary, *The Rationalisation of Hungarian Public Administration*, 11.

[117] Law 5 of 1878 established the first two categories; Law 40 of 1879 added the third. For a summary of the Csemegi code, see Krisztina Karsai and Zsolt Szomora, *Criminal Law in Hungary* (Alphen aan den Rijn, 2010), 35–6.

[118] Zlinszky, 'Hungarian Private Law in the 19th and 20th Centuries', 311; Gusztáv Schwarz, *Magánjogunk felépitése* (Budapest, 1893), 14.

[119] János Martonyi, *A közigazgatási biráskodás bevezetése, szervezete és hatékonysága Magyarországon (1867–1949)*, Acta Juridica et Politica, 20, no. 2 (Szeged, 1972), 3–4.

[120] See generally on this point, J.W.F. Allison, *A Continental Distinction in the Common Law: A Historical and Comparative Perspective on English Public Law* (Oxford, 2000).

that belonged to individuals and their relationship to the offices of state power. Of these, the most signal involved rights of association and assembly. There was, however, a similar legislative void in respect of the burgeoning number of land trusts (an individual right gifted by the monarch on the advice of the Minister of Justice) and the post office (a public body trusted with the delivery of private communications).[121] The law of mortmain (*holtkéz*), which affected the individual right to give property to the churches, which were conceived of as public bodies, remained notoriously without any guidance in modern statute. It was ultimately left to the Curia to determine that the restrictions on mortmain inherited from the Middle Ages had lapsed through desuetude.[122]

Even though the ITSz had been intended only as an interim measure, no civil code emerged to take its place. For decades, committees staffed by some of Hungary's most respected academic lawyers busied away at preparing drafts, but these never acquired legislative sanction. The composition of the committees and the scrupulous way that they went about their business partly explains their failure. Too many intellectual constituencies needed to be satisfied—the historical law school that conceived of the law as reflecting national traditions; the school of *Interessen-Jurisprudenz* that, under the influence of Jhering, saw the role of the law as reconciling interests in such a way as to permit the transformation of society; and an Anglophile group that pushed for the development of jurisprudence based on precedent and a yet-to-be-developed Common Law. Since, moreover, any new code required parliamentary approval, the lawyers had to be alert to political trends and accommodate, in particular, the conservatism of the Upper House.

The failure of the committee charged with drafting the civil law can be briefly told.[123] Established in 1869, but only really active from 1873, the committee divided up its work between its members. These produced individual sections on general principles and on the laws of property, obligations and inheritance.[124] The parts, however, did not mesh and were widely condemned as a medley of haphazard borrowings taken from other continental codes. In particular, the section on inheritance law, published in 1876, satisfied no one, since it assumed a midway position in respect of the contentious issue of collateral succession, while at the same time lifting parts of its text from the Saxon Civil Code of 1863. Its contents were the subject of earnest, but fruitless discussion for more than a dozen years, with the usual claims being raised that collateral inheritance at several degrees had to be acknowledged in law since it formed part of the national genius.[125] Meanwhile,

121 Mór Katona, *A magyar családi hitbizomány* (Budapest, 1894), 65–6; Gábor Kertész, 'A magyarországi postaszabályozás fejlődése a kezdetektől a rendszerváltásig', *Jogtörténeti Szemle*, (2008, no. 2), 31–41 (33–4).

122 MJL, iv, 175–6; on the status of the churches, see Andor Csizmadia, *Rechtliche Beziehungen von Staat und Kirche in Ungarn vor 1944* (Budapest, 1971), 26–8.

123 For this and much of what follows, see Helmut Coing, ed., *Handbuch der Quellen und Literatur der neueren europäischen Privatrechtsgeschichte*, 3 vols. in 8 parts (Munich, 1973–88), iii/2, 2165–88 (János Zlinszky). See also, Károly Szladits in MJL, ii, 551–5.

124 The work of this committee and of a separate drafting commission for parliamentary bills is frequently confused. The latter was established in 1872 but survived only two years.

125 Elemér Pólay, *Kisérlet a magyar öröklési jog önálló kodifikációja a XIX. század végén*, Acta Juridica et Politica, 21, no. 4 (Szeged, 1974), 8; János Zlinszky, 'Die historische Rechtsschule und

a marriage law that recognized civil unions eventually passed through parliament in the early 1890s (bringing down two governments on its way). By considering marriage separately, the parliament made it a domain of the law that operated outside the private law—a situation which unusually for continental jurisprudence prevails in Hungary today. For this we must partly blame the author of the marriage law, Béni Grosschmid, who pressed for its separate legislative treatment as a way of entrenching in statute some of the principles upon which any future civil code should rest.[126] Confusingly, however, the marriage law omitted consideration of marital property rights which continued to be treated as part of private law.

In 1894, a second committee was formed with the brief of 'elaborating a unified and systematic draft of the Civil Code, taking into consideration Hungary's statutes affecting the private law and its customary laws, the drafts that have been already compiled, Hungarian judicial opinion and literature, and legal developments in other civilized states'.[127] The committee took five years to produce a text running to more than 2,000 paragraphs. This was then published in a five-part edition, in 1901–2, and sent out for comment. A revised draft was commenced in 1909, which on account of the need to accommodate criticisms resulted in an expanded text—the section on inheritance law doubled to 1980 paragraphs. The amended version was put before the Lower House in 1913 and revised by a parliamentary committee in 1915, but on account of the war it never received legislative sanction.[128] An attempt undertaken after 1922 to rework the drafts into a new civil code 'reflective of the thousand-year development of our law', which was presented to parliament in 1928, similarly perished on account of the legislature's inertia.[129]

The failure to produce a code of civil law that regulated private legal relations was partly compensated for by textbooks. These, pre-eminently Imre Zlinszky's *Hungarian Private Law as Currently in Operation* (1880, and many subsequent editions), attempted to make sense of the law by welding together its fragments by reference to the Austrian Civil Code and other instruments that otherwise had no ostensible validity in Hungary.[130] The result was a mishmash of provisions that aimed at comprehensiveness but was epistemologically shallow. As Szászy-Schwarz observed of Zlinszky's text, 'Here he advances a genuine proposition in Hungarian law, here an old dead statute pulled from another context, here a recommendation taken from Hesse or Dresden.' Szászy-Schwarz recommended burning the lot, but his own solution was equally perverse—to re-found Hungarian private law on the

die Gestaltung des ungarischen Privatrechts im 19. Jahrhundert', *Acta Juridica et Politica*, 33, no. 30 (1985), 433–45 (443).

[126] Coing, *Handbuch der Quellen*, iii/2, 2168, 2187–8 (Zlinszky).

[127] Coing, *Handbuch der Quellen*, iii/2, 2169 (Zlinszky).

[128] Coing, *Handbuch der Quellen*, iii/2, 2170–1 (Zlinszky).

[129] Charles Szladits, 'Le Projet de code civil hongrois', *Acta Juris Hungarici*, 1, nos. 3–4 (1932), 213–21 (215).

[130] Imre Zlinszky, *A magyar magánjog mai érvényében, különös tekintettel a gyakorlat igényeire* (Budapest, 1880, and many subsequent editions).

basis of case law, thus forcing it to become akin to the English Common Law.[131] As it happened, a different way was found upon which to build the law and it was in this context that the idea of customary law re-emerged as a guiding principle in Hungarian jurisprudence. This was, however, a quite different type of customary law to the one that had prevailed in the kingdom before the mid-nineteenth century.

## RENDELET, COURT PRACTICE AND RHETORIC

With the advent in 1867 of constitutional rule, the executive power was apportioned to ministers, who might henceforward issue decrees or *rendelets* of their own volition.[132] This was considered a necessary means of empowering the administration in such a way as to achieve a balance within the constitution. From the very start, however, the system of legislation by ministerial rendelet was abused. First, parliamentary law making was invariably sloppy and more concerned with establishing general principles than with providing a thorough explication of the way in which the law should be applied. It was intended that ministerial rendelet would make up for deficiencies in the drafting process, fleshing out on an ad hoc basis the details that the legislative instrument lacked. The law of hunting illustrates this approach. The two statutes published in 1883 that regulated hunting and hunting grounds consisted of just a few pages of text, altogether just over 100 short paragraphs. Within eight years their statutory content had been amplified by several hundred ministerial interventions and rendelets that ran to almost 200 pages.[133] Year after year, issues of the *Woodland Gazette* (*Erdészeti Lapok*) and the *Hunting Almanach* (*Vadászati Zseb-Naptár*) carried pages of further administrative orders with which the dutiful huntsman and forester should comply. He was well advised to do so. Csemegi's criminal code of 1878–9 had not defined the offences that fell within the category of *kihágás* (*Verbrechen*). These were left blank, to be filled in by ministerial rendelet as the occasion arose.[134]

Secondly, rendelet was used not only to supplement existing legislation but also in place of it.[135] Whereas the French Revolutionary understanding of the law was that where the law was silent the citizen was free, in Hungary the reverse situation

131 Gusztáv Schwarz, *Magánjogunk felépitése*, 9, 16–23; Bernát Besnyő, *Szászy-Schwarz Gusztáv emlékezete* (Budapest, 1933), 31–5. On the larger cultural context, see László Országh, '"Anglomania" in Hungary, 1780–1900', *Angol-Filológiai Tanulmányok*, 12 (1979), 19–36.

132 The king might still issue decrees in the form of privileges for private persons or corporations, but these required ministerial counter-signature. See Katona, *A mai érvényű magyar magánjog*, 6–7.

133 Gyula Egervári Egerváry, *Vadászati ügyben hozott kormány-rendeletek*, 3rd edition (Budapest, 1891).

134 László Péter, 'The Autocratic Principle of the Law and Civil Rights in Nineteenth-Century Hungary', in Péter, *Hungary's Long Nineteenth Century: Constitutional and Democratic Traditions in a European Perspective* (Leiden and Boston, 2012), 281–304 (289–90), first published in *CEU History Department Yearbook, 1997–98* (Budapest, 1999), 11–34.

135 Gábor Máthé, *A magyar burzsoá igazságszolgáltatási szervezet 1867–1875* (Budapest, 1982), 64–5.

applied.[136] In the legislative gap, ministerial regulations held sway, which almost always worked to the state's advantage. Since ministerial regulations of this type were not explanatory of an existing legislative instrument, their legality could not be challenged in any court, which permitted all sorts of abuses. The ministerial requirement that associations fulfil only single purposes was therefore used to harass trade unions and to ban societies that promoted the cultural interests of national minorities.[137] Restrictions on assembly, imposed at ministerial discretion or on the Interior Minister's behalf by local police chiefs, often led to violent confrontations and deaths.[138] Parliamentary challenges to the discretionary power wielded by ministers almost invariably came to nothing.[139]

Where statute and rendelet were silent, the courts self-consciously filled the void.[140] It was their determinations that established the basic rules of commercial and domestic liability, the obligations of a mortgagee, rights to water, presumption of death in the event of disappearance, the period of legal prescription, that the obligatory portion applied to acquired as well as to inherited land, and so on.[141] The principle of mechanical jurisprudence thus gave way to judicial creativity, turning on its head the assumptions of the 1869 law. As a satirical verse of the time put it:

> We have many new laws, modern to a tee,
> It's to preserve social order, don't you see?
> Should something be lacking in any one line,
> The Curia will fill it, in record time![142]

It was partly in recognition of the inventiveness of the courts that the publication of judicial decisions, which had begun episodically in the 1820s, gathered pace, in editions that aimed to be comprehensive and which often amounted to several or more volumes each year.[143] These were accompanied by the publication of shorter compendiums, which contained decisions of the courts that were thought to be weightier, or else rearranged their content under convenient headings.[144] It was not intended, however, that these summaries of cases and judgments should act in the manner of case law, for Hungarian courts generally held to the conviction that similar judgments in similar cases needed to be given over a period of time to acquire cogency.[145] Nor was it at all obvious, moreover, what the grounds of

[136] István Kovács, 'A törvény és törvényerejű rendelet problematikájához', *Állam- és Jogtudomány*, 16, no. 3 (1973), 333–91 (349–51); Máthé, *A magyar burzsoá igazságszolgáltatási szervezet*, 64–5.

[137] Emil Vita, *Egyesületi jog* (Budapest, 1906), 21–2, 27–38.

[138] Attila Horváth, 'A gyülekezési jog elméletének és gyakorlatának története Magyarországon 1989-ig', *Jogtörténeti Szemle*, (2007, no. 1), 4–15 (10–11).

[139] Péter, 'The Autocratic Principle of the Law and Civil Rights', 294–301.

[140] See thus Dezső Márkus's introduction to *Felsőbirósagaink elvi határozatai*, ed. Márkus, 24 vols. (Budapest, 1891–1914), i, iii.

[141] Márkus, *Felsőbirósagaink elvi határozatai*, i, 436, 439, 442; Márkus, *Felsőbirósagaink elvi határozatai*, ii/2, 379–80, 389, 397; Márkus, *Felsőbirósagaink elvi határozatai*, iii, 203.

[142] Albert M. Kóssa, *Talmi aranykorunk. Tréfás szatirák versekben* (Budapest, 1886), 209.

[143] Some of these are listed in János Zlinszky and B. Szabó, 'Ungarn', in Filippo Ranieri, ed., *Gedruckte Quellen der Rechtsprechung in Europa (1800–1945)*, (Frankfurt a/M, 1992), 953–64 (957–8).

[144] Zlinszky and Szabó, 'Ungarn', 958–60.

[145] Zlinszky, *A magyar magánjog mai érvényében*, 37.

individual judgments were, for courts continued to eschew statements of principle lest these should subsequently prove restrictive. Their explanations for decisions were correspondingly vague, being usually confined to 'It is the understanding of judicial practice that *etc.*' or 'According to our public laws and received custom *etc.*' As Szászy-Schwarz lamented, the many volumes of decisions published from the 1870s barely ever disclosed legal reasoning that might serve to elucidate the law's actual content. He thus contrasted Hungarian judicial practice unfavourably with its English and German counterparts where an explanation *aus der Gründen* was an accepted part of the court's judgment.[146]

Certainly, by perusing sufficient cases, a mood or approach of the courts might be determined. On the whole, the courts tended towards the same sort of judicial expediency that had prevailed before, aiming at a balance between contending claims. This was particularly the case in respect of the estimation of damages, where the responsibility of the two parties tended to be weighed against each other rather than the matter resolved by reference to proximate cause.[147] It was impossible, however, to convert a mood into a substantive principle of law, particularly since courts retained the right to reject previous rulings.[148] The problem additionally arose that divergent practices began to emerge in the several layers of the judicial hierarchy or between courts. No attempts were made, however, to give the judgments of higher courts a binding authority, for these were limited to a 'guiding influence'.[149] Only a full session of the Curia, acting at the request of the president of the court or the Minister of Justice, could publish a decision to which other courts should yield.[150] Even so, since these Curia decisions still failed to give judicial grounds, their contribution to the development of substantive principles was slender.[151] It was only after the Second World War that judicial reasoning became an accepted part of court practice.[152]

In order to compensate for the absence of an alternative body of substantive law, the courts turned instead to the drafts that had been composed by the various committees as part of their work on the civil code. The volumes on the private law, published in 1901–2, were thus adopted by the courts, and subsequently influenced their judgments, especially in regard to the law of obligations. The revised 1928 draft was used in its turn during the inter-war period to guide judicial decisions. A similar use of draft instruments affected the criminal law. In 1871

146 Gusztáv Schwarz, *Magánjogunk felépitése*, 18–22.

147 Ernő Wittmann, 'Tanulmányok az angol magánjog köréből. Kárteritési jog', *Jogállam*, 5, nos. 7–8 (1906), 513–28, 588–608, 682–99, 736–63 (753–4); Martyn Rady, 'England and Hungarian Jurisprudence: Questions of Public and Private Law', in László Péter and Rady, eds., *British-Hungarian Relations since 1848* (London, 2004), 315–27 (324). See also Márkus, *Felsőbiróságaink elvi határozatai*, i, 439, on cesspits.

148 Márkus, *Felsőbiróságaink elvi határozatai*, i, 209.

149 Grosschmid, *Magánjogi előadások*, 782–803.

150 See Law LIV of 1912, para. 76.

151 Gyula Eörsi, 'Richterrecht und Gesetzesrecht in Ungarn. Zum Problem der Originalität eines Zivilrechts', *Rabels Zeitschrift für ausländisches und internationales Privatrecht*, 30 (1966), 117–40 (122–7); *Polgári Jogi Határozatok Tára* (Budapest, 1918 etc.).

152 See thus Mihály Antalfy, Dezső Nagy (ifj.) and Miklós Újlaki, eds., *Magánjogi Döntvénytár*, NS, i (1946–7) (Budapest, 1948).

Csemegi had written a proposal on criminal procedure, with the aim of replacing Tivadar Ortvay's textbook on criminal law, which had until this time been all that there was to guide the courts.[153] The draft proposal went to the parliament but was held up in committees. Rather than allow Ortvay's manual to retain its pre-eminence by default, the Justice Minister sent out Csemegi's draft to the courts, with the recommendation that they follow its advice on a temporary basis. For almost thirty years, the so-called 'Yellow Book' (*Sárga könyv*) determined the manner of proceeding in criminal cases, and was primarily responsible for introducing to Hungary the institution of the investigating magistrate. It was finally superseded in 1896 by a statutory code of procedure, which came into effect in 1900.[154]

Hungarian law in the late nineteenth- and early-twentieth centuries consisted, therefore, of two types. The first was statutory law that had received parliamentary sanction. The second was extra-statutory. It comprised a variety of sources—rendelet, the decisions of the courts, and what might broadly be understood as juridical opinion, either in the form of the ITSz or of various drafts of intended legislation that had never made it onto the statute book. The authority of these non-statutory sources was not at all obvious and, indeed, they should by the terms of the 1869 Law on the Exercise of Judicial Power have been inefficacious. The 1869 Law had said nothing about the role of Curia judgments or legal drafts in guiding judgments. In respect of rendelet, the Law had presumed that ministerial decrees would be explanatory of statute rather than a substitute for it.

The solution was actually quite straightforward. The 1869 Law had permitted judgments by reference to custom, and so it was under this heading that non-statutory instruments were now conceived. There was a precedent for this, for the ITSz had similarly been a non-statutory instrument that was subsequently deemed to have gathered its authority from customary use. Lawyers and commentators were also able to use Werbőczy's statement on the way in which judgments were constitutive of customary law and the manner of the *Tripartitum*'s own reception to press home the point. Others found in the *Planum Tabulare* a bridge between the *Tripartitum* and their own time, thus demonstrating a spurious historical continuity in respect of the role of court decisions in determining arrangements of law.[155] The practice of the courts thus became conceived as identical to customary law. The ways that the courts sought to administer the law and the texts that they chose to use were accordingly given the legal sanction that they otherwise lacked. As Grosschmid (who really knew better) asked, were not judgments both the source and driving force of the law as well as its proof?[156] A few legal scholars realized that judicial practice needed to be embedded in something more than just what the courts did. Their response was either to consider court judgments as

[153] Tibor Király, 'Das Strafgesetzbuch von 1878. Der Csemegi-Kodex', in Gábor Máthé and Werner Ogris, eds., *Die Entwicklung der osterreichisch-ungarischen Strafrechtskodifikation im xix.–xx. Jahrhundert* (Budapest, 1996), 221–36 (222).

[154] Barna Mezey, *Magyar jogtörténet*, 2nd edition (Budapest, 1999), 378–9.

[155] Suhayda, *A magyar polgári anyagi magánjog rendszere*, 37; Zlinszky, *A magyar magánjog mai érvényében*, 37; Gyula Paraszkay, ifj, *A birói gyakorlat mint jogforrás* (Miskolc, 1929), 6–7, offprint of *Miskolci Jogászélet* (1929, no. 6).

[156] Grosschmid, *Magánjogi előadások*, 727.

reflexive, slowly shaping popular practice, or to invoke a new form of the *lex regia*—since the people were incapable of expressing themselves, their collective will was now articulated by the judiciary.[157] It belonged, however, to Károly Szladits, to point out the paradox that after centuries of being founded on written texts, and he included the *Tripartitum* in this category, Hungary's law was now being shaped by the unwritten law of judicial decision.[158]

A similar brand of intellectual legerdemain was applied to rendelet. Since executive orders had long been in use, they were considered to retain a customary authority in law. Moreover, so it was argued, the provisions of individual rendelets might in time become rooted in popular practice and thus accumulate a customary authority that gave them an additional persuasiveness in law. Nodding to the *tacitus consensus populi*, but plainly confusing tacit consent with dumb compliance, Gejza Ferdinandy averred that even those instruments published during the period of neo-absolutism might have 'silently' gathered authority in daily observance in much the same way as the provisions of the ITSz.[159] Gyula Moór put the case for the customary authority of rendelet even more strongly: 'Rendelets of the administration have their origin in the practice of government and retain a power that is equivalent to custom.'[160]

The explanation that non-statutory legislation held a customary authority was an attractive solution. It lent the kingdom's legal institutions a supposedly historical continuity, both emphasizing Hungary's unique place within the Habsburg Monarchy and comporting with the studied medievalism of the millennial celebrations of 1896. Whereas in the earlier part of the nineteenth century, the legislation of diet and parliament had been understood as providing the main vehicles for national renewal, the customary law was now invoked as the manifestation of Hungary's national mission. Werbőczy's memory was celebrated and his work in 'unifying' the nation admitted him to membership of the overcrowded pantheon of Hungarian heroes. Some portraits even gave him Kossuth's full beard, although this feature was missing from the statue erected in 1908 by the gift of Franz Joseph on what is now the Franciscans' Square.[161] In the Millennium edition of the CJH, which commenced its series with the *Tripartitum*, those parts of Werbőczy's text that were still deemed pertinent were printed in bold letters, thereby emphasizing their continued contribution to the living law of the nation. The entirety of the Prologue and about 70 of the 160 pages of the main text were rendered in this way.[162] Not a few jurists still held to the dogmatic view of statute as the proper

157 Katona, *A mai érvényű magyar magánjog*, 8.

158 Károly Szladits, 'A magyar magánjog jellegváltozásai az utolsó száz év alatt', in Ferenc Eckhart and Alajos Degré, eds., *Emlékkönyv Dr. Viski Illés József* (Budapest, 1942), 486–95 (490). Szladits typically overstates his case.

159 Gejza Ferdinandy, *Magyarország közjoga* (Budapest, 1902), 89.

160 Moór, *A különböző jogforrások, azok egyensúlya es rangfokozata a magyar jogrendszerben* (Budapest, 1932), 10.

161 DRMH 5, xliv. The statue was pulled down 'spontaneously' (a brass band in attendance) by a Communist gang on 6 May 1945, and has not been replaced. The name of Werbőczy Street (now Táncsics Mihály Street) has not been restored either, but retains its Communist designation.

162 *Magyar Törvénytár. Werbőczy István Hármaskönyve*, eds. Sándor Kolosvári and Kelemen Óvári (Budapest, 1897).

embodiment of the state and the single source of law, beside which customary law was an empty fiction. An increasing share, however, identified the customary law with national traditions and affirmed its equivalence or even superiority to statute law, the provisions of which it might annul.[163] By conflating customary law with the Common Law, a spurious parallel with the English constitutional tradition was even invoked. The customary law of which Hungarian lawyers now spoke was not, however, the same as Werbőczy had explained in the *Tripartitum*. It comprised extra-statutory instruments that proceeded out of the work of government and the courts, upon which the title of custom had been rhetorically bestowed.

There is nothing unusual in this. From no later than the sixteenth century, the name of customary law has often been attached in Europe and elsewhere to legislation imposed from above. Norms promoted by courts or by government are given the sanction of the past and, as in early modern France or more recently in Korea, legitimized by reference to historic practice.[164] During the nineteenth century, an analogous process of state-building and of the modernization of institutions resulted in Hungary in the expansion of the law. The law was built not only on statutory instruments but also on non-statutory ones and the legal system depended for its coherence on the successful coordination of the two spheres. In order to buttress the authority of non-statutory legislation, its origin was explained by reference to customary law, which had the advantage of comporting with notions of historic identity and traditions. The solution was effective and beguiling, but unconvincing in so far as it confused the customary authority of an instrument with the customary character of its content, and mistook obedience for consent. It remained, nevertheless, the proud contention of many Hungarian jurists until the period of Communist rule.[165]

[163] László Péter, 'The Primacy of *Consuetudo* in Hungarian Law', in CLCS, 101–12 (110–11).
[164] Jacques Krynen, 'The Absolute Monarchy and the French Unification of Private Rights', in Julius Kirsher and Laurent Mayali, eds., *Privileges and Rights of Citizenship: Law and the Juridical Construction of Civil Society* (Berkeley, 2002), 27–55; Marie Seong-Hak Kim, *Law and Custom in Korea* (Cambridge, 2012), 299.
[165] Péter, 'The Primacy of *Consuetudo* in Hungarian Law', 110–11.

# Conclusion
## Customary Law in Hungary

In 1959 Hungary obtained its first civil code, which was passed into law by a pliant Communist parliament. The authority of the new code rested upon statute, but as its authors explained, there were anterior sources of authority which also lent it cogency. The civil code's architect, Gyula Eörsi (a distinguished lawyer), and the minister of justice, Ferenc Nezvál (a former leather worker), spelled these out. First, the code looked towards the best examples of socialist law, not least the Russian Federation's civil code of 1923 and the legislative example of Hungary's Communist neighbours. Secondly, its authors had consulted previous court decisions, taking into account those judgments that embodied 'sound rulings'. Thirdly, the civil code sought to include popular understandings of the law's content. Its drafting had thus, so Eörsi averred, been preceded by 'nation-wide discussion', public debate and press commentary, to such an extent that the new civil code was 'tantamount to a plebiscite'.[1] In deference to the 'old, but deep-rooted, Hungarian civil law institutions' that still retained popular approbation, some traditional methods of inheritance had therefore, so Nezvál explained, been included in the civil code, even though they sat uneasily with socialist principles.[2]

It is easy to sneer at Eörsi and Nezvál's description of the way the 1959 Civil Code came into being—they were after all the regime's servants. Once we strip away, however, the statutory basis of the Civil Code, we are in respect of the authority claimed for its text, confronted with almost the same considerations as influenced the *Tripartitum*'s account of the origins of Hungarian customary law. First, the law was framed by its larger legal context—in the case of the 1959 code, by the *ius commune* of socialist practice. It originated thus in relation to a set of norms that transcended national boundaries, being products of a universal vision of the law. Secondly, the contents of the code depended upon those decisions of the courts that had been tested over time and deemed trustworthy. Finally, a part of the code derived from popular practice, thus depending upon common conduct and belief. In this way, Eörsi and Nezvál unwittingly drew together the separate sources of the historic Hungarian law—its location in common observance, its articulation by the courts, and the larger legal context to which it deferred. Notwithstanding the changes in Hungary after 1989 and the election in 2010 of a radical

[1] Gyula Eörsi, *Legal System and Administration of Justice in Hungary* (Budapest, 1958), 16, 33.

[2] *Civil Code of the Hungarian People's Republic* (Budapest, 1960), 165–82 (text of the Ministerial Motivation); Miklós Világhy and Gyula Eörsi, *Magyar polgári jog*, 2 vols. (Budapest, 1962), ii, 374.

right-wing government committed to a decisive break with the country's Communist legacy, the same considerations that inspired Eörsi and Nezvál may still be detected in the rhetoric of law making. The 2013 Civil Code, which replaced its (much amended) Communist predecessor, was thus advertised as having been based on the European 'social model' and the examples of codification elsewhere, and founded 'on solutions that have been tried and tested in real life and have been polished to perfection in decades of judicial practice'.[3]

In the preceding chapters, we have sought to explain the interplay between the various sources of Hungarian customary law. From the very start of the kingdom's legal history, the language of the law was shaped by a vocabulary and body of procedures that derived from Romano-canonical practice. It is to this that the *Tripartitum* refers in respect of its observation that 'almost all the laws of this kingdom have evolved from sources in pontifical and imperial law'. Romano-canonical principles and practices were diffused through the work of the chancellery and the *loca credibilia*, thus contributing to the kingdom's legal uniformity. The customary law of the kingdom was also moulded by statutory legislation. The written law was persuasive, however, only to the extent that its contents passed into practice and thus obtained a customary authority of their own. This was not a theoretical consideration but derived from the way that the written law was distributed and retained. The laws of the kingdom were all too often lost, inadequately circulated, forgotten or, on account of their ad hoc character, deemed no longer relevant. Accordingly, only those that were collected and recollected, passing into active use, retained a legal character. They eventually became a part of the Hungarian *Corpus Juris*. On account, however, of the way in which the content of the written law interacted with custom, authority lay not with the authentic, historical version but with the one that was used in the courts, even though its text was known to be corrupt. In this respect, the 'closed book' of the written law also took on the character of customary law.

A part of the customary law of the kingdom was built upon court practice. The courts determined what the law was in respect of the cases that came before them. The judgments of the kingdom's courts were on the one hand declaratory, insofar as the courts pronounced what the existing law was, and constitutive, since it was the courts that determined what customs were possessed of a normative quality. Two objections stand in the way, however, of Eörsi's contention that until the advent of socialism, judge-made law in the sense of *Richterrecht* prevailed in the kingdom.[4] First, the decisions of the courts were not communicated and for the most part they were unmotivated. The courts might recollect how they had previously arrived at a decision. Over time, a set of propositions emerged from their practice, to which the courts usually deferred. Nevertheless, there was no written body of past cases and decisions to which the courts might refer for guidance; nor did the perusal of previous judgments inform jurisprudence. On this account, the customary

[3] Statement by Tibor Navracics, Minister of Public Administration and Justice, 23 July 2012.

[4] Gyula Eörsi, *Fundamental Problems of Socialist Civil Law* (Budapest, 1970), 31. Discussed by Zdeněk Kühn, *The Judiciary in Central and Eastern Europe: Mechanical Jurisprudence in Transformation?* (Leiden and Boston, 2011), 5–6.

law of the kingdom did not crystallize around a sophisticated body of substantive propositions, communicated through court judgments, in the manner of Common Law jurisdictions. Some basic norms certainly influenced court decisions, in which respect judicial reasoning did not happen in a complete void. Beyond the framework of *aviticitas*, however, these were strikingly few, as a consequence of which a high degree of uncertainty attached to customary law adjudication. In this respect, Eörsi's qualification that *Richterrecht* in Hungary was on account of its malleability (*Verändlichkeit*) akin to *Kadijustiz* was not entirely inappropriate.[5]

Secondly, the composition of the courts affected the justice that they dispensed. It is frequently averred that it is the courts in customary law jurisdictions which determine the law's content and that their appeals to common observance and belief are only rhetorical. The problem of whether customary law originates in popular practices or whether it is institutionally derived is plain from the contradictions in the *Tripartitum*. As we have noted, in the Prologue Werbőczy assumed a strongly Bartolist position—'It is called custom, for it is, as it were, common practice and human use, because it is in common use.' In the main body of his text, however, Werbőczy located the origins of the customary law elsewhere—in Romano-canonical norms, statute, and the decisions of the courts. Although he subsequently qualified his account, readmitting popular practice as a source of customary law, he did so only obliquely and without discussion. Nevertheless, we have throughout this book been concerned to show that, in respect of the sources of customary law, the antithesis between the practice of the courts on the one hand and popular practice on the other is falsely conceived. On account of the numerousness of their composition, Hungary's courts conveyed the law as it was customarily understood. At the lower level, Hungarian courts were often akin to assemblies and they dispensed popular justice. At the higher level, in the courts of the Curia, proceedings took place in a more lawyerly fashion, largely under the influence of the protonotaries, but these courts also drew on a wider constituency than just law men. Moreover, the passage of persons and business between the higher and lower courts, particularly as a consequence of the development of appellate jurisdiction, meant that practices observed in the localities influenced court practice at the centre. The Hungarian law of bankruptcy is illustrative of this trend.

The composition of the courts and the manner in which they made their decisions stood in the way of jurisprudential growth. On account of their predominantly lay character, the courts were less concerned with dispensing a law that was principled as with reaching a solution that was just, expedient and lasting. It was on this account that so many remedies in law were built into the system of adjudication. For this reason too, the courts eschewed the sort of reasoning that might have yielded substantive propositions, preferring instead to adjudicate matters before them equitably, on a case by case basis. In attempting to expose the old Hungarian law as the antithesis of socialist law, Gyula Eörsi compared the customary law with the Common Law, both being in his opinion expressions of a

[5] Although it may do a disservice to Qadi courts. See Lawrence Rosen, 'Equity and Discretion in a Modern Islamic Legal System', *Law and Society Review*, 15, no. 2 (1980–1), 217–46.

similar type of *Richterrecht*. In fact, the two systems are at odds with one another. The Common Law seeks to build on previous decisions and to develop principles which will help to guide later judgments. The customary law is not led by past decisions, but aims at judgments that are more distributive, in the sense of being informed by what it is thought to be right at the time. In reality, the outcomes may be the same, being led by the court's intuition of the law, which the court subsequently grounds on a supposed principle.[6] The starting-points of the two systems and the claims that they make about the nature of adjudication are, however, quite different.

The interest of customary law courts in remedies and solutions rather than in judgments resting on substantive principles left the law uncertain. Even the most basic propositions of the system of *aviticitas* might thus be rejected in favour of outcomes that were deemed on occasion more equitable. We have indicated several decisions of this type, as well as the large areas of the law where matters were left without any guiding principles or rules. It was to make up for this deficiency that the *Tripartitum* was commissioned. Certainly, publication of the *Tripartitum* stabilized a part of the law, by in particular limiting the possibilities for the alienation of land and thereby reaffirming the basic propositions of *aviticitas*, to which Werbőczy's account of *proditio sanguinis* added special moral suasion. Nevertheless, its text was also customized, with some parts being disregarded in practice, while others acquired over time a special salience. By analogy and inference, the courts were, moreover, able to stretch the meaning of the *Tripartitum*'s individual parts, adapting its text to fit new circumstances. Although courts recognized that there were limits to judicial ingenuity, customary law could be moulded to fit new contingencies, in which respect it did not freeze the law or render it capable of only conservative decisions. The development of a commercial law of some sophistication is testament to the possibilities for innovation within a customary jurisdiction, in which respect the customary law was not responsible for a *végétation coutumière*.[7] Where the *Tripartitum* was silent, as in respect of the criminal law, courts imported texts from elsewhere or developed their own practices and institutions, which accumulated over time a customary authority.

The *Tripartitum* rapidly acquired a symbolic significance, embodying the rights of the noble nation and explaining historically the intimate and reciprocal bond that united monarch and nobility. The inclusion within its text of 'public law' clauses affirming the electoral character of Hungarian kingship and the nobility's right of resistance enhanced its status as emblematic of noble liberty. Many attempts were made to revise or even replace its text. All of these foundered not only on account of the magnitude of the task but also because the customary authority attaching to the *Tripartitum* hemmed in subsequent generations of law makers. As a consequence, attempts to reform the law often took the form of simply recasting

[6] See thus Karl N. Llewellyn, *The Bramble Bush: The Classic Lectures on the Law and Law School* (Oxford, 2006), 32 (first published in 1930).

[7] The expression originates in G. Le Bras, Ch. Lefebvre and J. Rambaud, *L'Age classique, 1140–1378: sources et théorie du droit* (Paris, 1965), 207. Noted in R.C. van Caenegem, *Law, History, the Low Countries and Europe* (London and Rio Grande, 1994), 98.

or amplifying its contents. The two most laboured attempts at the renewal of the law, by the Commissio Systematica and the Deputatio Juridica respectively, thus started with the premises of the *Tripartitum*, rearranging its headings but scarcely affecting its substance. Indeed, with the inclusion of the *Tripartitum* in the CJH and its repeated republication, not least in Szegedi's *Werbőczius Illustratus*, its text acquired a circulation and currency that ensured its perseverance both in common conviction and in the deliberations of the courts. In similar fashion, the structure of the courts remained largely unaltered, notwithstanding the procedural disassembly that took place in the sixteenth and seventeenth centuries.

The reputation attaching to the *Tripartitum* may be demonstrated in legal education. Even in the schools, Hungarian law as communicated in the *Tripartitum* assumed the most important place in the curriculum. For those learning the trade of a lawyer by pupillage (*in patvariis*), the *Tripartitum* was almost the only text from which they drew their legal knowledge. Since Hungarian law had already been homologated by the *Tripartitum*, Romanist solutions to the problems of the law's inconsistency were deemed unnecessary. Although we may detect some Romanist influence on judicial decision making, through the application of civilian brocards, Hungary did not experience a Roman Law reception. As a consequence, Hungarian customary law was not stiffened by the admission of substantive categories into which its content might be pressed. Although scholars have often presumed that Hungary's historic law may be best comprehended by imposing a pandectist scheme upon it, it is plain that its content continued to be negotiated rather than organized according to a set of fixed assumptions.

It was only in the nineteenth century that customary law was dislodged from its primacy. Parliamentary legislation took its place and this became the instrument of choice of reformers. Statute was, however, often crafted inadequately and failed to take in large areas of the law, which remained without any formal legislative provision. No new civil code was agreed, while arrangements that stood at the interface of public and private law were left in a legal void. In order to make up for these deficiencies, there was an increased reliance upon extra-statutory instruments, most notably the formal decisions of the courts and ministerial decree or *rendelet*. The nimbus attaching to the name of custom meant that the use of these discretionary instruments was justified by appeals to Hungary's customary law tradition. In this way, the notion persevered that Hungary was still a largely customary jurisdiction. Not for the first time, institutions of state deployed the authority of custom to impose a legal order that was far from customary in its content.

The customary law may be several things. It may be the rhetorical cloak by which governments standardize the law, appealing to the past as a way of justifying innovation. Or it may be the discussions of simple folk, articulating what they believe on occasion to be fair and in conformity with the moral order. Throughout the medieval and for much of the modern periods, however, the customary law of Hungary developed in the manner described in the *Tripartitum*. It was located in the interplay of the *ius commune* of the Romano-canonical tradition, the written law, and the decisions of the kingdom's courts, which articulated a collective and lay understanding of the law and its practice. The *Tripartitum* was itself an amalgam of the *ius commune*, statutory provision, lawyerly interpretation and popular conviction. It also reflexively influenced the language of the law, the procedures and practices of the courts, and the efficacy of legislation, for a long time acting as a block to any renewal of the kingdom's legal order. Because the law continued to be comprehended as customary, the *Tripartitum* was itself subsequently moulded by practice, in which respect it did not give fixity to court judgments or stabilize Hungarian jurisprudence upon a series of immutable propositions. The *Tripartitum* was a book of customary law, but it was also customizing in the sense of lending the name of custom to practices, and customized to the extent that its own content was altered by practice. The *Tripartitum* was, like the law of the kingdom more generally, customary, customizing and customized law. In this respect, it embodies an older jurisprudence that may by its appeal to a popular comprehension of the law still influence the reasoning of lawyers and politicians.

# *Bibliography*

## MANUSCRIPT COLLECTIONS


**HUNGARY**

**Magyar Nemzeti Levéltár, Országos Levéltár (Hungarian National Archive)**

Section B. Erdélyi kancelláriai levéltár (Transylvanian Chancellery Archive)
B 53, Index manualis in juridicis (1752–1827)
Section E. Magyar kincstári levéltárak (Hungarian Treasury Archives)
E 14, Acta Hungarica
E 21, Benignae Resolutiones
E 137, Relationes Commissariorum Regiorum
Section N. Regnicolaris levéltár (Regnicolaris Archive)
N 105, Deputatio Regnicolaris in Juridicis
Section O. Birósági levéltárak (Judicial Archives)
O 1, Processus Octavales
O 2, Processus Delegatorii
O 3, Mandata Judiciaria
O 4, Inquisitiones Juratorum
O 8, Protocolla Tabulae Septemviralis
O 9, Protocolla Tabulae Regiae
O 10, Normalia
O 11, Rescripta Regia (Ad Septemviralem)
O 18, Processus Tabulares
O 30, Büntető perkivonatok fogalmazványai
O 39, Decisiones Curiales
O 52, Váltótörvényszék
O 98, Acta Tavernici Antonii Cziráky
O 111, Dunántúli Keruleti Tábla levéltára. Szabályrendeletek, ügyviteli iratok
O 116, Dunantúli Kerületi Tábla levéltára. Tanácsülési jegyzőkönyvek
O 125, Országbirói Hivatal
O 142, Justizministerium. Akten-Ungern
Section P. Családok, személyek, testületek és egyesületek iratai (MSS of Families, Persons, Corporations and Associations)
P 88, Dessewffy család
P 275, Festetics család keszthelyi levéltár
Section Q. Mohács-előtti gyűjtemény (Pre-Mohács Collection)
DL. (Collection of medieval charters and MSS)

**Pest Megyei Levéltár (Pest County Archive, Budapest)**

Fond IV–87, Uriszéki iratok
Fóti uradalom
Gödöllői Grassalkovich uradalom
Fond V–180 Ráckeve
A (a) Ráckeve tanácsi iratai

**A Dunamelléki Református Egyházkerület Ráday Levéltára (Ráday Archive of the Danubian District of the Reformed Church, Budapest)**
C/67, Sárközy család levéltára
C/71, Sigray család levéltára

**Eötvös Loránd Tudományegyetem, Egyetemi Könyvtár (Library of Eötvös Loránd University, Budapest)**
MSS, Litterae et Epistolae Originales

**Országos Széchényi Könyvtár (National Széchényi Library, Budapest)**
Department of MSS

ROMANIA
**Serviciul Judeţean al Arhivelor Naţionale, Cluj-Napoca (County Branch of the National Archive, Cluj)**
Fond 3. Prefectura judeţului Cluj
16. Protocollum Marchalis Congregationis
126. Protocollum inclyti comitatus Colosiensis Generale
Fond 4. Comitatul Alba de Sus
Fond 363. Fond Familial Josika de Vlaha, no 28, Procese-verbale

**Serviciul Judeţean al Arhivelor Naţionale, Sibiu (County Branch of the National Archive, Sibiu)**
Fond Colecţia de Documente Medievale
Fond Colecţia Brukenthal

**Biblioteca Academiei Române Cluj-Napoca** (Library of the Romanian Academy, Cluj)
Biblioteca Colegiului unitarian de Cluj, MSS

## PRINTED BOOKS

The bibliography of printed books is confined to works on Hungarian legal history. It omits contextual and comparative studies as well as the standard nineteenth-century source editions, the titles of which are given in full in the footnotes. Items cited only once in the footnotes are generally also not included.

Acsády, Ignácz, *A pozsonyi és szepesi kamarák 1565–1604* (Budapest, 1894).
Acsády, Ignácz, *Régi magyar birtokviszonyok 1494–1598* (Budapest, 1894).
Bak, János M., *Königtum und Stände in Ungarn im 14.–16. Jahrhundert* (Wiesbaden, 1976).
Bak, János M., 'Tradition and Renewal in the Decretum Maius of King Matthias', in *Matthias Rex 1458–1490: Hungary at the Dawn of the Renaissance* (Budapest, 2013), unpaginated, online resource.
Bak, János M. et al., eds., *Decreta Regni Mediaevalis Hungariae—The Laws of the Medieval Kingdom of Hungary*, 5 vols. (Budapest, Los Angeles, Salt Lake City, Idyllwild, CA, 1989–2012). The first volume appeared in a second edition in 1999.
Balogh, János, *A magyar magánjog visszaállitásának kérdései* (Pest, 1861).
Banyó, Péter, 'Birtoköröklés és leánynegyed. Kisérlet egy középkori jogintézmény értelmezésére', *Aetas*, (2000, no. 3), 76–92.

Baranyai, Béla, 'Hoffmann János György magyar közjogi codex-tervezete (1698–90)', in Baranyai, *A lengyel királykoronázás. Négy közlemény a magyar jog- és alkotmány-történetéhez* (Karcag, 1927), 39–84.
Bartoniek, Emma, 'A koronázási eskü fejlődése 1526-ig', *Századok*, 51 (1917), 5–44.
Béli, Gábor, 'Degré Alajos és a régi gyámsági jog', in András Molnár, ed., *Levéltáros Elődeink. Degré Alajos és Szabó Béla munkassága* (Zalaegerszeg, 2006), 25–39.
Béli, Gábor, *Magyar jogtörténet. A tradicionális jog* (Budapest and Pécs, 2009).
Béli, Gábor, 'Strafrechtspraxis und Strafrechtswissenschaft in Ungarn im 18. Jh.', in Barna Mezey, ed., *Strafrechtsgeschichte an der Grenze des nächsten Jahrtausendes* (Budapest, 2003), 110–21.
Beňa, Jozef, and Tomáš Gábriš, *History of Law in Slovakia I. (Until 1918)* (Bratislava, 2008).
Benczédi, László, *Rendiség, absolutizmus és centralizáció a xvii. század végi Magyarországon (1664–1685)* (Budapest, 1980).
Benda, Kálmán, ed., *A magyar jakobinusok elleni felségsértési és hűtlenségi per iratai 1794–95* (*A Magyar Jakobinusok*, 2) (Budapest, 1952).
Bertényi, Iván, *Az országbirói intézmény és működése a xiv. században* (Budapest, 1976).
Blazovich, László, 'A Szász tükör és a Zipser Willkür', *Jogtörténeti Szemle*, (2004, no. 1), 1–4.
Blazovich, László, 'A Tripartitum és forrásai', *Századok*, 141 (2007), 1011–23.
Bodnárová, Michaela, 'Iuxta morem patrium. Ungarische Krönungen der Jagiellonen 1490/1508 und Ferdinands I. von Habsburg 1527', in Florin Ardelean, Christopher Nicholson and Johannes Preiser-Kapeller, eds., *Between Worlds: The Age of the Jagiellonians* (Frankfurt a/M, 2013), 21–36.
Bónis, György, *A birósági szervezet megújitása III. Károly korában (Systematica Commissio)* (Budapest, 1935).
Bónis, György, *Buda és Pest birósági gyakorlata a török kiűzése után 1686–1708* (Budapest, 1962).
Bónis, György, *Einflüsse des römischen Rechts in Ungarn* (*Ius Romanum Medii Aevi*, 5, no. 10) (Milan, 1964).
Bónis, György, *Hűbériség és rendiség a középkori magyar jogban*, 2nd edition (Budapest, 2003).
Bónis, György, *A jogtudó értelmiség a Mohács előtti Magyarországon* (Budapest, 1971).
Bónis, György, *Középkori jogunk elemei. Római jog, kánonjog, szokásjog* (Budapest, 1972).
Bónis, György, 'Men Learned in the Law in Medieval Hungary', *East Central Europe/L'Europe du centre-est*, 4, no. 2 (1977), 181–91.
Bónis, György, 'Petrus de Vinea leveleskönyve Magyarországon', *Filológiai Közlöny*, 4, nos. 1–2 (1958), 1–26, 173–93.
Bónis, György, 'Szent István törvényének önállósága', *Századok*, 72 (1938), 433–87.
Bónis, György, 'Törveny és szokás a Hármaskönyvben', *Acta Juridico-Politica*, 2 (1942), offprint.
Bónis, György, 'Ungarische Juristen am Ausgang des Mittelalters', in Roman Schur, ed., *Die Rolle der Juristen bei der Entstehung des modernen Staates* (Berlin, 1986).
Bónis, György, Alajos Degré and Endre Varga, *A magyar birósági szervezet és perjog története*, 2nd edition (Zalaegerszeg, 1996).
Bónis, György, Ferenc Döry, Géza Érszegi and Zsuzsanna Teke, eds., *Decreta Regni Hungariae, Gesetze und Verordnungen Ungarns 1458–1490* (Budapest, 1989).
Bónis, Péter, 'Bartolus in Medieval Hungary', *Fundamina*, 18, no. 2 (2012), 11–22.
Bónis, Péter, 'The commentators and the Hungarian law in the Middle Ages, with special regard to the Tripartitum', in Péter Antalóczy, ed., *Hagyomány és érték. Állam- és jogtudományi*

*tanulmányok a Károli Gáspár Református Egyetem fennállásának 20. évfordulójára* (Budapest, 2013), 116–26.

Bónis, Péter, 'A Tripartitum forrásai és az európai ius commune', in Gábor Máthé, ed., *A magyar jog fejlődésének fél évezrede. Werbőczy és a Hármaskönyv 500 esztendő múltán* (Budapest, 2014), 213–42.

Borovszky, Samu, and János Karácsonyi, eds., *Regestrum Varadiniense examinum ferri candentis* (Budapest, 1903).

Borsa, Iván, 'Irattipusok a középkori Magyarországon', *Levéltári Közlemények*, 64 (1993), 27–37.

Csekey, István, *Werbőczy és a magyar alkotmányjog*, Acta Juridico-Politica, 2 (Cluj, 1942).

Csekey, István, *Werbőczy István—A Tripartitum bibliográfiája*, Acta Juridico-Politica, 2 (Cluj, 1942).

Csemegi, Károly, *Az egyházi holtkéz a magyar törvények szerint* (Budapest, 1897).

Csizmadia, Andor, *Adam Franz Kollár und die ungarische rechtshistorische Forschung* (Vienna, 1982).

Csizmadia, Andor, 'Hungarian customary law before the bourgeois rebellion of 1848', *Journal of Legal History*, 4, no. 2 (1983), 3–37.

Csizmadia, Andor, *Jogi emlékek és hagyományok. Esszék és tanulmányok* (Budapest, 1981).

Csizmadia, Andor, 'Previous Editions of the Laws of Hungary', in János Bak, György Bónis and James Ross Sweeney, eds., *Decreta Regni Mediaevalis Hungariae—The Laws of the Medieval Kingdom of Hungary, 1000–1301*, Second edition (Idyllwild, CA, 1999), pp. xvii–xxxiii.

Dáné, Veronka, *'Az Őnagysága széki igy deliberála.' Torda vármegye fejedelemségkori bírósági gyakorlata* (Debrecen and Cluj, 2006).

Degré, Alajos, 'Az ellenállási jog története Magyarországon', *Jogtudományi Közlöny*, 35 (1980), 366–71.

Degré, Alajos, 'Elemente des römischen Rechtes im Vermögensrecht der ungarischen Leibeigenen', in György Antalffy, ed., *Einzelne Probleme der Rechtsgeschichte und des römischen Rechts*, Acta Juridica et Politica, 17 (Szeged, 1970), 27–35.

Degré, Alajos, *Feudális gyámsági jog Magyarországon. Kandidátusi Értekezés Tézisei* (Budapest, 1955).

Degré, Alajos, *A magyar gyámsági jog kialakulása a dualizmus korának gyámsági kódexéig* (Budapest, 1977).

Degré, Alajos, *A Négyeskönyv perjogi anyaga* (Budapest, 1935).

Degré, Alajos, 'A Planum Tabulare keletkezésével kapcsolatos kérdések', in *Emlékkönyv Kolosváry Bálint* (Budapest, 1939), 101–9.

Döry, Ferenc, György Bónis and Vera Bácskai, eds., *Decreta Regni Hungariae, Gesetze und Verordnungen Ungarns 1301–1457* (Budapest, 1976).

Eckhart, Ferenc, *A földesúri büntetőbíráskodás a xvi–xvii. században* (Budapest, 1954).

Eckhart, Ferenc, 'Jog- és alkotmánytörténet', in Bálint Hóman, ed., *A magyar történetirás új útjai* (Budapest, 1932), 269–320.

Eckhart, Ferenc, *A jog- és államtudományi kar története 1667–1935* (Budapest, 1936).

Eckhart, Ferenc, 'A pápai és császári kanczelláriai gyakorlat hatása Árpádkori királyi okleveleinek szövegezésében', *Századok*, 44 (1910), 13–24.

Eckhart, Franz (Ferenc), 'Die glaubwürdigen Orte Ungarns im Mittelalter', *Mitteilungen des Instituts für österreichische Geschichtsforschung*, Supplement 9 (1913–15), 395–558.

Ember, Győző, *Az újkori magyar közigazgatás története. Mohácstól a török kiűzéséig* (Budapest, 1946).

Ember, Győző, 'Mária Terézia urbérrendezés és az államtanács', *A Gróf Klebelsberg Kunó Magyar Történetkutató Intézet Évkönyve*, 5 (1935), 103–49.

Engel, Pál, 'Királyi emberek Valkó megyében', in Engel, *Honor, vár, ispánság. Válogatott tanulmányok* (Budapest, 2003), 578–99, first published in *Mediaevalia Transilvanica*, 3 (1999), 71–88.

Engel, Pál, 'Nagy Lajos ismeretlen adományreformja', *Történelmi Szemle*, 39, no. 2 (1997), 137–57.

Engel, Pál, *The Realm of St Stephen: A History of Medieval Hungary, 895–1526* (London and New York, 2001).

Eörsi, Gyula, 'Richterrecht und Gesetzesrecht in Ungarn. Zum Problem der Originalität eines Zivilrechts', *Rabels Zeitschrift für ausländisches und internationales Privatrecht*, 30 (1966), 117–40.

Fejérpataky, László, *A királyi kanczellária az Árpádok korában* (Budapest, 1885).

Fekete, György Galanthai, *Problemata Juridica seu Quaestiones in causis*, ed. János Csaplovics (Bratislava, 1814).

Felhő, Ibolya, 'A szabad királyi városok és a magyar kamara a xvii. században', *Levéltári Közlemények*, 24, no. 1 (1946), 208–67.

Fraknói, Vilmos, *Werbőczi István életrajza* (Budapest, 1899).

Frank, Ignácz, *Ősiség és elévülés* (Buda, 1848).

Fügedi, Erik, *The Elefánthy: The Hungarian Nobleman and his Kindred* (Budapest and New York, 1998).

Gábor, Gyula, *A megyei intézmény alakulása és működése Nagy Lajos alatt* (Budapest, 1908).

Gábriš, Tomáš, *Maintaining Peace and Justice in Árpádian Hungary: Punishment and Settlement of Disputes*, unpublished MA thesis (Central European University, Dept of Medieval Studies, 2007) (online CEU eTD Collection).

Gál, Alexander, ed., *Die Summa Legum brevis levis et utilis*, 2 vols. (Weimar, 1926).

Gerics, József, 'A magyar királyi kúriai biráskodás és központi igazgatás Anjou-kori történetéhez', in Gerics, *Egyház, állam és gondolkodás Magyarországon a középkorban* (Budapest, 1995), 295–318, first published in *Jogtörténeti Tanulmányok*, 1 (1966), 285–306.

Gönczi, Katalin, *Die europäischen Fundamente der ungarischen Rechtskultur* (Frankfurt a/M, 2008).

Gönczi, Katalin, 'Jogászképzés a királyi akadémiákon a felvilágosodás korában és a reformkorban', *Jogtörténeti Szemle*, (2006, no. 2), 1–3.

Gönczi, Katalin, 'Werbőczy's Reception in Hungarian Legal Culture', in Martyn Rady, ed., *Custom and Law in Central Europe* (Cambridge, 2003), 87–99.

Gray, R.W., 'Etching the Law on the Land: The Role of Landscape and Custom in Defining the Space of the Hungarian Village in the Eighteenth and Nineteenth Centuries', *Central Europe*, 11, no. 2 (2013), 82–101.

Gray, Robert W., 'Bringing the Law Back In: Land, Law and the Hungarian Peasantry before 1848', *Slavonic and East European Review*, 91, no. 3 (2013), 511–34.

Grosschmid, Béni, *Magánjogi előadások. Jogszabálytan* (Budapest, 1905).

Grosschmid, Béni, *Werbőczy és az angol jog* (Budapest, 1928).

Hajdú, Lajos, *Az első (1795-ös) magyar büntetőkódex-tervezet* (Budapest, 1971).

Hajdú, Lajos, *Bűntett és büntetés Magyarországon a xviii. század utolsó harmadán* (Budapest, 1985).

Hajnal, István, *L'Enseignement de l'écriture aux universités médiévales*, 2nd edition (Budapest, 1959).

Hajnik, Imre, *A király birósági személyes jelenléte és ennek helytartója a vegyesházakbeli királyok korszakában* (Budapest, 1892).

Hajnik, Imre, *A magyar birósági szervezet és perjog az Árpád- es a vegyes-házi királyok alatt* (Budapest, 1899).

Hajnik, Imre, *A perdöntő eskü és az előzetes tanúbizonyitás a középkori magyar jogban* (Budapest, 1881).

Hamza, Gábor, ed., *Tanulmányok Werbőczy Istvánról* (Budapest, 2001).

Hamza, Gábor, *Wege der Entwicklung des Privatrechts in Europa* (Passau, 2007).

Händel, Béla, 'A tehérvállalás középkori jogrendünkben', *Századok*, 78 (1944), 373–418.

Hermann, Zsuzsanna, *Az egyetemi könyvtár Werbőczi-kéziratai és az 'Analecta Saeculi XVI Hungarica'* (Budapest, 1983).

Holub, József, 'A vásárolt fekvő jószág jogi természete régi jogunkban', *Emlékkönyv Károlyi Árpád* (Budapest, 1933), 246–54.

Holub, József, *Zala megye története a középkorban* (Pécs, 1929).

Homoki-Nagy, Mária, *Az 1795. évi magánjogi tervezetek* (Szeged, 2004).

Homoki-Nagy, Mária, 'Az Osztrák Polgári Törvénykönyv hatása a magyar magánjogra', in Péter Antalóczy et al., eds., *Kormányzás és kodifikáció. Tanulmányok az újkori Európa jogfejlődéséről* (Budapest, 2006), 227–47.

Homoki-Nagy, Mária, *A magyar magánjog történetének vázlata 1848*-ig (Szeged, 2010).

Homoki-Nagy, Mária, 'Megjegyezések Banyó Péter: Birtoköröklés és leánynegyed cimű tanulmányára', *Aetas*, (2001, no. 2), 189–93.

Homoki-Nagy, Mária, 'A szabad költözködési jog biztositása Magyarországon', *Tanulmányok Dr Veres József 70. születésnapjára*, Acta Juridica et Politica, 55 (Szeged, 1999), 122–31.

Homoki-Nagy, Mária, 'A törvényes öroklés jogi szabályozása Magyarországon 1861-ig', *Acta Juridica et Politica*, 59 (2000), 211–31.

Horváth, Attila, 'A gyülekezési jog elméletének és gyakorlatának története Magyarországon 1989-ig', *Jogtörténeti Szemle*, (2007, no. 1), 4–15.

Hunyadi, Zsolt, 'Administering the Law: Hungary's *Loca Credibilia*', in Martyn Rady, ed., *Custom and Law in Central Europe* (Cambridge, 2003), 25–35.

Hunyadi, Zsolt, '*Maiores, Optimates, Nobiles*. Semantischen Fragen zur Frühgeschichte des ungarischen Adels', *East Central Europe/L'Europe du Centre-Est*, 29, nos. 1–2 (2002), 134–43.

Hunyadi, Zsolt, '"Scripta manent." Archival and Manuscript Resources in Hungary', *Annual of Medieval Studies at CEU 1997–1998* (Budapest, 1999), 231–40.

Ibbetson, David, 'Custom in the Tripartitum', in Martyn Rady, ed., *Custom and Law in Central Europe* (Cambridge, 2003), 13–23.

Illés, József, *Bevezetés a magyar jog történetébe. A források története* (Budapest, 1910).

Illés, József, *A magyar házassági vagyonjog az Árpádok korában* (Budapest, 1900).

Illés, József, *A Quadripartitum közjogi interpolátiói* (Budapest, 1931).

Istványi, Géza, 'A generalis congregatio', *Levéltári Közlemények*, 17 (1939), 50–83; *Levéltári Közlemények*, 18–19 (1940–1), 179–207.

Iványi, Béla, *Mossóczy Zakariás és a magyar Corpus Juris keletkezése* (Budapest, 1926).

Jánosi, Monika, *Törvényalkotás a korai Árpád-korban* (Szeged, 1996).

Jánossy, Dénes, 'Reformtörekvések a polgári peres eljárás terén a xviii. században', *Századok*, 77 (1943), 41–77.

Kadlec, Karel, *Verbőczyovo Tripartitum a soukromé právo uherské i chorvatské šlechty v něm obsažené* (Prague, 1902).

Kállay, István, *Úriszéki biráskodás a xviii–xix. században* (Budapest, 1985).

Kállay, István, 'Világos adóssági per és csődeljárás az úriszékben', *Jogtörténeti Tanulmányok*, 5 (1983), 129–41.

Kálmár, János, and János J. Varga, eds., *Einrichtungswerk des Königreichs Hungarn (1688–1690)* (Stuttgart, 2010).

Karácsonyi, János, 'Katonai becsületbíróság 1515–1516', *Hadtörténeti Közlemények*, 2 (1891), 482–8.

Karbić, Damir, and Marija Karbić, *The Laws and Customs of Medieval Croatia and Slavonia: A Guide to the Extant Sources*, ed. Martyn Rady (London, 2013) (electronic resource).

Károlyi, Árpád, *Illésházy István hűtlenségi pöre* (Budapest, 1883).

Károlyi, Árpád, *A magyar alkotmány fölfüggesztése 1673-ben* (Budapest, 1883).

Kassics, Ignác, *Enchiridion seu Extractus Benignarum Normalium Ordinationum Regiarum*, 3 vols. (Pest, 1825).

Katona, Mór, *A magyar családi hitbizomány* (Budapest, 1894).

Katona, Mór, *A mai érvényű magyar magánjog vezérfonala* (Bratislava, 1899).

Kelemen, Emericus, *Historia Juris Hungarici Privati*, 2nd edn., 4 vols. (Buda, 1818).

Kérészy, Zoltán, 'A Corpus Juris Hungarici mint irott jogi kútfő', *A Magyar Királyi Erzsébet Tudományegyetem 1934/35. tanévi irataiból*, 2 (1935), 11–45.

Király, Tibor, 'Das Strafgesetzbuch von 1878. Der Csemegi-Kodex', in Gábor Máthé and Werner Ogris, eds., *Die Entwicklung der osterreichisch-ungarischen Strafrechtskodifikation im XIX.–XX. Jahrhundert* (Budapest, 1996), 221–36.

Kiss, István R., *A magyar helytartótanács I. Ferdinand korában és 1549–1551. évi leveleskönyve* (Budapest, 1908).

Komáromy, Andor, *Magyarországi boszorkányperek oklevéltára* (Budapest, 1910).

Kovachich, M.G., *Formulae Solennes Styli* (Pest, 1799).

Kovács, András W., *The History of the Wass de Czege Family* (Hamburg, 2005).

Kovács, István, 'A törvény és törvényerejű rendelet problematikájához', *Állam- és Jogtudomány*, 16, no. 3 (1973), 333–91.

Králik, Dani, 'A királyi kincstár képviselője a perben', in *Emlékkönyv Grosschmid Béni* (Budapest, 1912).

Králik, Lajos, *A magyar ügyvédség. Az ügyvédi kar*, 2 vols. (Budapest, 1903).

Kristó, Gyula, Pál Engel and Ferenc Makk, *Korai magyar történeti lexikon, 9–14. sz.* (Budapest, 1994).

Kubinyi, András, 'Adatok a Mátyás-kori királyi kancellária és az 1464. évi kancelláriai reform történetéhez', in L.F. Lendvai, ed., *Tiz éves a bölcsészképzés a miskolci egyetemen* (Miskolc, 2004), 25–58.

Kubinyi, András, 'Die Beisitzer des königlichen Rates aus dem mittleren Adel unter den Jagiellonen', in Kubinyi, *Stände und Ständestaat in spätmittelalterlichen Ungarn* (Herne, 2011), 232–51 (243). Also published in Hungarian in *Mályusz Elemér Emlékkönyv* (Budapest, 1984), 257–68.

Kubinyi, András, 'Isten bárányát ábrázoló törvénybeidéző pecsét (billog)', *Folia Archaeologica*, 35 (1984), 139–59.

Kubinyi, András, 'István Werbőczy als Politiker vor Mohács (1526)', in Balázs Nagy and Marcell Sebők, eds., *Festschrift for János M. Bak* (Budapest and New York, 1999), 558–82.

Kubinyi, András, 'Királyi kancellária és udvari kápolna Magyarországon a xii. század közepén', *Levéltári Közlemények*, 46, no. 1 (1975), 59–121.

Kumorovitz, Bernát L., *Die erste Epoche der ungarischen privatrechtlichen Schriftlichkeit im Mittelalter (xi–xii. Jahrhundert)*, Studia Historica, 21 (Budapest, 1960).

Kumorovitz, Bernát L., *A magyar pecséthasználat története a középkorban* (Budapest, 1993).

Kurucz, György, *Keszthely grófja. Festetics György* (Budapest, 2013).

Mádl, Ferenc, 'Kodifikation des ungarischen Privat- und Handelsrecht im Zeitalter des Dualismus', in Andor Csizmadia and Kálmán Kovács, eds., *Die Entwicklung des Zivilrechts in Mitteleuropa* (Budapest, 1970), 87–119.

Magina, Adrian, 'From Custom to Written Law: *Ius Valachicum* in the Banat', in Martyn Rady and Alexandru Simon, eds., *Government and Law in Medieval Moldavia, Transylvania and Wallachia* (London, 2013), 71–7.

Magina, Livia, *Instituția judelui sătesc în Principatul Transilvaniei (sec. XVI–XVIII)*, PhD thesis (Babeș-Bolyai University of Cluj-Napoca, 2013). Published under the same title (Cluj, 2014).

Maksay, Ferenc, *Urbáriumok. XVI–XVII. század* (Budapest, 1959).

Mályusz, Elemér, *Királyi kancellária és krónikairás a középkori Magyarországon* (Budapest, 1973).

Marczali, Henrik, *A magyar történet kútfőinek kézikönyve* (Budapest, 1901).

Márkus, Dezső, ed., *Felsőbiróságaink elvi határozatai*, 24 vols. (Budapest, 1891–1914).

Márkus, Dezső, ed., *Magyar Jogi Lexikon*, 6 vols. (Budapest, 1898–1907).

Máthé, Gábor, ed., *A magyar jog fejlődésének fél évezrede. Werbőczy és a Hármaskönyv 500 esztendő múltán* (Budapest, 2014).

Mezey, Barna, ed., *Magyar jogtörténet*, 2nd edition (Budapest, 1999).

Meznerics, Iván, *A megyei büntető igazságszolgáltatás a 16–19. században* (Budapest, 1933).

Mikó, Gábor, 'Ismeretlen országgyűlési emlék a Jagelló-korból', *Történelmi Szemle*, 56, no. 3 (2013), 455–80.

Mollay, Karl (Károly), ed., *Das Ofner Stadtrecht. Eine deutschsprachige Rechtssammlung des 15. Jahrhunderts aus Ungarn* (Budapest, 1959).

Nagy, Ferenc Szentpáli, *Verbötzi István törvény könyvének compendiuma* (Cluj, 1798), first published in 1701.

Nagy, Imre, *A Pécz nemzetségbeliek öröködési pere. 1425–1433* (Budapest, 1892).

Nagy, István, and Erzsébet F. Kiss, *A magyar kamara és egyéb kincstári szervek* (Budapest, 1995).

Nánási, László, 'Ügyészek a rendi Magyarországon', *Jogtörténeti Szemle*, (2009, no. 3), 34–41.

Neumann, Tibor, 'Werbőczy István származása és pályakezdése', in Gábor Máthé, ed., *A magyar jog fejlődésének fél évezrede. Werbőczy és a Hármaskönyv 500 esztendő múltán* (Budapest, 2014), 31–57.

Nizsalovszky, Endre, 'Deák Ferenc és a magyar polgári magánjog kialakulása', *Tanulmányok Deák Ferencről* (*Zalai Gyűjtemény*, 5) (Zalaegerszeg, 1976), 61–84.

Papp, László, 'A birtokba-iktatás (statutio) lefolyása', in *Emlékkönyv Szentpétery Imre* (Budapest, 1938), 372–84.

Papp, László, *A hiteleshelyek története és működése az újkorban* (Budapest, 1936).

Paraszkay (ifj), Gyula, *A birói gyakorlat mint jogforrás* (Miskolc, 1929), offprint of *Miskolci Jogászélet* (1929, no. 6).

Párniczky, Mihály, and János Bátyka, *A magyar Corpus Juris (Az első kiadások forrásai)* (Budapest, 1936).

Pesty, Frigyes, Adrian Magina and Livia Magina, eds., *Diplome privind istoria comitatului Timiș și a orașului Timișoara—Oklevelek Temesvármegye és Temesvár város történetéhez 1430–1470* (Cluj, 2014).

Péter, László, 'The Autocratic Principle of the Law and Civil Rights in Nineteenth-Century Hungary', in Péter, *Hungary's Long Nineteenth Century: Constitutional and Democratic Traditions in a European Perspective* (Leiden and Boston, 2012), 281–304, first published in *CEU History Department Yearbook, 1997–98* (Budapest, 1999), 11–34.

Péter, László, 'Die Verfassungsentwicklung in Ungarn', in Helmut Rumpler and Peter Urbanitsch, eds., *Die Habsburger Monarchie*, vol. 8 (*Verfassung und Parlamentarismus*), 2 parts (Vienna, 2000), i, 239–540.

Péter, László, 'The Holy Crown of Hungary, Visible and Invisible', *Slavonic and East European Review*, 81, no. 3 (2003), 421–510.

Péter, László, 'The Hungarian *Diœtalis Tractatus* and the Imperial Constitutional Systems: A Comparison', *Central Europe*, 6, no. 1 (2008), 47–64.

Péter, László, 'The Irrepressible Authority of the *Tripartitum*', in János Bak, Péter Banyó and Martyn Rady, eds., *Stephen Werbőczy, The Customary Law of the Renowned Kingdom of Hungary in Three Parts (The Tripartitum)* (Decreta Regni Mediaevalis Hungariae, 5) (Budapest and Idyllwild, CA, 2005), pp. xi–xxvi.

Péter, László, '*Ius resistendi* in Hungary', in Péter and Martyn Rady, eds., *Resistance, Rebellion and Revolution in Hungary and Central Europe: Commemorating 1956* (London, 2008), 41–55.

Péter, László, 'Montesquieu's Paradox on Freedom and Hungary's Constitutions 1790–1990', in Péter, *Hungary's Long Nineteenth Century: Constitutional and Democratic Traditions in a European Perspective. Collected Studies* (Leiden and Boston, 2012), 152–82, first published in *History of Political Thought*, 16 (1995), 77–104.

Péter, László, 'The Primacy of Consuetudo in Hungarian Law', in Martyn Rady, ed., *Custom and Law in Central Europe* (Cambridge, 2003), 101–11.

Pólya, Jakab, 'A magyar birtok- és örökösödési jognak fejlődése', *Magyar Gazdaságtörténelmi Szemle*, 1 (1894), 60–5, 136–45.

*Quadripartitum Opus Juris Consuetudinarii Regni Hungariae* (Zagreb, 1798).

Rady, Martyn, ed., *Custom and Law in Central Europe* (Cambridge, 2003).

Rady, Martyn, 'Justice Delayed? Litigation and Dispute Settlement in Fifteenth-Century Hungary', *Central Europe*, 2, no. 1 (2004), 3–14.

Rady, Martyn, *Medieval Buda: A Study of Municipal Government and Jurisdiction in the Kingdom of Hungary* (Boulder, CO and New York, 1985).

Rady, Martyn, *Nobility, Land and Service in Medieval Hungary* (Basingstoke and New York, 2000).

Rady, Martyn, 'The Prologue to Werbőczy's *Tripartitum* and its Sources', *English Historical Review*, 121, no. 490 (2006), 104–45.

Rady, Martyn, 'Stephen Werbőczy and his *Tripartitum*', in János Bak, Péter Banyó and Martyn Rady, eds., *Stephen Werbőczy, The Customary Law of the Renowned Kingdom of Hungary in Three Parts (The Tripartitum)* (Decreta Regni Mediaevalis Hungariae, 5) (Budapest and Idyllwild, CA, 2005), pp. xxvii–xliv.

Rady, Martyn, '"They brought in an ox as king: they elected and installed him": The royal succession in later medieval Hungary', in Frédérique Lachaud and Michael Penman, eds., *Making and breaking the rules: succession in medieval Europe, c. 1000–c. 1600* (Turnhout, 2008), 61–9.

Rady, Martyn, 'The "Title of New Donation" in Medieval Hungarian Law', *Slavonic and East European Review*, 79, no. 4 (2001), 638–52.

Rady, Martyn, 'Warranty and Surety in Medieval Hungarian Land Law', *Journal of Legal History*, 23, no. 1 (2002), 23–36.

Ráth, György, *Az országbirói értekezlet a törvénykezés tárgyában*, 2 vols. (Pest, 1861).

Sápi, Vilmos, 'Községi biráskodásunk a feudalizmus utolsó évszázadaiban', *Jogtudományi Közlöny*, NS, 21 (1966), 466–72.

Schwarz, Gusztáv, *Magánjogunk felépitése* (Budapest, 1893).

Solymosi, László, *Irásbeliség és társadalom az Árpád-korban* (Budapest, 2006).

Štenpien, Erik, *Tripartitum* (Bratislava, 2008).
Stipta, István, *A magyar bírósági rendszer története*, 2nd edition (Debrecen, 1998).
Szabó, Béla P., 'A jogtudós Honterus – Az európai 'ius commune' közvetitője', in Ágnes W. Salgó and Ágnes Stemler, eds., *Honterus Emlékkönyv* (Budapest, 2001), 28–56.
Szabó, Béla P., 'Stephanus Werbőczy' in Michael Stolleis, ed., *Juristen. Ein biographisches Lexikon. Von der Antike bis zum 20. Jahrhundert* (Munich, 2001), 668–9.
Szabó, Béla P., 'A szepesi jog forrásai', *Jogtörténeti Tanulmányok*, 8 (2005), 443–63.
Szabó, Béla P., *A Zipser Willkür (Szepesi jog) 13 kéziratának összehasonlító elemzése és fordítása*, on-line Project Report, OTKA, 2007.
Szabó, Imre, *A burzsoá állam- és jogbölcselet Magyarországon*, 2nd edition (Budapest, 1980).
Szegedi, János, *Tripartitum Juris Hungarici Tyrocinium* (Košice, 1764).
Szentpétery, Imre, *Magyar oklevéltan* (Budapest, 1930).
Szijárto, István M., *A diéta. A magyar rendek és az országgyűlés 1708–1792* (Budapest, 2005).
Szilágyi, Loránd, 'A királyi secretariusok intézménye és az újkori magyar állam', *Emlékkönyv Domanovszky Sándor* (Budapest, 1937), 547–61.
Szilágyi, Loránd, *A magyar királyi kancellária szerepe az államkormányzatban 1458–1526* (Budapest, 1930).
Szladits, Charles, 'A Comparison of Hungarian Customary Law with English Case Law', *Journal of Comparative Legislation and International Law*, 3rd series, 19, no. 4 (1937), 165–78.
Tagányi, Károly, *Magyar erdészeti oklevéltár*, 3 vols. (Budapest, 1896).
Teszelszky, Kees, *Az ismeretlen korona. Jelentések, szimbólumok es nemzeti identitás* (Pannonhalma, 2009).
Tringli, István, 'A magyar szokásjog a malomépitésről', in Tibor Neumann, ed., *Analecta Mediaevalia 1* (Budapest, 2001), 251–68.
Varga, Endre, 'A hivatásos ügyvédi osztály kialakulása', *Emlékkönyv Domanovszky Sándor* (Budapest, 1937), 624–42.
Varga, Endre, *A királyi Curia 1780–1850* (Budapest, 1974).
Varga, Endre, 'Polgári peres eljárás a királyi curián 1724–1848/49', *Levéltári Közlemények*, 39, no. 2 (1968), 269–309.
Varga, Endre, and Miklós Veres, *Bírósági levéltárak 1526–1869* (Budapest, 1989).
Varga, János J., 'Berendezési tervezetek Magyarországon a török kiűzésének időszakában. Az Einrichtungswerk', *Századok*, 125 (1991), 449–88.
Vécsey, Tamás, *Széchenyi és a magyar magánjog* (Budapest, 1895).
Waldapfel, Eszter, 'Nemesi birtokjogunk kialakulása a középkorban', *Századok*, 65 (1931), 134–67, 259–72.
Wallaszky (Valaszky), Paul, *De Stephano Verbőczio icto celeberrimo dissertatio* (Leipzig, 1768).
Wenzel, Gusztáv, *Visszapillantás az előbbi magyar királyi curiának 1724–1769-iki működésére* (Budapest, 1875).
Windisch, Éva V., *Kovachich Márton György, a forráskutató* (Budapest, 1998).
Wittmann, Ernő, *Tanulmányok az angol magánjog köréből*, (Budapest, 1907).
Wittmann, Ernő, 'Tanulmányok az angol magánjog köréből. Kárteritési jog', *Jogállam*, 5, nos. 7–8 (1906), 513–28, 588–608, 682–99, 736–63.
Závodszky, Levente, *A Szent István, Szent László és Kálmán korabeli törvények és zsinati határozatok forrásai* (Budapest, 1904).
Zlinszky, Imre, *A magyar magánjog mai érvényében különös tekintettel a gyakorlat igényeire*, 4th edition, ed. Sándor Dárday (Budapest, 1891).

Zlinszky, János, *Az ügyvédség kialakulása Magyarországon és története Fejér megyében* (Székesfehérvár?, 1976?).
Zlinszky, János, 'Die historische Rechtsschule und die Gestaltung des ungarischen Privatrechts im 19. Jahrhundert', *Acta Juridica et Politica*, 33, no. 30 (1985), 433–45.
Zlinszky, János, 'Ein Versuch zur Rezeption des römischen Rechts in Ungarn', in Franz Horak and Wolfgang Waldstein, eds., *Festgabe für Arnold Herdlitczka* (Munich and Salzburg, 1972), 315–26.
Zlinszky, János, 'Kodifikation und Gesetzgebung des allgemeinen Privatrechts in Ungarn', in Helmut Coing, ed., *Handbuch der Quellen und Literatur der neueren europäischen Privatrechtsgeschichte*, 3 vols. in 8 parts (Munich, 1973–88), iii/2, 2141–213, 2819–38.
Zlinszky, János, 'Legal Studies and works of János Baranyai Decsi', in *'Igniculi Sapientiae'. János-Baranyai-Decsi-Festschrift* (Budapest, 2004), 104–18.
Zlinszky, János, 'Werbőczy jogforrástana', *Jogtudományi Közlöny*, 48, no. 10 (1993), 374–6.
Zsoldos, Attila, 'II. András Aranybullája', *Történelmi Szemle*, 53 (2011), 1–38.
Zsoldos, Attila, *A szent király szabadjai. Fejezetek a várjobbágyság történetéből* (Budapest, 1999).

# Index

All place names are rendered in their current form, as may be found on a modern map, with alternative names given in brackets. Sometimes this will grate, but to do otherwise could cause offence. Buda and Pest are retained as separate entries.

The manufacturer's authorised representative in the EU for product safety is Oxford University Press España S.A. of el Parque Empresarial San Fernando de Henares, Avenida de Castilla, 2 – 28830 Madrid (www.oup.es/en or product.safety@oup.com). OUP España S.A. also acts as importer into Spain of products made by the manufacturer.

www.ingramcontent.com/pod-product-compliance
Lightning Source LLC
Chambersburg PA
CBHW071300180926
51613CB00001B/85
*9780198743910*